THE BELOVED'S MAJESTY

Quranic Verses in Praise of the Holy Prophet ﷺ

ISLAMIC LIFESTYLE SOLUTIONS

Published by **Islamic Lifestyle Solutions**
500 Ridge Rd, Overport, 4067, Durban, South Africa
(+27)31 207 7276 · ils@hotmail.co.za
www.islamiclifestylesolutions.co.za

ISBN 978-0-620-55180-9

Print-on-Demand Edition (November 2012)

Original Work *Shaan'e-Habībur-Rahmān min Āyātil-Qurān*

Author Mufti Ahmed Yaar Khan Naeemi ؒ

Translated by Mufti Omar Dawood Qadri Moeeni
(Islamic Lifestyle Solutions, South Africa)

Typing &Typesetting Maulana Omar Sayed
(www.islamic-literature.com)

Cover by Catalyst Studios
(+27)83 747 8828

*'O Muhammad ﷺ, soon your Lord will make you stand
at a place where all will praise you.'*

– Surah Bani Israel (17), Verse 79

CONTENTS

Author's Note – Pg. 1

Introduction – Pg. 5

Quranic Verses in Praise of the Holy Prophet ﷺ

Verse 1

هُوَ الْاَوَّلُ وَالْآخِرُ وَالظَّاهِرُ وَالْبَاطِنُ ، وَهُوَ بِكُلِّ شَيْءٍ عَلِيْمٌ

'He is the first; he is the last; he is the open; he is the hidden;
and he has knowledge of everything.'
– Surah Hadīd (57), Verse 3 [Pg. 11]

Verse 2

وَاِنْ كُنْتُمْ فِيْ رَيْبٍ مِّمَّا نَزَّلْنَا عَلٰى عَبْدِنَا فَأْتُوْا بِسُوْرَةٍ مِّن مِّثْلِه ، وَادْعُوْا شُهَدَاءَكُمْ مِّنْ دُوْنِ اللهِ اِنْ كُنْتُمْ صٰدِقِيْنَ

'And if you have any doubt as to what We have sent down
upon Our (exalted) servant, bring just one chapter like it and call
upon all your helpers besides Allah ﷻ if you are truthful.'
– Surah Baqarah (2), Verse 23 [Pg. 15]

Verse 3

يُخٰدِعُوْنَ اللهَ وَالَّذِيْنَ آمَنُوْا وَمَا يَخْدَعُوْنَ اِلَّا أَنْفُسَهُمْ وَمَا يَشْعُرُوْنَ

'They seek to deceive Allah ﷻ and the believers, but in fact they
deceive none but themselves, and yet they perceive not.'
– Surah Baqarah (2), Verse 9 [Pg. 17]

Verse 4

وَعَلَّمَ اٰدَمَ الْاَسْمَاءَ كُلَّهَا ثُمَّ عَرَضَهُمْ عَلَى الْمَلَائِكَةِ

'Allah ﷻ taught Adam ﷺ the names of all things,
then He showed them to the angels.'
– Surah Baqarah (2), Verse 31 [Pg. 18]

Verse 5

فَتَلَقّٰى اٰدَمُ مِن رَّبِّه كَلِمٰتٍ فَتَابَ عَلَيْهِ ، اِنَّه هُوَ التَّوَّابُ الرَّحِيْمُ

'Then Adam ﷺ learnt certain words (of repentance) from
his Lord and He (Allah ﷻ) accepted his repentance. Surely

He is the Most Relenting, Most Merciful.'
– Surah Baqarah (2), Verse 37 [Pg. 20]

Verse 6

يَأَيُّهَا الَّذِيْنَ آمَنُوْا لَا تَقُوْلُوْا رَاعِنَا وَقُوْلُوا انْظُرْنَا وَاسْمَعُوْا ، وَلِلْكٰفِرِيْنَ عَذَابٌ اَلِيْمٌ

'O you who believe, don't say (to Allah's ﷻ Messenger) 'Ra'ina', but say,
'Unzurna'. From the beginning, listen attentively (to his disclosure), and
for the disbelievers is a painful punishment.'
– Surah Baqarah (2), Verse 104 [Pg. 22]

Verse 7

اِنَّا اَرْسَلْنٰكَ بِالْحَقِّ بَشِيْرًا وَّنَذِيْرًا ، وَلَا تُسْئَلُ عَنْ أَصْحٰبِ الْجَحِيْمِ

'Indeed We have sent you (O Muhammad ﷺ) with the
truth, a bearer of glad tidings and a warner. And you will not
be questioned regarding the inmates of Hell.'
– Surah Baqarah (2), Verse 119 [Pg. 24]

Verse 8

رَبَّنَا وَابْعَثْ فِيْهِمْ رَسُوْلًا مِّنْهُمْ يَتْلُوْا عَلَيْهِمْ اٰيٰتِكَ وَيُعَلِّمُهُمُ الْكِتٰبَ وَالْحِكْمَةَ وَيُزَكِّيْهِمْ ، اِنَّكَ اَنْتَ الْعَزِيْزُ الْحَكِيْمُ

'O our Lord, send among them a Messenger ﷺ from themselves who will recite
to them Your verses and teach them the scripture & wisdom, and purify them.
Surley You are the Most Exalted, the Wise.'
– Surah Baqarah (2), Verse 129 [Pg. 25]

Verse 9

وَكَذٰلِكَ جَعَلْنٰكُمْ أُمَّةً وَّسَطًا لِّتَكُوْنُوْا شُهَدَاءَ عَلَى النَّاسِ وَيَكُوْنَ الرَّسُوْلُ عَلَيْكُمْ شَهِيْدًا

'And so We made you an exalted community
among all the nations so that you may be a witness over
the people and the Messenger ﷺ a witness over you.'
– Surah Baqarah (2), Verse 143 [Pg. 27]

Verse 10

قَدْ نَرٰى تَقَلُّبَ وَجْهِكَ فِى السَّمَاءِ ، فَلَنُوَلِّيَنَّكَ قِبْلَةً تَرْضٰهَا

'Surely We have observed you turning your face (O
Muhammad ﷺ) towards Heaven repeatedly, and We will
surely turn you to a qibla with which you will be pleased.'
– Surah Baqarah (2), Verse 144 [Pg. 29]

Verse 11

تِلْكَ الرُّسُلُ فَضَّلْنَا بَعْضَهُمْ عَلَى بَعْضٍ ، مِّنْهُم مَّن كَلَّمَ اللهُ ، وَرَفَعَ بَعْضَهُمْ دَرَجَٰتٍ

*'Of these messengers We have excelled some over others. To some of them
Allah ﷻ spoke, and one is he who's raised high in degrees over all.'*
– Surah Baqarah (2), Verse 253 [Pg. 31]

Verse 12

مَنْ ذَا الَّذِيْ يَشْفَعُ عِنْدَهُ إِلَّا بِإِذْنِهِ ، يَعْلَمُ مَا بَيْنَ أَيْدِيهِمْ وَمَا خَلْفَهُمْ ، وَلَا يُحِيطُونَ بِشَيْءٍ مِّنْ عِلْمِهِ إِلَّا بِمَا شَاءَ

*'Who is there that can intercede with Him except by His permission? He knows
all that was before and all that will happen after; and they can encompass
nothing of His knowledge except for what He wills.'*
– Surah Baqarah (2), Verse 255 [Pg. 32]

Verse 13

قُلْ إِنْ كُنْتُمْ تُحِبُّونَ اللهَ فَاتَّبِعُونِيْ يُحْبِبْكُمُ اللهُ وَيَغْفِرْ لَكُمْ ذُنُوبَكُمْ ، وَاللهُ غَفُورٌ رَّحِيْمٌ

*'Please declare (O Beloved ﷺ), "If you love Allah ﷻ, follow me.
(Only then) Allah ﷻ will love you and forgive you for your faults. And
Allah ﷻ is Most Forgiving, Most Merciful.'*
– Surah Ale-Imran (3), Verse 31 [Pg. 35]

Verse 14

وَإِذْ أَخَذَ اللهُ مِيْثَاقَ النَّبِيِّيْنَ لَمَا اٰتَيْتُكُم مِّن كِتٰبٍ وَّحِكْمَةٍ ثُمَّ جَاءَكُمْ رَسُوْلٌ مُّصَدِّقٌ لِّمَا مَعَكُمْ لَتُؤْمِنُنَّ بِهِ
وَلَتَنصُرُنَّهُ ، قَالَ ءَأَقْرَرْتُمْ وَأَخَذْتُمْ عَلَى ذٰلِكُمْ إِصْرِى ، قَالُوا أَقْرَرْنا ، قَالَ فَاشْهَدُوا وَأَنَا مَعَكُم مِّنَ الشَّهِدِيْنَ

*'And recall when Allah ﷻ took from the Prophets ﷺ their
covenant, that, "I should give you a Book and Wisdom; then comes to
you a Messenger ﷺ confirming what is with you; assuredly you will believe
in him and help him." Then He said, "Do you agree and take this as my firm
agreement as binding on you?" They said, "We've agreed." Allah ﷻ then
said, "Then be witness, and I am with you among the witnesses.'*
– Surah Ale-Imran (3), Verse 81 [Pg. 37]

Verse 15

لَقَدْ مَنَّ اللهُ عَلَى الْمُؤْمِنِيْنَ إِذْ بَعَثَ فِيهِمْ رَسُوْلًا مِّنْ أَنْفُسِهِمْ يَتْلُوا عَلَيْهِمْ اٰيٰتِهِ وَيُزَكِّيْهِمْ
وَيُعَلِّمُهُمُ الْكِتٰبَ وَالْحِكْمَةَ وَإِنْ كَانُوا مِنْ قَبْلُ لَفِيْ ضَلٰلٍ مُّبِيْنٍ

*'Certainly Allah ﷻ conferred (great) favor upon the
believers that He sent a Messenger ﷺ from among them who recites
to them the verses, purifies them and teaches them the Book & wisdom;
and previous to that they were clearly in error.'*
– Surah Ale-Imran (3), Verse 164 [Pg. 39]

Verse 16

مَا كَانَ اللهُ لِيَذَرَ الْمُؤْمِنِيْنَ عَلَى مَا أَنْتُمْ عَلَيْهِ حَتَّى يَمِيْزَ الْخَبِيْثَ
مِنَ الطَّيِّبِ ، وَمَا كَانَ اللهُ لِيُطْلِعَكُمْ عَلَى الْغَيْبِ وَلٰكِنَّ اللهَ يَجْتَبِىْ مِنْ رُّسُلِهِ مَنْ يَّشَاءُ

'Allah ﷻ will not leave the believers in the state which you are
in until He separates the impure from the pure. And it doesn't befit the
dignity of Allah ﷻ to reveal to you all the secrets of the unseen; but
Allah ﷻ chooses of His Messengers ﷺ whom He pleases.'
– Surah Ale-Imran (3), Verse 179 [Pg. 41]

Verse 17

وَلَوْ أَنَّهُمْ إِذْ ظَّلَمُوْا أَنْفُسَهُمْ جَاءُوْكَ فَاسْتَغْفَرُوا اللهَ وَاسْتَغْفَرَ لَهُمُ الرَّسُوْلُ لَوَجَدُوا اللهَ تَوَّابًا رَّحِيْمًا

'And if they are unjust to their souls, then (O Beloved ﷺ), they should come
to you and beg forgiveness of Allah ﷻ, and the Messenger ﷺ should intercede
for them. Then surely they will find Allah ﷻ Most Relenting, Merciful.'
– Surah Nisā (4), Verse 64 [Pg. 42]

Verse 18

فَلَا وَرَبِّكَ لَا يُؤْمِنُوْنَ حَتّى يُحَكِّمُوْكَ فِيْمَا شَجَرَ بَيْنَهُمْ ثُمَّ لَا يَجِدُوْا فِىْ أَنْفُسِهِمْ حَرَجًا مِّمَّا قَضَيْتَ وَيُسَلِّمُوْا تَسْلِيْمًا

'Then (O Beloved ﷺ), by your Lord, they will not be Muslims until they make
you judge in all their disputes and find in their souls no resistance against your
decisions, but accept them with the fullest conviction.'
– Surah Nisā (4), Verse 65 [Pg. 45]

Verse 19

مَنْ يُّطِعِ الرَّسُوْلَ فَقَدْ أَطَاعَ اللهَ ، وَمَنْ تَوَلّٰى فَمَا أَرْسَلْنٰكَ عَلَيْهِمْ حَفِيْظًا

'He who obeys the Messenger ﷺ has indeed obeyed Allah ﷻ. But (as for)
anyone who turns his face away, We have not sent you to save them.'
– Surah Nisā (4), Verse 80 [Pg. 46]

Verse 20

وَأَنْزَلَ اللهُ عَلَيْكَ الْكِتٰبَ وَالْحِكْمَةَ وَعَلَّمَكَ مَا لَمْ تَكُنْ تَعْلَمُ ، وَكَانَ فَضْلُ اللهِ عَلَيْكَ عَظِيْمًا

'And Allah ﷻ has revealed to you the Book & wisdom, and taught you
what you did not know. And great is the grace of Allah ﷻ upon you.'
– Surah Nisā (4), Verse 113 [Pg. 48]

Verse 21

وَمَنْ يُّشَاقِقِ الرَّسُوْلَ مِنْ بَعْدِ مَا تَبَيَّنَ لَهُ الْهُدٰى وَيَتَّبِعْ غَيْرَ سَبِيْلِ
الْمُؤْمِنِيْنَ نُوَلِّهِ مَا تَوَلّٰى وَنُصْلِهِ جَهَنَّمَ ، وَسَاءَتْ مَصِيْرًا

*'And as for he who opposes the Messenger ﷺ after
guidance has become clear and follows a way other than the way
of the Muslims, We will leave him in his own condition and will
cause him to enter Hell. What an evil destination that is.'*
– Surah Nisā (4), Verse 115 [Pg. 51]

Verse 22

يَأَيُّهَا النَّاسُ قَدْ جَاءَكُم بُرْهَنٌ مِّن رَّبِّكُمْ وَأَنزَلْنَا إِلَيْكُمْ نُورًا مُّبِينًا

*'O people, there has indeed come to you a manifest proof from Allah ﷻ,
and We have sent down to you a manifest light (Noor).'*
– Surah Nisā (4), Verse 174 [Pg. 52]

Verse 23

الْيَوْمَ أَكْمَلْتُ لَكُمْ دِينَكُمْ وَأَتْمَمْتُ عَلَيْكُمْ نِعْمَتِي وَرَضِيتُ لَكُمُ الْإِسْلَمَ دِينًا

*'This day I have perfected your religion for you, completed My
favor upon you and have chosen Islam as your way of life.'*
– Surah Māida (5), Verse 3 [Pg. 57]

Verse 24

قَدْ جَاءَكُم مِّنَ اللهِ نُورٌ وَكِتَبٌ مُّبِينٌ

*'Undoubtedly there has come to you from
Allah ﷻ a light and a luminous book.'*
– Surah Māida (5), Verse 15 [Pg. 58]

Verse 25

إِنَّمَا وَلِيُّكُمُ اللهُ وَرَسُولُهُ وَالَّذِينَ امَنُوا الَّذِينَ يُقِيمُونَ الصَّلَوةَ وَيُؤْتُونَ الزِّكَوةَ وَهُمْ رَكِعُونَ

*'Only Allah ﷻ is your friend, and His Messenger ﷺ and the believers who
establish prayer, pay Zakaat and bow down (before Allah ﷻ).'*
– Surah Māida (5), Verse 55 [Pg. 61]

Verse 26

يَأَيُّهَا الرَّسُولُ بَلِّغْ مَا أُنزِلَ إِلَيْكَ مِن رَّبِّكَ ، وَإِن لَّمْ تَفْعَلْ فَمَا بَلَّغْتَ رِسَالَتَهُ ، وَاللهُ يَعْصِمُكَ مِنَ النَّاسِ

*'O Beloved Messenger ﷺ propagate what has been revealed to you from your
Lord. And if you are unable to do so, then you have not conveyed any message.
And Allah ﷻ will protect you from the people.'*
– Surah Māida (5), Verse 67 [Pg. 62]

Verse 27

وَأَطِيعُوا اللهَ وَأَطِيعُوا الرَّسُوْلَ وَاحْذَرُوا ، فَإِنْ تَوَلَّيْتُمْ فَاعْلَمُوْا أَنَّمَا عَلى رَسُوْلِنَا الْبَلَغُ الْمُبِيْنُ

'And obey Allah ﷻ and obey the Messenger ﷺ and
be careful. Then if you turn back, know then that the duty of
Our Messenger ﷺ is only to deliver the message clearly.'
– Surah Māida (5), Verse 92 [Pg. 64]

Verse 28

يَأَيُّهَا الَّذِيْنَ امَنُوْا لَا تَسْئَلُوا عَنْ اَشْيَاءَ اِنْ تُبْدَ لَكُمْ تَسُؤْكُمْ وَإِنْ تَسْئَلُوا عَنْهَا
حِيْنَ يُنَزَّلُ الْقُرْانُ تُبْدَ لَكُمْ عَفَا اللهُ عَنْهَا ، وَاللهُ غَفُوْرٌ حَلِيْمٌ

'O Believers, question not things that, if disclosed, may
displease you. And if you will ask while the Quran is being revealed,
they will be made clear to you. Allah ﷻ has already pardoned them.
And Allah ﷻ is the Forgiving, the Forbearing.'
– Surah Māida (5), Verse 101 [Pg. 65]

Verse 29

قَدْ نَعْلَمُ اِنَّهُ لَيَحْزُنُكَ الَّذِيْ يَقُوْلُوْنَ ، فَإِنَّهُمْ لَا يُكَذِّبُوْنَكَ وَلكِنَّ الظّٰلِمِيْنَ بِاياتِ اللهِ يَجْحَدُوْنَ

'We know that what they say grieves you; they belie you not,
but the evildoers deny the signs of Allah ﷻ.'
– Surah An'ām (6), Verse 33 [Pg. 67]

Verse 30

وَمَا قَدَرُوا اللهَ حَقَّ قَدْرِه اِذْ قَالُوا مَا اَنْزَلَ اللهُ عَلى بَشَرٍ مِّنْ شَيْءٍ

'And they (the Jews) could not visualize the respect
of Allah ﷻ as was necessary to be visualized. Then they said,
"Allah ﷻ had not revealed anything on any man.'
– Surah An'ām (6), Verse 91 [Pg. 70]

Verse 31

اَلَّذِيْنَ يَتَّبِعُوْنَ الرَّسُوْلَ النَّبِيَّ الْأُمِّيَّ الَّذِيْ يَجِدُوْنَهُ مَكْتُوبًا عِنْدَهُمْ فِى التَّوْرٰةِ وَالْاِنْجِيْلِ يَأْمُرُهُمْ بِالْمَعْرُوْفِ وَيَنْهٰهُمْ
عَنِ الْمُنْكَرِ وَيُحِلُّ لَهُمُ الطَّيِّبٰتِ وَيُحَرِّمُ عَلَيْهِمُ الْخَبٰئِثَ وَيَضَعُ عَنْهُمْ إِصْرَهُمْ وَالْأَغْلٰلَ الَّتِيْ كَانَتْ عَلَيْهِمْ

'Those who serve the unlettered Messenger ﷺ (the one who
hasn't learnt from anyone), who they will find with them written in
the Torah and the Injīl (New Testament), he will bid them to do good
and will forbid them from doing evil, and he will make lawful for them
clean things and will forbid for them unclean things, and will take off
from them the burden and shackles which they were upon.'
– Surah A'rāf (7), Verse 157 [Pg. 72]

Verse 32

قُلْ يَأَيُّهَا النَّاسُ اِنِّ رَسُوْلُ اللهِ اِلَيْكُمْ جَمِيْعًا

'Say (O Beloved ﷺ), 'O Mankind, I'm a Messenger ﷺ to you all from Allah ﷻ.'
– Surah A'rāf (7), Verse 158 [Pg. 75]

Verse 33

وَمَا رَمَيْتَ اِذْ رَمَيْتَ وَلٰكِنَّ اللهَ رَمٰى

'And (O Beloved ﷺ) the dust that you threw, you did
not [truly] throw; but Allah ﷻ threw.'
– Surah Anfāl (8), Verse 17 [Pg. 77]

Verse 34

يَأَيُّهَا الَّذِيْنَ اٰمَنُوا اسْتَجِيْبُوا للهِ وَلِلرَّسُوْلِ اِذَا دَعَاكُمْ لِمَا يُحْيِيْكُمْ

'O believers! Respond to the calling of Allah ﷻ and the Messenger ﷺ
when the Messenger ﷺ calls you to that which gives you life.'
– Surah Anfāl (8), Verse 24 [Pg. 80]

Verse 35

وَمَا كَانَ اللهُ لِيُعَذِّبَهُمْ وَأَنْتَ فِيْهِمْ

'And Allah ﷻ isn't one to punish them while
you (O Beloved ﷺ) are in their midst.'
– Surah Anfāl (8), Verse 33 [Pg. 84]

Verse 36

وَلَوْ اَنَّهُمْ رَضُوا مَا اٰتٰهُمُ اللهُ وَرَسُوْلُه ، وَقَالُوا حَسْبُنَا اللهُ سَيُؤْتِيْنَا اللهُ مِنْ فَضْلِه وَرَسُوْلُه ، اِنَّا اِلَى اللهِ رٰغِبُوْنَ

'If only they had been content with what Allah ﷻ and His Messenger ﷺ had
given them and said, "Sufficient for us is Allah ﷻ. Allah ﷻ will give us of His
bounty. To Allah ﷻ do we turn in submission.'
– Surah Tauba (9), Verse 59 [Pg. 85]

Verse 37

يَحْلِفُوْنَ بِاللهِ لَكُمْ لِيُرْضُوْكُمْ ، وَاللهُ وَرَسُوْلُه اَحَقُّ اَنْ يُّرْضُوْهُ اِنْ كَانُوا مُؤْمِنِيْنَ

'They swear by Allah ﷻ before you that you may be
pleased. And Allah ﷻ and the Messenger ﷺ had a greater
right that they should please him if they had faith.'
– Surah Tauba (9), Verse 62 [Pg. 86]

Verse 38

أَلَمْ يَعْلَمُوا أَنَّهُ مَن يُحَادِدِ اللهَ وَرَسُولَهُ فَأَنَّ لَهُ نَارَ جَهَنَّمَ خَالِدًا فِيْهَا ، ذٰلِكَ الْخِزْيُ الْعَظِيْمُ

*'Are they not aware that, concerning whoever opposes Allah ﷻ
and His Messenger ﷺ, for such a person is the fire of Hell in which
he will abide forever? This is a great humiliation.'*
– Surah Tauba (9), Verse 63 [Pg. 88]

Verse 39

خُذْ مِنْ أَمْوَالِهِمْ صَدَقَةً تُطَهِّرُهُمْ وَتُزَكِّيْهِمْ بِهَا وَصَلِّ عَلَيْهِمْ ، إِنَّ صَلوٰتَكَ سَكَنٌ لَّهُمْ ، وَاللهُ سَمِيْعٌ عَلِيْمٌ

*'(O Beloved Prophet ﷺ) Realize the poor-due (Zakaat) out of their wealth to
purify and cleanse them therewith, and pray good for them. No doubt your
prayer is solace for their hearts. And Allah ﷻ Hears, Knows.'*
– Surah Tauba (9), Verse 103 [Pg. 89]

Verse 40

لَقَدْ جَاءَكُمْ رَسُوْلٌ مِّنْ أَنْفُسِكُمْ عَزِيْزٌ عَلَيْهِ مَا عَنِتُّمْ حَرِيْصٌ عَلَيْكُمْ بِالْمُؤْمِنِيْنَ رَؤُوْفٌ رَّحِيْمٌ

*'Surely there has come to you a Messenger ﷺ from among yourselves.
Heavy upon him is your suffering, and he ardently desires your welfare.
To the believers he is most kind and merciful.'*
– Surah Tauba (9), Verse 128 [Pg. 91]

Verse 41

قُلْ يَأَيُّهَا النَّاسُ قَدْ جَاءَكُمُ الْحَقُّ مِن رَّبِّكُمْ

'Say (O Beloved ﷺ), 'The truth has come from your Lord.''
– Surah Yunus (10), Verse 108 [Pg. 96]

Verse 42

أَلَا بِذِكْرِ اللهِ تَطْمَئِنُّ الْقُلُوْبُ

'Behold, in the remembrance of Allah ﷻ is there satisfaction of hearts.'
– Surah Ra'ad (13), Verse 28 [Pg. 97]

Verse 43

وَلَقَدْ أَرْسَلْنَا رُسُلًا مِّنْ قَبْلِكَ وَجَعَلْنَا لَهُمْ أَزْوَاجًا وَّذُرِّيَّةً

*'And undoubtedly We have sent Messengers before you and
assigned to them wives and children.'*
– Surah Ra'ad (13), Verse 38 [Pg. 100]

Verse 44

لَعَمْرُكَ إِنَّهُمْ لَفِىْ سَكْرَتِهِمْ يَعْمَهُوْنَ

'(O My Beloved ﷺ) By your life, indeed they are wandering
about in their intoxication.'
– Surah Hijr (15), Verse 72 [Pg. 101]

Verse 45

سُبْحٰنَ الَّذِىٓ أَسْرٰى بِعَبْدِهِ لَيْلًا مِّنَ الْمَسْجِدِ الْحَرَامِ إِلَى الْمَسْجِدِ الْأَقْصَا الَّذِىْ بَرَكْنَا حَوْلَهُ لِنُرِيَهُ مِنْ ءايٰتِنَا ، إِنَّهُ هُوَ السَّمِيْعُ الْبَصِيْرُ

'Glory be to He Who carried His bondsman by night from the sacred Musjid to
the Aqsa Musjid around which We've put blessings that We may show him
Our grand signs. No doubt He is the All-Hearing, All-Seeing.'
– Surah Bani Israel (17), Verse 1 [Pg. 102]

Verse 46

وَمِنَ الَّيْلِ فَتَهَجَّدْ بِهِ نَافِلَةً لَّكَ ، عَسٰى أَن يَّبْعَثَكَ رَبُّكَ مَقَامًا مَّحْمُوْدًا

'And offer Tahajjud in some portion of the night, this is
particularly and additionally for you. It's near that your Lord
may make you stand at a place where all will praise you.'
– Surah Bani Israel (17), Verse 79 [Pg. 110]

Verse 47

قُلْ لَّوْ كَانَ الْبَحْرُ مِدَادًا لِّكَلِمٰتِ رَبِّىْ لَنَفِدَ الْبَحْرُ قَبْلَ أَن تَنْفَدَ كَلِمٰتُ رَبِّىْ وَلَوْ جِئْنَا بِمِثْلِهِ مَدَدًا

'Say (O Beloved ﷺ), "If the sea was the ink for the words of my Lord, then
necessarily the sea would be exhausted while the words of my Lord would not
come to an end, though We may bring the like of it for help."'
– Surah Kahf (18), Verse 109 [Pg. 113]

Verse 48

قُلْ إِنَّمَا أَنَا بَشَرٌ مِّثْلُكُمْ يُوْحٰى إِلَىَّ أَنَّمَا إِلٰهُكُمْ إِلٰهٌ وَّاحِدٌ

'Say (O Beloved ﷺ), 'I'm a man like you. I receive
revelation that your God is one God."
– Surah Kahf (18), Verse 110 [Pg. 117]

Verse 49

فَإِنَّمَا يَسَّرْنٰهُ بِلِسَانِكَ لِتُبَشِّرَ بِهِ الْمُتَّقِيْنَ وَتُنْذِرَ بِهِ قَوْمًا لُّدًّا

'So We made this Quran easy on your tongue so that you may give
glad-tidings to the God-fearing and warn thereby a contentious people.'
– Surah Maryam (19), Verse 97 [Pg. 125]

Verse 50

طه ، مَا أَنْزَلْنَا عَلَيْكَ الْقُرْآنَ لِتَشْقَى

*"Tāhā. O Beloved ﷺ, We didn't send this Quran
upon you that you may be troubled."*
– Surah Tāhā (20), Verses 1-2 [Pg. 127]

Verse 51

وَمَا أَرْسَلْنَاكَ إِلَّا رَحْمَةً لِّلْعَالَمِينَ

'And We didn't send you but as a Mercy for the Worlds.'
– Surah Ambiya (21), Verse 107 [Pg. 129]

Verse 52

اللهُ نُورُ السَّمَوَاتِ وَالْأَرْضِ ، مَثَلُ نُورِهِ كَمِشْكَوةٍ فِيهَا مِصْبَاحٌ ، الْمِصْبَاحُ فِي زُجَاجَةٍ

*'Allah ﷻ is the light (Noor) of the Heavens and the Earth. The likeness of His
Light is a niche wherein is a lamp. The lamp is in a chandelier (of glass).'*
– Surah Noor (24), Verse 35 [Pg. 133]

Verse 53

لَا تَجْعَلُوا دُعَاءَ الرَّسُولِ بَيْنَكُمْ كَدُعَاءِ بَعْضِكُمْ بَعْضًا

*'Make not the summoning of the Messenger ﷺ among
yourselves the way one calls the other among you.'*
– Surah Noor (24), Verse 63 [Pg. 134]

Verse 54

تَبَارَكَ الَّذِي نَزَّلَ الْفُرْقَانَ عَلَى عَبْدِهِ لِيَكُونَ لِلْعَالَمِينَ نَذِيرًا

*'Immensely Great is He Who sent down the Quran
to His bondsmen that he may warn the worlds.'*
– Surah Furqān (25), Verse 1 [Pg. 137]

Verse 55

وَتَوَكَّلْ عَلَى الْعَزِيزِ الرَّحِيمِ ، الَّذِي يَرَاكَ حِينَ تَقُومُ ، وَتَقَلُّبَكَ فِي السَّاجِدِينَ

*'And rely upon Him Who's the Mighty, the Most Merciful; Who sees you when
you stand and your movements amongst those who offer prayer.'*
– Surah Shuarā (26), Verses 217-9 [Pg. 140]

Verse 56

حَتَّى إِذَا أَتَوْا عَلَى وَادِ النَّمْلِ قَالَتْ نَمْلَةٌ يَأَيُّهَا النَّمْلُ ادْخُلُوا مَسَاكِنَكُمْ لَا يَحْطِمَنَّكُمْ سُلَيْمَنُ وَجُنُودُهُ

وَهُمْ لَا يَشْعُرُونَ ، فَتَبَسَّمَ ضَاحِكًا مِّن قَوْلِهَا

'Until they came to the valley of the ants, and one ant said, "O Ants! Enter your homes lest Sulaiman ﷺ and his armies crush you unknowingly." Thereupon he smilingly laughed at her proclamation.'
– Surah Naml (27), Verses 18-9 [Pg. 141]

Verse 57

وَمَا كُنتَ تَتْلُوا مِن قَبْلِهِ مِن كِتَابٍ وَّلَا تَخُطُّهُ بِيَمِينِكَ ، إِذًا لَّارْتَابَ الْمُبْطِلُونَ

'And you did not recite any Book before, nor did you write anything with your hand. In that case, the followers of falsehood would've doubted.'
– Surah Ankabūt (29), Verse 48 [Pg. 145]

Verse 58

النَّبِيُّ أَوْلَى بِالْمُؤْمِنِينَ مِنْ أَنْفُسِهِمْ ، وَأَزْوَاجُهُ أُمَّهَتُهُمْ

'The Prophet (Muhammad ﷺ) is more worthy of the believers than their own selves, and his wives are their mothers.'
– Surah Ahzāb (33), Verse 6 [Pg. 149]

Verse 59

لَقَدْ كَانَ لَكُمْ فِي رَسُولِ اللهِ أُسْوَةٌ حَسَنَةٌ لِّمَن كَانَ يَرْجُوا اللهَ وَالْيَوْمَ الْاخِرَ وَذَكَرَ اللهَ كَثِيرًا

'Certainly you have an excellent model in the following of the Messenger of Allah ﷺ for him who hopes in Allah ﷺ and the Last Day and (who) remembers Allah ﷺ in abundance.'
– Surah Ahzāb (33), Verse 21 [Pg. 153]

Verse 60

يَنِسَاءَ النَّبِيِّ لَسْتُنَّ كَأَحَدٍ مِّنَ النِّسَاءِ

'O Wives of the Prophet ﷺ, you are not like other women.'
– Surah Ahzāb (33), Verse 32 [Pg. 156]

Verse 61

وَمَا كَانَ لِمُؤْمِنٍ وَّلَا مُؤْمِنَةٍ إِذَا قَضَى اللهُ وَرَسُولُهُ أَمْرًا أَنْ يَكُونَ لَهُمُ الْخِيَرَةُ مِنْ أَمْرِهِمْ

'And it's not befitting for a Muslim man and a Muslim woman when Allah ﷺ and His Messenger ﷺ have decreed something that they should have any choice in their matters.'
– Surah Ahzāb (33), Verse 36 [Pg. 159]

Verse 62

مَا كَانَ مُحَمَّدٌ اَبَا اَحَدٍ مِّنْ رِّجَالِكُمْ وَلٰكِنْ رَّسُوْلَ اللهِ وَخَاتَمَ النَّبِيِّیْنَ

'Muhammad ﷺ isn't the father of any of your men, but he's the
Messenger of Allah ﷻ and the Seal of the Prophets.'
– Surah Ahzāb (33), Verse 40 [Pg. 162]

Verse 63

يٰاَيُّهَا النَّبِیُّ اِنَّا اَرْسَلْنٰكَ شَاهِدًا وَّمُبَشِّرًا وَّنَذِيْرًا ، وَّدَاعِيًا اِلَى اللهِ بِاِذْنِهِ وَسِرَاجًا مُّنِيْرًا

'O Prophet (the communicator of unseen news), surely We
have sent you as a witness, a bearer of glad tidings, a warner, an inviter
towards Allah ﷻ by His command and an illuminating lamp.'
– Surah Ahzāb (33), Verses 45-46 [Pg. 166]

Verse 64

يٰاَيُّهَا الَّذِيْنَ اٰمَنُوْا لَا تَدْخُلُوْا بُيُوْتَ النَّبِیِّ اِلَّا اَنْ يُّؤْذَنَ لَكُمْ اِلٰى طَعَامٍ غَيْرَ نٰظِرِيْنَ اِنٰهُ

'O Believers, don't enter the houses of the Prophet ﷺ unless you receive
permission for a meal, not that you wait for its preparation.'
– Surah Ahzāb (33), Verse 53 [Pg. 174]

Verse 65

اِنَّ اللهَ وَمَلٰئِكَتَهٗ يُصَلُّوْنَ عَلَى النَّبِیِّ ، يٰاَيُّهَا الَّذِيْنَ اٰمَنُوْا صَلُّوْا عَلَيْهِ وَسَلِّمُوْا تَسْلِيْمًا

'Undoubtedly Allah ﷻ and His angels send blessings on the Prophet ﷺ. O
Believers, send blessings upon him and salute him fairly well in abundance.'
– Surah Ahzāb (33), Verse 56 [Pg. 175]

Verse 66

وَمَا اَرْسَلْنٰكَ اِلَّا كَآفَّةً لِّلنَّاسِ بَشِيْرًا وَّنَذِيْرًا وَّلٰكِنَّ اَكْثَرَ النَّاسِ لَا يَعْلَمُوْنَ

'And (O Beloved ﷺ), We have not sent you but for the entire mankind as
a bearer of good news and a warner, but most of the people don't know.'
– Surah Saba (34), Verse 28 [Pg. 183]

Verse 67

اِنَّا اَرْسَلْنٰكَ بِالْحَقِّ بَشِيْرًا وَّنَذِيْرًا ، وَاِنْ مِّنْ اُمَّةٍ اِلَّا خَلَا فِيْهَا نَذِيْرٌ

'(O Beloved Prophet ﷺ) Surely We have sent you
with truth, as a bearer of good news and as a warner. And
for every nation a warner has been appointed.'
– Surah Fātir (35), Verse 24 [Pg. 184]

Verse 68

يس ، وَالْقُرْآنِ الْحَكِيمِ ، إِنَّكَ لَمِنَ الْمُرْسَلِينَ

'Yaseen, by the wise Quran, Undoutedly you are of the sent ones.'
– Surah Yaseen (36), Verses 1-3 [Pg. 187]

Verse 69

قُلْ يِعِبَادِىَ الَّذِينَ أَسْرَفُوا عَلَى أَنْفُسِهِمْ لَا تَقْنَطُوا مِنْ رَحْمَةِ الله

'(O My Beloved ﷺ), Say, 'O my slaves who have committed excesses against their own souls, don't despair of the mercy of Allah ﷻ.'
– Surah Zumar (39), Verse 53 [Pg. 187]

Verse 70

إِنَّا فَتَحْنَا لَكَ فَتْحًا مُبِينًا ، لِيَغْفِرَ لَكَ الله مَا تَقَدَّمَ مِنْ ذَنْبِكَ وَمَا تَأَخَّرَ

'Undoubtedly We have granted you a clear victory [so] that Allah ﷻ may forgive sins of your formers and of your latters.'
– Surah Fat'h (48), Verses 1-2 [Pg. 189]

Verse 71

إِنَّا أَرْسَلْنَاكَ شهدًا وَمُبَشِّرًا وَنَذِيرًا ، لِتُؤْمِنُوا بِالله وَرَسُولِهِ وَتُعَزِّرُوه وَتُوَقِّروه وَتُسَبِّحوه بُكْرَةً وَأَصِيلًا

'Certainly We have sent you as a witness, a bearer of glad-tidings and a warner so that people should believe in Allah ﷻ and His Messenger ﷺ and honor him, and that you may glorify Him morning and evening.'
– Surah Fat'h (48), Verses 8-9 [Pg. 194]

Verse 72

إِنَّ الَّذِينَ يُبَايِعُونَكَ إِنَّمَا يُبَايِعُونَ اللهَ يَدُ اللهِ فَوْقَ أَيْدِيهِمْ

'Surely those who swear allegiance to you indeed swear allegiance to Allah ﷻ. The hand of Allah ﷻ is above their hands.'
– Surah Fat'h (48), Verse 10 [Pg. 196]

Verse 73

لَقَد رَضِىَ الله عَنِ الْمُؤْمِنِينَ إِذْ يُبَايِعُونَكَ تَحْتَ الشَّجَرَةِ فَعَلِمَ مَا فِي قُلُوبِهِمْ فَأَنْزَلَ السَّكِينَةَ عَلَيْهِمْ وَأَثَابَهُمْ فَتْحًا قَرِيبًا

'Certainly Allah ﷻ was pleased with the believers when they were pledging allegiance to you under the tree, and He knew what was in their hearts. So, He sent down on them tranquility and rewarded them with an expedition's victory.'
– Surah Fat'h (48), Verse 18 [Pg. 203]

Verse 74

هُوَ الَّذِى أَرْسَلَ رَسُولَه بِالْهُدى وَدِينِ الْحَقِّ لِيُظْهِرَه عَلَى الدِّينِ كُلِّه ، وَكَفى بِاللهِ شَهِيْدًا ، مُحَمَّدٌ رَسُوْلُ اللهِ ، وَالَّذِيْنَ مَعَه أَشِدَّاءُ عَلَى الْكُفَّارِ رُحَمَاءُ بَيْنَهُمْ ، تَرَاهُمْ رُكَّعًا سُجَّدًا يَبْتَغُوْنَ فَضْلًا مِّنَ اللهِ وَرِضْوَانًا

'It's He Who sent His Messenger ﷺ with guidance and the religion
of truth so that He may make it present over all other religions; and Allah ﷻ
suffices as a witness. Muhammad ﷺ is the Messenger of Allah ﷻ, and those
with him are severe against the infidels but compassionately tender among
themselves. You will see them bowing and prostrating themselves (in power)
seeking grace from Allah ﷻ and His pleasures.'
– Surah Fat'h (48), Verses 28-9 [Pg. 205]

Verse 75

يَأَيُّهَا الَّذِيْنَ امَنُوا لَا تُقَدِّمُوا بَيْنَ يَدَيِ اللهِ وَرَسُوْلِه ، وَاتَّقُوا اللهَ ، إِنَّ اللهَ سَمِيْعٌ عَلِيْمٌ ، يَأَيُّهَا الَّذِيْنَ امَنُوا لَا تَرْفَعُوا أَصْوَاتَكُمْ فَوْقَ صَوْتِ النَّبِيِّ وَلَا تَجْهَرُوا لَه بِالْقَوْلِ كَجَهْرِ بَعْضِكُمْ لِبَعْضٍ أَنْ تَحْبَطَ أَعْمَالُكُمْ وَأَنْتُمْ لَا تَشْعُرُوْنَ

'O Believers! Don't commit any excess before Allah ﷻ and
His Messenger ﷺ, and fear Allah ﷻ. Surely Allah ﷻ hears, knows.
O Believers, don't raise your voices above the voice of the Prophet ﷺ
and don't speak aloud in his presence as you speak to one another,
lest your deeds become in vain while you are unaware.'
– Surah Hujarāt (49), Verses 1-2 [Pg. 212]

Verse 76

وَالنَّجْمِ إِذَا هَوَى ، مَا ضَلَّ صَاحِبُكُم وَمَا غَوَى ، وَمَا يَنْطِقُ عَنِ الْهَوَى ، إِنْ هُوَ إِلَّا وَحْيٌ يُوْحَى

'By the brightly shining star (i.e. the Holy Prophet ﷺ) when he
descended from the Ascension (i.e. Mi'rāj). Your companion (the Holy
Prophet ﷺ) has not strayed nor was he misled. And he does not speak of
his own desire. It's no less than revelation revealed to him.'
– Surah Najm (53), Verses 1-4 [Pg. 215]

Verse 77

مَا كَذَبَ الْفُؤَادُ مَا رَأَى ، أَفَتُمَارُوْنَه عَلَى مَا يَرَى ، وَلَقَدْ رَآهُ نَزْلَةً أُخْرَى ، عِنْدَ سِدْرَةِ الْمُنْتَهَى

'The heart lied not in what it saw. Do you then
dispute with him concerning what he has seen? And indeed,
he saw that splendid sight twice; near the farthest Lote-tree.'
– Surah Najm (53), Verses 11-14 [Pg. 217]

Verse 78

إِقْتَرَبَتِ السَّاعَةُ وَانْشَقَّ الْقَمَرُ

'The Hour neared and the moon was split.'
– Surah Qamar (54), Verse 1 [Pg. 219]

Verse 79

الرَّحْمنُ ، عَلَّمَ الْقُرْآنَ ، خَلَقَ الْإِنْسَنَ ، عَلَّمَهُ الْبَيَانَ

*'The Most Affectionate; Taught the Quran; He created
(the soul of) mankind; He taught him expression.'*
– Surah Rahmān (55), Verses 1-4 [Pg. 221]

Verse 80

يَأَيُّهَا الَّذِينَ آمَنُوا اتَّقُوا الله وَآمِنُوا بِرَسُولِهِ يُؤْتِكُمْ كِفْلَيْنِ مِن رَّحْمَتِهِ وَيَجْعَل لَّكُمْ نُورًا تَمْشُونَ بِهِ وَيَغْفِرْ لَكُمْ ، والله غَفُورٌ رَّحِيْمٌ

*'O Believers! Fear Allah ﷻ and believe His Messenger ﷺ. He will give you a
two-fold portion of His mercy, will provide a light by which you will walk, and
will grant you forgiveness. And Allah ﷻ is Most Forgiving, Most Merciful.'*
– Surah Hadīd (57), Verse 28 [Pg. 223]

Verse 81

لَا تَجِدُ قَوْمًا يُؤْمِنُونَ بِاللهِ وَالْيَوْمِ الْآخِرِ يُوَادُّونَ مَنْ حَادَّ الله وَرَسُولَهُ وَلَوْ كَانُوا آبَاءَهُمْ أَوْ أَبْنَاءَهُمْ أَوْ إِخْوَنَهُمْ أَوْ عَشِيرَتَهُمْ

*'You will not find a people who believe in Allah ﷻ and the Last Day loving
those who act in opposition to Allah ﷻ and His Messenger ﷺ, even though they
may be their fathers, sons, brothers, or their kinsmen.'*
– Surah Mujādalah (58), Verse 22 [Pg. 224]

Verse 82

وَمَا اتكُمُ الرَّسُوْلَ فَخُذُوه وَمَا نَهْكُمْ عَنْهُ فَانْتَهُوا

*'And whatever the Messenger of Allah ﷺ gives you, take it; and
stay away from that which he prohibits you from.'*
– Surah Hashr (59), Verse 7 [Pg. 225]

Verse 83

هُوَ الَّذِى أَرْسَلَ رَسُوْلَهُ بِالْهُدَى وَدِيْنِ الْحَقِّ لِيُظْهِرَهُ عَلَى الدِّيْنِ كُلِّهِ وَلَوْ كَرِهَ الْمُشْرِكُوْنَ

*'It's He Who sent His Messenger ﷺ with guidance and the
true religion so that He may cause it to dominate over all religions,
even though the polytheists may hate it.'*
– Surah Saff (61), Verse 9 [Pg. 226]

Verse 84

وَللهِ الْعِزَّةُ وَلِرَسُوْلِهِ وَلِلْمُؤْمِنِيْنَ وَلكِنَّ الْمُنفِقِيْنَ لَا يَعْلَمُوْنَ

'And to Allah ﷻ belongs the dignity, and to His Messenger ﷺ

and the believers, but the Hypocrites don't know.'
– Surah Munafiqūn (63), Verse 8 [Pg. 228]

Verse 85

ن ، وَالْقَلَمِ وَمَا يَسْطُرُوْنَ ، مَا أَنْتَ بِنِعْمَةِ رَبِّكَ بِمَجْنُوْنَ ، وَإِنَّ لَكَ لَأَجْرًا غَيْرَ مَمْنُوْنَ

'Nūn; By the Pen and what they write; By the grace of your Lord, you
are not at all insane; and surely for you is an endless reward.'
– Surah Qalam (68), Verses 1-3 [Pg. 232]

Verse 86

وَإِنَّكَ لَعَلى خُلُقٍ عَظِيْمٍ

'And indeed, you are upon great manners.'
– Surah Qalam (68), Verse 4 [Pg. 238]

Verse 87

عَلِمِ الْغَيْبِ فَلَا يُظْهِرُ عَلى غَيْبِهِ أَحَدًا ، إِلَّا مَنِ ارْتَضى مِن رَّسُوْلٍ

'He is the Knower of the unseen. He does not reveal
His secrets to any except His chosen Messengers.'
– Surah Jinn (72), Verses 26-7 [Pg. 240]

Verse 88

يَأَيُّهَا الْمُزَّمِّلُ ، قُمِ الَّيْلَ إِلَّا قَلِيْلًا

'O you enwrapped one! Stand praying at night except a small portion thereof.'
– Surah Muzammil (73), Verses 1-2 [Pg. 243]

Verse 89

إِنَّا أَرْسَلْنَا إِلَيْكُمْ رَسُوْلًا شَهِدًا عَلَيْكُمْ كَمَا أَرْسَلْنَا إِلى فِرْعَوْنَ رَسُوْلًا

'Surely We have sent to you a Messenger 🕌 who is a witness
against you, as We sent a Messenger towards Pharaoh.'
– Surah Muzammil (73), Verse 15 [Pg. 244]

Verse 90

إِنَّ رَبَّكَ يَعْلَمُ أَنَّكَ تَقُوْمُ أَدْنى مِن ثُلُثَيِ الَّيْلِ وَنِصْفَهُ وَثُلُثَهُ وَطَائِفَةٌ مِّنَ الَّذِيْنَ مَعَكَ ،
وَاللهُ يُقَدِّرُ الَّيْلَ وَالنَّهَارَ ، عَلِمَ أَن لَّنْ تُحْصُوْهُ فَتَابَ عَلَيْكُمْ ، فَاقْرَؤُوا مَا تَيَسَّرَ مِنَ الْقُرْآنِ

'Surely your Lord knows that you remain standing in
devotion nearly two-thirds of the night, sometimes half of it, and
sometimes a third of it, along with a party of your Companions 🕌 with
you. And Allah 🕌 measures the night and the day. He knows that you

(O Muslims) are not able to calculate it. So, He has turned to you
(mercifully). Therefore, recite how much is easy of the Quran.'
– Surah Muzammil (73), Verse 20 [Pg. 245]

Verse 91

يَاۤأَيُّهَا الْمُدَّثِّرُ ، قُمْ فَأَنْذِرْ ، وَرَبَّكَ فَكَبِّرْ ، وَثِيَابَكَ فَطَهِّرْ

'O you who enfolded yourself in your mantle. Arise and warn; and
glorify the dignity of your Lord; and purify your garments.'
– Surah Mudath'thir (74), Verses 1-4 [Pg. 246]

Verse 92

لَا تُحَرِّكْ بِهِ لِسَانَكَ لِتَعْجَلَ بِهِ ، إِنَّ عَلَيْنَا جَمْعَهُ وَقُرْآنَهُ ، فَإِذَا قَرَأْنَاهُ فَاتَّبِعْ قُرْآنَهُ ، ثُمَّ عَلَيْنَا بَيَانَهُ

'(O Beloved ﷺ) Don't move your tongue with it (the Quran) that
you may hasten to learn it. Undoubtedly, it's upon Us to preserve and
recite it. Therefore, when We have recited it, follow the recitation.
Then on Us is the explaining of its minute detail.'
– Surah Qiyaamat (75), Verses 16-9 [Pg. 247]

Verse 93

عَبَسَ وَتَوَلَّى ، أَن جَاءَهُ الْأَعْمَى ، وَمَا يُدْرِيْكَ لَعَلَّهُ يَزَّكَّى

'He frowned and turned aside because the
blind man came to him; but what could convince you
that he may be seeking to purify himself?'
– Surah Abasa (80), Verses 1-3 [Pg. 248]

Verse 94

لَا أُقْسِمُ بِهَذَا الْبَلَدِ ، وَأَنْتَ حِلٌّ بِهَذَا الْبَلَدِ ، وَوَالِدٍ وَّمَا وَلَدَ

'I swear by this city (Makkah) as (O Beloved ﷺ) you dwell in this city, and by
your father (Sayyiduna Ibrahim السلام) and his progeny (i.e. Rasoolullah ﷺ).'
– Surah Balad (90), Verses 1-3 [Pg. 251]

Verse 95

وَالضُّحَى ، وَاللَّيْلِ إِذَا سَجَى ، مَا وَدَّعَكَ رَبُّكَ وَمَا قَلَى ، وَلَلْآخِرَةُ خَيْرٌ لَّكَ مِنَ الْأُولَى ، وَلَسَوْفَ يُعْطِيْكَ رَبُّكَ فَتَرْضَى

'By the brightness of the morning, and by the night when it covers,
your Lord has not forsaken you nor is He displeased. And undoubtedly
the Hereafter is better for you than the former. And indeed soon your
Lord will give you so much that you'll be satisfied.'
– Surah Duhā (93), Verses 1-5 [Pg. 255]

Verse 96

وَوَجَدَكَ ضَالًّا فَهَدَى

'He (Allah ﷻ) saw you deeply immersed in your love, so He guided you.'
– Surah Duhā (93), Verse 7 [Pg. 258]

Verse 97

أَلَمْ نَشْرَحْ لَكَ صَدْرَكَ ، وَوَضَعْنَا عَنكَ وِزْرَكَ ، الَّذِي أَنقَضَ ظَهْرَكَ

'Have We not expanded your chest for you? And removed your
burden from you? [That] which had broken your back?'
– Surah Sharh (94), Verses 1-3 [Pg. 260]

Verse 98

وَرَفَعْنَا لَكَ ذِكْرَكَ

'And have We not elevated your remembrance?'
– Surah Sharh (94), Verse 4 [Pg. 261]

Verse 99

وَالْعَصْرِ ، إِنَّ الْإِنسَانَ لَفِي خُسْرٍ

'By the time (of My Beloved ﷺ), indeed man is in a state of loss.'
– Surah Asr (103), Verses 1-2 [Pg. 265]

Verse 100

إِنَّا أَعْطَيْنَاكَ الْكَوْثَرَ

'(O Beloved ﷺ), undoubtedly We've bestowed upon you
Kauthar (an abundance of good).'
– Surah Kauthar (108), Verse 1 [Pg. 266]

Verse 101

قُلْ أَعُوذُ بِرَبِّ الْفَلَقِ

'(O Beloved ﷺ), Say, 'I seek refuge with the Lord of the daybreak.''
– Surah Falaq (113), Verse 1

قُلْ أَعُوذُ بِرَبِّ النَّاسِ

'(O Beloved ﷺ), Say, 'I seek refuge with the Lord of mankind.''
– Surah Naas (114), Verse 1 [Pg. 269]

Verse 102

اَلْحَمْدُ لِلَّهِ رَبِّ الْعٰلَمِيْنَ

'All praise be to Allah ﷻ, the Lord of the Worlds.'
– Surah Fatiha (1), Verse 1 [Pg. 271]

Verse 103

اِهْدِنَا الصِّرَاطَ الْمُسْتَقِيْمَ ، صِرَاطَ الَّذِيْنَ أَنْعَمْتَ عَلَيْهِمْ غَيْرِ الْمَغْضُوْبِ عَلَيْهِمْ وَلَا الضَّالِّيْنَ

'Guide us on the straight path, the path of those whom You have favored. Not those who have earned Your anger, nor of those who have gone astray.'
– Surah Fatiha (1), Verses 6-7 [Pg. 272]

SUPPLEMENTARY

The Friends of Allah ﷻ – Pg. 275

The Martyrs – Pg. 301

AUTHOR'S NOTE

بسم الله الرحمن الرحيم
نحمده ونصلى على حبيبه الكريم

Praise is reserved uniquely for the Sustainer of the Worlds Who created the entire creation by the command of "Be" (کن). He created man with a handful of sand and placed on his head the crown of honor,

ولقد كرمنا بني آدم
'And indeed We honored the children of Adam عليه السلام.'
– Surah Bani Israel (17), Verse 70

Subhanallah! How Compassionate, Merciful and Gracious is Allah ﷻ, that He showered us with blessings out of His grace? If we ever tried to count His blessings, we would never be able to do so.

To grant honor to this 'handful of sand', Allah ﷻ then sent the Prophets عليهم السلام to them, and indeed this is the greatest blessing of all His benedictions. An infinite amount of Durood be on the Beloved of the Lord of Duroods, the Beloved whose existence is the reason for the entire creation coming into existence. The entire creation was made for this Beloved. Sayyiduna Adam عليه السلام, his children, and all that is created is existent by means of this Beloved.

Subhanallah! How powerful a king is this Beloved, this Leader of the Prophets, this sympathizer of sinners, this intercessor on the Day of Resurrection, this Mercy of the Almighty, the helper of the helpless, this strength of the weak, this support of the destitute, whose remembrance is solace for troubled hearts?! How merciful is he that at the time of his birth, he remembered us sinners, during his Ascension (معراج) he kept us transgressors in mind, and he even moved his lips for us wrongdoers in his grave after his demise! – *Madaarijun-Nubuwwah*

On the Day of Qiyaamat, everyone will be worried and be thinking of themselves, yet on that Day, this Beloved will worry and think of everyone.

'Where a mother will forsake her only child (on the Day of Account),
He (Rasoolullah ﷺ) will be there, calling out, "Come to me!"'
– Alahadrat Imam Ahmed Raza Khan ﵀

After the praise of Allah ﷻ and Durood of His Messenger ﷺ, it should be known that the true purpose of human life is to recognize our Lord and perform His worship,

وما خلقت الجن والانس الا ليعبدون

'I have not created the jinn and the human but that they worship Me.'
– Surah Zāriyāt (51), Verse 56

Only he who knows the grand glory of Allah's ﷻ Beloved ﷺ can recognize Allah ﷻ Himself. Jews, Christians and polytheists can worship Allah ﷻ for years, but they cannot become people who have understanding of His Recognition (عارفین) or servants dedicated to His worship (عابدین). Why? Simple! They perform their worship, etc. without the understanding of the King of Madina, Muhammad Mustapha ﷺ. In several places of the Holy Quran, Allah ﷻ Himself presented His recognition through the means of His Beloved Prophet ﷺ,

هو الذي أرسل رسوله بالهدى ودين الحق

'It is He (Allah ﷻ) Who sent His Messenger ﷺ
with guidance and the true religion.'
– Surah Tauba (9), Verse 33

Allah ﷻ also states,

هو الذي بعث في الأميين رسولا منهم

'It is He Who sent among the unlettered a
Messenger ﷺ from among themselves.'
– Surah Jumua (62), Verse 2

If a person recognizes Allah ﷻ in Him being the Creator of the Heavens and the Earth, he's still incomplete in his Divine recognition (عرفان), yet he who recognizes Allah ﷻ in Him being the Creator of Muhammad ﷺ is a complete believer (مؤمن).

In short, Allah ﷻ demonstrates His complete admiration for His Beloved ﷺ, because He teaches us several times, "If you wish to see My glory, My wonderful workmanship, then look at My glorious and unique creation, Muhammad'ur-Rasoolullah ﷺ."

The skill of a workman is recognized by his production. The intensity of knowledge possessed by a scholar is understood through his best student. Likewise, the greatness of Allah ﷻ is seen in the splendor of Rasoolullah's ﷺ

beauty. The being of the Holy Prophet ﷺ is the manifestation (مظهر) of Allah Almighty ﷻ.

Allah ﷻ is the unrivalled Creator and Muhammad Mustapha ﷺ is the matchless creation. The follower of any religion cannot present a personality like the Holy Messenger ﷺ. Complete research and study on this will be presented later.

In the present era, among the things Muslims have become negligent of is the glory of our master, Muhammad Mustapha ﷺ. Unfortunately, there has also emerged an irreligious group of outward 'Muslims' who have made degrading the status of Rasoolullah ﷺ their religion. They've begun calling the Holy Prophet ﷺ a man like them, their 'big brother', and Allah ﷻ knows well their other disrespectful pronouncements. Simple and innocent Muslims have become ensnared in their traps after seeing them in their religious apparel of jubbas and turbans. When a passionate, religiously-inclined Muslim sees this condition in the believers, he has no other alternative but to cry tears of blood.

Seeing this state of affairs, my respected and honored Haji Iqdaam Ahmed, trustee and manager of Musjid'e-Gulzar'e-Madina, due to his compassionate and sympathetic nature towards Muslims, requested that I compile a book on Quranic verses which explicitly explain the glory of Rasoolullah ﷺ and briefly elucidate them in a manner which will cause the hearts of Muslims to become bright with Imaan. [He explained that] this book should be able to grant believers who read it solace of heart & knowledge of the Holy Prophet's ﷺ eminence, and that if it's read by even the hardest enemy of Islam & the Holy Messenger ﷺ, he will have no other option (after reading of the Prophet's ﷺ excellence) but to become his admirer. However, I was entirely mindful of my deficiency in knowledge and of my unworthiness for such a task. Where am I, an unsuitable human, and where is the excellence of the master of jinn and mankind?

Regarding the possessions of the world, Allah ﷻ states,

قل متاع الدنيا قليل

'Tell them (O Beloved ﷺ), 'The possessions of this world are little."
– Surah Nisā (4), Verse 77

Still, no one can count them,

وإن تعدوا نعمة الله لا تحصوها

'And if you have to count the bounties of Allah ﷻ,
you would be unable to do so.'
– Surah Nahl (16), Verse 18

Regarding the manners of Rasoolullah ﷺ, however, the Holy Quran states,

وإنك لعلى خلق عظيم

'And indeed, you are a person of great manners.'
– Surah Qalam (68), Verse 4

When the entire mankind cannot count that which has been mentioned as 'little' in the Holy Quran, who then has the power and ability to measure the excellences of the person with great manners, the greatest Beloved ﷺ?!

So, only with the intention of my name entering the list of those who have praised the Holy Prophet ﷺ, with these humble words I wish to be so fortunate that I be resurrected at the feet of those who carry the blessed sandals of Hadrat Hasan ibn Thaabit ؓ. I also pray that writing the praise of Rasoolullah ﷺ becomes compensation for my sins. Placing my trust in Allah ﷻ, I began this blessed task, and while *I* have started it, it is only Allah ﷻ Who will end it on goodness. Ameen.

This book was commenced on the 18th of Jamaadul-Ula, 1361 A.H, corresponding to Thursday, the 3rd of June, 1942. I name this book *Shaan'e-Habībur-Rahmān min Āyātil-Quran* (The Glory of the Most Merciful's ﷻ Beloved ﷺ from Verses of the Quran).

وما توفيقى الا بالله عليه توكلت واليه انيب وهو حسبى ونعم الوكيل ولا حول ولا قوة الا بالله العلى العظيم

Ahmed Yaar Khan Badaayuni

بسم الله الرحمن الرحيم

In truth, one sees that when the Holy Quran is studied with Imaan, from the beginning to the end, it is *all* the praise (نعت) of the master of the world, Muhammad Mustapha ﷺ. Whether it be while discussing the hand of Allah ﷻ or in the dissemination of beliefs, stories of the previous Prophets عليهم السلام & their nations or the Islamic Laws, every subject matter of the Holy Quran contains the praise and epithet of he who gave us the Holy Book – Rasoolullah ﷺ. Examples of this include Surah Ikhlās (which seemingly only mentions the Qualities of Allah ﷻ) and Surah Lahab (which discusses the disbeliever Abu Lahab and his wife). If careful attention is paid to even these Surahs, it becomes evident that they consist of the Holy Prophet's ﷺ praise.

In Surah Ikhlās (112), the Holy Prophet ﷺ is commanded, "(O Beloved ﷺ, *you*) say, 'Allah ﷻ is One, Allah ﷻ is Independent from every need, etc.'" However, with just one word, "Say" (قل), the Prophet's ﷺ praise is enjoined to the entire Surah! It was Allah's ﷻ wish that the subject being discussed be His Being & Qualities, while the speaker be His Most Beloved ﷺ!

"O Beloved ﷺ, you inform the world of My Qualities and I'll inform them of your calibre and attributes. You say,

الله احد
'Allah ﷻ is One.'
– Surah Ikhlās (112), Verse 1

"And I will say,

محمد رسول الله
'Muhammad ﷺ is the Messenger of Allah ﷻ.'
– Surah Fat'h (48), Verse 29

In other words, "You declare, 'Laa ilaaha illallaah' (There is no being worthy of worship besides Allah ﷻ), and I will say, 'Muhammad'ur-Rasoolullah ﷺ' (Muhammad is the Messenger of Allah ﷻ). I desire to hear of My Qualities from you.' On the Day of Covenant (the day wherein Allah ﷻ asked the souls if He was their Lord), the Holy Prophet ﷺ was the first to testify to Allah's ﷻ

Oneness. Just as how he is Beloved in being, so too is his blessed speech and utterance beloved to Allah ﷻ. This is why Allah ﷻ made Rasoolullah ﷺ recite the Quran to His creation.

Another reason why 'You say' in the verse was used is because Allah ﷻ is saying, "O Beloved ﷺ, say to the people that Allah ﷻ is One, so that if any human wishes to know and accept My Qualities without first being your slave, he can never be someone who recognizes Me (عارف) or one who believes in My Oneness (موحد). He can only be these things after pledging allegiance to you and *then* accepting My Oneness as taught by you." This is why the first Kalima (كلمة طيبة) is also called 'Kalimatut-Tauheed', since it comprises of Allah's ﷻ remembrance as well as 'Muhammad'ur-Rasoolullah ﷺ'. The first part speaks of Allah's ﷻ Oneness and the second part mentions the name of the teacher and propagator of this Oneness. Without the assistance of prophethood, Imaan (faith) on the true Oneness of Allah ﷻ cannot be reached.

Surah Lahab (111) also includes the praise of Rasoolullah ﷺ. In Surah Ikhlās (112), his praise was enjoined to the entire chapter through the word 'Say', yet in Surah Lahab, it's by *not* using the word 'Say'. Once, Abu Lahab ibn Abdul-Muttalib said to the Holy Prophet ﷺ, "May you be destroyed!" In response to such a cursed, foul statement, Allah ﷻ Himself ordered,

تبت يدا ابى لهب وتب

'The hands of Abu Lahab are destroyed, and he too is destroyed.'
– Surah Lahab (111), Verse 1

In other words, "O Beloved ﷺ, don't respond to him, because I Myself will answer him." Thereafter, by mentioning the punishment, dissension and ruin, etc, of Abu Lahab, we understand the grand eminence the Holy Prophet ﷺ possesses in the court of Allah ﷻ – that the person who utters even the slightest statement of insolence towards him becomes the enemy of *even Allah ﷻ!* It's reported in a Hadith'e-Qudsi,

من عادى لى وليا فقد اذنته بالحرب

'Allah ﷻ states, 'I declare war against anyone who has enmity for my friends.'
– Mishkaat, with ref. to Bukhari

The excellence of the Sahaabah, Ahle-Bait, Makkah Sharif, Madina Sharif, etc. mentioned in the Holy Quran is actually the praise of the Holy Messenger ﷺ. Praise of a king's slave and admiration of a king's crown & throne are in fact praise of the king himself. Furthermore, the censoring of idol-worshippers and the evils of the disbelievers is *also* the praise of the king (through whose opposition they become cursed and rejected).

If one studies Quranic verses dealing with Islamic Laws, he will find that the praise of Rasoolullah 🕊 is also apparent in all of them. In several places, the Holy Quran states, 'Perform Salaah', 'Give Zakaat', 'Hajj is compulsory upon you,' etc, but in no place does it say how Salaah should be read or how many rakaats should be completed. It doesn't say who must give Zakaat or how much should be given. The Holy Quran commands that Hajj be made but it doesn't explain the rules of the entire pilgrimage. The intent behind this is, "O People, We've given you the orders. If you wish to now know the details and methodology of these actions, look at the blessed rulings and practices of My Beloved 🕊. His blessed life is a complete elucidation of all My commands."

The reality is that Salaah, fasting, Hajj, etc, are the practices of the Noble Messenger 🕊. His practices are beloved, and if they are performed by us with sincerity, these practices of ours too become accepted. If a person recites the Holy Quran in the position of ruku or sajda in Salaah, or reads 'At-Tahiyaat...' while standing (i.e. he changes the sequence of Salaah as taught by the Holy Prophet 🕊), his Salaah will not be complete. Why? Simply because although he performed the positions of Salaah, he didn't present himself in the way taught by the Holy Prophet 🕊. O Muslims! Use the language of the Beloved 🕊 and you'll be rewarded for it (even if you don't understand it). If Salaah was a mere obligation and supplication, it could've been performed in *any language* since Allah ﷻ knows each one!

What occurs in Hajj? Remaining in a certain place, running in a certain place, throwing stones, making Tawaaf, etc. Why did these things become acts of worship on these dates? Simple – they are the practices of those who have proximity to Allah ﷻ. A Hadith states,

من تشبه بقوم فهو منهم
'Whoever resembles a particular nation is from amongst them.'

This is the case in Salaah and all other forms of worship. It's hoped that they gain a likeness to Rasoolullah 🕊 so that Allah ﷻ forgives us through their means.

Our sajdas are copies of those accepted sajdas. In brief, all Quranic verses of Islamic rulings are the praise of Rasoolullah 🕊.

Similarly, whatever action dissatisfies the Holy Messenger ﷺ is a sin. Allah ﷻ states,

والذين يؤذون رسول الله لهم عذاب اليم

'And those who hurt the Messenger ﷺ, for them is a painful torment.'
– Surah Tauba (9), Verse 61

By giving 'for them' (لهم) precedence, it's known that only those who hurt and trouble the Holy Prophet ﷺ will be punished. Rasoolullah ﷺ is hurt and troubled by the disbelief of every non-Muslim and the sin of the believers. If he isn't content with a particular form of worship, that act becomes a sin, and if he's satisfied with a certain faltering, that mistake becomes an act of worship completely! Hadrat Abu Bakr ﷺ allowing the snake to bite him in the cave was not considered suicide, but an act of worship. Abu Umayya Damari uttering a statement of disbelief while under duress wasn't considered evil, and Hadrat Ali ﷺ foregoing his Asr Salaah in Khaibar was also not a sin but an act of worship. All of these actions became good because Rasoolullah ﷺ was satisfied with them. However, Hadrat Ali ﷺ marrying another woman while in the Nikah of Sayyidah Fathima Zahra ﷺ would've been a sin because the Noble Messenger ﷺ was troubled by this, while his action of making Maghrib Salaah *qadā* in Arafat became an act of worship because the Holy Prophet ﷺ was satisfied with it.

In this book, however, we will discuss only those Quranic verses which are *directly* the praise of Rasoolullah ﷺ. On that note, let us begin the praise of our master and end this introduction!

Ahmed Yaar Khan Naeemi

THE BELOVED'S MAJESTY

بسم الله الرحمن الرحيم

VERSE 1

هُوَ الْأَوَّلُ وَالْآخِرُ وَالظَّاهِرُ وَالْبَاطِنُ ، وَهُوَ بِكُلِّ شَيْءٍ عَلِيْمٌ

'He is the first; he is the last; he is the open; he is the hidden;
and he has knowledge of everything.'
– Surah Hadīd (57), Verse 3

In the khutba of the book *Madaarijun-Nubuwwah*, Shaikh Abdul-Haqq Muhaddith Dehlwi ﷺ states that this verse is both the praise of Allah ﷻ *and* the praise of His Beloved ﷺ. The Holy Prophet ﷺ is the first of all, the last of all, he is evident to all, he is obscured, and he has knowledge of everything.

The Holy Prophet ﷺ is the first of all – Before the world, Hereafter and everything else, the first thing created was the Noor of Rasoolullah ﷺ,

اول ما خلق الله نوري
'The first thing Allah ﷻ created was my Noor.'

In the case of his physical body, Sayyiduna Adam عليه السلام is the father of Rasoolullah ﷺ, but in reality Rasoolullah ﷺ is the source of Sayyiduna Adam عليه السلام. A tree bears flowers even though the tree itself is from a flower. The flower of this orchard of creation is Rasoolullah ﷺ. Prophethood was first bestowed to him, as he himself states,

كنت نبيا وآدم بين الطين والماء
'I was already a prophet when Adam عليه السلام was between sand
and water (i.e. in the process of being created).'

On the Day of Covenant, when it was asked by Allah ﷻ, "Am I not your Lord?", the Holy Prophet ﷺ was the first to reply, "Indeed You are." – *Surah A'rāf (7), Verse 172*

On the Day of Qiyaamat, Rasoolullah's ﷺ grave will be opened first. He'll be commanded first to both make sajda and intercede (شفاعة). Bear in mind that the door of intercession will only be opened by the Holy Prophet ﷺ. He'll also be the first to open the doors of Jannah and enter it. All the other Prophets عليهم السلام will enter after him. It will be Rasoolullah's ﷺ Ummah to first enter

Jannah, and the other nations will follow us into Paradise. In short, the crown of being the first and having precedence is set on his blessed head. The first day (i.e. Jumua, Friday) was bestowed to the Holy Prophet ﷺ. Yet in spite of all these things, the Holy Messenger ﷺ is also last.

The Holy Prophet ﷺ is the last of all – Rasoolullah's ﷺ advent was the last – *The Seal & Final of Prophets* (خاتم النبیین) is a title which belongs to him. He was given the Final Book and the Final Deen, both of which will remain until Qiyaamat.

> *'Who knows how many stars were opened, then concealed?*
> *Yet never has, nor will, our Prophet ﷺ ever set.'*

> *'The Salaah of the Mi'rāj (Ascension) reveals the*
> *meaning of the first and the last.'*

> *'Behind, standing with folded hands are present those*
> *who already had dominion.'*
> – Alahadrat Imam Ahmed Raza ﵀

The Holy Prophet ﷺ is both open and hidden – Rasoolullah ﷺ has always been, and will always be, open and manifest to all because Muslims believe in him (and even non-Muslims recognize him),

> الذین ءاتینهم الکتب یعرفونه کما یعرفون ابناءهم
> *'Those to whom We gave the scripture recognize him (Prophet*
> *Muhammad ﷺ) as they recognize their own sons.'*
> – Surah Baqarah (2), Verse 146

Recognizing the Holy Prophet ﷺ here is equaled to knowing one's son, not with knowing a father. There are three reasons for this,

1. A son knows his father without proof (he recognizes him by the professing of people). However, the father knows his son through proof, e.g. the Nikah, his son's period in the womb, birth, etc. Likewise, non-Muslims also know Rasoolullah ﷺ through proof, not merely as hearers.

2. A son recognizes his father only after birth, while the father recognizes his son before birth. Likewise, non-Muslims knew of the Holy Prophet ﷺ before his blessed birth (and would even supplicate for his coming!).

3. The son doesn't recognize his father as soon as he's born. He recognizes him only after gaining comprehension. On the other hand, the father knows the child from the very first day. Similarly, the entire creation knew the Holy Prophet ﷺ from his infancy – mountains used to greet him, stones gave glad-tidings about him, trees bent to shade him, the moon conversed with him, non-Muslims testified to his prophethood, and even animals knew him (e.g. camels prostrated to him, while wild deers asked him to provide safety for them). Both the sun and the moon demonstrated their recognition of him – the moon split in two for him, and the set sun rose up on his gesture. Likewise, the inmates of the Heavens and the Earth knew him – as soon as Sayyiduna Adam عليه السلام opened his eyes, he saw the name of the Beloved ﷺ written next to Allah's ﷻ on the pillars of His Great Throne. So do the residents of Jannah know him – the Kalima is written on every leaf of Jannah, in the eyes of its maidens, on the chests of the male servants – in short, every place in Paradise.

Even the inmates of Jahannam profess,

قالوا لم نك من المصلين

'They said, 'We used to not offer prayer.''
– Surah Mudath'thir (74), Verse 43

(They'll say that them opposing the Holy Prophet ﷺ was what brought them to where they are.) In brief, wherever the remembrance of Allah ﷻ is present, the remembrance of the Holy Prophet ﷺ will be there with it. The entire creation is filled with his Noor, and in every place is his manifestation. Every countenance of the Beloved ﷺ is known to all until Qiyaamat. Every moment of his blessed life – from his infancy, his milk-drinking period, his childhood, events before the proclamation of prophethood, after the proclamation, his private and public life, his talking, walking, eating, sleeping, smiling, crying, etc. – in short, *every stage* of Rasoolullah's ﷺ life is open to all in all parts of the world. Where in the world haven't the books of Ahadith reached? This is his glory of being manifest.

Still, no one knew his reality besides Allah ﷻ. All of the above is the glory of him being open, while his reality is the glory of him being hidden.

Maulwi Qasim Nanotwi, famed as the founder of Darul Uloom Deoband, writes,

رہا جمال پہ تیرے حجاب بشریت

نہ جانا کون ہے کچھ بھی کس نے بجز ستار

سوا خدا کے بھلا کوئی تجھ کو کیا جانے

تو شمس نور ہے شپر نمط اولو الابصار

'The veil of humanity remained on your beauty and splendor.
Besides the Almighty, no one truly knew you.'

'Who can truly know you but Him? You are the sun of Noor,
unable to be seen even by those with vision.'
– Qasāid'e-Qasimi

His humanity (بشریت) was disclosed to the sight of humanity, but none besides the Creator knows the true reality of Muhammad Mustapha ﷺ. Just as how the light of the sun blocks the sun itself so that no one can see it completely, so too does the Prophet ﷺ being made of Noor (نورانیت) become a veil for us. This is why Allah ﷻ used the word 'Noor' for Rasoolullah ﷺ,

قد جاءکم من اللہ نور وکتب مبین

'Indeed there has come to you from Allah ﷻ a light
and a luminous book.'
– Surah Māida (5), Verse 15

A discussion on this verse will follow later.

The Holy Prophet ﷺ has knowledge of everything – Rasoolullah ﷺ has complete understanding of the Being (ذات) and Qualities of Allah ﷻ, and all former and latter creation's sciences of knowledge are encompassed by him. Within creation, he holds the highest rank with regards to the verse,

فوق کل ذی علم علیم

'And above every man of knowledge, there is someone more knowledgeable.'
– Surah Yusuf (12), Verse 76

On the night of Mi'rāj, the eye of the Holy Prophet ﷺ saw his Creator. How then can the creation be hidden from his vision?

'(O Rasoolullah ﷺ) How can anything be hidden from you,
When Allah ﷻ Himself wasn't hidden from you?'
– Alahadrat Imam Ahmed Raza Khan ؓ

Insha-Allah ﷻ, the study on this Divine vision will be presented later. [Also, a more comprehensive study on the knowledge of the Holy Prophet ﷺ can be found in verse 47 of this book].

VERSE 2

وَاِنْ كُنْتُمْ فِىْ رَيْبٍ مِّمَّا نَزَّلْنَا عَلٰى عَبْدِنَا فَأْتُوْا بِسُوْرَةٍ مِّنْ مِّثْلِهٖ ، وَادْعُوْا شُهَدَاءَكُمْ مِّنْ دُوْنِ اللّٰهِ اِنْ كُنْتُمْ صٰدِقِيْنَ

'And if you have any doubt as to what We have sent down
upon Our (exalted) servant, bring just one chapter like it and call
upon all your helpers besides Allah ﷻ if you are truthful.'
– Surah Baqarah (2), Verse 23

The disbelievers of Makkah would say, "Muhammad invents the Holy Quran on his own and then recites it to people." The above verse was a reply to this statement. The recognition of a product created by humans is that another person can make a product just like it, but when this is impossible, it's understood that it is Allah's ﷻ product and creation. Even though ants and fireflies are weak, no one says that they are created by humans. On the other hand, while trains and airplanes are strong, everyone knows humans made them. Why is this? Simple – because today there are *hundreds* of factories manufacturing trains and airplanes, yet there isn't one factory making ants and fireflies. Similarly, in this verse, it's said that if you believe the Holy Quran is a product of a human being, you should produce another like it.

Visibly, it seems that it's the Holy Quran alone that's being praised here, yet after paying careful attention, it becomes apparent that the praise of this verse also includes the *Saahibul-Quran* (Muhammad Mustapha ﷺ). Rasoolullah ﷺ isn't the student of anyone in creation. Still, he has come to this world as the ultimate teacher. Allah ﷻ is directly the teacher of His Messenger ﷺ, and Rasoolullah ﷺ is the student of Allah ﷺ. Bear in mind that the student of an excelled teacher becomes exceptional in his own right. When Allah ﷻ is the teacher of Rasoolullah ﷺ, imagine how proficient he is in knowledge and wisdom! This is why the verse says, "Call all your helpers (i.e. gather every scholar of the world you encounter, you'll still be unsuccessful [in finding a teacher like him])." This is because every scholar learnt from creation to become a scholar, so they are all students of creation. How then can they challenge he who's the student of the Creator and the teacher of creation himself?!

This verse proves that Rasoolullah ﷺ purifies the servants of Allah ﷻ. He purifies them from polytheism, disbelief, sin and moral degeneration.

Commentators of the Holy Quran have also asserted the following meaning to this verse: The pronoun (ضمیر) in 'like it' (مثله) relates to the Holy Messenger ﷺ. So, the verse will mean, "Bring just one chapter which has likeness to a chapter that emanates from the blessed mouth of Muhammad'ur-Rasoolullah ﷺ." In other words, "First search for a glorious beloved like Muhammad ﷺ, then make him recite such a chapter." – *Khaazin, Madaarik, etc.*

The meaning of this verse is that you can neither find anyone as glorious as the Holy Prophet ﷺ nor will you be able to present such speech like the Holy Quran. This proves that Rasoolullah ﷺ is matchless and unrivalled. The Prophet ﷺ himself once asked,

ایکم مثلی

'Which of you is like me?!'
– Bukhari Sharif

At another juncture, he said,

ولکنی لست کاحد منکم

'However, I am not like you.'

Intelligence also demands that there can be no equal to Rasoolullah ﷺ for the following reasons,

1. We are believers, while the Messenger ﷺ *is* belief (Imaan).

2. We are recognized as truthful, while Rasoolullah ﷺ is truth from head to toe.

3. People gain knowledge, while the Holy Prophet ﷺ is knowledge himself (since knowing or recognizing him is regarded as knowledge).

4. Our urine and excretion is impure, while the discharges of Rasoolullah ﷺ are clean for the Ummah. – *Shaami, Vol. 1*

5. Our sleep breaks our wudhu while his sleep doesn't.

6. We believe in Jannah, Jahannam, and Allah's ﷻ Being & Qualities after hearing of them. So, our faith is based on what we hear. Rasoolullah's ﷺ faith is based on what he *saw*.

7. Only five Salaah are compulsory on us, but a sixth Salaah (i.e. Tahajjud) was compulsory on him,

ومن اليل فتهجد به نافلة لك

'And offer Tahajjud in some portion of the night; this is especially for you in addition.'
– Surah Bani Israel (17), Verse 79

8. Five pillars of Islam are enjoined on every Muslim, but only four are compulsory on Rasoolullah ﷺ (Zakaat wasn't). – *Shaami, Kitaabuz-Zakaat*

9. We may keep up to four wives in Nikah, but there is no such restriction on Rasoolullah ﷺ.

10. Our wealth will be distributed after our death as inheritance, but not the wealth of any prophet.

11. After our death, our wives can remarry, but after the demise of Rasoolullah ﷺ, his wives couldn't. Allah ﷻ states,

ولا ان تنكحوا ازواجه من بعده ابدا

'Nor should you ever marry his wives after him.'
– Surah Ahzāb (33), Verse 53

There are several further differences in acts of worship (among other things). How then can it be said that we are men (بشر) like Rasoolullah ﷺ? A more detailed study on this will be presented later.

VERSE 3

يُخْدِعُوْنَ الله وَالَّذِيْنَ آمَنُوا وَمَا يَخْدَعُوْنَ إِلَّا أَنْفُسَهُمْ وَمَا يَشْعُرُوْنَ

'They seek to deceive Allah ﷻ and the believers, but in fact they

deceive none but themselves, and yet they perceive not.'
– Surah Baqarah (2), Verse 9

Although the Hypocrites (منافقين) are being censored and their faults are being disclosed here, the greatness of Rasoolullah ﷺ is also firmly established in it. Under this verse, Imam Khaazin ؓ states, "How can the Hypocrites deceive Allah ﷻ?" The answer given is,

ذكر نفسه واراد به رسوله وفى ذلك تفخيم لامره وتعظيم لشانه

'Allah ﷻ mentioned His being but intended His Messenger ﷺ by doing so.'

In other words, the Hypocrites wish to deceive Allah ﷻ by intending to deceive Rasoolullah ﷺ. This proves the nearness the Holy Prophet ﷺ has to Allah ﷻ, that trying to deceive him is regarded as deceiving Allah ﷻ.

Tafseer Madaarik states, "This verse is similar to the verse of allegiance, in which it was stated, "(O Beloved ﷺ,) Those who swear allegiance to you swear allegiance to Allah ﷻ. The hand of Allah ﷻ is over their hands." – *Surah Fat'h (48), Verse 10*

It was also said, "(O Beloved ﷺ,) You did not throw the stone you threw. It was Allah ﷻ [Who threw it]." – *Surah Anfāl (8), Verse 17*

Subhanallah! Allah ﷻ made the action of Rasoolullah ﷺ His own act!

VERSE 4

وَعَلَّمَ اٰدَمَ الْاَسْمَاءَ كُلَّهَا ثُمَّ عَرَضَهُمْ عَلَى الْمَلَائِكَةِ

*'Allah ﷻ taught Adam عليه السلام the names of all things,
then He showed them to the angels.'*
– Surah Baqarah (2), Verse 31

The greatness of Sayyiduna Adam عليه السلام and his surplus of knowledge are being discussed in this verse. Allah ﷻ showed him all former and latter, major and minor things and informed him of their names. He also taught him each object's harm and benefit, as well as its state and condition. – *Tafseer Madaarik*

We can also deduce that Sayyiduna Adam عليه السلام was informed of every name of every thing in every language that will come until Qiyaamat. For example, water is *maa* in Arabic, *aab* in Farsi, *jal* in Hindi, and *paani* in Urdu.

18

Likewise, other languages have different words for it, and Sayyiduna Adam ﷺ was taught all of these names. – *Tafseer Kabeer*

In short, everything was made apparent to Sayyiduna Adam ﷺ, and based on this excellence of knowledge, Allah ﷻ placed the crown of His deputyship (خلافة) on his blessed head and made him the object of sajda for the angels. However, this verse also demonstrates the praise of Rasoolullah ﷺ in the following manner: It's an accepted fact that Rasoolullah ﷺ possesses the collective sciences of knowledge (علوم) held by *all* the other Prophets ﷺ. Rather, it was actually from *his blessed hands* that the Prophets ﷺ attained every blessing of Allah ﷻ. The Holy Prophet ﷺ states,

الله المعطى وانا قاسم
'Allah ﷻ is the giver and I am the distributor.'
– Bukhari Sharif

Allah ﷻ also states,

اولئك الذين هدى الله ، فبهداهم اقتده
'These are those whom Allah ﷻ has guided. Then you follow their path.'
– Surah An'ām (6), Verse 90

So, the Holy Messenger is the collection of every quality of all the Prophets ﷺ.

This verse doesn't mean that Rasoolullah ﷺ must be obedient to the former Prophets ﷺ with regards to the deen. In matters of belief, submission to someone (تقليد) isn't permissible even for an ordinary Muslim (it's necessary for him to do research (تحقيق) himself). This is why Allah ﷻ established rational proofs concerning His Oneness, granting of prophethood, and resurrection (حشر ونشر) in the Holy Quran. So, how can the Leader of Prophets submit to others in beliefs?

Concerning religious practices, indeed the deen of Rasoolullah ﷺ is what nullifies previous deens. When Islam is the nullifier of deens, how can it follow them?

Therefore, 'their path' in this verse refers to the personal and unique excellences of the Prophets ﷺ. Rasoolullah ﷺ was bestowed the gratefulness of Sayyiduna Nuh ﷺ, the tradition of Sayyiduna Ibrahim ﷺ, the sincerity of Sayyiduna Musa ﷺ, the truthfulness of Sayyiduna Ismail ﷺ, the patience of Sayyiduna Ayub ﷺ and Sayyiduna Yaqub ﷺ, the repentance of Sayyiduna Dawud ﷺ, and the humility of Sayyiduna Sulaiman ﷺ and Sayyiduna Esa

صلى الله عليه وسلم. So, 'their path' means, "Become the collection of every excellence of the previous Prophets عليه السلام." – *Roohul-Bayaan (in the begininng of Surah Nuh)*

> *'You possess the beauty of Yusuf* عليه السلام, *the spirit of Esa* عليه السلام,
> *and the marvel of the bright hand. Whatever excellence*
> *we individually possess, you are their collection.'*

Imam Busairi رحمة الله عليه states,

فانك شمس فضل هم كواكبها ، يظهرن انوارها الناس فى الظلم

> *'O Beloved* صلى الله عليه وسلم, *you are the sun of greatness while all the*
> *Prophets* عليه السلام *are your stars. Everyone takes from you and*
> *demonstrates your Noor to people in darkness.'*
> – Qasida Burda Sharif

Also, Maulwi Qasim Nanotwi writes, "All former and latter knowledge is encompassed in the knowledge of Rasoolullah صلى الله عليه وسلم. Just as how the knowledge of sight and sound are both individual but collective in a being, so too is the Holy Prophet صلى الله عليه وسلم the True & Real Knower (عالم حقيقى) while the other Prophets عليه السلام are Knowers who have gained knowledge (عالم بالفرض). – *Tahzeerun-Naas*

And Shaikh'e-Akbar Ibn Arabi رحمة الله عليه states, "Sayyiduna Adam عليه السلام was the first Khalifa and deputy of Rasoolullah صلى الله عليه وسلم." – *Futoohaat'e-Makkiya, Chapter 10*

These Quranic verses, Ahadith, and statements by the Islamic Scholars clearly prove that although the knowledge of Sayyiduna Adam عليه السلام was very extensive, it was but a drop in the ocean compared to the knowedge of Rasoolullah صلى الله عليه وسلم, or a line in the journal of his knowledge. How extensive is Rasoolullah's صلى الله عليه وسلم knowledge? This is known only by Rasoolullah صلى الله عليه وسلم and He Who granted him that knowledge. A study on this will be presented later.

Sayyiduna Adam عليه السلام was made the object of sajda for the angels and was bestowed the crown of Allah's عز وجل deputyship. These are all the blessings of the Noor of Muhammad صلى الله عليه وسلم which was present in his forehead. It was this Noor that was actually made the object of sajda, and it's through its blessings that these branches of knowledge were granted to Sayyiduna Adam عليه السلام. – *Refer to Madaarijun-Nubuwwah, Vol. 2.*

VERSE 5

فَتَلَقَّى آدَمُ مِن رَّبِّهِ كَلِمَاتٍ فَتَابَ عَلَيْهِ ، إِنَّهُ هُوَ التَّوَّابُ الرَّحِيْمُ

> *'Then Adam* عليه السلام *learnt certain words (of repentance) from*

his Lord and He (Allah ﷻ) accepted his repentance. Surely
He is the Most Relenting, Most Merciful.'
– Surah Baqarah (2), Verse 37

This verse explains the incident of the acceptance of Sayyiduna Adam's ﷺ repentance. After his mistake and descent to Earth, Sayyiduna Adam ﷺ didn't look up towards the Heavens for 300 years, and he cried so much that if the tears of the entire world were collected, they would still not equal his.

There are five individuals who cried excessively in this world,

1. Imam Zainul-Ābideen ﷺ after the incident of Karbala.

2. Sayyidah Fathima Zahra ﷺ after the demise of Rasoolullah ﷺ.

3. Sayyiduna Yahya ﷺ in the fear of Allah ﷻ.

4. Sayyiduna Yaqub ﷺ during his separation from Sayyiduna Yusuf ﷺ.

5. Sayyiduna Adam ﷺ on his mistake.

Thereafter, a few words of dua were placed by Allah ﷻ in the heart of Sayyiduna Adam ﷺ, and it was only when he used these words in dua that Divine Mercy assisted him.

And what were the words of this dua? There are several opinions regarding them.

Tibrani, Haakim, Abu Nuaim and *Baihaqi* narrate from Hadrat Ali ﷺ, "One day, after much crying, the heart of Sayyiduna Adam ﷺ inspired him, causing him to say, 'When I was created, I saw written on the pillars of the Throne, "لا اله الا الله محمد رسول الله There is none worthy of worship besides Allah ﷻ; Muhammad ﷺ is the Messenger of Allah ﷻ." I understood that Muhammad'ur-Rasoolullah ﷺ was the accepted beloved of the Divine Court since Allah ﷻ wrote his name next to His.' Sayyiduna Adam ﷺ then submitted, 'O Allah ﷻ, I seek forgiveness of my mistake through the means of that blessed being. I ask You to pardon me.' At that exact moment, the mercy of Allah ﷻ pardoned Sayyiduna Adam ﷺ for his mistake." – *Roohul-Bayaan (under the commentary of this verse) & Madaarijun-Nubuwwah (Beginning of Vol. 2)*

Subhanallah! What a merciful name is possessed by Rasoolullah 鷺?! The Holy Prophet 鷺 made his father (Sayyiduna Adam عليه السلام) both the object of sajda for the angels *and* saved him from his grief!

"If the name 'Muhammad 鷺' was not used as the intercessor, neither would Adam عليه السلام have attained (the acceptance of his) repentance nor would '*We have saved...*' have been used concerning Nuh عليه السلام and the drowning." – *Allama Jaami* رحمه الله

The children of Adam عليه السلام are now also commanded, "If you commit sin, disbelief or oppression, present yourselves to Rasoolullah 鷺 and request intercession from him. Go to him and repent to Allah ﷻ, and when the Holy Prophet 鷺 intercedes for you, your repentance will be accepted. Allah ﷻ states,

ولو انهم اذ ظلموا انفسهم جائوك فاستغفروا الله واستغفر لهم الرسول لوجدوا الله توابا رحيما

'And if they do injustice unto their souls, then O Beloved 鷺, they should come to you and then beg forgiveness from Allah ﷻ, and the Messenger 鷺 should intercede for them. Then surely they will find Allah ﷻ Most Relenting, Merciful.'
– Surah Nisā (4), Verse 64

This doesn't mean that we must go only to Madina. Rather, it means, "Turn towards the Holy Prophet's 鷺 merciful being because he is present (حاضر) at all places." A more thorough discussion on this will be presented later.

This verse also establishes that, nevermind us, even the Prophets عليهم السلام are needy of Rasoolullah 鷺. Allah ﷻ is the Lord of Creation (رب العالمين) and Rasoolullah 鷺 is the Mercy unto Creation (رحمة للعالمين). In other words, he is mercy for everything Allah ﷻ is the Lord of.

VERSE 6

يَأَيُّهَا الَّذِيْنَ آمَنُوا لَا تَقُوْلُوْا رَاعِنَا وَقُوْلُوا انْظُرْنَا وَاسْمَعُوْا ، وَلِلْكٰفِرِيْنَ عَذَابٌ أَلِيْمٌ

'O you who believe, don't say (to Allah's ﷻ Messenger) 'Ra'ina', but say, 'Unzurna'. From the beginning, listen attentively (to his disclosure), and for the disbelievers is a painful punishment.'
– Surah Baqarah (2), Verse 104

At first glance, it seems as if it's the Muslims who are being given a command in this verse, but in fact it's clear proof of the greatness of Rasoolullah 鷺. The background behind the revelation of this verse is as follows: the Companions of the Prophet ﷺ would say 'Ra'ina' (O Prophet of Allah ﷺ, take care of us!) whenever Rasoolullah ﷺ said something that was incomprehensible to them. In other words, "Repeat what you said, O Rasoolullah ﷺ!".

However, the word 'Ra'ina' was also a swear word in the language of the Jews, so they [the Jews] began to use this in the Prophet's ﷺ court with a bad intention. Hence, this verse was revealed and Muslims were now commanded to say 'Unzarna' instead of 'Ra'ina', even though the Companions' usage of 'Ra'ina' was with good intention.

Subhanallah! The grandeur of the Holy Prophet ﷺ is clearly proven by this! Allah ﷻ desires to extend the glory of His Beloved ﷺ to such an extent that He doesn't even permit the usage of a word which others can misuse with the intention of disrespect! We come to know from this that to utter something negligible about the Holy Prophet ﷺ is an act of disbelief, even if it was said with no bad intention. In fact, Jurists have stated that the person who shows disrespect to *even the blessed sandal* of the Holy Prophet ﷺ becomes a non-Muslim!

The following incident about Imam Abu Yusuf ؓ is recorded in the book *Sharah Fiqh'e-Akbar*: *Kaddu* (pumpkin/gourd/calabash) was once cooked and served on the table of Hārūn Rashid. Someone at the table said, "The Holy Prophet ﷺ liked *kaddu*," resulting in another saying, "But I don't like it." Hearing this, Imam Abu Yusuf ؓ drew out his sword to slay the neck of the man and said, "You've become an apostate (مرتد) for mentioning your dislike in comparison to something Rasoolullah ﷺ was fond of!" He then left the man only after he repented.

> If his advent hadn't occurred in Arabia, who would've known about the Ka'ba and Madina? Arabia doesn't have any fancy tourist attractions, green scenery or beautiful landscape, yet the entire world is drawn to it! Why?

The people of Egypt taunted Sayyiduna Yusuf عليه السلام for being a slave even though he had power over them. In reply, Allah ﷻ sent such a drought to them that people from all countries sacrificed their properties, their wealth, and ultimately their lives for Sayyiduna Yusuf عليه السلام. Sayyiduna Yusuf عليه السلام then freed them; resulting in the entire world being his freed slaves, and he their master. Who now dares call him a slave?!

We also come to know from this verse that people in this time who've spoken or published disrespectful statements about the Holy Prophet ﷺ are people with no Islam in them.

VERSE 7

إِنَّا أَرْسَلْنَاكَ بِالْحَقِّ بَشِيرًا وَّنَذِيرًا ، وَلَا تُسْئَلُ عَنْ أَصْحٰبِ الْجَحِيْمِ

*'Indeed We have sent you (O Muhammad ﷺ) with the
truth, a bearer of glad tidings and a warner. And you will not
be questioned regarding the inmates of Hell.'*
– Surah Baqarah (2), Verse 119

This verse explains several excellences of the Holy Prophet ﷺ.

Seeing the condition of the disbelievers and his refuters, Rasoolullah ﷺ used to be saddened. Out of his mercy, he desired that all people bring Imaan and become inmates of Jannah. However, Allah ﷻ declared, "O Beloved ﷺ, those who are your enemies and speak ill of you will not attain even the *fragrance* of Jannah." In short, seeing the stubbornness and disbelief of the non-Muslims, the blessed heart of Rasoolullah ﷺ would become saddened. This verse, then, was revealed to bring solace and contentment to him, i.e. "O Beloved ﷺ, your obligation was propagation, and you fulfilled it. You will not be questioned on the Last Day as to why people didn't become believers. You are not responsible for them."

Allah ﷻ shows in this verse that He didn't enjoy seeing the Holy Prophet ﷺ sad. Is the greatness of the Holy Prophet ﷺ not proven here?

Let's now examine the verse more thoroughly. It begins with, "Indeed We have sent you," establishing that the coming of the Noble Messenger ﷺ is a gift to the bondsmen from Allah ﷻ. Understand also that a royal gift is the pinnacle of all gifts. So, from all the Divine blessings, this is the most excellent.

Secondly, only that which is initially in the proximity of someone is sent. So, we can ascertain that before coming to the world, Rasoolullah ﷺ was present (حاضر) in the special court of his Lord. And what was the manner of him being present there? The following narration sheds some light on this: The Holy Prophet ﷺ once asked Sayyiduna Jibrael عليه السلام how old the angel was. Sayyiduna Jibrael عليه السلام replied, "I cannot say, but I do know that a star would shine every 70,000 years, and I saw that star 72,000 times." The Holy Prophet

⚜ replied, "Indeed that star was me." – *Tafseer Roohul-Bayaan (Surah Tauba, Verse 128)*

When this was the manner of the Holy Prophet's ⚜ presence in the court of Allah ﷻ, can anyone now hope to fathom his excellence?! A sesame seed spends only one night by a flower before attaining its fragrance. So, why can't the Holy Prophet ⚜ not become the manifestation of Allah's ﷻ Qualities? In the khutba of the book *Madaarijun-Nubuwwah*, Shaikh Abdul-Haqq ⚜ himself states that Rasoolullah ⚜ is the manifestation of Allah's ﷻ Qualities. The Friends of Allah ⚜, too, demonstrate control by the power of Allah ﷻ. – *Mishkaat, Baabu Fadhliz-Zikr*

The verse also states that Rasoolullah ⚜ didn't come empty-handed. Rather, he brought three things,

1.   Truth.

2.   Glad-tidings for believers.

3.   Warnings of punishment for the refuters.

The verse then states [in other words], "O Beloved ⚜, you will not be questioned like others as to why a certain person didn't believe, or why he didn't do good." A Hadith states that every person will be asked, "Why didn't your children, spouses, dependants and even servants join the path of salvation?" But the Holy Prophet ⚜ will not face such questioning. Also, the previous nations will say on the Day of Judgment, "No prophet even came to us." The prophet sent to them will say, "O Allah ﷻ, we did propagate Your commands to them." These nations will become plaintiffs and the Prophets عليهم السلام defendants, while the Ummah of Rasoolullah ⚜ will be the witnesses of the previous Prophets عليهم السلام. On that Day, no disbeliever will have the courage to say such a thing against the Holy Prophet ⚜.

VERSE 8

رَبَّنَا وَابْعَثْ فِيهِمْ رَسُوْلًا مِّنْهُمْ يَتْلُوْا عَلَيْهِمْ اٰيٰتِكَ وَيُعَلِّمُهُمُ الْكِتٰبَ وَالْحِكْمَةَ وَيُزَكِّيْهِمْ ، اِنَّكَ اَنْتَ الْعَزِيْزُ الْحَكِيْمُ

'O our Lord, send among them a Messenger ⚜ from themselves who will recite to them Your verses and teach them the scripture & wisdom, and purify them. Surley You are the Most Exalted, the Wise.'
– Surah Baqarah (2), Verse 129

This verse concerns the construction of the Holy Ka'ba. When Sayyiduna Ibrahim عليه السلام and Sayyiduna Ismail عليه السلام completed its construction, they supplicated to Allah ﷻ, saying, "We have made this house. Now send to this city the prophet who will cherish it and purify Your servants." This supplication was accepted when Muhammad Mustapha ﷺ was born in the city of Makkah, from the lineage of Sayyiduna Ismail عليه السلام, in the home of Hadrat Abdullah ﷺ, and from the womb of Sayyidah Amina ﷺ. He shone so brightly from here that his radiance will exist until Qiyaamat. He himself states, "I am the supplication of Ibrahim عليه السلام, the glad-tidings of Esa عليه السلام and the dream of my mother." – *Mishkaat, Baabu Fadhaaili Sayyidil-Mursaleen*

Two points emerge from this verse,

1. The earlier Prophets عليهم السلام supplicated and expressed their hope for the Holy Prophet ﷺ.

2. Although the Holy Ka'ba was constructed by Sayyiduna Ibrahim عليه السلام, it was in fact through the Holy Messenger ﷺ that it attained honor and reverence. It became cherished because of Rasoolullah ﷺ.

Everyone knows that prior to the advent of the Holy Prophet ﷺ, the polytheists (مشرکین) of Makkah kept idols in the Holy Ka'ba specifically and began idolating there. Others besides Allah ﷻ were being worshipped in the House of Allah ﷻ. So, the Ka'ba too anxiously awaited the arrival of Rasoolullah ﷺ, because it was his arrival that would cleanse it from the filth of idols until the Day of Qiyaamat.

The Ka'ba is the House of Allah ﷻ and Rasoolullah ﷺ is the light (نور) of Allah ﷻ. It's light that brightens a home. What's the Holy Ka'ba when even the highest elevation of Jannah gained adornment because of Rasoolullah ﷺ,

> *'It's a point of amazement that the Holy Paradise has been*
> *created by Allah ﷻ but populated by Muhammad ﷺ.'*
> – Dr. Iqbal

This verse also proves that Rasoolullah ﷺ purifies the servants of Allah ﷻ. He purifies them from polytheism, disbelief, sin and moral degeneration. If you desire purification, submerge yourself in his ocean of mercy and you will be cleansed. Water cleans only the outer body while the blessed sight of the Mercy unto Creation ﷺ cleans the outer *and* inner parts, including the heart, senses and mouth.

وَكَذَٰلِكَ جَعَلْنَٰكُمْ أُمَّةً وَّسَطًا لِّتَكُوْنُوْا شُهَدَاءَ عَلَى النَّاسِ وَيَكُوْنَ الرَّسُوْلُ عَلَيْكُمْ شَهِيْدًا

*'And so We made you an exalted community
among all the nations so that you may be a witness over
the people and the Messenger 🌺 a witness over you.'*
– Surah Baqarah (2), Verse 143

This verse apparently praises the Ummah of Rasoolullah 🌺, but it's obvious that whatever we (the Ummah) have gained in honor is only through us being the slaves of our master, Muhammad Mustapha 🌺.

On the Day of Qiyaamat, the nations of previous Prophets 🌺 will say in the Divine Court, "O Allah 🌺, no prophet of Yours came to us, and no one communicated Your commands to us." The Prophets 🌺 will reply, "O Allah 🌺, they are liars! We did communicate Your commands to them but they didn't accept them." Allah 🌺 will then instruct the Prophets 🌺 to present a witness for their claim, and they in turn will present the Ummah of the Holy Prophet 🌺. This Ummah will testify, "O Allah 🌺, Your Prophets 🌺 are true and these disbelievers are liars. These Prophets 🌺 truly completed the propagation of Your commands." The disbelievers will object to this and point out, "You weren't present in our time. In fact, you came centuries after us. How can you testify without having seen anything?" The Muslims will answer, "We heard from the one who *has* seen (i.e. our Beloved Prophet 🌺)." After this, Rasoolullah 🌺 will come to verify the Muslims' testimony and will say, "O Allah 🌺, indeed I said to them that the previous Prophets 🌺 propagated to their respective nations." This statement will bring the decision in favor of the Prophets 🌺.

This is the incident being referred to in this verse, and it establishes the following points,

1. This Ummah (i.e. the Muslims) is witness for the Prophets 🌺. The witness is loved by the person he supports. So, this Ummah is the beloved of all the Prophets 🌺.

2. The Holy Prophet 🌺 saw the affairs of those before him. Otherwise, testimony based on hearing had already been given by the Muslims; there was no need for an eye-witness to further present his testimony. This is why the Ascension (Mi'rāj) of Rasoolullah 🌺 occurred – everybody else's testimony regarding Jannah, Jahannam,

and Allah's ﷻ Being & Qualities is based on hearing, while the Holy Messenger's ﷺ testimony is based on seeing these things.

3. Rasoolullah ﷺ is aware of the actions and condition of every follower (امّتی) of his at all times. On the Day of Judgment, he will bear witness to two things: first, that the Muslims are correct, and the second, that they are worthy of being witnesses (i.e. they are not open transgressors of Islamic Law). The testimony of an open transgressor is not credible according to Islam. 'Alaa' (علی) was used in the verse because 'witness' incorporates the meaning of overseer here. So, that person whose faith is testified to by Rasoolullah ﷺ is truly an inmate of Jannah. The faith of Hadrat Abu Bakr Siddique ؓ and Hadrat Umar ؓ is definite because the witness of Allah ﷻ (i.e. the Holy Prophet ﷺ) testified to it. In fact, whoever rejects their faith rejects Allah ﷻ.

The above verse can also mean, "O Muslims! You can [collectively] become the witness of all people on Earth." It's for this reason that in an Islamic court, the testimony of a Muslim in a non-Muslim's case will be accepted, but the testimony of non-Muslims will not be accepted in the cases of Muslims. This is the honor of this Ummah.

A third meaning of this verse can be, "If Muslims regard any living or deceased being to be good, then that individual is also good in the sight of Allah ﷻ; and if they regard someone to be bad, then he or she is also bad in the sight of Allah ﷻ." It's reported that once, a funeral procession passed by the Holy Messenger ﷺ. When he heard that the Muslims were praising the deceased, he replied, "Jannah is necessary for him." Another funeral procession then passed, and when Rasoolullah ﷺ heard the Muslims speaking ill of the deceased, he replied, "Jahannam is necessary for him." A short while later, he said, "You are the witnesses of Allah ﷻ on the Earth." – *Mishkaat, Baabul-Mashyi bil-Janaazah*

So, the Muslim who's believed to be a Friend of Allah ﷻ by the general body of Muslims is truly a Saint and Friend of Allah ﷻ.

We may also deduce from this verse that whatever is not prohibited in Islamic Law and is regarded to be a good act in the sight of Muslims is also a good act in the sight of Allah ﷻ, such as gatherings in celebration of the Holy Prophet's ﷺ birth (میلاد), Fatiha (conveying *thawāb* to the deceased) and other acts of goodness. A Hadith states,

ما راه المؤمنون حسنا فهو عند الله حسن

'Whatever the Muslims deem good is good in the sight of Allah ﷻ.'

Muslims are the witnesses of Allah ﷻ in everything in both worlds.

VERSE 10

قَدْ نَرَى تَقَلُّبَ وَجْهِكَ فِى السَّمَاءِ ، فَلَنُوَلِّيَنَّكَ قِبْلَةً تَرْضٰهَا

'Surely We have observed you turning your face (O Muhammad ﷺ) towards Heaven repeatedly, and We will surely turn you to a qibla with which you will be pleased.'
– Surah Baqarah (2), Verse 144

Although outwardly this verse commands the changing of the direction for Salaah, if it's seen with Imaan, it becomes apparent that the glory of Rasoolullah ﷺ is being discussed here. This verse states that the Beloved Prophet ﷺ is the Ka'ba of even the Holy Ka'ba. Being the Ka'ba for all is something, but being the Ka'ba's Ka'ba is something else entirely.

The reason for the revelation of this verse is as follows: Salaah was made compulsory on the night of Mi'rāj in the city of Makkah, and the Holy Ka'ba was appointed as the direction for it. After the migration, Muslims were ordered to face Baitul-Muqaddas (Jerusalem) instead. Baitul-Muqaddas was the qiblah for the Jews and Christians. So, the Jews began to taunt, "In all laws and commands, Muhammad opposes us, yet he prays facing our qiblah!" Based on this objection, and due to the fact that the Ka'ba was constructed by Sayyiduna Ibrahim السلام عليه (an ascendant of Rasoolullah ﷺ), the Prophet ﷺ desired that the Ka'ba become his qiblah once again. Seventeen months had passed facing Baitul-Muqaddas for Salaah, until one day, Rasoolullah ﷺ said to Sayyiduna Jibrael السلام عليه, "My heart desires that I face the Ka'ba and perform Salaah." Sayyiduna Jibrael السلام عليه replied, "O Beloved of Allah ﷺ, I'm a humble servant of Allah ﷻ. Without His command I cannot say anything. You are the Beloved of Allah ﷺ, and so your dua will never be rejected. O Rasoolullah ﷺ, you supplicate to Him." After saying this, Sayyiduna Jibrael السلام عليه left. While awaiting revelation afterwards, the Prophet ﷺ began to turn his blessed face towards the Heavens, thinking that the command for the qiblah to be changed will be revealed. This action of his was beloved to Allah ﷻ, and so

> We believe in Jannah, Jahannam, and Allah's ﷻ Being & Qualities after hearing of them. So, our faith is based on what we hear. Rasoolullah's ﷺ faith is based on what he *saw*.

He replied, "O Beloved 🕌, We see this graceful mannerism of yours, that you repeatedly lift your face towards the Heavens. So We now make the qiblah that which you wish to be so." – *Tafseer Roohul-Bayaan (under the commentary of this verse)*

We can deduce the following from this,

1. All people are bound by Divine Law, but Divine Law awaits the desire of the Holy Beloved 🕌.

2. The honor of the Ka'ba – that even Saints prostrate in its direction and revere it – is all through the means (صدقة) of Rasoolullah 🕌. His desire made the Ka'ba the qiblah of the believers until Qiyaamat.

3. Sometimes the person who prostrates is more excellent than that which he's prostrating to. Sayyiduna Yaqub عليه السلام made sajda towards Sayyiduna Yusuf عليه السلام whereas Sayyiduna Yaqub عليه السلام is more excellent than him. Likewise, the Holy Prophet 🕌 made sajda towards the Ka'ba even though he's more excellent than it.

Rule – If a person is performing fardh or optional (نفل) Salaah and the Holy Prophet 🕌 calls him, it's compulsory (واجب) on the person to leave his Salaah and present himself in the court of the Prophet 🕌. – *Mishkaat, Baabu Fadhaailil-Quran*

This will be discussed in detail under Surah Anfāl (8), Verse 24 [Verse 34 of this book].

In fact, some are of the opinion that if the person reading Salaah leaves it and presents himself in the service of Rasoolullah 🕌, he may return and complete it – even if he spoke to the Holy Prophet 🕌 and turned his chest away from the Ka'ba, still too will his Salaah not be squandered or broken. Refer to *Qastalaani Sharah Bukhari*, Kitaabut-Tafseer, Surah Anfāl (8) under the commentary of this verse.

Though the chest of the one reading Salaah turned away from the qiblah, one has to ask: where did it then turn to? It turned towards he who is the qiblah of the qiblah! Although the one reading Salaah spoke, who did he speak to? He spoke to he on whom it's compulsory to make Salaam to in Salaah (refer to the wording of At-Tahiyaat). Even the Holy Ka'ba made sajda towards the Maqaam'e-Ibrahim on the night of the Prophet's 🕌 blessed birth. – *Madaarijun-Nubuwwah, Vol. 2, Discussion on Wilaadat*

It's therefore proven that the Holy Messenger ﷺ is the Ka'ba of even the Holy Ka'ba.

VERSE 11

تِلْكَ الرُّسُلُ فَضَّلْنَا بَعْضَهُمْ عَلَى بَعْضٍ ، مِّنْهُم مَّن كَلَّمَ اللهُ ، وَرَفَعَ بَعْضَهُمْ دَرَجَٰتٍ

'Of these messengers We have excelled some over others. To some of them Allah ﷻ spoke, and one is he who's raised high in degrees over all.'
– Surah Baqarah (2), Verse 253

This verse states that the Prophets علّيهم السّلام have been sent to the world for the salvation of the creation. They aren't equal in excellence (i.e. some have excellence over others). One is the Speaker with Allah ﷻ (Sayyiduna Musa علّيه السّلام), one the Close Friend of Allah ﷻ (Sayyiduna Ibrahim علّيه السّلام), one the Spirit of Allah ﷻ (Sayyiduna Esa علّيه السّلام), and some are those whom Allah ﷻ granted great rank and excellence.

The Commentators of the Holy Quran state, "...he who's raised high in degrees (of honor) over all," refers to our Beloved Master, Muhammad Mustapha ﷺ. So, the verse would mean, "Rasoolullah ﷺ has been granted such great honor and status that none can comprehend it. Only the Lord Who bestowed him with it and the Prophet ﷺ who received it know." It's evident that Rasoolullah ﷺ has received and possesses all the greatness and excellences possessed by the previous Prophets علّيهم السّلام. In fact, he possesses *even more* excellence than this.

To speak of Rasoolullah's ﷺ complete glory and excellence isn't within human capacity. However, we'll try to mention some of these excellences here in brief,

1. Other Prophets علّيهم السّلام were sent to specific nations and people, but the prophethood of Rasoolullah ﷺ is for all whose lord is Allah ﷻ. This is why his quality is 'the Mercy unto Creation' (رحمة للعلمين).

2. Rasoolullah ﷺ is the Prophet of all Prophets علّيهم السّلام, and all the Prophets علّيهم السّلام are his Ummatis and followers. A detail discussion on this follows under Surah Ale-Imran (3), Verse 81 [Verse 14 in book].

3. The Holy Messenger ﷺ is the Final (and Seal) of Prophets ﷺ. No new prophet can come after him.

4. Rasoolullah ﷺ is the prophet who went for Mi'rāj (the Ascension). No other prophet was granted this.

5. All the Prophets ﷺ wish for the desire of Allah ﷻ in every affair, but Allah ﷻ wishes for the pleasure of His Beloved ﷺ,

فلنولينك قبلة ترضاها

'We will surely turn you to a qiblah with which you will be pleased.'
– Surah Baqarah (2), Verse 144

ولسوف يعطيك ربك فترضى

'And soon your Lord will give so much that you
(O Beloved ﷺ) will be pleased."
– Surah Duhā (93), Verse 5

6. Other Prophets ﷺ were bestowed with a few miracles, but our Beloved Prophet ﷺ was granted innumerable miracles. In fact, he's a miracle from head to toe!

7. The Divine Book given to Rasoolullah ﷺ (i.e. the Holy Quran) annuls all previous books, but the Quran itself cannot be annulled by another.

8. On the Day of Judgment, Rasoolullah ﷺ will be adorned with the greatest ability to intercede (الشفاعة الكبرى).

9. Rasoolullah's ﷺ Ummah is the most excellent of Ummahs, etc.

VERSE 12

مَنْ ذَا الَّذِىْ يَشْفَعُ عِنْدَه إِلَّا بِإِذْنِه ، يَعْلَمُ مَا بَيْنَ اَيْدِيْهِمْ وَمَا خَلْفَهُمْ ، وَلَا يُحِيْطُوْنَ بِشَيْءٍ مِّنْ عِلْمِه إِلَّا بِمَا شَاءَ

'Who is there that can intercede with Him except by His permission? He knows
all that was before and all that will happen after; and they can encompass
nothing of His knowledge except for what He wills.'
– Surah Baqarah (2), Verse 255

These are three sentences of Ayatul-Kursi (the Verse of the Throne). From its beginning until the end, Ayatul-Kursi mentions eleven qualities of Allah ﷻ. Under its commentary, however, *Tafseer Roohul-Bayaan* states that the above verses contain three qualities of the Holy Messenger ﷺ. Before this passage, five qualities of Allah ﷻ are mentioned, and after it, three. Between them, the qualities of Rasoolullah ﷺ are being mentioned (similar to the

Kalima, wherein Allah's ﷻ name is mentioned at both the beginning and the end, while the Holy Prophet's ﷺ in the middle).

In the first sentence, the Holy Prophet's ﷺ greatest ability to intercede (الشفاعة الكبرى) is mentioned. On the Day of Qiyaamat, when even the Prophets عليهم السلام will proclaim, "To each his own (نفسى نفسى)," what can possibly be said about *our* condition on that day?! However, after the doors of intercession are opened by the blessed hand of Rasoolullah ﷺ, Islamic scholars, children, the Ka'ba, the Holy Quran, and even the month of Ramadaan will intercede.

> 'The only reason the Day of Resurrection has been co-ordinated is so
> that the Holy Prophet's ﷺ glory of belovedness is demonstrated.'
> – Maulana Hasan Raza ﷜

Although others will intercede, the doors of intercession will be initially opened by Rasoolullah's ﷺ hands.

Bear in mind that intercession is of four types,

1. A greater person interceding for someone to a less esteemed being,

2. A person interceding for someone to his equal,

3. A less esteemed person interceding for someone to a greater being but with coercion.

The above categories of intercession are impossible in the court of Allah ﷻ (non-Muslims believed in these forms). The verse itself negates these types of intercession.

4. A lesser being interceding in the court of a greater being, doing so merely in the latter's mercy and love. This is known as Intercession by Permission (شفاعة بالاذن). The beloveds of Allah ﷻ complete this type of intercession.

The next sentence of Ayatul-Kursi ('*He knows all that was before and all that will happen after.*') states that this Intercessor of Sinners, Muhammad Mustapha ﷺ, knows the condition and state of these people, i.e. he knows what was their condition in the world, whether they were Muslims, non-Muslims or Hypocrites (منافقين), and what their future condition will be. He knows whether they will be inmates of Jannah or Jahannam and even what rank they will be worthy of within it.

For Rasoolullah ﷺ to know so is necessary, because if a doctor doesn't know whether a patient is treatable or not, how can he prescribe medicine? Likewise, if the Intercessor of Sinners doesn't know and recognize who's worthy of intercession and who isn't, how will he carry it out? Rasoolullah ﷺ has already informed many in the world that they would be either inmates of Jannah or Jahannam. Besides informing the Ten Individuals (عشرة مبشرة), Sayyidah Fathima Zahra ؓ, Imam Hasan ؓ and Imam Husain ؓ, etc. that they would reside in Jannah, he also informed Sayyidah Fathima Zahra ؓ that she would be the leader of womenfolk in Jannah, and that Imam Hasan ؓ and Imam Husain ؓ would be the Leaders of the Youth in Jannah.

In one battle, a Muslim was fiercely slaying non-Muslims, leading some of the Companions to praise him. Regardless, Rasoolullah ﷺ said, "Even with all this, he will be an inmate of Jahannam." This was because he eventually committed suicide.

Once, the Holy Prophet ﷺ came to his Companions with two books in his hands and said, "This book mentions the names of the inmates of Jannah as well as the names of their fathers and tribes. The other mentions the names of the inmates of Jahannam along with the names of their fathers and tribes." He then totaled the number of both. – *Mishkaat, Baabul-Imaan bil-Qadr*

OBJECTION A Hadith states that the Hypocrites will come to the Fountain of Kauthar but will be stopped from nearing it. Rasoolullah ﷺ will say, "O angels, let them come. They are my companions." The angels will submit, "You don't know what they committed after you."

Answer – How can Rasoolullah ﷺ not know on the Day of Qiyaamat who will enter Jannah while he informed us of these things here in the world?

I've comprehensively explained this Hadith in my book, *Ja'al-Haqq*. Refer to it there.

The third sentence states that people do not grasp the knowledge of the Intercessor of Sinners except the amount which he wishes for them to acquire. In other words: Saints, and even the Prophets ﷺ and angels, cannot fully encompass the knowledge of the Holy Prophet ﷺ. On the contrary, he informs them of the amount he wishes for them to know. Actually, the knowledge of Rasoolullah ﷺ is an ocean, and the amount taken from it varies according to the vessels different individuals use. Some used a jug, while others used smaller vessels – so is the difference in the amount of knowledge they possess. Hadrat Abu Bakr Siddique ☙, Hadrat Umar ☙, Hadrat Uthman ☙ and Hadrat Ali ☙ all attained blessings from the ocean of Rasoolullah ☙, but all according to the ability of their bearing. Imam Busairi ☙ eloquently states,

وكلهم من رسول الله ملتمس ، غرفا من البحر او رشفا من الديم

'And all request from the Messenger of Allah ☙,
A scoop from the ocean or a drink from continuous rain.'
– Qasida Burda Sharif

Maulwi Qasim Nanotwi has explained the above discussion clearly in his treatise *Tahzeerun-Naas*. In short, this verse has clearly mentioned intercession, knowledge, and the Holy Prophet's ☙ bestowal of it.

VERSE 13

قُلْ اِنْ كُنْتُمْ تُحِبُّوْنَ الله فَاتَّبِعُوْنِىْ يُحْبِبْكُمُ الله وَيَغْفِرْ لَكُمْ ذُنُوْبَكُمْ ، وَالله غَفُوْرٌ رَّحِيْمٌ

'Please declare (O Beloved ☙), "If you love Allah ☙, follow me.
(Only then) Allah ☙ will love you and forgive you for your faults. And
Allah ☙ is Most Forgiving, Most Merciful.'
– Surah Ale-Imran (3), Verse 31

This verse clearly explains the path of attaining and reaching Allah ☙, and through it the glory of Rasoolullah ☙ is clearly demonstrated to all. The disbelievers of Makkah used to say, "We are the beloveds of Allah ☙." So, they were commanded, "If you truly love Allah ☙, become the slaves of His Beloved ☙. The benefit of doing so is that until now, you claim to have love for Allah ☙ and say that He's your beloved, but when you become the slaves of Allah's ☙ Beloved, Muhammad Mustapha ☙, Allah ☙ will love you, make you His beloveds, and forgive you for your sins."

We can deduce from this verse that even a rejected person becomes the beloved of Allah ☙, and the sinful are forgiven, all through the blessings of being the slaves of Rasoolullah ☙.

Follow (اتباع) means 'to walk behind'. So, the verse states, "If you desire Allah's ☙ love, follow [i.e. walk behind] the Holy Beloved ☙; don't walk in line with him thinking yourself to be his brother, or walk ahead of him thinking yourself to be his superior. Become his slave and follow him from behind. The carriages of a train are only beneficial if they are connected to its engine. Also, the engine pays no attention to whether the first-class or third-class is joined to it. All it's concerned with is the carriage. First-class or not, the engine moves them equally on condition that the carriage is joined and on the railway track. It's as if the engine is saying to the carriage, "Even though you are weak, I'm strong." So, the Quran is saying, "Follow the Prophet ﷺ. No matter how you do it, I look not at you but at the connection you have with him."

Maulana Jalaaluddin Rumi ؓ states,

'Cast into the fire the pages of the hundred books you may have,
Turn the face of the heart towards he who is the heart's beloved.'
– Mathnawi Sharif

Obedience (اطاعة) is of three kinds,

1. Obedience out of fear

2. Obedience out of greed

3. Obedience out of love

This verse intends the third kind (obedience of love), because the other categories of obedience are carried out by Hypocrites. This is the reason why the verse started with love. Bear in mind that love is also of three kinds,

1. Love shown to someone smaller than you, e.g. the love a parent has for his or her child.

2. Love shown to an equal, e.g. the love a husband has for his wife.

3. Love shown with honor to a greater being.

We deduce from 'you should follow me' in the verse that the third kind of love should be present.

Thereafter, greatness (عظمة) is of two kinds,

1. Religious.

2. Worldly.

We learn from 'Allah ﷻ will love you' in the verse that the greatness of Rasoolullah ﷺ is religious, meaning one has to love and honor him based on his prophethood, not think of him as our big brother.

VERSE 14

وَإِذْ أَخَذَ اللهُ مِيثَاقَ النَّبِيِّينَ لَمَا اٰتَيْتُكُمْ مِّنْ كِتٰبٍ وَّحِكْمَةٍ ثُمَّ جَآءَكُمْ رَسُوْلٌ مُّصَدِّقٌ لِّمَا مَعَكُمْ لَتُؤْمِنُنَّ بِهٖ وَلَتَنْصُرُنَّهٗ ، قَالَ ءَاَقْرَرْتُمْ وَاَخَذْتُمْ عَلٰى ذٰلِكُمْ إِصْرِىْ ، قَالُوْٓا اَقْرَرْنَا ، قَالَ فَاشْهَدُوْا وَاَنَا مَعَكُمْ مِّنَ الشّٰهِدِيْنَ

'And recall when Allah ﷻ took from the Prophets ﷺ their covenant, that, "I should give you a Book and Wisdom; then comes to you a Messenger ﷺ confirming what is with you; assuredly you will believe in him and help him." Then He said, "Do you agree and take this as my firm agreement as binding on you?" They said, "We've agreed." Allah ﷻ then said, "Then be witness, and I am with you among the witnesses."
– Surah Ale-Imran (3), Verse 81

The pledge taken from the Prophets ﷺ on the Day of Covenant is mentioned in this verse. It also proves the greatness of Muhammad Mustapha ﷺ to the extent few are able to comprehend.

The incident of this pledge is as follows: Sayyiduna Adam ﷺ was sent to the [Sarandeep] mountain of Colombo (in present-day Sri Lanka) from Jannah while Sayyidah Hawa ﷻ was placed in Jeddah (Arabia). Through the blessings of the Holy Prophet's ﷺ name, after three hundred years, their repentance was accepted. This has already been explained under Verse 5 in the book. On the mountain of Nu'mān, the souls of all of Sayyiduna Adam's ﷺ children were brought out from his spine, and three pledges were then taken from them. The first was, "Am I not your Lord?" (asked to the entire creation). They replied, "Yes, You are our Lord." The second pledge of agreeing to propagate the commands of Allah ﷻ was taken from the religious scholars, and the third pledge was taken from the Prophets ﷺ (as mentioned in the verse). On that day, Allah ﷻ said to the Prophets ﷺ, "When I will grant you Divine revelation (i.e. the Holy Books), adorn your heads with the crown of prophethood, make My servants your followers, and when the sun of your prophethood's glory shines bright and

> His teaching created an Abu Bakr Siddique ﷺ, an Umar Farooq ﷺ, etc. No other teaching is as comprehensive as the Holy Prophet's ﷺ. When a student enters a school, he goes to various teachers to learn different subjects, but when a person came to the Holy Prophet ﷺ, there was no need for another.

your name dominates the world, if in that time this Final Messenger 🌸 comes to the world, it's obligatory on you and your followers to become his followers (Ummatis). As soon as he arrives, your Deen and Book is annulled." The Prophets ﷺ agreed to this, but Allah ﷻ didn't stop there. He said, "Become witnesses on one another," meaning Sayyiduna Adam ﷺ should become a witness for Sayyiduna Nuh ﷺ, etc. He also said, "My Divine testimony is included with your witnessing. I'm also a witness to your pledge."

When Allah ﷻ took the pledge of His Lordship, everyone agreed by saying, "Yes," and the matter ended. But, here, Allah ﷻ made the Prophets ﷺ not only agree, He even made them witnesses on each other's affirmation, *and* included His own testimony with theirs! It was indeed in Allah's ﷻ knowledge that no prophet would be in the era of Rasoolullah 🌸, yet He still took this pledge from them, that if the Beloved Messenger 🌸 comes in their time, they must follow him. It can be understood that every prophet declared faith on this. Also, if their followers, after hearing about this incident from them, lived in the Final Messenger's 🌸 era, they should also believe in him. On the night of Mi'rāj, every prophet confirmed this pledge by following Rasoolullah 🌸 in Salaah in Baitul-Muqaddas.

> *'The Salaah of the Mi'rāj (Ascension) reveals the*
> *meaning of the first and the last. Behind, standing with folded*
> *hands are present those who already had dominion.'*
> – Alahadrat Imam Ahmed Raza ﷺ

Subhanallah! What a Salaah this must have been?! A Salaah in which all the followers are the Prophets ﷺ, and the Leader of Prophets, the Imam! To act upon this very pledge, Sayyiduna Esa ﷺ will come to the world as the follower (Ummati) of Rasoolullah 🌸 to protect and help the deen of our Beloved Messenger 🌸. He'll save the believers from enemies.

In the presence of Rasoolullah 🌸, why will all the Prophets' ﷺ deens be annulled? It's the norm of the world that everything stops when it reaches its source. In fact, it even loses itself in its source. The moon shines bright the entire night, but when the sun rises, it stops, because the moon attains its brightness from the sun itself. Rivers too rush towards the ocean (since they're made by it, formed by clouds also developed from the ocean). While the river returns to its source, it rushes so speedily that it overcomes any building or bridge that wishes to stop it. However, when it nears the ocean, it slows down; and when it meets it, the river becomes so annihilated by it that it's as if it didn't exist in the first place. This metaphorically states,

'I've become you, you've become me. I've become
the body and you the soul. So, no one should say after this
convergence that I'm separate or that you are different."
– Khwaja Amīr Khusro ◌

The Prophets ◌ are rivers and Rasoolullah's ◌ the ocean. All prophethoods were rushing towards his direction, and if any Pharaoh or Nimrod stood in their way, they crushed them. But, when they merged with the ocean of prophethood, they annihilated themselves in it.

This verse proves that all the Prophets ◌ are the followers (Ummatis) of Rasoolullah ◌, and that he's the leader of them.

VERSE 15

لَقَدْ مَنَّ اللهُ عَلَى الْمُؤْمِنِيْنَ إِذْ بَعَثَ فِيْهِمْ رَسُوْلًا مِّنْ أَنْفُسِهِمْ يَتْلُوْا عَلَيْهِمْ ايْتِه وَيُزَكِّيْهِمْ
وَيُعَلِّمُهُمُ الْكِتبَ وَالْحِكْمَةَ وَإِنْ كَانُوْا مِنْ قَبْلُ لَفِيْ ضَلٰلٍ مُّبِيْنٍ

'Certainly Allah ◌ conferred (great) favor upon the
believers that He sent a Messenger ◌ from among them who recites
to them the verses, purifies them and teaches them the Book & wisdom;
and previous to that they were clearly in error.'
– Surah Ale-Imran (3), Verse 164

This verse is clear praise of Rasoolullah ◌. Allah ◌ bestowed humanity with innumerable favors, and every blessing is so precious that even if the wealth of the world is spent, the blessings granted to us would still not be equaled. Our eyes, feet, noses, ears, the Earth, sky, sun, moon, etc. are all Divine blessings. Our bodies have many strands of hair, each with an infinite number of blessings, and every blessing is such that without it, life would be very difficult. Although the Holy Quran mentioned these things several times, not once does it boast about conferring such favors. It doesn't say, "O Muslims! We have shown you great favor by giving you eyes, ears, the Earth, etc."

The word 'manna' (to confer favor) was used in this verse. So, it'll mean, "By this single blessing of giving My Beloved ◌ to the Muslims for their salvation, I (Allah ◌) have conferred a great favor upon them." This proves that the advent of the Holy Prophet ◌ is the greatest of all blessings. There are three reasons for this,

1. Everything can be given to others in the world, but an individual cannot give away his beloved. Rasoolullah ﷺ going for Mi'rāj (his Ascension to the Heavens) isn't surprising (because the Beloved ﷺ is shown such favor). However, Rasoolullah ﷺ returning to the world from Allah's ﷻ presence *is* amazing, because the Beloved ﷺ was once again granted to the creation.

2. The world and all the blessings of it exist through the means (صدقة) of the Holy Messenger ﷺ. A Hadith states,

لو لاك لما خلقت الافلاك

*'Allah ﷻ states, "(O Beloved ﷺ,) Had it not been for you,
I would not have created the Heavens."'*

3. The eyes, ears and mouth, etc. of a person are only beneficial to him during his lifetime. When he dies, all of these blessings cease to benefit him (even his wealth is given away to others). Yes, people will still show mercy to him, but only until his grave. However, the person who's beneficial to us in life, the grave, the Hereafter, in Jannah, at the time of death, and at every juncture of our existence is our Beloved Master, Muhammad Mustapha ﷺ. Temporal blessings have no value in comparison to perpetual blessings,

قل متاع الدنيا قليل

'Say (O Beloved ﷺ), 'The possessions of the world are insignificant."
– Surah Nisā (4), Verse 77

4. If wealth, human senses, body parts, etc. are used correctly, only then do they act as blessings. If not, they are trouble and an inconvenience. If a tongue completes its purpose (such as mentioning Allah ﷻ), it's praised, but if it speaks ill of things and backbites, it's frowned upon and causes difficulties for the speaker. Definitely, it's the Holy Prophet ﷺ who taught us the correct usage of these blessings. In other words, he made them the blessings that they are. Otherwise, they would have been nothing but inconveniences. If our body parts are used to sin, our very eyes, feet, etc. will testify against us on the Day of Qiyaamat. We may even call them the 'secret agents' of the Almighty ﷻ.

Returning to the verse, the words 'purifies them' teaches us that the Holy Prophet ﷺ purifies Muslims from every inner and outer impurity. Only the practices (اعمال) that are accepted by the Holy Prophet ﷺ are correct.

'Teaches them the Book & wisdom' explains that the Holy Quran is such an intricate book, Allah ﷻ sent His Beloved ﷺ to teach it. Intricate knowledge is taught by an accomplished teacher. Therefore, to understand the Holy Quran, there is the need of the Hadith.

'Previous to that, they were in clear error' tells us that the teaching of Rasoolullah ﷺ is so complete that it doesn't merely remove those who are astray from the path of transgression but makes them *complete* believers. His teaching created an Abu Bakr Siddique ؓ, an Umar Farooq ؓ, etc. No other teaching is as comprehensive as the Holy Prophet's ﷺ. When a student enters a school, he goes to various teachers to learn different subjects, but when a person came to the Holy Prophet ﷺ, there was no need for another teacher.

VERSE 16

مَا كَانَ اللهُ لِيَذَرَ الْمُؤْمِنِيْنَ عَلى مَا أَنْتُمْ عَلَيْهِ حَتّى يَمِيْزَ الْخَبِيْثَ
مِنَ الطَّيِّبِ ، وَمَا كَانَ اللهُ لِيُطْلِعَكُمْ عَلَى الْغَيْبِ وَلكِنَّ اللهَ يَجْتَبِى مِن رُّسُلِه مَن يَّشَاءُ

'Allah ﷻ will not leave the believers in the state which you are
in until He separates the impure from the pure. And it doesn't befit the
dignity of Allah ﷻ to reveal to you all the secrets of the unseen; but
Allah ﷻ chooses of His Messengers ﷺ whom He pleases.'
– Surah Ale-Imran (3), Verse 179

This verse is the explicit praise of the Holy Prophet ﷺ. The background of its revelation is that once, Rasoolullah ﷺ said, "My Ummah was presented to me in their appearances and form before their birth just as how the children of Adam السلام عليه were shown to him. I've also been given the knowledge of who'll bring faith on me and who won't." Hearing this, the Hypocrites mocked, "Muhammad claims he knows who's a Muslim and who's a non-Muslim before their birth. We are with him, pretending to be Muslims, yet he doesn't recognize us." The Holy Prophet ﷺ then ascended the *mimbar* and said in a discourse, "What's the condition of people who mock my knowledge?! I'll answer anything you ask me from now until Qiyaamat!" Hearing this, Hadrat Abdullah ibn Huzaifa ؓ seized the moment, stood up and asked, "O Beloved of Allah ﷺ, who's my father?" Rasoolullah ﷺ answered, "Huzaifa." Thereafter, Hadrat Umar ؓ stood up and said, "O Rasoolullah ﷺ, we are satisfied with the Lordship of Allah ﷻ, your prophethood, and Islam. We ask for your forgiveness." The Holy Messenger ﷺ then said, "Now will you stop?" and he finally descended. – *Tafseer Khaazin, Khazaainul-Irfaan*

The following can be deduced from this verse,

1. To mock Rasoolullah's ﷺ knowledge of the unseen (غیب) or say, "He didn't have knowledge of a certain thing," is the conduct of Hypocrites. It's compulsory on Muslims to accept, without question, all of the amazing qualities of the Holy Prophet ﷺ.

2. Allah ﷻ granted our Beloved Master ﷺ the knowledge of everything until Qiyaamat. Rasoolullah ﷺ said, "Whoever wishes to ask anything may do so," and this statement can be made only by he whose knowledge is complete.

3. Even that which we secretly do in the confines of our homes isn't hidden from the sight of Rasoolullah ﷺ. The father of Hadrat Abdullah ؓ was Huzaifa, and this was a hidden matter. A father is he from whose seed a child is born. To know this is the glory of the being whose sight is on every particle of this world. Actually, why can't the eyes that saw the Creator on the night of Mi'rāj not see the creation? This will be discussed in the commentary of Surah Najm, Insha-Allah ﷻ.

   Are worldly objects more advanced and superior to Allah ﷻ?

   > 'How can anything be hidden from you (O Rasoolullah ﷺ), when even Allah ﷻ didn't remain hidden from you. Upon you be millions of Durood.'
   > – Alahadrat Imam Ahmed Raza ؓ

4. Rasoolullah ﷺ has knowledge of every Muslim, non-Muslim and Hypocrite until the Day of Judgment. If he didn't disclose anyone's fault, it wasn't because he was unaware of it, but that he is the Prophet ﷺ who hides the mistakes and faults of others. He's the manifestation (مظهر) of Allah's ﷻ attribute *as-Sattār* (the Coverer). This knowledge and awareness didn't diminish with his demise, because after death, the knowledge (and every sense of a being) is intensified.

VERSE 17

وَلَوْ أَنَّهُمْ إِذ ظَّلَمُوا أَنفُسَهُمْ جَاءُوكَ فَاسْتَغْفَرُوا اللَّهَ وَاسْتَغْفَرَ لَهُمُ الرَّسُولُ لَوَجَدُوا اللَّهَ تَوَّابًا رَّحِيمًا

'And if they are unjust to their souls, then (O Beloved ﷺ), they should come

to you and beg forgiveness of Allah ﷻ, and the Messenger ﷺ should intercede
for them. Then surely they will find Allah ﷻ Most Relenting, Merciful.'
– Surah Nisā (4), Verse 64

This verse explains to Muslims the method of repenting and how to get our sins forgiven, but indeed the eminence of the Holy Prophet ﷺ is clearly established by it. It lists three conditions for repentance to be accepted,

1. Presenting oneself in Rasoolullah's ﷺ court.

2. Repenting from one's sins there.

3. The Holy Prophet ﷺ interceding.

If any of these three conditions aren't found, one's repentance being accepted is not hoped.

The following points emerge from this verse,

1. Rasoolullah ﷺ is the official and powerful lawyer in Allah's ﷻ court. Sin against Allah ﷻ was committed, yet here we are commanded to go to the Holy Prophet ﷺ. For our understanding, let's consider this example: a crime is committed against the government, but we are sent to a lawyer or a court for the case. In the courts of this world, proceedings don't start without the lawyer. Similarly, without the Holy Prophet ﷺ, proceedings don't start in the court of Allah ﷻ. This is why the name of Rasoolullah ﷺ is definitely found in Salaah, etc.

> *'O [wretches], your intending to separate*
> *Rasoolullah's ﷺ remembrance from Allah's ﷻ is not the*
> *remembrance of truth. Rather, it's the key to Hell-fire.'*

> *'Saying 'Allah ﷻ bestows without the Prophet's ﷺ means'*
> *is totally wrong and the false love of he who is without vision.'*
> – Alahadrat Imam Ahmed Raza ؓ

2. The doorway of Rasoolullah ﷺ is the Divine threshold. When a beggar begs, he doesn't stand on the roof or behind the house. Rather, he comes to its door to ask for help. Likewise, if you want help from Allah ﷻ, go to His doorway, i.e. the court of the Holy Prophet ﷺ, and then ask. Whatever you will attain from Allah ﷻ will

only be through this august court and by Rasoolullah's ﷺ blessed hands.

3. Presenting oneself in Madina isn't necessary for intercession, because the verse didn't say, "Present yourselves in Madina." Rather, the directive is, "Wherever you may be, turn your heart to his court, because every heart is his citadel of presence."

> *'It's said that the master lives only in Madina.*
> *This is wrong, because he resides in the hearts of lovers.'*

4. This command of 'presenting oneself' is for sinners and criminals until Qiyaamat, not just during Rasoolullah's ﷺ lifetime on the Earth. This is why *Fatawa Alamghiri* states that when a person comes to the Rauda Sharif, he should recite this verse. – *Kitaabul-Hajj*

Tafseer Madaarik and *Khazaainul-Irfaan* state, "After Rasoolullah's ﷺ demise, a person came to his Rauda Sharif, recited this verse and submitted, "O Rasoolullah ﷺ, I have heard this command and indeed I've been oppressive on myself. Seeking forgiveness from Allah ﷻ, I've presented myself at your door. Please pardon my sins from Allah ﷻ." Upon this, he heard a call from the Rauda Sharif saying, "You've been forgiven."

The following rules of Islamic Jurisprudence are extracted from this verse and incident,

1. Using a beloved of Allah ﷻ as an intermediary (wasīla) to Allah ﷻ is a means of success.

2. Going to the graves of the spiritual luminaries for the attainment of one's purpose is permissible and falls under 'they should come to you' in the verse.

3. Calling out to accepted servants of Allah ﷻ after their demise with "O [so-and-so], etc." (ي) is permissible.

4. A Hadith states, "Forty high-ranking friends of Allah ﷻ (Abdāls) are found in Syria. Through their blessings, it rains, victory is attained over enemies, and punishment is kept away from its people." – *Mishkaat*

Imam Shafi ﷺ also states, "At the time of any need, I present myself at the grave of Imam Abu Hanifa ﷺ and make dua." – *Introduction of Shaami*

5. "…injustice unto their souls" in the verse tells us that no matter what kind of sinner or criminal (even if he's a disbeliever or Muslim sinner) comes to the Holy Prophet ﷺ and repents, Allah's ﷺ mercy will help him. Rasoolullah ﷺ is akin to an ocean. No matter how impure a person may be, if he submerges himself in it, he becomes pure. No ill person was ever turned away from the Prophet ﷺ and told, "I cannot help you." Here in this verse, every sinner is commanded, "Go to the Prophet ﷺ. You'll attain whatever you wish for."

> *'Your mercy is upon everyone wherever*
> *they may be. Such a Mercy unto Creation you are.'*
> – Huzoor Muhaddith'e-Azam'e-Hind Kichochwi ﷺ

VERSE 18

فَلَا وَرَبِّكَ لَا يُؤْمِنُوْنَ حَتّٰى يُحَكِّمُوْكَ فِيْمَا شَجَرَ بَيْنَهُمْ ثُمَّ لَا يَجِدُوْا فِيْ اَنْفُسِهِمْ حَرَجًا مِّمَّا قَضَيْتَ وَيُسَلِّمُوْا تَسْلِيْمًا

'Then (O Beloved ﷺ), by your Lord, they will not be Muslims until they make you judge in all their disputes and find in their souls no resistance against your decisions, but accept them with the fullest conviction.'
– Surah Nisā (4), Verse 65

This verse explains how to be a Muslim and informs us of a Muslim's identity. However, it too contains the praise of Rasoolullah ﷺ.

The background of its revelation is that the people of Madina would irrigate their lands with the water running from the mountain. As the lands of Hadrat Zubair ﷺ and another Companion were close to one another, an argument ensued concerning the water (i.e. who should water his land first). Their case was eventually presented to the Holy Prophet ﷺ. Rasoolullah's ﷺ decision was that Hadrat Zubair ﷺ should water his land first as it was higher than that of the others. The other Companion was unhappy with this decision and said, "Zubair ﷺ is the son of your paternal aunt (i.e. you decided in his favor because he's a relative of yours)." This verse was then revealed wherein it was said, "O Beloved ﷺ, no one can be a true believer until he accepts you as the judge in his every dispute and sincerely accepts your every ruling."

This beggar, the reciter of praise of his Beloved ﷺ, Ahmed Yaar Khan ؓ [the author of this book. – *Translator*], states that 'By your Lord' in the verse is so absorbing that I cannot help myself from becoming ecstatic. Allah ﷻ took an oath on Himself yet He didn't use his name. He didn't say, "By Allah ﷻ," or, "By the Most Merciful." Rather, He joined His remembrance to the Beloved's ﷺ and said, "O Beloved ﷺ, oath on your Lord." Marvel at the statement and its uniqueness. How great is the Lord of the Beloved ﷺ?! Only he who's familiar with this type of love will attain the relish of this statement. Thereafter, Allah ﷻ says, "Only he who possesses the stamp of My Beloved's ﷺ slavehood will attain the certification of Imaan from My court."

The truth is that true obedience to Rasoolullah ﷺ is the worship of Allah ﷻ, martyrdom and spiritual strife (رياضة).

> '[O Rasoolullah ﷺ], Sacrificing life in your path is martyrdom; and being buried in your vicinity is called Jannah.
>
> 'Spiritual strife is to come and go in your presence. To remain t hinking about you is the worship of Allah ﷻ.'
> – Alahadrat Imam Ahmad Raza ؓ

Anyone who emplaces his own opinion over the decision of the Holy Prophet ﷺ on a matter is someone with no Islam in him.

A Hypocrite (someone posing as a Muslim) once had a quarrel with a Jew. In this matter, it was the Jew who was correct. So, the case was presented to the Holy Prophet ﷺ and he naturally ruled in favor of the Jew. This was disliked by the Hypocrite, so he sought a second opinion from Hadrat Umar ؓ. At this juncture, the Jew informed Hadrat Umar ؓ that the Holy Prophet ﷺ had already decided the case in his favor, but this Hypocrite was unwilling to accept it. So, they were now before him. Hadrat Umar ؓ immediately beheaded the Hypocrite and said, "This is the decision for he who's not happy with the ruling of the Messenger ﷺ." From that day onwards, Hadrat Umar ؓ gained the title of *Farūq* (i.e. he who distinguishes between truth & falsehood). – *Background of Revelation of Surah Nisā (4), Verse 60*

VERSE 19

مَن يُطِعِ الرَّسُوْلَ فَقَدْ اَطَاعَ اللهَ ، وَمَنْ تَوَلَّى فَمَا اَرْسَلْنَاكَ عَلَيْهِمْ حَفِيْظًا

'He who obeys the Messenger ﷺ has indeed obeyed Allah ﷻ. But (as for) anyone who turns his face away, We have not sent you to save them.'
– Surah Nisā (4), Verse 80

This verse is also the praise of Rasoolullah ﷺ. The reason for its revelation was that once, the Holy Prophet ﷺ said, "He who obeys me, obeys Allah ﷻ." In response to this, some Hypocrites remarked, "The Prophet ﷺ wants us to accept him as our Lord, just as how the Christians accepted Sayyiduna Esa علیہ السلام as their Lord." So, this verse was revealed, in which the Holy Prophet's ﷺ statement was certified. The following points emerge from this,

1. Regarding the respect of the Holy Prophet ﷺ to be 'making partners with Allah ﷻ' is the conduct of Hypocrites. Respect and worship are two different things, and every form of respect cannot be said to be worship.

2. The Holy Prophet ﷺ has a unique closeness in the Divine court. He who is truly the slave of Rasoolullah ﷺ has the right of being the slave of Allah ﷻ.

3. Before obedience to Allah ﷻ comes obedience to the Holy Prophet ﷺ. In this verse, obedience to the Holy Messenger ﷺ is mentioned first and spoken of as a condition. The obedience of Allah ﷻ was made the compensation of this condition and was mentioned afterwards. This is a fact, because when the Holy Prophet ﷺ proclaims, "O Muslims, Allah ﷻ has made five Salaah compulsory and revealed this verse in the Holy Quran," we accept it. Keep in mind that this is firstly obedience to the Holy Prophet ﷺ and *then* obedience to Allah's ﷻ command. In the Kalima, although the name of Rasoolullah ﷺ comes after 'Laa ilaaha illallaah,' bringing Imaan on him has precedence in Imaan. Only when we accept Muhammad ﷺ as the Messenger of Allah ﷺ are the secrets of 'Laa ilaaha illallaah' opened to us. Accepting Allah ﷻ as One but not bringing faith on Rasoolullah ﷺ isn't enough for a person to be a monotheist (موحد). Don't some Christians and Jews, etc. also regard the Creator to be One? Why then are they still disbelievers?

4. It's not necessary to obey anyone in creation besides Rasoolullah ﷺ. If parents, teachers and Shaikhs, etc. are obeyed, it's only because the Holy Prophet ﷺ commanded that they be so. A Hadith states that once, Sayyiduna Jibrael علیہ السلام came to the Holy Prophet ﷺ and submitted, "What is Islam? What is Imaan? When will the Day of Judgment occur?" These questions were posed in the gathering of some Companions when Rasoolullah ﷺ answered them. However, Sayyiduna Jibrael علیہ السلام didn't himself say to the Companions, "This is

Islam. This is Imaan. Perform Salaah like this, etc." because he knew that Muslims wouldn't be obligated to do these things by him saying so. Yes! When *the Holy Prophet* ﷺ utters these things, they become obligatory and commands of Islamic Law. We also come to know that merely propagating the message of Allah ﷻ isn't uniquely the quality of a prophet, but even the responsibility of Sayyiduna Jibrael ﷺ. The Prophets ﷺ are in fact the ministers of Allah's ﷻ governance and emplacers of His commands. The responsibilities of a Commentator of the Hadith and a Jurist can be understood likewise. The former is he who propagates the Hadith while a Jurist (عالم ، فقيه) understands and emplaces the commands of the Hadith. This is why it has been stated in another verse,

اطيعوا الله واطيعوا الرسول واولى الامر منكم

*'Obey Allah ﷻ, obey the Messenger ﷺ, and
those of command among you.'*
– Surah Nisā (4), Verse 59

Here, the obedience of three has been mentioned,

1. Allah ﷻ.

2. The Holy Prophet ﷺ.

3. Those with command/authority (i.e. the Scholars).

So, it's said that Rasoolullah ﷺ is the deputy (خليفة) of Allah ﷻ, and the Scholars are the successors of the Holy Prophet ﷺ.

VERSE 20

وَأَنْزَلَ اللهُ عَلَيْكَ الْكِتَبَ وَالْحِكْمَةَ وَعَلَّمَكَ مَا لَمْ تَكُنْ تَعْلَمُ ، وَكَانَ فَضْلُ اللهِ عَلَيْكَ عَظِيمًا

*'And Allah ﷻ has revealed to you the Book & wisdom, and taught you
what you did not know. And great is the grace of Allah ﷻ upon you.'*
– Surah Nisā (4), Verse 113

This verse mentions several qualities of the Holy Prophet ﷺ. They are as follows,

1. The Book (meaning the Holy Quran) was revealed to him.

2. Rasoolullah ﷺ was granted wisdom.

3. The knowledge of the unseen (علم الغيب) was also granted to him.

4. The grace of Allah ﷻ is great upon him.

By mentioning the Book and wisdom, we come to know that the speech of the Holy Prophet ﷺ (i.e. the Hadith) is also revelation from Allah ﷻ (وحى). Yes, the Quran is visible (ظاهر) revelation (in its wording and theme) while the Hadith is secret (خفى) revelation (its theme is revelation but its wording is the Holy Prophet's ﷺ). This is why laws are attained from the Hadith, and why the Quran's commands can be annulled by it. The permissibility of performing sajda out of respect is proven from the Holy Quran but has been annulled by the Hadith. Similarly, we come to know from the Holy Quran that the estate of a deceased individual will be taken by his inheritors. However, the Hadith explains that neither do the Prophets عليهم السلام take the inheritance of their family members nor do their family members take their inheritance. In short, the Hadith is also a type of revelation from Allah ﷻ. Otherwise, why is 'wisdom' mentioned with 'the Book'? *Tafseer Khazaainul-Irfaan* states that the Prophet's ﷺ teachings (Sunnah) is what is meant by wisdom.

> Each and every strand of the Holy Prophet's ﷺ blessed hair was a miracle. When a strand of it remained in the hat of Hadrat Khalid ibn Waleed ؓ, he always attained victory over his enemies. Hadrat Ameer Muawiyah ؓ wished that the blessed hair and nail-cuttings of the Prophet ﷺ be placed on his eyes and lips after being given ghusl to ease the accounting in the grave. We understand from this that the Prophet's ﷺ hair eases even the difficulties in the grave!

We further come to know that knowledge of the unseen is also among the various qualities granted by Allah ﷻ to the Holy Prophet ﷺ. This verse doesn't say that only knowledge of the commands of Islamic Law was given. Rather, it says, "…what you did not know." Rasoolullah ﷺ was taught whatever he never knew. It's established that knowledge of every particle and matter was bestowed to the Holy Prophet ﷺ. Allah ﷻ states that He bestowed the knowledge of everything, and the Holy Prophet ﷺ declares that he attained this bestowal. Who now can snatch this gift from Allah ﷻ from the Holy Messenger ﷺ? Refer to my book, *Ja'al-Haqq*, for a complete discussion on this.

The verse further states, "And great is the grace of Allah ﷻ upon you." Who now has the authority to limit this 'great grace' of Allah ﷻ upon the Holy Prophet ﷺ? Speaking about Allah's ﷻ quality, He states,

وهو العلى العظيم

'*And He alone is the Most Exalted, the Great.*'
– Surah Baqarah (2), Verse 255

And regarding the Holy Messenger ﷺ, He states,

وانك لعلى خلق عظيم

'*And indeed you have great manners.*'
– Surah Qalam (68), Verse 4

The grace upon the Holy Prophet ﷺ has been described as 'great' (عظيم) in this verse, whereas the blessings of the world have all been referred to as 'little' (قليل),

قل متاع الدنيا قليل

'*Tell them (O Beloved ﷺ), 'The possessions of this world are little.*"
– Surah Nisā (4), Verse 77

We can deduce that just as how the greatness of Allah ﷻ cannot be comprehended, so too is the greatness of Rasoolullah ﷺ (bestowed upon him by Allah ﷻ) incomprehensible by the creation. This is why Imam Busairi ؓ states,

دع ما ادعته النصارى فى نبيهم ، واحكم بما شئت مدحا فيه واحتكم
فان فضل رسول الله ليس له ، حد فيعرب عنه ناطق بفم

'*Besides calling the Holy Prophet ﷺ 'god' or 'the son of god', ascribe whatever honor and greatness as praise to him, because the excellence of the Holy Prophet ﷺ has no limit that can be emplaced by a person's utterance.*'
– Qasida Burda Sharif

From the beginning until the end, including on the Day of Judgment, the angels, Prophets ◌ and humanity have spoken – and will speak – about the qualities and praise of the Holy Prophet ﷺ, but the reality is that not even a speck of the journal of his excellence will be completed. This is because whatever has been or will be spoken is within a limit, and Rasoolullah's ﷺ qualities are seemingly beyond limit. Allah's ﷻ true praise can only be made by Sayyiduna Ahmed ﷺ (i.e. the Holy Prophet ﷺ), and the correct praise of Muhammad ﷺ can only be made by Allah ﷻ. We cannot praise Allah ﷻ nor recite the praise of Rasoolullah ﷺ as it's truly supposed to be made.

In the commentary of this verse, Allama Ismail Haqqi ؒ states that the Holy Prophet ﷺ is the favor of Allah ﷻ for the world, and that the Being (ذات) of Allah ﷻ is the favor of Allah ﷻ for Rasoolullah ﷺ. So, the verse can also mean, "Indeed Allah ﷻ is Great, and His Being is His favor upon you."

VERSE 21

وَمَن يُشَاقِقِ الرَّسُولَ مِن بَعْدِ مَا تَبَيَّنَ لَهُ الْهُدَى وَيَتَّبِعْ غَيْرَ سَبِيلِ
الْمُؤْمِنِينَ نُوَلِّهِ مَا تَوَلَّى وَنُصْلِهِ جَهَنَّمَ ، وَسَاءَتْ مَصِيرًا

'And as for he who opposes the Messenger ﷺ after
guidance has become clear and follows a way other than the way
of the Muslims, We will leave him in his own condition and will
cause him to enter Hell. What an evil destination that is.'
– Surah Nisā (4), Verse 115

The reason for the revelation of this verse is as follows: a person in Madina named Ta'maa ibn Abeeraq stole something but accused someone else of stealing it. When the truth of the matter became apparent, Rasoolullah ﷺ ordered that Ta'maa's hand be cut. When Ta'maa heard this, he fled to Makkah at night, joined the disbelievers there and adopted their religion as his own. He also later died as one of them. This verse was revealed concerning him. – *Tafseer Roohul-Bayaan*

This verse is clear praise of the Holy Prophet ﷺ, and the following points can be derived from it,

1. In verses before this, we were informed that only he who obeys the Holy Prophet ﷺ is a true and obedient servant of Allah ﷻ, and he who opposes the Holy Messenger ﷺ is rejected in the court of Allah ﷻ. This is also apparent here.

2. He who's rejected in the Holy Prophet's ﷺ court cannot remain in safety – not among the creation and not too in the sight of the Creator. There was a person who used to transcribe revelation but later insulted the Holy Prophet ﷺ, became an apostate and joined the non-Muslims. When he died and was buried, even the *earth* didn't accept his corpse (but spat him out instead). After trying to bury him

numerous times afterwards, the earth continued to spit the body out!
– *Mishkaat*

We can therefore say that he who's rejected by the Holy Prophet ﷺ is cursed.

3. If you wish to be steadfast on the path of salvation, remain in the path of the general body of Muslims. If a person invents a new path and follows it, Shaitaan will destroy him the way a sheep which strays away from the flock is destroyed by wolves. The path of the general body of Muslims is the path of the Glorious Companions, Ahle-Bait, Islamic Scholars, Shaikhs and general body of Muslims. Its name is the Ahle-Sunnah wal-Jamaah. Whichever sect or movement rises in opposition against it is the path to Jahannam.

4. Opposing the pious servants of Allah ﷻ (or having contempt against and rejecting an Islamic command) destroys Imaan. Such was the result of Ta'maa. We should pay heed to this.

VERSE 22

يَا أَيُّهَا النَّاسُ قَدْ جَاءَكُم بُرْهَانٌ مِّن رَّبِّكُمْ وَأَنزَلْنَا إِلَيْكُمْ نُورًا مُّبِينًا

'O people, there has indeed come to you a manifest proof from Allah ﷻ, and We have sent down to you a manifest light (Noor).'
– Surah Nisā (4), Verse 174

This verse is a collection of Rasoolullah's ﷺ praise, and although it isn't within human capacity to thoroughly discuss it, we will attempt to for the attainment of blessings,

Attention should be given to four things mentioned in this verse,

1. O People,

2. There has indeed come to you,

3. Manifest proof,

4. And manifest light.

It's obvious that when 'O believers' is said, only Muslims are being addressed, while 'O people' refers to even Jews, Christians, fire-worshippers…in short, the entire mankind. In this verse, "O people," was used. So, we come to know that everyone is being addressed here. A person calls out to those whose attention he wishes to draw. Doctors call out to their patients, teachers to their students, etc. The advent of the Holy Prophet ﷺ was for the entire mankind. So, the entire mankind is being addressed here.

We also come to know that his arrival and prophethood isn't for a specific nation, country or time (as it was with other Prophets ﷺ), but that everyone who's the servant of Allah ﷻ becomes the follower (Ummati) of the Holy Prophet ﷺ. This is apparent from the words 'there has indeed come to you,' i.e. Rasoolullah ﷺ didn't just come to the Arabian Peninsula and stay there. He is wherever we are – in our homes, our hearts, our thoughts, and even our minds. Yes, he is unseen while you are visible.

> 'My friend is closer to me than I am to myself.
> It is indeed strange that I am far from him.'

Burhaan in this verse means 'proof by which a claim is strengthened'. This refers to the Prophet's ﷺ miracles. Rasoolullah ﷺ has been bestowed with all the miracles granted to the previous Prophets ﷺ (along with several others unique to him). In fact, the truth is that from head to toe, the Holy Prophet ﷺ himself is the proof of Allah's ﷻ Oneness, Being and Qualities. So, 'proof' here really refers to the blessed being of the Holy Messenger ﷺ. The complete being of other Prophets ﷺ were not miracles. Rather, certain body parts and effects were ascribed as such, e.g. the hand and staff of Sayyiduna Musa ﷺ, the breath of Sayyiduna Esa ﷺ, etc. However, each and every strand of the Holy Prophet's ﷺ blessed hair was a miracle. When a strand of it remained in the hat of Hadrat Khalid ibn Waleed ؓ, he always attained victory over his enemies, and as long as it remained in the turban of Hiraqal, he experienced comfort from the severe headache he had. Hadrat Amr ibn 'As ؓ stated before his passing that he wished for the blessed hair of Rasoolullah ﷺ to be placed in his kafn so that the hardship of the grave was overcome, and Hadrat Ameer Muawiyah ؓ wished that the blessed hair and nail-cuttings of the Prophet ﷺ be placed on his eyes and lips after being given ghusl to ease the accounting in the grave. We understand from this that the Prophet's ﷺ hair eases even the difficulties in the grave!

The Companions would also give water which touched the Prophet's ﷺ blessed hair to the sick to drink. Once, the hair of Rasoolullah ﷺ was brought to the home of Hadrat Talha ؓ. He narrates that he heard holy recitations being made by angels the entire night thereafter. – *Madaarijun-Nubuwwah, Mawaahibul-Ladunya*

The miracle of the Holy Prophet's ﷺ blessed eye is that he saw every event until the Day of Judgment. He saw Jannah, Jahannam, the Throne (عرش), the Kursi…even Allah ﷻ Himself! He was also able to see Jannah and Jahannam while in *Salaatul-Kusoof* and see what those who were reading behind him were doing.

The miracle of Rasoolullah's ﷺ blessed nose is that he smelled the fragrance of love emitting from Yemen. – *Tafseer Roohul-Bayaan (under this verse)*

The miracle of his blessed tongue is that its utterances were the revelation of Allah ﷻ and the key to unlock everything. His saliva brought blessings to the food of Hadrat Jabir ؓ and increased the flour it was placed in, allowing it to feed thousands of Companions (with the same amount remaining at the end)!

> The miracle of the Holy Prophet's ﷺ blessed eye is that he saw every event until the Day of Judgment. He saw Jannah, Jahannam, the Throne (عرش), the Kursi…even Allah ﷻ Himself!

Sayyiduna Musa عليه السلام struck a rock with his staff and caused water to emerge from it, but by placing his blessed saliva in the pot of Hadrat Jabir ؓ, Rasoolullah ﷺ caused *fountains* of meat and curry to emerge! Bear in mind that the curry had all the ingredients found within it, e.g. butter, spices, etc. So, this is indeed a unique miracle. During the Battle of Khaibar, Rasoolullah's ﷺ blessed saliva was placed on the sore eye of Hadrat Ali ؓ and alleviated his pain. The snake in the cave of Hira bit Hadrat Abu Bakr's ؓ leg, yet the Companion received comfort after the Prophet's ﷺ saliva was applied to it. This blessed saliva even turned a salty well sweet!

Rasoolullah's ﷺ blessed hand is also proof [from Allah ﷻ]. In the Battle of Badr, he took a handful of stones and threw them at the non-Muslims. Allah ﷻ revealed,

وما رميت اذ رميت ولكن الله رمى

'And (O Beloved ﷺ,) you didn't throw [the stones]. We threw them.'
– Surah Anfāl (8), Verse 17

It was those very hands wherefrom pebbles recited the Kalima. Also, when allegiance was pledged on these hands, Allah ﷻ said,

يد الله فوق ايديهم

'The hand of Allah ﷻ is over their hands.'
– Surah Fat'h (48), Verse 10

Even the fingers of these hands are a miracle. When they were placed in a bowl of water, five fountains emerged from them.

'The fingers are benevolent, the thirsty rush passionately;
Five rivers of mercy are flowing, how grand!'
– Alahadrat Imam Ahmed Raza ؓ

The Prophet's ﷺ blessed feet are also miracles. If he walks on a rock, it accepts its footprint. These feet not only walked the Earth, they even walked the Heavens!

In short, every body part of Rasoolullah ﷺ, including each strand of hair, is a proof to recognize Allah ﷻ.

Even the blessed perspiration is a miracle as it contained an unrivalled fragrance. His sleeping and being awake is a miracle, because his sleep didn't break his wudhu. The entire blessed body was protected from having a shadow so that none could tramp it. He is the shadow of Allah ﷻ, how then can he have a shadow?

Everyone's urine and excreta is impure (نجس), but the Prophet's ﷺ is pure for the Ummah. – *Shaami, Baabul-Anjaas*

Every quality of the Holy Messenger ﷺ is a miracle, and he's the proof of Allah's ﷻ power in every condition. This is why the word 'burhaan' (proof) was used for him.

Even the *name* of the Holy Messenger ﷺ is a miracle for the following reasons,

1. Every person is given a name by his or her parents, his community gives him a title and he's addressed by the power of the day. However, the name, titles and attention of the Holy Prophet ﷺ were all from Allah ﷻ. Through the instruction of angels, Hadrat Abdul-Muttalib ؓ kept his name 'Muhammad ﷺ'.

2. Every person is named on the seventh day after his or her birth, but Allah ﷻ named His Beloved ﷺ even before the creation of man!

Sayyiduna Adam ﷺ saw this name written on the pillars of the Throne; Sayyiduna Nuh's ﷺ ark became complete through it; during his era, Sayyiduna Esa ﷺ announced Rasoolullah ﷺ to have the name 'Ahmed'; and the Prophets ﷺ supplicated through its blessed means.

3.   Other Prophets' ﷺ names don't have the grand meanings possessed by the name of the Holy Prophet ﷺ, Muhammad ﷺ, which means 'without fault and worthy of praise in every way.'

4.   Through the blessings of this name, a non-Muslim of decades becomes a believer the way ice is melted by the sun.

5.   Through the name of the Holy Prophet ﷺ, a person attains success in the test of the grave and safety on the Day of Resurrection.

The name of the Noble Messenger ﷺ also has the power to change the condition of a person. Anyone who wishes to dishonor it is destroyed by the wrath of Allah ﷻ.

The miracles of all other Prophets ﷺ are only narratives now, but a few miracles of Rasoolullah ﷺ exist to this day, e.g. the Holy Quran, the sound Hadith, his strands of hair found in different locations which remain objects of visiting, his complete biography through chains of narrations, etc. Besides Rasoolullah ﷺ, no one has been granted these things.

In this verse, Rasoolullah ﷺ is addressed as a 'proof', and in another, he's called 'Noor.' This is because proof and light is understood by the intellect and the eye respectfully. Philosophers and intellectuals recognized the Prophet ﷺ through proofs, while the laymen recognized him by sight. The monk Buhaira ؓ brought Imaan after seeing him, while Hadrat Salmaan Farsi ؓ brought Imaan after using his intellect.

With regards to '… We have sent down to you a manifest light (Noor),' *Noor* here either refers to the Holy Quran or the being of the Holy Prophet ﷺ. In other words, Rasoolullah ﷺ is both the proof *and* the Noor. Proof is understood by the intellect, and Noor is seen by the eye. So, if you look at the Holy Prophet ﷺ, you'll see Noor (as his every body part is Noor). However, if you use your intelligence to recognize him, you'll also find him to be the proof of Allah ﷻ. The discussion on Noor will follow, Insha-Allah ﷻ.

VERSE 23

اَلۡیَوۡمَ اَکۡمَلۡتُ لَکُمۡ دِیۡنَکُمۡ وَاَتۡمَمۡتُ عَلَیۡکُمۡ نِعۡمَتِیۡ وَرَضِیۡتُ لَکُمُ الۡاِسۡلَمَ دِیۡنًا

*'This day I have perfected your religion for you, completed My
favor upon you and have chosen Islam as your way of life.'*
– Surah Māida (5), Verse 3

At first sight, this verse speaks about Islam being perfected, but it too is the praise of the Holy Prophet ﷺ. The background of its revelation is as follows: It was the year of the Final Hajj of the Prophet ﷺ. The day was Friday, the 9th of Zul-Hijjah, after the time of Asr Salaah. Rasoolullah ﷺ was on a camel delivering the sermon of Hajj when this verse was revealed. Coincidentally, six *Eids* (occasions of happiness) occurred simultaneously on that day, 3 for Muslims and 3 for other nations. It was the 25th of December, celebrated by Christians, Jews and Magians (fire worshippers). For Muslims, it was the day of Jumuah (which is an Eid), the day of Hajj, and the opportunity of seeing their Holy Beloved ﷺ (undoubtedly the greatest Eid). The entire world was in happiness. Since then, the world has never seen so many eids gathered in one day.

The following points are deduced from this verse,

1. When the verse was revealed, all other deens and religions (whether it be the deen of Sayyiduna Musa الله or of Sayyiduna Esa الله etc.) were nullified. They were temporarily placed in the world and thereafter annulled. The deen of Islam is so perfected that no one can add or deduct from it, no one can change the Holy Quran, no one can come as a prophet, and never will it be annulled! An example to understand this is that a child is firstly given formula as his primary food and drink. When he becomes stronger, he is fed bread and other foods, and then the formula stops.

2. Just as how the deen of Islam is the most complete of all religions, so too is the founder of Islam, Muhammad Mustapha ﷺ, the most excellent and revered of all initiators of religions. Islam is the most perfect deen because he who's the perfect of all is its founder. The students of a Madrassah study under various teachers in primary classes and advance after passing. However, they leave a Madrassah as complete (with a certificate) only after learning under the head teacher of the institute. This is the person responsible for completing the education of the students.

3. Without choosing the religion of Islam and adopting obedience to the Holy Prophet ﷺ, no good deed is accepted in the court of Allah ﷻ. They are rejected because disbelief (کفر) is like a lethal poison. If it's found in food, no matter how wholesome the food may look, a person will still die if he eats it. It's useless giving water and sunshine to the leaves of the tree when the root has already been uprooted. Likewise, if obedience to the Holy Prophet ﷺ isn't found, whatever good work a person does is totally futile.

4. In the verse, Islam has been described as 'perfected' and favor has been described as 'completed.' Decrease and increase cannot occur in something which is 'perfected'. Therefore, the principles (اصول) of Islam cannot be extended or lessened. Regarding something which is 'completed', increase can occur in it, but not decrease. So, whether 'blessing' refers to the rules of Islamic Law or to victory over enemies, increase can occur here.

5. If Allah ﷻ is content with Islam, He's definitely more than content with the founder of Islam, Muhammad Mustapha ﷺ; and through his blessings, Allah ﷻ is pleased with us. May Allah ﷻ keep us steadfast on Islam and Imaan. Aameen.

VERSE 24

قَدْ جَاءَكُم مِّنَ اللهِ نُورٌ وَّكِتَبٌ مُّبِينٌ

'Undoubtedly there has come to you from
Allah ﷻ a light and a luminous book.'
– Surah Māida (5), Verse 15

This verse is great praise of the Holy Prophet ﷺ. The People of the Scriptures (Jews and Christians) are being addressed in it, being told, "O servants of Allah ﷻ, a glorious being of Noor and a manifest book has reached you." Rasoolullah ﷺ is declared to be Noor in this verse. *Noor* is defined as 'that which is bright and brightens others'. The sun is noor; light isn't needed to look at it because it's bright itself and brightens whatever it focuses on. People in the world become famous due to their family background, occupation or power. Rasoolullah's ﷺ popularity, however, is not due to any of these things. He was Noor himself, and such a Noor that others were illuminated by him. This is why his birth didn't occur in a royal or wealthy family. In fact, his father met his demise before his birth. Nearly all of Rasoolullah's ﷺ close relatives passed away before the proclamation of his prophethood, and those who remained after the proclamation had enmity for him. So, no one can now say that Rasoolullah's ﷺ popularity is due to his family and relatives. This was the background of Rasoolullah ﷺ, yet the entire world recognizes him. Before his blessed birth, the world knew that the era of the Final Prophet of Allah ﷻ was near. Well-wishers rejoiced and enemies expressed sadness. This can be likened to the light that appears on the horizon preceding the appearance of the sun. What are people when even animals and stones recognized him in his childhood as the Final Messenger ﷺ?!

When the nurse, Sayyidah Halima رضى الله عنها, took Rasoolullah ﷺ to her home, the mule that she was traveling on said, "O Halima رضى الله عنها! The Final Messenger ﷺ of Allah ﷻ rides on me." – *Madaarijun-Nubuwwah*

The state of Noor (نورانیت) of Rasoolullah ﷺ is so intense that the Heavens and the Earth recognize him and present themselves in his service, the set sun returns for him, and the moon splits into two pieces on his gesture. They do so because they recognize the Final Prophet ﷺ of Allah ﷻ.

It's been approximately 1,400 years since the demise of the Noble Messenger ﷺ, yet in every part of the world, his name is taken, his Sunnah is emulated, and every aspect of his blessed life is presented to people. There were many cherished personalities that came to this world; powerful kings and rulers, people of wisdom and discernment, yet their names are not remembered today.

'What do we know of the amount of stars that shone and diminished?
But never had and never will our Beloved Prophet ﷺ decline.'
– Alahadrat Imam Ahmed Raza Khan رضى الله عنه

The above referred to Rasoolullah ﷺ being himself manifest and cherished. Now the question is, "How did others gain distinction through his blessings?" A concise reply is that many esteemed monarchs, people of power and authority came to this world. Some of them constructed mansions and initiated the writing of voluminous works of literature, etc. just to keep their names alive – yet in spite of these attempts, their names were forgotten through the passage of time. However, the blessed parents of Rasoolullah ﷺ, his grandfather, and likewise those who took care of him gained distinction in the world until Qiyaamat. How? Simply because they were connected to the being of Rasoolullah ﷺ. So, the Prophet ﷺ gave distinction to his family and country. The piece of earth his blessed foot touched is the object of visitation for the entire Muslim Ummah. If his advent hadn't occurred in Arabia, who would've known about the Ka'ba and Madina? Arabia doesn't have any fancy tourist attractions, green scenery or beautiful landscape, yet the entire world is drawn to it! Why? Simply because a fragrant flower which scented the entire world has bloomed from the flower-garden of Sayyiduna Ibrahim عليه السلام there. That fragrant flower, which is the object of visitation for all, is found in Madina. The hands of time crush everyone, but the person who aligns himself to the Holy Prophet ﷺ is saved from this fate!

Even those who displayed enmity towards Rasoolullah ﷺ became noted in the world, e.g. Abu Jahl, etc.

The above was a researched study on the meaning of Noor. Now follow two important points.

Why was Noor spoken about with the 'Book'? Simple: no book is read in darkness, because light is needed to read it. Likewise, he who has the Noor of Allah جل جلاله in his heart can understand the Book of Allah جل جلاله. The Quran is understood after Noor enters the heart.

The nūnation (تنوین) of 'Noor' in the verse is for reverence, and it refers to Rasoolullah ﷺ. How is Rasoolullah ﷺ a great light? The light of the sun increases and decreases on Earth. We have a little light at dawn, more at noon, less in the evening and nothing at all at night. The Holy Prophet's ﷺ Noor, however, never decreases. The light of the sun brightens only half of the Earth while his Noor brightens the entire Earth (and even the Heavens). The light of the sun brightens only the outer body while his Noor brightens the mind, heart, soul and thoughts. If a person wishes to escape the sun's light by concealing himself in a basement, he will be successful. The Noor of the Holy Prophet ﷺ, however, reaches every portion of the dominion of Allah جل جلاله. It doesn't deprive anyone of its blessings. He who doesn't want to take benefit from it is truly and unfortunately wretched.

The birth of the Beloved Messenger ﷺ occurred in Makkah Sharif, situated at the centre of the Earth. Lights found at the corners of gatherings brighten only the area they are placed in while the main lighting which brightens the entire gathering is found at the centre. The other Prophets عليهم السلام were lights found at the corners of creation, giving guidance to specific nations and tribes. On the other hand, Rasoolullah ﷺ is Noor for the entire creation – hence his birth in a central place. It's for this reason that the Holy Quran states,

یایها الناس انی رسول الله الیکم جمیعا

'O mankind, I've come as the Messenger ﷺ of Allah جل جلاله to all of you.'
– Surah A'rāf (7), Verse 158

In this section's verse, Rasoolullah ﷺ has been addressed as 'Noor,' and the Holy Quran has been called 'Mubeen' (i.e. something which opens another). What's the difference between Noor and Mubeen? Noor is seen by the eye (even blind people experience something when close to it). The Holy Messenger ﷺ is Noor in this regard, that even the blind like Abu Jahl, etc. acknowledged him,

یعرفونہ کما یعرفون ابناءہم

'They recognize him the way they recognize their sons.'
– Surah Baqarah (2), Verse 146

Only he who brings Imaan, however, can understand the Quran; and only he who possesses knowledge and deeply understands its injunctions (i.e. has the ability to make juristic reasonings such as *ijtihād*) can deduce rules from it. To gain the Holy Quran isn't everyone's part. Allah ﷻ states,

فانھم لا یکذبونک ولکن الظلمین بایت اللہ یجحدون

'They belie you not, but the evil doers deny the signs of Allah ﷻ.'
– Surah An'ām (6), Verse 33

We come to know that even the non-Muslims regarded Rasoolullah ﷺ as truthful, honest and trustworthy, but yes, they never accepted the Holy Quran. This is the difference between Noor and Mubeen. Understand it in this way: Rasoolullah ﷺ brightened the Holy Quran because he was Noor. The Holy Quran mentioned his qualities in several places because it (the Holy Quran) is something which makes open (i.e. Mubeen).

VERSE 25

اِنَّمَا وَلِیُکُمُ اللہ وَرَسُوْلُہ وَالَّذِیْنَ اٰمَنُوا الَّذِیْنَ یُقِیْمُوْنَ الصَّلٰوۃَ وَیُؤْتُوْنَ الزَّکٰوۃَ وَھُمْ رٰکِعُوْنَ

'Only Allah ﷻ is your friend, and His Messenger ﷺ and the believers who establish prayer, pay Zakaat and bow down (before Allah ﷻ).'
– Surah Māida (5), Verse 55

Although Muslims are given an important command in this verse, the verse also proclaims the honor and greatness of the Holy Prophet ﷺ. The background of its revelation was that Hadrat Abdullah ibn Salaam ﵁ (who was a scholar of the Jews) accepted Islam. In response to this, the tribes which he belonged to (i.e. the Banu Quraiza and the Banu Nadheer) held a meeting and decided that he be socially boycotted. The Companion came to the Holy Prophet ﷺ complaining that he was now an outcast among them, and so the above verse was revealed, saying to Hadrat Abdullah ⬥, "If the non-Muslims have distanced themselves from you, why do you grieve? You have now attained the love of Allah ﷻ, the Messenger ﷺ, and the Muslims and are not at a loss in this situation. By leaving the disbelievers, you've attained Allah ﷻ, are under the shade of Rasoolullah's ﷺ mercy, and have gained the friendship of believers."

The following points emerge from this,

1. It's not a sin to have affinity and friendship with others besides Allah ﷻ, e.g. the Holy Prophet ﷺ and Muslims.

2. The help and friendship of Allah ﷻ and His Messenger ﷺ are sufficient against everybody else's.

3. A Hadith states that only a person who loves and hates solely for Allah's ﷻ sake can attain the relish of Islam. In other words, he should love the pious servants of Allah ﷻ and stay away from the enemies of the deen.

4. Love for the Friends of Allah, the Mashaaikh (plural of Shaikh), Scholars, Companions of Rasoolullah and the Ahle-Bait ⬥ is a great blessing of Allah ﷻ since these personalities are not just believers, but masters of believers. This is why Surah Fatiha states,

اهدنا الصرط المستقيم ، صرط الذين انعمت عليهم
'Guide us on the straight path; the path of
those whom You have favored.'
– Surah Fatiha (1), Verse 6-7

The truth of the matter is that we love Muslims and the Friends of Allah ⬥ in the love of Rasoolullah ﷺ because they are the means of attaining his nearness.

VERSE 26

يَاَيُّهَا الرَّسُوْلُ بَلِّغْ مَا اُنْزِلَ اِلَيْكَ مِنْ رَّبِّكَ ، وَاِنْ لَّمْ تَفْعَلْ فَمَا بَلَّغْتَ رِسَالَتَه ، وَاللهُ يَعْصِمُكَ مِنَ النَّاسِ
'O Beloved Messenger ﷺ propagate what has been revealed to you from your
Lord. And if you are unable to do so, then you have not conveyed any message.
And Allah ﷻ will protect you from the people.'
– Surah Māida (5), Verse 67

This verse ultimately commands the Holy Prophet ﷺ to propagate the message of Islam, but it also proclaims his praise. Rasoolullah ﷺ is told in this verse, "O My Beloved Messenger ﷺ, propagate the deen without any fear. Have no concern for any enemy, because I (Allah ﷻ) am your Guardian." Previous Prophets عليهم السلام were martyred by non-Muslims and attempts to stop their propagation were made, but the honor and majesty of Rasoolullah ﷺ is protected by Allah ﷻ! Who can now harm the Holy Prophet ﷺ?! Therefore, he's commanded to effectively propagate the message.

The reason for the revelation of this verse is that the Jews of Madina said to Rasoolullah ﷺ, "We are large in number and are very powerful. If you stop propagating Islam, we'll honor and serve you. If you don't, we'll murder you." For this reason, 100 men from the Sahaabah remained with Rasoolullah ﷺ as guardians. When this verse was revealed, the Holy Prophet ﷺ said to them, "Return to your homes. My Lord has taken the responsibility of protecting me." – *Tafseer Roohul-Bayaan*

Subhanallah! Regarding the deen of Islam and the Holy Quran, Allah ﷻ states,

انا نحن نزلنا الذكر وانا له لحفظون

'No doubt, We have sent down this Quran,
and We most surely are its Guardian.'
– Surah Hijr (15), Verse 9

And, regarding the Quran personified, Sayyiduna Muhammad Mustapha ﷺ, Allah ﷻ states, "I will protect you from people." There was no responsibility of protection made on the lives of the previous Prophets عليهم السلام or their deens. This is why their deens have become corrupted and their Books have been changed. Here, the Quran is protected along with Islam and its rules. In fact, everything about the deen has been protected. It was the effect of this very protection that although the disbelievers of Makkah and the Jews of Madina tried hard to martyr Rasoolullah ﷺ, they were unsuccessful in achieving their goal. Allah ﷻ protected the Holy Messenger ﷺ in the Cave of Thūr by the web of a spider. This protection is not unique to that blessed era, because the honor and glory of the Holy Prophet ﷺ is protected until the Day of Qiyaamat. Even today, people write against kings, but few infidels have the courage to slander the Holy Prophet ﷺ. If any wretch does so, he immediately meets his punishment and doom. This is the protection of Allah ﷻ.

Sayyiduna Esa ﷺ was troubled by the Jews, so he was given protection by being taken to the Fourth Heaven. Greater than this is that Rasoolullah ﷺ was left among his enemies and was instructed, "Effectively propagate the message." The public couldn't be influenced by the awe of the governor, so the king summoned him to the royal palace. Another governor was able to control them, so he was effectively commanded to stay there and govern the people while every type of royal aid was given to him. It's apparent that the second governor projected greater awe.

We come to know that the person who says that the Holy Prophet ﷺ didn't reveal the Caliphate of Hadrat Ali ﷺ out of fear for Hadrat Umar ﷺ is someone without deen and a non-Muslim. Rasoolullah ﷺ has propagated all the commands that were to be propagated.

VERSE 27

وَأَطِيعُوا اللهَ وَأَطِيعُوا الرَّسُوْلَ وَاحْذَرُوا ، فَإِن تَوَلَّيْتُمْ فَاعْلَمُوا أَنَّمَا عَلَى رَسُوْلِنَا الْبَلغُ الْمُبِيْنُ

'And obey Allah ﷻ and obey the Messenger ﷺ and
be careful. Then if you turn back, know then that the duty of
Our Messenger ﷺ is only to deliver the message clearly.'
– Surah Māida (5), Verse 92

In this verse, Muslims are commanded to obey Allah ﷻ and the Messenger ﷺ, and are also shown further praise of the Holy Prophet ﷺ. Firstly, Allah ﷻ mentioned His obedience separately to His Messenger's ﷺ, granting it distinction. There's great wisdom in this – that accepting only the Quran is

> Islam is the most perfect deen because he who's the perfect of all is its founder.

not sufficient for salvation. To regard the Hadith of Rasoolullah ﷺ as unnecessary is clearly not Islam. There are certain actions which have been commanded by the Holy Prophet ﷺ but not mentioned in the Quran. However, the Ummah still completes them, regarding them to be prophetic actions. Accepting and acting on both the Quran and the Hadith is necessary in Islam. To refute the Holy Quran is disbelief (كفر). Likewise, to intentionally disregard and reject the Hadith of Rasoolullah ﷺ is also disbelief. Yes, credible doubting of a statement being a Hadith (due to its chain of narration, etc) and refuting its reference is something else, and this is clearly understood by the scholars of the Science of Hadith. However, to negate or have ill-feelings for a Hadith which has been undoubtedly established to be an utterance of the Holy Prophet ﷺ makes a person a non-Muslim. Hadrat Abu Bakr Siddique ﷺ heard the Messenger ﷺ say that the estate of the Prophets عليه isn't distributed, and whatever wealth they leave behind is charity (صدقة). So, the Holy Prophet's ﷺ estate was not distributed even though proof of distributing one's estate is found in the Holy Quran. Even Hadrat Ali ؓ didn't distribute the inheritance of Rasoolullah ﷺ during his Caliphate. The land and gardens he left behind were used as *waqf* (just like during the periods of Hadrat Abu Bakr Siddique ؓ and Hadrat Umar ؓ).

A point of note is that there is a difference between Allah's جل جلاله obedience and obedience to the Holy Prophet ﷺ. Obedience to Allah جل جلاله must be made in His proclamations and declarations, not in his actions. Obedience to Rasoolullah ﷺ, however, must be demonstrated in three things – his declarations (قول), his actions (فعل) and his silence regarding an issue (سكوت). In other words, we are to accept whatever he says, whatever he does, and whatever action he saw and didn't object to. On the other hand, obedience must not be shown to the workings of Allah جل جلاله and specific declarations. Allah's جل جلاله command is that the disbelievers should not be assisted and helped, yet He Himself gives them sustenance and comfort. In fact, He sometimes even grants them victory against Muslims in battle! If someone says, "When Allah جل جلاله is granting them blessings, we should also be kind to them," that person will be wrong. Sometimes Allah جل جلاله seemingly rebukes His Prophets عليهم السلام, but if we were to use those very words for them, it would be an act of pure disbelief, since these words are from the actions of Allah جل جلاله. The commands of Allah جل جلاله are binding on us. He has commanded us to not help the disbelievers and to obey His Prophet ﷺ. Due to there being a difference between obedience to Allah جل جلاله and obedience to the Messenger ﷺ, the word 'obey' (اطيعوا) came twice.

Another point to note is that the verse states [in other words], "Don't think that if you show disobedience to the Holy Prophet ﷺ, it will be his loss. No, he has fulfilled the obligation of propagating Islam, and so the consequence of disobedience will now be on you. Neither does he benefit from you if you are obedient nor does he lose anything if you are not. He is a content king, but yes, you are needy of him."

VERSE 28

يَأَيُّهَا الَّذِيْنَ اٰمَنُوْا لَا تَسْئَلُوْا عَنْ اَشْيَاءَ اِنْ تُبْدَ لَكُمْ تَسُؤْكُمْ وَاِنْ تَسْئَلُوْا عَنْهَا حِيْنَ يُنَزَّلُ الْقُرْاٰنُ تُبْدَ لَكُمْ عَفَا اللهُ عَنْهَا ، وَاللهُ غَفُوْرٌ حَلِيْمٌ

'O Believers, question not things that, if disclosed, may displease you. And if you will ask while the Quran is being revealed, they will be made clear to you. Allah جل جلاله has already pardoned them.

And Allah ﷻ is the Forgiving, the Forbearing.'
– Surah Māida (5), Verse 101

This verse is a collection of praise for the Beloved Prophet ﷺ.

There are two opinions regarding the reason for its revelation. One opinion is that some people would ask the Holy Prophet ﷺ pointless questions until, one day, he said, "Ask me whatever you wish. I'll answer every question." Someone then asked him what his result will be, and the Prophet ﷺ replied, "Jahannam." Another asked who his father was, and Rasoolullah ﷺ replied, "You are from the seed of Sadāqah (i.e. he was illegitimate because his mother wasn't the wife of Sadāqah)." This verse was revealed on this occasion, stating [in other words], "O Muslims! Don't divulge secrets using My Beloved ﷺ which may lead to your embarrassment." – *Tafseer Ahmadi*

The narration found in Muslim Sharif states that it was on this occasion that Abdullah ibn Huzaafa Sahmi asked, "Who is my father?" and the Holy Prophet ﷺ replied that it was Huzaafa. When the mother of Abdullah heard this, she said to Abdullah, "You are very unfortunate. What do you know about the condition of women during the Period of Ignorance? If your mother was at fault in any way, imagine the shame she would face."

The second opinion is that this verse was revealed on this occasion: a narration found in Muslim Sharif states that once, the Holy Messenger ﷺ said, "Hajj is compulsory on Muslims." A person stood up and asked if it was compulsory every year, but the Holy Prophet ﷺ remained silent. This person then posed the question several times, leading the Prophet ﷺ to say, "If I said 'yes' at that time, performing Hajj every year would've become compulsory, and you wouldn't be able to fulfill it annually." Here, Muslims are told not to ask questions bearing restrictions they cannot shoulder.

The following praise of the Holy Prophet ﷺ is disclosed from this verse,

1. So great is the excellence of Rasoolullah ﷺ in the sight of Allah ﷻ that Allah ﷻ Himself teaches His servants the etiquette of interacting with him, i.e. how to speak, sit, ask questions, etc. The Holy Prophet ﷺ had no need to teach others how to respect him.

'Even Jibrael ﷺ doesn't enter their home
without permission. Those with insight know the glory and
esteem of the Prophet's ﷺ household (Ahle-Bait).'
– Maulana Hasan Raza Khan ﷺ

2. From the first narration, it's apparent that Rasoolullah ﷺ knows well the origin and fate of all people. He knows whose son a person is, who's in Jannah, and who's in Jahannam. This is the meaning of him being present and seeing/aware (حاضر وناظر). However, he covers the faults of people and doesn't open the condition of all, but let that not misguide you into thinking he doesn't know.

3. From the second narration, we see that Rasoolullah ﷺ has been made the one in control (مالك) of Islamic commands (احكام). Whatever he utters is accepted as the law in the sight of Allah ﷻ. We are obliged by Islamic Law, but the movement of the Prophet's ﷺ blessed lips is actually what Islamic Law is.

4. If Islamic Law hasn't classified something as impermissible, it is permissible. A Hadith states, "Halaal is that which Allah ﷻ has made halaal, and haraam is that which Allah ﷻ has made haraam. Whatever He hasn't spoken of is forgiven." – *Mishkaat, Kitaabul-At'imah*

   So, gatherings celebrating the Holy Prophet's ﷺ birth, Fatiha of the pious, the establishment of religious Madrassahs, etc. were all non-existent during the era of the Holy Prophet ﷺ but are all permissible, because Islamic Law has not declared them to be haraam. This is spoken of in the verse being discussed, "Allah ﷻ has already pardoned them."

5. If a pious individual prescribes a *wazifa* or *amal* without any restrictions, don't unnecessarily ask for restrictions to be emplaced. The Bani Israel were told to slaughter a cow and hit a person who was killed with its meat, causing the person to return to life and disclose who had killed him. However, they began asking questions like, "What type of cow should it be?", What's its colour?", and, "What's its age?" If they'd slaughtered any ordinary cow without questioning anything, it would've been sufficient. Likewise, don't ask and inadvertently emplace restrictions on yourself.

VERSE 29

قَدْ نَعْلَمُ إِنَّهُ لَيَحْزُنُكَ الَّذِى يَقُوْلُوْنَ ، فَإِنَّهُمْ لَا يُكَذِّبُوْنَكَ وَلٰكِنَّ الظّٰلِمِيْنَ بِاٰيٰتِ اللهِ يَجْحَدُوْنَ

'We know that what they say grieves you; they belie you not,

but the evildoers deny the signs of Allah ﷻ.'
– Surah An'ām (6), Verse 33

This verse proclaims the praise of Rasoolullah ﷺ, and his proximity to Allah ﷻ is known from it. The reason for its revelation is as follows: Akhaas ibn Qais was a very close friend of Abu Jahl. Once, he met with him and asked, "O Abul-Hikam [i.e. 'the father of knowledge' – this was the appellation of Abu Jahl], we are alone and none are aware of what we are saying to one another. Answer truthfully: is Muhammad true in his claim of being Allah's Messenger or not?" Abu Jahl replied, "Oath on my lord, Muhammad is definitely true. Never has he uttered anything false. It's just that he comes from the Qasee tribe and his family already includes all eminent personalities: the steward of the Holy Ka'ba's water and the chamberlain of the Ka'ba, etc. are all from them. When prophethood has come to them, what honor is left for other people of the Quraish?" The above verse was revealed because of this. – *Tafseer Khaazin*

Hadrat Ali ؓ reports that once, Abu Jahl came to the Holy Messenger ﷺ and said, "We do not belie you, we belie the Book that you have brought." This verse is said by others to have been revealed because of this. – *Tirmidhi*

The following points of excellence regarding the Holy Prophet ﷺ is established here,

1. Rasoolullah ﷺ is such a great Beloved ﷺ of Allah ﷻ that if any statement causes grief to his blessed heart, it is *Allah ﷻ Himself* Who consoles him! Disbelievers used to say that the Holy Prophet ﷺ wasn't a prophet, and these words would hurt him, hence the tone in which Allah ﷻ states, "O Beloved ﷺ, they do not belie you, they belie Me and My signs. Why then do you grieve?"

2. The life of Rasoolullah ﷺ was so pure that, nevermind his friends, *even his enemies* accepted him to be trustworthy and truthful. If there's anyone in the world who didn't speak a single lie (even in jest or forgetfulness), that person is only our Beloved Prophet ﷺ. It is the norm of society that a person's countrymen and, especially his childhood friends, are aware of his outer and inner personality. A person can gain great acceptance among outsiders and unrelated people, but it's very difficult for him to be accepted among his own and familiar people – yet it's the being of the Holy Prophet ﷺ whose childhood friend, Hadrat Abu Bakr Siddique ؓ, brought Imaan on him as soon as he announced his prophethood. Even the wife of the

Noble Messenger ﷺ, Sayyidah Khadija ؓ, brought Imaan on him. Whoever *did* refute his prophethood did so solely based on envy, since they couldn't ascribe a fault to his blessed character.

3. The verse can also mean, "O My Beloved ﷺ, rejection of your prophethood, objecting to your greatness, and displaying abhorrence to your praise is actually a rejection of Me (Allah ﷻ) and My signs." If a king has to appoint someone to control his subjects and they show disobedience to this person, they are actually opposing the king himself (and are then rejected as rebels). So, whoever rejects the greatness of Rasoolullah ﷺ indirectly rejects the miraculous signs of Allah ﷻ.

4. 'Sign' (آية) in the verse refers to the sign of Allah ﷻ by which He is recognized. 'Signs' (آيات) is its plural. Rasoolullah ﷺ is a collection of the signs of Allah's ﷻ Being, and his qualities are a means of recognizing Allah ﷻ. The disbelievers rejected Rasoolullah's ﷺ prophethood and messengership, and Allah ﷻ proclaimed, "They have rejected the signs of Allah ﷻ."

5. Everything in this world is a sign of Allah's ﷻ power and nature. However, every object is a sign of only one quality of Allah ﷻ. The sun articulates the Noor of Allah ﷻ and the wind and water gesture to His generosity, but Rasoolullah ﷺ is the greatest reflection (مظهر) of Allah's ﷻ Being & Qualities. If you wish to see the knowledge of Allah ﷻ, look at the knowledge of Rasoolullah ﷺ. If you desire to see Allah's ﷻ generosity, look at Rasoolullah's ﷺ generosity.

'Rasoolullah ﷺ is the king of both worlds. Even though he keeps nothing with him, the blessings of both are in his empty hands.'
– Alahadrat Imam Ahmed Raza ؓ

After Rasoolullah ﷺ made dua for blessings for Hadrat Anas ؓ, while everyone else's orchard would continue to bear fruit just once a year, Hadrat Anas' ؓ orchard would produce fruit twice! – *Mishkaat, Baabul-Karaamaat*

The Holy Prophet ﷺ gave Hadrat Jabir ؓ and Hadrat Abu Hurairah ؓ a small amount of grain which didn't deplete for thirty years! – *Mishkaat, Baabul-Mujizaat*

The Holy Messenger ﷺ also placed his fingers in a bowl of water and fountains of water began to flow from them. Thousands of people made wudhu and ghusl, gave their animals water from it to drink and even filled their leather-bags! Rasoolullah ﷺ fed all the people of Madina in the home of Hadrat Jabir ؓ from only a small amount of flour. This is the generosity of the Holy Prophet ﷺ.

If you wish to see the power of Allah ﷻ, look at the power of the Holy Prophet ﷺ. He brought back the set sun after gesturing to it. – *Shaami*

He split the moon into two pieces. – *The Holy Quran*

He joined trees that were apart in distance so that he could relieve himself.

And, if you wish to see the Noor of Allah ﷻ, look at the beauty of the Holy Messenger ﷺ. Hadrat Jabir ؓ narrates, "It was a moonlit night and the Holy Prophet ﷺ was dressed in a *jubbah*. I would sometimes look at the moon of the sky and sometimes cast my eye towards the moon of Madina. By Allah ﷻ! The face of the Holy Prophet ﷺ was much more radiant and brighter than the moon!"

> *'I'm not a poet who calls his face a moon;*
> *I sacrifice the moon on the impressions of his feet.'*

In short, Rasoolullah ﷺ is a collection of the signs of Allah ﷻ. Whoever rejects him rejects Allah ﷻ, and whoever accepts him gains the recognition of Allah ﷻ.

VERSE 30

وَمَا قَدَرُوا اللهَ حَقَّ قَدْرِهٖ إِذْ قَالُوا مَا أَنْزَلَ اللهُ عَلَى بَشَرٍ مِّن شَىْءٍ

'And they (the Jews) could not visualize the respect of Allah ﷻ as was necessary to be visualized. Then they said, "Allah ﷻ had not revealed anything on any man.'
– Surah An'ām (6), Verse 91

This verse has seemingly been revealed to rebuke the Jews, but if a person looks at it with Imaan, it is fragranced with the praise of the Holy Prophet ﷺ.

The reason for the revelation of this verse is as follows: once, a group of Jews, headed by the leader of their scholars Malik ibn Saif, came to debate with the Holy Prophet ﷺ. Rasoolullah ﷺ said to him, "I implore you, under the oath of the Lord who revealed the Torah (Old Testament) to Musa عليه السلام, have you seen the verse in the Torah which says that Allah ﷻ regards an obese scholar to be an enemy?" Malik ibn Saif answered in the affirmative, after which the Prophet ﷺ replied, "You are an obese scholar. According to the Torah, you're the enemy of Allah ﷻ." This angered Malik ibn Saif, who then said, "Allah ﷻ has not sent revelation to any man." The above verse was thereafter revealed in reply to this, in which Allah ﷻ explains, "These wretches have not valued Allah ﷻ at all by rejecting His Books and Prophets ﷺ. So, who revealed the Torah then to Musa ﷺ?" Malik ibn Saif was removed as the head scholar by the Jews after this. – *Madaarik, Khaazin*

The following qualities of the Holy Prophet ﷺ are apparent in this verse,

1. Rasoolullah ﷺ is the knower of Inspired Knowledge (علم لدنی). He didn't gain knowledge or guidance from any person, yet the exquisite manner in which he held the debate made even the skilled and experienced debaters of the opposition lower their heads in submission. In other words, before presenting any proof in the debate, the Prophet ﷺ proved Malik ibn Saif to be one without religion (even his own). So, how could the debate continue?

2. The Torah was in the Hebrew language. Rasoolullah ﷺ had neither learnt the Torah from anyone nor did he learn the language of the Book. Marvel at his blessed knowledge, however, that he is aware of the Torah's verses and even knows the language of Hebrew. The Prophets ﷺ are born with awareness. As soon as Sayyiduna Adam ﷺ gained life, he read the Kalima written on the pillars of the Throne and asked, "O Allah ﷻ, whose name is written next to Yours?" Allah ﷻ answered, "O Adam ﷺ, it's the name of that personality who, had I not created him, I wouldn't have created you."

How did Sayyiduna Adam ﷺ read the written proclamation on the pillars of the Throne without learning to read and write? He read it through the Noor of his prophethood. – *Madaarijun-Nubuwwah*

The Holy Quran states,

وما ارسلنا من رسول الا بلسان قومه

'And We have sent each Messenger in the language of his own people.'
– Surah Ibrahim (14), Verse 4

The Holy Prophet ﷺ is the Messenger ﷺ of all nations. So, we can deduce that he is aware of every language. The Holy Quran states that Allah ﷻ taught Sayyiduna Adam ﷺ the names of all things, leading the Commentators of the Quran (مفسرين) to state that Sayyiduna Adam عليه السلام was taught all languages. Rasoolullah's ﷺ knowledge is far greater than Sayyiduna Adam's عليه السلام. So, it's established that Allah ﷻ *also* granted the Holy Messenger ﷺ the knowledge of every language! The Holy Prophet ﷺ once asked Hadrat Salmaan Farsi رضي الله عنه, "*Shikum dard?*" This is the language of Farsi (Persian).

3. Malik ibn Saif didn't reject the Being of Allah ﷻ. He refuted the Book of Allah ﷻ and the Prophet ﷺ, yet Allah ﷻ revealed, "They could not visualize the respect of Allah ﷻ." This proves that to not accept the Holy Prophet ﷺ is actually the rejection of Allah ﷻ. This is because Allah's ﷻ quality is Lord of the Worlds (رب العلمين). 'Lord' (Rubb) is he who fulfils the visible and inner worldly and religious needs of the servants. To fulfill worldly needs, Allah ﷻ has created parents, doctors, food, medicine, the Earth, the sky, etc, and for religious guidance, He has granted the world Prophets عليهم السلام, the Saints رضي الله عنهم, Mashaaikh رضي الله عنهم, Scholars, the Quran, the Hadith, good deeds, wazifas, etc. Now, he who rejects the Book or the Prophets ﷺ is similar to someone who says, "Allah ﷻ has not fulfilled our religious matters." This is equivalent to rejecting Allah's ﷻ Lordship.

VERSE 31

الَّذِيْنَ يَتَّبِعُوْنَ الرَّسُوْلَ النَّبِيَّ الْأُمِّيَّ الَّذِي يَجِدُوْنَهُ مَكْتُوْبًا عِنْدَهُمْ فِي التَّوْرَاةِ وَالْإِنْجِيْلِ يَأْمُرُهُمْ بِالْمَعْرُوْفِ وَيَنْهٰهُمْ عَنِ الْمُنْكَرِ وَيُحِلُّ لَهُمُ الطَّيِّبٰتِ وَيُحَرِّمُ عَلَيْهِمُ الْخَبٰئِثَ وَيَضَعُ عَنْهُمْ إِصْرَهُمْ وَالْأَغْلٰلَ الَّتِي كَانَتْ عَلَيْهِمْ

'Those who serve the unlettered Messenger ﷺ (the one who hasn't learnt from anyone), who they will find with them written in the Torah and the Injīl (New Testament), he will bid them to do good and will forbid them from doing evil, and he will make lawful for them clean things and will forbid for them unclean things, and will take off from them the burden and shackles which they were upon.'
– Surah A'rāf (7), Verse 157

Many qualities of the Holy Prophet ﷺ are mentioned in this verse. He has been mentioned by three titles here: Prophet (نبي), Messenger (رسول), and Unlettered (أمي). A Messenger is he who's a means between the Creator and creation, meaning he takes guidance from Allah ﷻ and passes it to creation; or he implores the Creator to forgive the sins and mistakes of the creation; or, by saving the creation from disbelief and polytheism, he makes them reach Allah ﷻ. This quality is clearly demonstrated by the Holy Messenger ﷺ. His advent occurred in a land like Arabia and he was able to make from its inhabitants the truthful Hadrat Abu Bakr ؓ, the just Hadrat Umar ؓ, etc.

There are two meanings to the word 'prophet' (نبي). It can mean a person with great rank, and truly the rank of Rasoolullah ﷺ is so great that, nevermind humans, even angels cannot know it. He alone knows Allah ﷻ, and only Allah ﷻ knows His Beloved ﷺ.

The words which we utter cannot justly praise the Holy Prophet ﷺ according to his right. No human thinking can reach his excellence.

ما ان مدحت محمدا بمقالتي ، لكن مدحت مقالتي بمحمد

'I have not praised Muhammad ﷺ with my words. Rather, I have made my words worthy of being praised using his name.'
– The Sahaabi Hadrat Hasan ibn Thaabit ؓ

Prophet (نبي) also means 'the communicator of the unseen'. It's a real occurrence that Rasoolullah ﷺ communicated Jannah, Jahannam, Qiyaamat, and each and every occurrence until the Last Day. Indeed, this is information of the unseen.

There are several meanings of the word 'unlettered' (أمي). *Umm* means 'mother' and 'source'. Therefore, Ummi can mean 'the Prophet ﷺ from an eminent mother.' Every person born in this world has a mother, but no one has a mother like the mother Allah ﷻ blessed the Holy Prophet ﷺ with.

> We are obliged by Islamic Law, but the movement of the Prophet's ﷺ blessed lips is actually what Islamic Law is.

Sayyidah Maryam ؓ was also a mother, but just as how Rasoolullah ﷺ is matchless, so too is his mother unrivalled. The oyster which has an expensive pearl inside it is treasured along with the pearl. So, how blessed is Sayyidah Amina ؓ, the mother who housed in her womb the leader of creation, Muhammad Mustapha ﷺ?!

Another meaning of Ummi is 'someone who's unlettered', i.e. from the time he was born, the Prophet ﷺ didn't learn from anyone.

The third meaning of Ummi is related to Ummul-Quraa, i.e. a person who is a resident of Makkah.

The fourth meaning is 'the source of all creation.'

The qualities of Rasoolullah 饝 spoken of in this verse are documented in the Torah and the Injīl. The Jewish scholars who embraced Islam and gained the honor of being the Holy Prophet's 饝 Companions (such as Hadrat Abdullah ibn Salaam 饝, Hadrat Ka'ab Ahbaar 饝, etc) mentioned the qualities of the Holy Messenger 饝 found in the Torah. Hadrat Abdullah ibn Salaam 饝 himself recited the following qualities mentioned in it, "O Prophet 饝, We [i.e. Allah 饝] have made you as a witness, a bearer of glad-tidings, a warner, and sent you. You are the protector of the weak; you are My servant and Messenger 饝. I have kept your name 'Mutawakkil'. You do not possess bad characteristics, you are not harsh in your disposition, and you do not shout out in the market place. You will not avenge bad with bad, but in fact you will forgive those who have erred. Allah 饝 will call you from the Earth only when, through your blessings, those who are afflicted can now lead the deen and people proclaim the Kalima. Through your blessings, blind eyes will gain sight, deaf ears will begin to hear, and hearts wrapped in coverings will become open."

A similar description is also reported from Hadrat Ka'ab Ahbaar 饝. Christians have tried to remove all the qualities of Rasoolullah 饝 mentioned in the Injīl (New Testament). In the present day Bible, however (which has experienced much alteration and interpolation), the following qualities of the Holy Prophet 饝 can still be found within,

> *'And I will ask the Father and He will give you another*
> *Helper that He may abide with you forever.'*
> – John, Chapter 14, Verse 16

This is the praise of Rasoolullah 饝, mentioning within it the fact that he's the Final Messenger 饝 (خاتم النبيين).

> *'I will no longer talk much with you, for the ruler of this world*
> *is coming and he has nothing in me.'*
> – John, Chapter 14, Verse 30

> *'Nevertheless, I tell you the truth. It's to your advantage that I go away, for if I*
> *do not, the Helper will not come to you, but if I depart, I will send Him to you.'*
> – John, Chapter 16, Verse 7

> *'However, when He, the spirit of truth, has come, he will guide you into all*
> *truth, for he will not speak on his own authority, but whatever he hears he will*
> *speak and he will tell you things to come.'*
> – John, Chapter 16, Verse 13

After Sayyiduna Esa عليه السلام, who else came to this world adorned with these qualities besides the Holy Prophet ﷺ?

The second quality mentioned in the Quranic verse is that Rasoolullah ﷺ will 'bid them to do good.'

The third quality mentioned is he will 'forbid them from doing evil.'

The fourth quality is that he will 'make lawful for them clean things.'

And the fifth quality is that he will 'forbid them from unclean things.'

We come to know that Allah ﷻ granted the Holy Messenger ﷺ authority with regards to making things halaal and haraam. Rasoolullah ﷺ is Shār'ee (i.e. the possessor of Islamic law) and is also the controller of it. Many Ahadith have been narrated illustrating this. Due to their sins, certain good things were made impermissible on the Bani Israel, such as the skin of halaal animals, etc. Through the blessings of the Holy Prophet ﷺ, however, they became halaal. Likewise, other impure things were halaal for them – but the Noble Messenger ﷺ made them impermissible until Qiyaamat.

The sixth quality mentioned is that Rasoolullah ﷺ will 'take off the burden from them,' referring to the previous strong commands which humans couldn't bear (i.e. the giving of one fourth of wealth as Zakaat, not being able to make tayammum in place of wudhu, to perform Salaah in designated places of worship and nowhere else, war-booty being impermissible, the body or clothes of a person having to be cut out or burnt if an impurity comes into contact with it, etc.) All of these commands were emplaced on the Bani Israel, but through the blessings of the Holy Prophet ﷺ, they were removed (e.g. only 2½ % of wealth is given as Zakaat, if wudhu cannot be made, tayammum will suffice, Salaah can be read anywhere, war-booty has been classified as permissible, etc.) All this ease is through the means of the Holy Prophet's ﷺ blessings.

VERSE 32

قُلْ يَأَيُّهَا النَّاسُ اِنِّى رَسُوْلُ اللّٰهِ اِلَيْكُمْ جَمِيْعًا

'Say (O Beloved ﷺ), 'O Mankind, I'm a Messenger ﷺ to you all from Allah ﷻ.'
– Surah A'rāf (7), Verse 158

This is explicit praise of the Holy Prophet ﷺ. Allah ﷻ is saying in this verse, "O Beloved ﷺ, say to all people, whether they be Christians, Jews, fire-worshippers, easterners, westerners, northerners or southerners, 'I am a Messenger ﷺ of Allah ﷻ to you all." So, whoever is the servant of Allah ﷻ is now the follower (Ummati) of the Holy Prophet ﷺ. Just as how the fatherhood of Sayyiduna Adam عليه السلام is general, so too is the prophethood of Rasoolullah ﷺ general. In fact, the truth is that the Prophets عليهم السلام, their nations, the jinns, and the angels عليهم السلام, etc. are all counted as the Ummah of the Noble Messenger ﷺ, and he's the Prophet ﷺ of all Prophets (نبی الانبیاء). This has already been explained.

Bear in mind that 'Ummah' is defined as those to whom a Prophet ﷺ is sent for propagation. The previous Prophets عليهم السلام used to be sent to specific nations or people (it wasn't necessary on other nations to follow them). When Sayyiduna Musa عليه السلام went to Sayyiduna Khidr عليه السلام, Sayyiduna Khidr عليه السلام said, "O Musa عليه السلام, your knowledge is something and my knowledge is something else. You are the prophet of the Bani Israel and you won't be able to show patience with me."

What he meant was, "You are not my prophet and your obedience isn't compulsory upon me. I will oppose you in many actions which you won't be able to bear and you'll object to me." This proves that Sayyiduna Musa عليه السلام was the prophet of only one nation. However, if our Holy Prophet ﷺ was to be grateful to Sayyiduna Khidr عليه السلام and meet him, Sayyiduna Khidr عليه السلام would've been obliged to adhere to his deen. A Hadith states, "If Musa عليه السلام would've been with us today, he would've had to be obedient to me."

'Ummah' is now of two types: *Ummat'e-Dawat* and *Ummat'e-Ijābat*. The first refers to those to whom propagation was made but who didn't accept the deen of Islam. Those who accepted it are regarded as the second type. Muslims are the Ummat-Ijābat of the Holy Prophet ﷺ while the non-Muslims and Hypocrites are the Ummate-Dawat. Whether people obey the Holy Prophet ﷺ or not, they'll still be regarded as in his Ummah.

Everyone is Allah's ﷻ servant, whether he's an obedient Muslim or an insolent non-Muslim. Similarly, whether people accept the commands [of Islam] or not, they are still Ummatis, and obedience to the Holy Prophet ﷺ is compulsory on all. The parents of Rasoolullah ﷺ were neither Christians nor Jews, because Sayyiduna Musa عليه السلام and Sayyiduna Esa عليه السلام were prophets to the Bani Israel (the children of Sayyiduna Is'hāq عليه السلام). Yes, the Prophet's ﷺ parents were initially believers in the Oneness of Allah ﷻ and later became Muslims after believing in Sayyiduna Muhammad Mustapha ﷺ. They weren't disbelievers, polytheists or idol-worshippers. A detailed discussion on this will be given later [Verse 40 in book].

VERSE 33

وَمَا رَمَيْتَ إِذْ رَمَيْتَ وَلَكِنَّ اللهَ رَمَى

'And (O Beloved ﷺ) the dust that you threw, you did not [truly] throw; but Allah ﷻ threw.'
– Surah Anfāl (8), Verse 17

This verse is clear praise of Rasoolullah ﷺ. Firstly, what is the incident being referred to here? And secondly, how is it the praise of the Holy Prophet ﷺ?

This incident took place during the Battle of Badr (2 A.H). In it, many well-equipped disbelievers of Makkah came to attack Madina, whose people had nothing but the help of Allah ﷻ and the blessings of the Holy Prophet ﷺ. The non-Muslims numbered approximately 1,000 while the Muslims numbered only 313. The non-Muslims had all types of food and drink while the Muslims fasted the entire day and recited the Holy Quran at night. The non-Muslims had swords, arrows, spears and shields, while the Muslims had sticks, wearing nothing but torn clothes and with blisters on their feet. The non-Muslims had people to sing and the sound of music; the Muslims had proclamations of 'Allahu Akbar' and the recitation of the Holy Quran. At night, the non-Muslims were intoxicated with liquor, while the Muslims were immersed in the remembrance of Allah ﷻ and intoxicated with Divine Love. In short, the non-Muslims were the army of Shaitaan while the Muslims were the army of *Rahmān* (The Most Gracious).

Seeing this visible condition of the Muslims, Rasoolullah ﷺ prostrated in the Divine Court and submitted, "O Allah ﷻ, only this small group of destitute Muslims without provisions truly worship You on the face of this Earth. If You don't help them and they are defeated and destroyed, there won't be anyone in the world to truly take Your name." The Holy Prophet ﷺ cried so much at this juncture that even the stones of that place became moist with his tears. He then lifted his head from sajda, took a handful of sand and threw it in the direction of the disbelievers. Allah ﷻ knows what handful of sand it was – that it reached all of them and caused each person to rub their eyes!

Through the grace of Allah ﷻ, this small group of provision-less Muslims was later able to defeat the well-equipped army of disbelievers so thoroughly that it's spoken about even until today. Great leaders of the opposition were killed in this battle and many were taken as prisoners.

This is the incident being referred to in the verse. It states, "O Beloved ﷺ, regarding the incident wherein you threw a handful of sand towards the non-Muslims and it reached their eyes: you didn't throw it. Rather, your Lord threw it." In other words, it was your hand but the action was Allah's ﷻ.

Allah ﷻ loved an action of the Holy Prophet ﷺ to such an extent that He said, "You did not do this, I did." The following points emerge from this,

1. Annihilation in Allah ﷻ (فنا فى الله) is an elevated rank in spirituality (Tasawwuf). When a servant becomes annihilated and remains only by Allah ﷻ (باقى بالله), although he's in his own form and appearance, the love of Allah ﷻ flows through his veins so profusely that this servant's every action is related to his Lord. Maulana Jalaaluddin Rumi ◌ gestures towards this in the following couplet,

> 'When he speaks, although it's the tongue of
> the servant, the speech is truly Allah's ﷻ.'
> – Mathnawi Sharif

When Sayyiduna Musa عليه السلام went to the Mountain of Tūr to converse with Allah ﷻ, the following was heard from a tree,

يا موسى انى انا الله رب العلمين

> 'O Musa عليه السلام, I am Allah ﷻ, the Lord of the entire world.'
> – Surah Qasas (28), Verse 30

So, was this the voice of a tree? Was the tree itself saying, "I'm Allah."? Definitely not! Rather, it was the speech of Allah ﷻ, and the tree was the point of its manifestation.

> 'When 'I'm Allah ﷻ' is allowed to be heard from a tree,
> why won't it be allowed from a person of piety?!'

Likewise, if a lump of coal is placed in a fire, the fire has such an effect on it that the coal becomes hot itself. Whatever touches it is burnt. So, if a person affected by a jinn says, "So-and-so is my name; I'm the jinn of a certain area; I have this power, etc," do these statements belong to the man? No, they are merely from the tongue of the person who's made to utter these things. The statement itself belongs to the being who has gained influence over him.

These were just examples for purposes of understanding. We must now recognize that by attaining this rank, some Gnostics (عارفین) have made the following proclamations, "I am Allah ﷻ," "I am the Truth," etc. These statements are actually not theirs. It's only their tongues that speak it, but it's the speech of another. This is the difference between Pharaoh and Hadrat Mansoor Hallaj ؓ both claiming to be Allah ﷻ. When Pharaoh said,

انا ربکم الاعلی

"I'm your lord, the highest one."
– Surah Nāziāt (79), Verse 24

he became a disbeliever because it emanated from his own being. However, when Hadrat Mansoor ؓ proclaimed, "I am the Truth [i.e. I am Allah ﷻ]," he said so after annihilating his self [in the worship of Allah ﷻ]. So, his proclamation didn't emanate from his own being.

By saying, "I am the Truth," Hadrat Mansoor ؓ became a person whose killing is compulsory (واجب القتل). Look at the power of control (ضبط) possessed by the Holy Prophet ﷺ however. He proclaimed, "I'm only the servant," at every juncture of his blessed life. Yes, but his Lord said, "O My Beloved ﷺ, you are adorned with such a station of annihilation in My remembrance that your every utterance and action is Mine." Sayyiduna Musa عليه السلام saw the radiance of Allah's ﷻ Qualities and lost consciousness. But marvel at the blessed eyes of the Holy Messenger ﷺ, that during the Ascension (Mi'rāj), he saw the radiance of Allah ﷻ and remained with a smile on his face!

'Consciousness left Musa عليه السلام through the radiance
of a single spark of Quality. You however, (O Rasoolullah ﷺ),
marveled at Allah ﷻ Himself with a smile.'

Allah ﷻ didn't speak this way in this verse alone. He also says in other places,

وما ینطق عن الهوی ، ان هو الا وحی یوحی

'And he (the Holy Prophet ﷺ) doesn't speak of his own desire.
It's no less than revelation sent down to him.'
– Surah Najm (53), Verses 3-4 [Verse 76 in Book]

ان الذین یبایعونک انما یبایعون الله ید الله فوق ایدیهم

'Surely those who swear allegiance to you swear allegiance to Allah ﷻ. The hand of Allah ﷻ is over their hands.'
– Surah Fat'h (48), Verse 10 [Verse 72 in Book]

2. The person who disrespects any action, statement or something related to the Holy Prophet ﷺ is a non-Muslim. In fact, this disrespect is indirectly disrespect towards Allah ﷻ. If a person worships Allah ﷻ for hundreds of years but disrespects even the blessed shoes of the Holy Prophet ﷺ once, all of his worship will be wasted, irrespective of his knowledge, standing or surface-piety. This has been explained in *Shifaa Sharif* and *Raddul-Muhtaar*. In fact, the Holy Quran itself states,

ولا تجهروا له بالقول كجهر بعضكم لبعض ان تحبط اعملكم وانتم لا تشعرون

'And do not speak in his presence as you speak aloud to one another lest your deeds become in vain while you are unaware.'
– Surah Hujarāt (49), Verse 2

May Allah ﷻ grant us the ability to revere the Holy Prophet ﷺ. Aameen.

VERSE 34

يَأَيُّهَا الَّذِيْنَ آمَنوا اسْتجِيْبوا لله وللرَّسُوْل إِذَا دَعَاكُمْ لِمَا يُحْيِيكُمْ

'O believers! Respond to the calling of Allah ﷻ and the Messenger ﷺ when the Messenger ﷺ calls you to that which gives you life.'
– Surah Anfāl (8), Verse 24

The praise of the Holy Prophet ﷺ is clearly evident in this verse. It's Allah ﷻ Himself Who teaches the Sahaabah the manner and respect they must demonstrate towards the Holy Prophet ﷺ and his blessed court. Allah ﷻ didn't instruct Rasoolullah ﷺ to teach them this. Rather, He Himself commanded, "O Muslims, the respect of My Beloved's ﷺ court is that if he calls you at any time, immediately present yourself before him and don't delay in doing so – irrespective of the condition you may be in." Let's see how the Sahaabah fulfilled this command.

A Companion was once being intimate with his wife when the Holy Prophet ﷺ called for him outside his home. Before completing intimacy, he immediately rushed to the calling of the Noble Messenger ﷺ and was asked by him, "Have I put you in haste?" The Companion replied, "Yes." Rasoolullah ﷺ then commanded him to go and perform ghusl. – *Tahaawi, Baabul-Ghusl*

From this incident, the Jurists (فقهاء) establish the rule that if a person has intercourse with a woman and stops without ejaculation, ghusl is still obligatory on him. When Hadrat Hanzalah Ghasīlul-Malāikah ﷺ (the individual who was given ghusl by the angels) went to his wife on the first nuptial night, he hadn't even made ghusl when the command of Rasoolullah ﷺ reached him to prepare leaving for Jihad. Still without ghusl, Hadrat Hanzalah ﷺ joined the army and was ultimately martyred in battle. When his body was brought forward from all the other bodies, drops of water were seen falling from it. The Holy Prophet ﷺ explained, "The angels gave him ghusl." This is where his title 'Ghasīlul-Malāikah' came from.

Hadrat Ubai ibn Ka'ab ﷺ was once performing Salaah when the Noble Messenger ﷺ called for him. He quickly completed his Salaah and came to him. When Rasoolullah ﷺ asked concerning what delayed him from coming straight away, the Companion replied that he was in Salaah. The Beloved Prophet ﷺ then asked, "Have you not heard the verse,

استجيبوا لله وللرسول اذا دعاكم
'Respond to the call of Allah ﷻ and the Messenger ﷺ
when the Messenger ﷺ calls you.'
– Surah Anfāl (8), Verse 24

We come to know that it's necessary upon a person even performing Salaah to leave it and present himself on the calling of the Noble Messenger ﷺ! Many Jurists have stated that if the person reading Salaah answers the calling of Rasoolullah ﷺ, he remains in Salaah even though he carries out the service of the Holy Prophet ﷺ. – *Qastalaani Sharah Bukhari, Kitaabut-Tafseer, Surah Hijr (15)*

Indeed, this statement of the Jurists is true! If the person reading Salaah talks [to the Holy Prophet ﷺ while in his service], he talks to the individual upon whom sending Salaam is compulsory in Salaah! – *See the Tashahud of Salaah*

If his chest moves away from the Ka'ba, it moves towards he who is the Ka'ba's Ka'ba!

If he goes to the court of Rasoolullah ﷺ or represents his court, this is an act of worshipping Allah ﷻ in itself. So, why would his Salaah be broken by doing such a thing? If a person's wudhu breaks while he's in Salaah, it is permissible for him to go to water, move away from the Ka'ba, and even perform actions that nullify Salaah. However, he'll still be regarded as being in Salaah. Rasoolullah ﷺ is the ocean of Allah's ﷻ mercy, why then would going towards him nullify Salaah?

If the word *believers* in the verse is taken as 'those who have faith on the Day of Judgment', even non-Muslims would be included in this matter. So, the obedience of Rasoolullah ﷺ is truly necessary on all of creation.

Every type of creation was obedient to the Holy Prophet ﷺ. – *Mishkaat, Baabul-Mu'jizaat*

Even trees responded to his calling. This verse remains in the Holy Quran for the purpose of proclaiming his greatness. Otherwise, the Prophet's ﷺ visible calling isn't found anymore. Indirect calling could also be meant here.

Rule – To stop performing Salaah is permissible in the following cases,

1. If a person sees himself being harmed or experiencing loss, he may break his Salaah.

2. If one needs to remove any difficulty from a Muslim.

3. If a blind person is about to fall into a well, the one making Salaah may break his Salaah and guide him.

4. If a person is performing optional (نفل) Salaah and his mother calls him (not knowing that he's in Salaah), the individual may stop the Salaah and answer her call.

5. If a person commenced an obligatory (fardh) Salaah alone and the takbeer for congregational Salaah is made, he may break his individual Salaah and join the congregation. – *Roohul-Bayaan (under the commentary of this verse) & Shaami, Vol. 1, Baabu Idraakil-Fareedha*

However, in all of these cases, *qadā* for the Salaah must be made.

The Quran has mentioned two callers in this verse, Allah ﷻ and Rasoolullah ﷺ. It's apparent that Allah ﷻ doesn't call anyone directly, and no one hears His voice by ear. So, indisputably, Rasoolullah ﷺ will be the caller, because his calling is the calling of Allah ﷻ. This is why the singular verb is used later in 'he calls you' (دعاكم).

The verse continues, "The Messenger ﷺ calls you to that which gives you life." We come to know that the Holy Prophet ﷺ gives life to those who are dead. He gives life to even the hearts of those who are alive, and grants existence to thoughts. To drown Pharaoh, Sayyiduna Jibrael عليه السلام rode a horse, the hoof of which caused the piece of earth it touched to grow grass. A member from the Bani Israel, Sāmiri, picked up this sand and, after the death of Pharaoh, placed it in the mouth of the golden calf, causing life to set into it too! Sayyiduna Jibrael's عليه السلام body touched the horse, the horse touched the sand, and the sand caused life to set in the golden calf – this is why Sayyiduna Jibrael عليه السلام is called *Roohul-Ameen*, because *rooh* (the soul) is attained through him. The sight of Rasoolullah ﷺ poses several Jibraeli strengths, so why can't the dead also attain life and existence through his gestures?

> Everything in this world is a sign of Allah's ﷻ power and nature. However, every object is a sign of only one quality of Allah ﷻ. The sun articulates the Noor of Allah ﷻ and the wind and water gesture to His generosity, but Rasoolullah ﷺ is the greatest reflection of Allah's ﷻ Being & Qualities. If you wish to see the knowledge of Allah ﷻ, look at the knowledge of Rasoolullah ﷺ. If you desire to see Allah's ﷻ generosity, look at Rasoolullah's ﷺ generosity.

Madaarijun-Nubuwwah records many incidents wherein the Holy Prophet ﷺ gave life to the dead. Rasoolullah ﷺ was once invited to the house of Hadrat Jabir ؓ, and the Companion slaughtered a goat to feed his noble guest. However, at that time, one of his sons killed the other son. So, he hid on the roof of the house in fear of his father, but slipped while on it and fell to his death. Hadrat Jabir's ؓ wife hid the bodies of both children so as not to disturb the invitation. Later, when the Holy Prophet ﷺ sat down to eat, he said, "O Jabir ؓ, call your children. I'll eat with them." The Sahaabi related the entire incident to him, after which the Prophet ﷺ brought them back to life (and ate with them).

The Prophet ﷺ once wiped his blessed hands on the tablecloth of Hadrat Anas ؓ. Whenever the tablecloth became dirty, Hadrat Anas ؓ would put it in a burning oven, which wouldn't harm the tablecloth. Rather, it would become clean. – *Mathnawi Sharif*

The Holy Prophet ﷺ once went somewhere on an invitation for a meal. A goat was slaughtered there, and Rasoolullah ﷺ instructed those present, "Eat the meat but don't break the bones of the animal." After the meal, the bones of the goat were gathered together. Rasoolullah 🌸 made dua, and the animal then came back to life! – *Madaarijun-Nubuwwah, Fasl Mu'jizaat*

In short, the Beloved Prophet 🌸 gave life to animals, humans – even stones and sticks! He gave life to stones and made them recite the Kalima, and sticks cried due to being separated from him. Sayyiduna Esa الـعليه gave life to dead humans, but Rasoolullah 🌸 gave life to lifeless objects. This is the meaning of 'he calls you to that which gives you life.'

VERSE 35

وَمَا كَانَ اللهُ لِيُعَذِّبَهُمْ وَأَنتَ فِيهِمْ

'And Allah ﷻ isn't one to punish them while
you (O Beloved 🌸) are in their midst.'
– Surah Anfāl (8), Verse 33

This verse is the praise of Rasoolullah 🌸, and it mentions his quality of being the Mercy to the Creation (رحمة للعالمين). The reason for its revelation is that on one occasion, the disbelievers said, "O God! If this Quran is true and we choose not to believe in it, make it rain stones from Heaven upon us or send some other punishment." The above verse was then revealed wherein Allah ﷻ says, "O Beloved Messenger 🌸, these people supplicate for their death on their own, but you are amidst them and have been sent as the Mercy unto Creation. Mercy and punishment cannot be joined, so no punishment will befall them while you are with them."

The following points emerge from this,

1. Through the blessings of the Holy Prophet 🌸, there's safety from the punishment of Allah ﷻ.

2. General punishment cannot befall Muslims until the Day of Qiyaamat. The general forms of punishment that previous nations underwent were that they were pelted with stones from the Heavens, submerged in the earth, and even drowned, etc. We come to know that Rasoolullah 🌸 is amongst the believers until the Last Day.

3. This also proves that the Holy Prophet's 🌸 presence isn't restricted in Madina. Rather, he's present wherever Muslims are found, because if punishment will not come wherever he's present, and since Muslims don't receive general punishment, we come to know that Rasoolullah 🌸 is present in all places.

84

4. Sayyiduna Esa عليه السلام was called to the Heavens and Sayyiduna Idris عليه السلام was called to Jannah. Our Holy Prophet ﷺ, however, remains in this world because its workings are due to him, and his going away would therefore be a problem for us. – *Roohul-Bayaan (under the commentary of this verse)*

VERSE 36

وَلَوْ اَنَّهُمْ رَضُوْا مَا اٰتٰهُمُ اللهُ وَرَسُوْلُه ، وَقَالُوْا حَسْبُنَا اللهُ سَيُؤْتِيْنَا اللهُ مِنْ فَضْلِه وَرَسُوْلُه ، اِنَّا اِلَى اللهِ رٰغِبُوْنَ

'If only they had been content with what Allah ﷻ and His Messenger ﷺ had given them and said, "Sufficient for us is Allah ﷻ. Allah ﷻ will give us of His bounty. To Allah ﷻ do we turn in submission.'
– Surah Tauba (9), Verse 59

This verse is clear praise of Rasoolullah ﷺ. The reason for its revelation is that once, the Holy Prophet ﷺ was distributing war-booty when a person named Harqoos ibn Zuhair stood up and said, "O Muhammad! Be fair in this distribution!" The Holy Prophet ﷺ replied, "If I'm not fair, who in the world will be fair?" Hadrat Umar ؓ then passionately offered, "O Rasoolullah ﷺ, will you allow me to kill this person who has no deen?!" He replied, "Let him be, as Allah ﷻ has willed a nation to emerge from him. The Salaah and surface piety of this nation will seem greater than your Salaah and piety. However, they'll leave the deen just as how an arrow leaves a hunter's bow. They will recite the Quran but the Quran won't go beyond their throats." Due to this, this verse and a few others were revealed. In the above, Allah ﷻ says, "If these people were content with what Allah ﷻ and Rasoolullah ﷺ gave them and said, 'Allah ﷻ will grant us more through His grace,' it would've been better for them."

The following points emerge from this,

1. To object to any action of the Holy Prophet ﷺ is an act of disbelief (کفر). This is why Hadrat Umar Farooq ؓ sought permission to kill the man, because an apostate (مرتد) is someone necessary to be killed (واجب القتل).

2. The Holy Prophet ﷺ is *Malik & Mukhtar* (i.e. one with authority). If he wishes to emplace a specific command upon a person, he may do so.

3. Allah ﷻ has bestowed the Holy Messenger ﷺ with the Knowledge of the Five Secrets (علوم خمسة). Through the vision of prophethood, Rasoolullah ﷺ saw what the offspring of this man will be, and that it's the planning of Allah ﷻ that such people will emerge. So, he said [in other words], "O Umar ؓ, don't kill him, because doing so is contrary to the will of Allah ﷻ."

4. The Holy Prophet ﷺ distributes the blessings of Allah ﷻ. The verse states, "…what Allah ﷻ and His Messenger ﷺ had given them." So, if a person says, "Allah ﷻ and His Rasool ﷺ has given me honor, Imaan, life or wealth," this will not be equating the Holy Prophet ﷺ to Allah ﷻ, because it is permissible to ask from he who gives. The Prophet ﷺ also said, "Allah ﷻ is the Giver and I am the distributor." – *Bukhari, Kitaabul-Ilm*

    Hadrat Rabia ibn Ka'ab Aslami ؓ was instructed by the Holy Prophet ﷺ, "Ask." The Companion submitted, "I ask to be in your service in Jannah." Rasoolullah ﷺ then said, "Do you ask for anything else?" He answered, "That is sufficient for me." – *Muslim; Mishkaat, Baabus-Sujood*

    Under the commentary of this Hadith, Mulla Ali Qaari ؓ and Shaikh Abdul-Haqq Muhaddith Dehlwi ؓ state in *Mirqaat* and *Ashiatul-Lam'aat* respectively, "We can deduce that the blessings of Allah ﷻ are in the control of the Holy Prophet ﷺ. He can bestow whatever amount he wishes to whomever he wishes."

VERSE 37

يَحْلِفُونَ بِاللهِ لَكُمْ لِيُرْضُوكُمْ ، وَاللهُ وَرَسُولُهُ أَحَقُّ أَنْ يُرْضُوهُ إِنْ كَانُوا مُؤْمِنِينَ

'They swear by Allah ﷻ before you that you may be pleased. And Allah ﷻ and the Messenger ﷺ had a greater right that they should please him if they had faith.'
– Surah Tauba (9), Verse 62

The praise of the Holy Prophet ﷺ is explicitly proven by this verse. The reason for its revelation is that Hypocrites would mock and criticize Rasoolullah ﷺ in their gatherings. When they came among Muslims, however, they'd deny doing such things and swear false oaths to prove their innocence. This verse was revealed regarding this issue, and in it Allah ﷻ says, "Greater than swearing oaths to make Muslims content is to make Allah ﷻ and His Messenger ﷺ pleased. If they were believers, why did they do what they did? This action was a means of gaining Allah ﷻ and His Messenger's ﷺ displeasure."

The following points emerge from this,

1.   Allah ﷻ is displeased and angry with whatever is the Holy Prophet's ﷺ displeasure. The Hypocrites didn't speak drivel against Allah ﷻ (just His Messenger ﷺ), yet Allah ﷻ *also* became displeased.

2.   If you wish to extinguish the fire of Allah's ﷻ anger, please and satisfy the Holy Prophet ﷺ. In the verse, the Hypocrites were told to please Allah ﷻ *and* the Messenger ﷺ, and it's apparent that they cannot go to Allah ﷻ. So, to appease Him, they would have to come to the court of the Holy Messenger ﷺ.

3.   To intend appeasing Rasoolullah ﷺ in a good work and displaying it to him is neither considered show nor polytheism (forming partners with Allah ﷻ). If a person intends attaining the pleasure of Allah ﷻ and Rasoolullah ﷺ by performing Salaah (meaning he performs the worship of Allah ﷻ but completes it because it's the command of the Holy Prophet ﷺ and contains within it the pleasure of both), this is an admirable, good act. In this verse, command is given to please two beings, Allah ﷻ and Rasoolullah ﷺ.

     Under the commentary of 'And We gave Dawud ﷺ the scripture' – Surah Nisā (4), Verse 163 or Surah Isrā (17), Verse 55 – *Tafseer Roohul-Bayaan*, *Khaazin* and *Madaarik* all record the following Hadith. Once, the Holy Prophet ﷺ said to Hadrat Abu Musa Ash'ari ﷺ, "Tonight I heard your recitation of the Holy Quran. Allah ﷻ has granted you the sweet voice of Sayyiduna Dawud ﷺ." The Companion submitted, "O Rasoolullah ﷺ, if I had known that the Quran personified (i.e. the Holy Prophet ﷺ) was listening to me, I would've attempted to recite better than that." Subhanallah! Salaah and the recitation of the Holy Quran is the worship of Allah ﷻ, yet Hadrat Abu Musa Ash'ari ﷺ wished to please the Holy Beloved ﷺ in Allah's ﷻ worship itself!

     The Hadith about the Holy Prophet's ﷺ final illness states that Hadrat Abu Bakr Siddique ﷺ was leading the congregational Salaah in the Holy Prophet's ﷺ place [i.e. as the Imam]. During the Salaah, the Holy Messenger ﷺ arrived – and Hadrat Abu Bakr ﷺ

immediately became the follower of him (i.e. Rasoolullah ﷺ took up being the Imam of the Salaah). – *Bukhari, Muslim, etc.*

This is respect for the Holy Prophet ﷺ in Salaah.
'The remembrance of Allah ﷻ which you wish to be separate from the Prophet's ﷺ remembrance, O [wretches]...by Allah ﷻ! It's not the remembrance of truth, but the key to Hell-fire!'
– Alahadrat Imam Ahmad Raza ☙

4. To please the Holy Prophet ﷺ is part of Imaan. The verse states, "...if they had faith." When Rasoolullah's ﷺ name is included in every verbal act of worshipping Allah ﷻ, why would attaining his pleasure not be part of Imaan? The name of the Holy Prophet ﷺ is present and found in the Kalima, Salaah, the Khutba, the Azaan and in every dua. Hadrat Hasan ibn Thaabit ☙ states,

ضم الاله اسم النبى باسمه ، اذ قال فى الخمس المؤذن اشهد

'Allah ﷻ joined the name of the Holy Prophet ﷺ with His, and this is established by the name of Rasolullah ﷺ uttered five times daily by the Muazzin.'

VERSE 38

اَلَمۡ يَعۡلَمُوۡۤا اَنَّه مَن يُّحَادِدِ اللهَ وَرَسُولَه فَاَنَّ لَه نَارَ جَهَنَّمَ خٰلِدًا فِيۡهَا ، ذٰلِكَ الۡخِزۡيُ الۡعَظِيۡمُ

'Are they not aware that, concerning whoever opposes Allah ﷻ and His Messenger ﷺ, for such a person is the fire of Hell in which he will abide forever? This is a great humiliation.'
– Surah Tauba (9), Verse 63

The honor and greatness of the Holy Prophet ﷺ is proclaimed in this verse. It also severely censors those who oppose Allah ﷻ and His Rasool ﷺ. This verse states that to displease Allah ﷻ or His Messenger ﷺ ultimately results in disbelief (كفر). In other words, to displease Allah ﷻ is an act of disbelief, and to oppose the Holy Prophet ﷺ its *also* an act of disbelief. If a person causes trouble to his parents, causes displeasure to other creation, etc. he will not become a non-Muslim (just a sinner). But again, if he opposes the Holy Prophet ﷺ, he becomes a disbeliever (كافر).

Shaitaan was commanded to make sajda to Sayyiduna Adam عليه السلام but refused. He didn't refute the Oneness of Allah ﷻ or the act of performing sajda to Him. Rather, he rejected the greatness of the prophet who had in his spine the Noor of Muhammad'ur-Rasoolullah ﷺ. This resulted in the worship of Allah ﷻ he had performed his entire life being wasted, and in him becoming the object of Allah's ﷻ curse.

Presenting oneself in the Holy Prophet's ﷺ court and seeking his intercession will please Allah ﷻ, but tell me, if the Holy Prophet ﷺ is displeased with you, whom can you turn to then? Rasoolullah ﷺ is the *intercessor*. If a person is apprehended by Allah ﷻ, Allah ﷻ forgives him through the intercession of the Holy Messenger ﷺ, but if a person is seized by Rasoolullah ﷺ, who then will save him?

It has been stated by the Jurists that if a person becomes insolent towards Allah's ﷻ glory, he'll leave the fold of Islam and should be executed. However, if he repents, he'll be forgiven. On the other hand, if a person becomes insolent towards *the Holy Prophet's* ﷺ honor, he must be executed even if he repents, because Allah's ﷻ right can be forgiven through repentance, but not the rights of creation. – *Durre-Mukhtaar, Baabdul-Murtaddeen*

> As soon as Sayyiduna Adam عليه السلام gained life, he read the Kalima written on the pillars of the Throne and asked, "O Allah ﷻ, whose name is written next to Yours?" Allah ﷻ answered, "O Adam عليه السلام, it's the name of that personality who, had I not created him, I wouldn't have created you."

We can deduce that there is severe punishment in worldly commands for he who's disrespectful to the Holy Messenger ﷺ.

There was a person who used to write revelation but later became an apostate. He accused the Holy Prophet ﷺ of concocting the Holy Quran and said that he knew this because he was the scribe for that very purpose. When he died and was buried, even the earth refused to accept him (and spat his body out). When his grave was dug deeper and deeper several times afterwards, the body continued to be spat out on every instance. – *Madaarijun-Nubuwwah*

We come to know that a person apprehended by the Beloved Prophet's ﷺ anger will never attain safety anywhere.

VERSE 39

خُذْ مِنْ اَمْوَالِهِمْ صَدَقَةً تُطَهِّرُهُمْ وَتُزَكِّيْهِمْ بِهَا وَصَلِّ عَلَيْهِمْ ، إِنَّ صَلٰوتَكَ سَكَنٌ لَّهُمْ ، وَاللهُ سَمِيْعٌ عَلِيْمٌ

'(O Beloved Prophet ﷺ) Realize the poor-due (Zakaat) out of their wealth to purify and cleanse them therewith, and pray good for them. No doubt your prayer is solace for their hearts. And Allah ﷻ Hears, Knows.'
– Surah Tauba (9), Verse 103

The reason for the revelation of this verse is that a group of sincere believers were unable to partake in the Battle of Tabuk due to their business commitments. They repented with great remorse, so much so that some of them even tied themselves to the pillars of Musjidun-Nabawi, saying that they wouldn't have themselves freed until the Holy Prophet ﷺ untied them himself with his blessed hands! When Rasoolullah ﷺ heard this, he said, "By Allah ﷻ, I won't untie them until Allah ﷻ orders their freedom!"

Allah ﷻ did eventually command their freedom. So, these individuals were untied and thereafter came to the Holy Prophet ﷺ presenting their wealth, saying, "It's due to this wealth that we stopped ourselves from partaking in Jihad. So, O Rasoolullah ﷺ, it's now being presented as compensation for our non-participation." The Holy Prophet ﷺ replied, "I've not been commanded to take it." The above verse was then revealed on this occasion. – *Khazaainul-Irfaan*

Rasoolullah ﷺ was commanded in the verse, "O Beloved ﷺ, accept this wealth of theirs and supplicate for them because your remembrance is the solace of their hearts. Whatever they are, they are yours. If you become upset, who'll then be theirs to purify them?"

The praise of the Holy Prophet ﷺ is established here through the following points,

1. Deeds may be profuse in quantity, but their acceptance is through the attention of the Holy Prophet ﷺ. Giving charity is the worship of Allah ﷻ, but if it *is* accepted, it is through the *means* of Rasoolullah ﷺ.

2. The Sahaabah believed that sin is forgiven through the Holy Prophet ﷺ. This is why they came to Musjidun-Nabawi and desired that he set them free.

3. Rasoolullah ﷺ purifies Muslims from every impurity, sin, etc, and good deeds are a means of purification. Here Rasoolullah ﷺ is commanded to purify them by accepting their charity. If the worship of Allah ﷻ is great in quantity but doesn't attain acceptance in the

Prophetic court, it's useless, and the doer of these good deeds is still impure.

4. Allah's ﷻ habit is that whenever He wishes to send or bestow mercy, He says to His Beloved ﷺ, "You ask this for them from Me, then I will send it." This is why the verse says, "...supplicate for them." Allah ﷻ definitely has the power to send to them without His Beloved's ﷺ supplication, but He chooses not to. Rather, He states, "O Beloved ﷺ, you supplicate and I will then demonstrate mercy." The Holy Prophet ﷺ said in a Hadith, "Every Monday and Friday, all Books of Deeds are presented to me and I supplicate for everyone's forgiveness from sin." Why then are these Books of Deeds presented (even until today)? Simple! Their condition of acceptance is the dua of the Holy Prophet ﷺ.

5. Through the dua of the Prophet ﷺ, the Sahaabah would attain solace. However, even though humans are blessed with intelligence, we see that even inanimate objects and animals attain solace from the Holy Prophet ﷺ. The pillar of Hanānah cried due to being separated from Rasoolullah ﷺ, and even camels demonstrated their peace when he was nearby. Once, a deer trapped in the net of a hunter submitted to Rasoolullah ﷺ, "My children are hungry. If you grant me permission, I can feed them and return." – *Mishkaat Sharif, Dalaailul-Khairaat, Madaarijun-Nubuwwah*

In short, the being of the Holy Messenger ﷺ is the solace of the heart for the entire creation. He who doesn't attain relief from his blessed name is someone deprived of his natural disposition, like a sick person who finds even sweet things sour.

VERSE 40

لَقَدْ جَاءَكُمْ رَسُوْلٌ مِّنْ اَنْفُسِكُمْ عَزِيْزٌ عَلَيْهِ مَا عَنِتُّمْ حَرِيْصٌ عَلَيْكُمْ بِالْمُؤْمِنِيْنَ رَؤُوْفٌ رَّحِيْمٌ

'Surely there has come to you a Messenger ﷺ from among yourselves.
Heavy upon him is your suffering, and he ardently desires your welfare.
To the believers he is most kind and merciful.'
– Surah Tauba (9), Verse 128

This verse is a collection of Rasoolullah's ﷺ praise. It speaks about his *Mīlad* (blessed birth), since 'Mīlad' is to mention the coming and advent of the Holy Messenger ﷺ. Everyone knew Rasoolullah ﷺ came to the world, so why mention something that was already known to all? Simple – it's a chance to mention the blessed birth itself (ولادة) and demonstrate his grandeur. The previous Prophets عليهم السلام also gave glad-tidings to their respective nations about Rasoolullah's ﷺ birth. We come to know that celebrating this event is a practice of the Prophets عليهم السلام – and even the way of Allah ﷻ Himself!

Six attributes of the Holy Prophet ﷺ have been mentioned in this verse,

1. He's a Messenger,

2. He's from amongst us,

3. Our hardship is hard on him,

4. He's someone who strives for us (حريص),

5. He's kind to believers,

6. And he's merciful to them.

Accepting Rasoolullah ﷺ to have come to this world as a Messenger is the foundation of Imaan. By regarding him to be merely a man, an equal, or our brother doesn't make a person a Muslim. Abu Lahab observed happiness on the birth of the Holy Prophet ﷺ thinking him to be his nephew, and Abu Talib thought the same whenever he saw him. If they did what they'd done due to him being the *Messenger* ﷺ, they would've been not just Muslims, but amongst the Sahaabah!

In this verse, the word 'Messenger ﷺ' has been used, and in the verse of the Ascension (Mi'rāj), the word 'servant' (عبد) was used. This is because when the Holy Prophet ﷺ presented himself in Allah's ﷻ court, he went with his glory of servanthood, but when he came to us, he came with the grandeur of prophethood. 'A manifest proof', a 'Noor', 'the ultimate blessing of Allah ﷻ', etc. are all titles used at appropriate occasions. He who addresses the Holy Prophet ﷺ as a 'servant' is similar to a wife who calls her husband 'son'.

'Messenger' can either mean a distinguished Messenger, or that particular Messenger (referred to on the Day of Covenant). There are two ways to read the ف in the words من انفسكم. One can either read it with a *fat'ha* or a *dumma*. If the former is recited, the meaning will be 'he came to the best group of you'. In this case, we come to know that the Arab nation is the most excellent of all the world's nations. Among them, the Quraish is the most excellent, and among them, the Banu Hashim (because the Holy Prophet ﷺ was born in this family). Similarly, the best language is Arabic, because the Quran was revealed in it, the language of the Hereafter is in Arabic, the language of the inmates of Jannah is in Arabic, and the Holy Prophet's ﷺ language was also Arabic.

Likewise, the most excellent city is Makkah, since it's the birthplace of the Beloved Prophet ﷺ. Also, from all the genealogies, Rasoolullah's ﷺ genealogy is the most pure. None of his ancestors, from Sayyiduna Adam عليه السلام to (his father) Hadrat Abdullah رضى الله عنه, was ever involved in fornication. The Holy Prophet ﷺ shined bright from the foreheads of the best people in every era. This is attested to by the first Hadith found in *Mishkaat, Baabu Fadhaaili-Sayyidil-Mursaleen.*

Also, no ancestor of the Holy Prophet ﷺ, from Sayyiduna Adam عليه السلام until Hadrat Abdullah رضى الله عنه, was ever a polytheist or an idol-worshipper. Sayyiduna Ibrahim's عليه السلام father was not Aazar, but in fact Tārikh رضى الله عنه. When the Quran called Aazar the father of Sayyiduna Ibrahim عليه السلام, it was in relation to him being his paternal-uncle. Likewise, the Hadith wherein the Holy Prophet ﷺ said,

ان ابى واباك فى النار

'Your father and my father are in Jahannam.'
– Muslim Sharif

'My father' here referred to Abu Talib.

Once, the Holy Prophet ﷺ went to the *qabr* of his blessed mother, Sayyidah Amina رضى الله عنها, wept profusely and said, "I asked for permission for my mother's grave and it was granted to me. I asked for permission to supplicate for her forgiveness but I was stopped from doing so." – *Mishkaat, Baabu Ziyaaratil-Qabr*

Based on this Hadith, some say that Sayyidah Amina رضى الله عنها was not a Muslim [Allah ﷻ forbid!]. This is incorrect, because the Prophet's ﷺ weeping was due to him being separate from her. It doesn't establish that she was a non-Muslim. Allah ﷻ stopped the Holy Prophet ﷺ from asking for her forgiveness because such a dua is only made for sinners, and Sayyidah Amina رضى الله عنها wasn't one. This is why the dua for forgiveness isn't made in the Salaatul-Janaazah of a child. The definition of a sinner is a person who acts contrary to the commands of the Holy Prophet ﷺ after receiving them. Hadrat Abdullah رضى الله عنه and Sayyidah Amina رضى الله عنها didn't see the era of the Holy Messenger ﷺ, and the deens of the previous Prophets عليهم السلام were changed, making their teachings inaccessible. So, what were the Prophet's ﷺ parents to practice now? This proves that they didn't sin, and dua is made for those who are sinful. Allah ﷻ forbid, if they *were* non-Muslims, the Holy Prophet ﷺ wouldn't have even been permitted to visit their graves, because visiting the graves of non-Muslims is haraam. The Holy Quran states,

ولا تقم على قبره ، انهم كفروا بالله ورسوله وماتوا وهم فسقون

'You shouldn't stand at their graves. No doubt, they disbelieved in Allah ﷻ and His Messenger ﷺ and died while they were disobedient.'
– Surah Tauba (9), Verse 84

Nevertheless, we have to accept that Hadrat Abdullah ؓ and Sayyidah Amina ؓ, the parents of the Holy Prophet ﷺ, weren't non-Muslims.

One question remains: which deen, then, did they adhere to? I've already submitted that Islam wasn't proclaimed in the world during their lifetimes, and the deens of previous Prophets السلام عليهم were changed. So, Hadrat Abdullah ؓ and Sayyidah Amina ؓ are counted as the *As'haabe-Fatrah* (in other words, to simply refrain from idolatry and accept Allah ﷻ as One is enough for them to be believers).

So, Hadrat Abdullah ؓ and Sayyidah Amina ؓ were from the As'haabe-Fatrah and met their demise as such. Thereafter, Rasoolullah ﷺ brought both of them back to life on the occasion of the Final Hajj and entered them into Islam. For this reason, they are now Muslims. Imam Jalaaluddin Suyuti ؓ has written an extensive treatise which supports this, and Alahadrat Imam Ahmad Raza Khan ؓ has also written a treatise on this topic. The name of the latter is *Shumūlul-Islam li Abā'il-Kirām*. The stomach of the fish in which Sayyiduna Yunus ؓ remained in is more excellent than the Throne of Allah ﷻ because the Ascension (Mi'rāj) of a prophet occurred there.

Likewise, the Companions of Rasoolullah ﷺ are the most excellent of all the companions of the previous Prophets السلام عليهم, his family is the greatest of all the Prophets' السلام عليهم families, and his era is the greatest of all eras. According to some Scholars, the day the Holy Prophet ﷺ was born (Monday) is the greatest of days, the month of his birth (Rabiul-Awwal) is greater than many months of the year, and the earth which is touching the blessed body of Rasoolullah ﷺ is more excellent than the Holy Ka'ba, the entire Earth, the Throne of Allah ﷻ (عرش) and the Kursi. Refer to *Shaami, Kitaabul-Hajj*.

In short, whatever gains a connection to the Holy Prophet ﷺ becomes excellent.

An issue on which Jurists deliberated is, "Which is the most excellent of waters?" Some claim that it's the water of Zam-Zam, but others say that the most excellent water is the water which flowed from the blessed fingers of the Holy Prophet 🕌 (when he placed his hand in a bowl during one of the battles). This is because Zam-Zam emanated at the feet of Sayyiduna Ismail عليه السلام while this water emerged from the hand of the Noble Messenger 🕌. Likewise, the food of Hadrat Jabir's 🕌 home (wherein Rasoolullah 🕌 placed his blessed saliva) is the most excellent of all foods.

If, on the other hand, the ف is read with a dumma, it gives the meaning 'from among your beings'. By this, it's established that this Prophet 🕌 hasn't come from among angels, jinns or non-Arabs. Rather, he has come from humans, and so effectively, humanity will have pride in this until the Day of Qiyaamat. His coming from Arabs also causes them to gain distinction.

It could also mean, "His coming to you is like the position of the soul in a body (which is present at all times yet obscured from our vision). Similarly, O Muslims, he remains in your hearts and thoughts but not in your sight."

> "I have not praised Muhammad 🕌 with my words. Rather, I have made my words worthy of being praised using his name."
>
> *The Companion Hadrat Hasan ibn Thaabit* 🕌

Regarding 'heavy upon him is your suffering' in the verse, the Holy Prophet 🕌 is shown to be distressed by your hardships. The meaning of this is clear to all. If Rasoolullah 🕌 has come to us the way a soul comes to a body, he surely experiences our hardship the way the soul experiences hardship when the body is hurt. We come to know that the Holy Prophet 🕌 is aware of every condition of the Muslims at all times. If not, how could he be distressed by our hardship?

'Has come to you' in the verse proves that the Holy Prophet 🕌 has come to all places, effectively establishing the belief in him being حاضر وناظر (able to see and assist us at all times). The verse also doesn't disclose where he came from. We come to know that he came from where there is no 'where', i.e. he came to a physical vicinity (مكان) from an unreachable space (لا مكان). The Holy Prophet 🕌 came from the Divine proximity where he remained for thousands of years.

'He ardently desires your welfare' means that some desire the comfort of their children, some honor, wealth and other things, but Rasoolullah ﷺ desires neither the comfort of his children nor his own personal comfort. He is only desirious of our welfare. This is why he remembered us on the occasion of his birth, during his Ascension (Mi'rāj), and at the time of his demise. When the Prophet ﷺ was lowered into his blessed *qabr*, Hadrat Abdullah ibn Abbas ؓ noticed that his lips were moving. When he paid attention to it, he heard the Holy Prophet ﷺ interceding for his Ummah.

Rasoolullah ﷺ used to even spend his nights awake, crying in supplication for his Ummah, saying, "O Allah ﷻ, if You punish them, they are Your servants, but if you forgive them, indeed You are Mighty and Wise."

On the Day of Judgment, everyone will be concerned with their own life, but the Holy Prophet ﷺ will be concerned with everyone else's. Every prophet will declare, "To each his own," but our Beloved Prophet ﷺ will proclaim, "My followers, I'm here for you."

VERSE 41

قُلْ يَأَيُّهَا النَّاسُ قَدْ جَاءَكُمُ الْحَقُّ مِن رَّبِّكُمْ

'Say (O Beloved ﷺ), 'The truth has come from your Lord.'
– Surah Yunus (10), Verse 108

This verse is also the praise of the Holy Prophet ﷺ. It states, "The truth has come from your Lord." 'Truth' here refers to the Holy Quran, the deen of Islam, or the being of the Holy Prophet ﷺ himself. We come to know that 'truth' is one of the names of the Holy Messenger ﷺ.

Another point that emerges is that people are on truth, but the Holy Prophet ﷺ *is* truth personified. He who has seen him has seen truth. People are those with Imaan (Mu'mins), but the Holy Prophet ﷺ is Imaan itself; people are Aarifs (Gnostics), but he is Irfaan (recognition itself); people are scholars, but he is knowledge personified – being aware of his qualities and epithets *is* knowledge.

'Spiritual excellence (رياضت) is to come and go in your proximity;
Being in your remembrance is the worship of Allah ﷻ.'
– Alahadrat Imam Ahmed Raza Khan ؓ

اَلَا بِذِكۡرِ اللهِ تَطۡمَئِنُّ الۡقُلُوۡبُ

'Behold, in the remembrance of Allah ﷻ is there satisfaction of hearts.'
– Surah Ra'ad (13), Verse 28

This verse is clear praise of Rasoolullah ﷺ. In it, the remedy for the believer's restlessness of heart is explained. Allah ﷻ states that through His remembrance, the heart attains satisfaction. 'Remembrance of Allah ﷻ' refers to either the Being of Allah ﷻ Himself or the Holy Prophet ﷺ, because one of the Prophet's ﷺ names is *Zikrullah* (the Remembrance of Allah ﷻ). Refer to *Dalaailul-Khairaat, Hizb Awwal*.

If the first meaning is applied, the verse will mean that through the remembrance of Allah ﷻ, the heart attains satisfaction. Its restlessness and dissatisfaction at most times is due to the scourge of sins. Maulana Rumi ﷺ says,

'Whatever grief and darkness you face is due to your insolence and arrogance.'
– Mathnawi Sharif

The Holy Quran states,

وما اصبكم من مصية فبما كسبت ايديكم ويعفوا عن كثير

'And whatever affliction reached you is due to what your hands have earned; and He pardons much.'
– Surah Shūrā (42), Verse 30

The remembrance of Allah ﷻ is to sin what water is to an impurity. When water's used to wash an impure object, it becomes clean. Likewise, the scourge of sin and its impurities are removed by the remembrance of Allah ﷻ. Sins are forgiven and despondency is removed.

This is why Islam encourages the remembrance of Allah ﷻ at the time of every affliction and hardship. When there's no rain, perform *Salaatul-Istisqā*; at the time of a lunar or solar eclipse, perform *Salaatul-Khusoof & Kusoof*; if you intend doing something, perform *Salaatul-Istikhāra*. In fact, carry out the remembrance of Allah ﷻ in every condition and state. When a baby is born, give the Azaan in his or her ear; teach your children to perform Salaah during their childhood; when you awake in the morning, perform Salaah; at night, perform it before sleeping; encourage the recital of the Kalima to a person nearing his or her demise; write it on the *kafn*; when placing the deceased in the grave, recite, 'Bismillah wa alā Millati Rasoolillah ﷺ,' etc. In short, remember Allah ﷻ in every condition.

The remembrance of Allah ﷻ performed by each part of the body is different and separate. His remembrance when carried out by the eye is to cry in His fear, to look at the Quran, the Ka'ba, one's parents or the Islamic Scholars. The remembrance of Allah ﷻ when carried out by the ear is to hear the name of Allah ﷻ and the Holy Quran. His remembrance by the hand is to touch the Holy Quran and the Ahadith, etc, and his remembrance by the feet is to go towards the musjid and other blessed places, etc.

The heart, however, attains satisfaction through every form of remembrance. Maulana Jalaaluddin Rumi ؓ states,

'If you desire an existence with honor, remember Him, remember Him, make His remembrance always.'

'His remembrance makes every beggar a king. His remembrance is the adornment of Imaan.'

Another explanation of how the heart attains satisfaction is as follows: A human being has two things, a body and a soul. The body is in its element but the soul isn't, because it belongs to the Realm of Souls (عالم الارواح). The soul is restricted within the prison of the physical body, and the remembrance of Allah ﷻ is a letter from the homeland. When a person is in a foreign land and receives a letter from his motherland, the foreigner attains satisfaction. Likewise, in the world, the remembrance of Allah ﷻ is the satisfaction of the heart and soul. The honor of a believer is through this remembrance. The covering of any Holy Quran and the ghilāf of the Holy Ka'ba are revered because they have a connection with the Quran and the Ka'ba. Similarly, if the heart and tongue of a believer becomes the citadel and fort of Divine remembrance, he's definitely honored in the world and in the Hereafter – wherever he may be! Maulana Jalaaluddin Rumi ؓ states,

'The will of he who becomes lost in the remembrance of Allah ﷻ is emplaced.'
– Mathnawi Sharif

If the second meaning of 'the remembrance of Allah ﷻ' is applied, the verse will mean, 'Restless hearts attain satisfaction through the Holy Prophet ﷺ.' Rasoolullah ﷺ is called 'the remembrance of Allah ﷻ' because a person remembers Allah ﷻ when he sees him. The Holy Quran states,

انما انت مذكر

"(O Beloved ﷺ) Indeed you are the one who causes
the remembrance [of Allah ﷻ]."
– Surah Ghāshiyah (88), Verse 21

Restless hearts attain satisfaction through the Holy Prophet ﷺ because he's the beloved of every Muslim, and it's well known that, "The cure of an illness is meeting the beloved friend." So, this necessitates the Prophet's ﷺ name to be the satisfaction of Muslims. The remembrance of the beloved is the cure for he who is lovesick. Secondly, Rasoolullah ﷺ is the source of the entire world,

انا نور من نور الله وكل الخلق من نوري

'I'm from the Noor of Allah ﷻ and the entire creation is from my Noor.'
– Hadith Sharif

Shaikh Sādi Shirazi ؓ states,

'(O Rasoolullah ﷺ) You are the source and origin of
everything. Everything exists secondary to you.'
– Bustaan

It's a rule that when an object reaches its source and origin, it attains rest and tranquility. A person remains uneasy in a foreign land and is happy when he returns home, and waters of rivers flow because they aren't in their element while the water of the ocean is still. The remembrance of the Holy Prophet ﷺ is the remembrance of our source. So, tranquility surely comes through it. It's an experienced and trusted practice that when a person experiences heart palpitations, he should write this verse (the verse being discussed) with his finger over his heart and say, "Ya Muhammad," continuously. In doing so, Insha-Allah ﷻ, he will attain comfort.

'For he who loves the Beloved Messenger ﷺ, whatever difficulty he may be in;
When Rasoolullah ﷺ is remembered, he forgets all sadness.'
– Alahadrat Imam Ahmed Raza ؓ

Humans have the faculty of intellect, but even animals, stones and sticks attain tranquility from Rasoolullah ﷺ. When a piece of bark cried out due to being separated from him, Rasoolullah ﷺ embraced it and caused it to settle.

A pious man was once writing an amulet (ta'wīz) for a sick person when an irreligious person said, "The writing of these amulets are only to fill one's stomach. Nothing occurs through them." The pious man replied, "Donkey! Dog!" and continued writing. Hearing this, the objector became furious and started saying nonsensical things. The pious man asked, "O friend, why are you angry? I only took the names of two creations of Allah ﷻ." The man replied, "Will those words not affect the heart of a person? People are definitely offended by them." The pious man then explained, "When the names of insignificant things can change a person's condition, why would the name of Allah ﷻ the Creator and the name of His Beloved ﷺ not have the ability to change the condition of a sick person?"

Actually, remembering Rasoolullah ﷺ is a way of concentrating his attention on us. Through his special care, the needs of us beggars are fulfilled.

'How can his mercy not be extended to a sinner?
Indeed the Most Merciful is diligent of he who is my benefactor.'
– Maulana Hasan Raza ؓ

VERSE 43

وَلَقَدْ اَرْسَلْنَا رُسُلًا مِّنْ قَبْلِكَ وَجَعَلْنَا لَهُمْ اَزْوَاجًا وَّذُرِّيَّةً

'And undoubtedly We have sent Messengers before you and assigned to them wives and children.'
– Surah Ra'ad (13), Verse 38

This verse is also the praise of the Holy Prophet ﷺ. The reason behind its revelation was that the non-Muslims would say, "If Muhammad ﷺ is a prophet of Allah ﷻ, why does he have children and a household? What relationship does a prophet need to have with the world? He should have affinity with Allah ﷻ alone, just like Sayyiduna Esa عليه السلام and Sayyiduna Yahya عليه السلام." The above verse was revealed for this reason. The praise of the Holy Messenger ﷺ is found within it for the following reasons,

1. An objection was raised against Rasoolullah ﷺ and Allah ﷻ answered it. The Holy Prophet ﷺ didn't have to say anything against it.

2. The objectors regarded worldly relationships as a defect while the verse states that worldly relationship is excellence entirely. Many Prophets عليهم السلام had worldly relationships. In fact, maintaining these relationships is a grand action. Also, whoever gains a connection or relationship with Rasoolullah ﷺ attains honor and greatness. Sayyiduna Esa عليه السلام was born without a father, so only his maternal

family and relatives gained honor through his being. Our Prophet ﷺ was born from a mother *and* a father. So, two groups of people effectively gained distinction through him. Likewise, all of his blessed wives and their families attained honor until Qiyaamat. Today, descendants of Rasoolullah ﷺ are looked at with respect throughout the world, and this will be the case until the Last Day, Insha-Allah ﷻ. If they weren't the descendants of the Prophet ﷺ, how would this group of people attain this distinction?

VERSE 44

لَعَمْرُكَ إِنَّهُمْ لَفِيْ سَكْرَتِهِمْ يَعْمَهُوْنَ

'(O My Beloved ﷺ) By your life, indeed they are wandering about in their intoxication.'
– Surah Hijr (15), Verse 72

This verse is the praise of Rasoolullah ﷺ because an oath on his life was taken in it. In the entire Holy Quran, Allah ﷻ doesn't mention an oath on any prophet besides Sayyiduna Rasoolullah ﷺ. In fact, Allah ﷻ takes an oath not only on his life, but on the Holy Prophet's ﷺ *city* (Makkah)…

لا اقسم بهذا البلد ، وانت حل بهذا البلد

'Indeed I swear by this city (Makkah) as you (O Beloved ﷺ) dwell in this city.'
– Surah Balad (90), Verse 1-2

his blessed era…

والعصر

'I swear by the time (of My Beloved ﷺ).'
– Surah Asr (103), Verse 1

and everything associated to him. We come to know that the Holy Prophet ﷺ and everything connected to him is valued and sacred in the sight of Allah ﷻ, because oaths are either taken on beloved things (e.g. a person swearing an oath on his life, his children, his mother, etc.) or on sacred things (such as Allah ﷻ and His Qualities).

Rule – There are two types of oaths,

1. **Shar'i Oath** Oaths on which Shariah rules (i.e. rules pertaining to Islamic Law) are enjoined, e.g. kaffarah. This oath can be taken on Allah's ﷻ Being, or Qualities of His on which oaths are traditionally

made, e.g. "Oath on Rahmān (The Most Merciful)! Oath on the Quran!"

2. **Urfī Oath** Oaths on which Shariah rules are not enjoined. This oath is made to add emphasis to speech, e.g. "Oath on my life/mother/father/children, etc.!"

When the Holy Quran takes an oath on something, it wishes to demonstrate its honor and greatness, either from a religious or worldly point of view. The Quran has taken an oath on the *zaitūn* (olive-oil), figs, etc. because they have several worldly benefits. People, especially Arabs, find much benefit in them. Oaths have therefore also been taken on the Holy Prophet 🕌, his blessed city, etc. because they are embellished with greatness until the Day of Judgment.

VERSE 45

سُبْحٰنَ الَّذِى أَسْرٰى بِعَبْدِهٖ لَيْلًا مِّنَ الْمَسْجِدِ الْحَرَامِ إِلَى الْمَسْجِدِ الْأَقْصَا الَّذِى بٰرَكْنَا حَوْلَهٗ لِنُرِيَهٗ مِنْ ءايٰتِنَا ، إِنَّهٗ هُوَ السَّمِيْعُ الْبَصِيْرُ

'Glory be to He Who carried His bondsman by night from the sacred Musjid to the Aqsa Musjid around which We've put blessings that We may show him Our grand signs. No doubt He is the All-Hearing, All-Seeing.'
– Surah Bani Israel (17), Verse 1

This verse is clear praise of the Holy Prophet 🕌, and it mentions an honor which was conferred upon no other prophet besides him, i.e. the Ascension (or *Mi'rāj*).

The following questions should be kept in mind concerning the incident of Mi'rāj,

1. Why did it occur?

2. How and when did it occur?

3. What are the points of wisdom found in this verse?

There are hundreds of wise points found in the incident of Mi'rāj. The following four points alone are clearly apparent,

1. The Holy Prophet 🕌 has been bestowed the rank and miracles of every prophet. In fact, he has been granted much more. Several examples of this have already been presented. Sayyiduna Musa عليه السلام was granted the honor of conversing with Allah ﷻ at the Mountain

of Tūr, Sayyiduna Esa عليه السلام was elevated to the fourth Heaven, while Sayyiduna Idris عليه السلام was raised to Jannah. Our Beloved Prophet ﷺ was blessed with the Mi'rāj, and on this journey, he conversed with Allah ﷻ, traveled the Heavens *and* inspected Jannah and Jahannam! In short, the excellences of the other Prophets عليهم السلام mentioned earlier were all encompassed on that single journey.

> *'No prophet has attained the rank you have.'*

Another point to bear in mind is that Sayyiduna Musa عليه السلام used to *go* to the mountain to speak to Allah ﷻ, but Rasoolullah ﷺ was *called* for the Mi'rāj to speak to Him!

2.   All of the Prophets عليهم السلام bore witness to Allah ﷻ, Jannah, Jahannam, etc. and made their respective nations declare, "I bear witness that there's no being worthy of worship besides Allah ﷻ." However, none of their testimonies were based on actually *seeing* these things; they were only a result of what they heard. Testimony is actually based on seeing. Therefore, there was a need for a unique personality from the respected group of Prophets عليهم السلام to see all of these things and bear witness to them. This personality's testimony will complete the witnessing of others. Muhammad Mustapha ﷺ is that blessed personality whose testimony is so. This is gestured to in the verse,

يايها النبى انا ارسلنا شهدا

'O Prophet of Allah ﷺ, surely we have sent you as a witness.'
– Surah Ahzāb (33), Verse 45

All the Prophets عليهم السلام gave testimony, but they were supported by the Holy Prophet ﷺ. This is why Rasoolullah ﷺ is the Seal of Prophets (خاتم النبيين), because the culmination of testimony by hearing is through testimony by sight. If his advent had to occur first, other Prophets عليهم السلام wouldn't have been embellished with prophethood. Also, there wouldn't have been a need for any other prophet after him, because what purpose does testimony by hearing serve after testimony by sight has already taken place?

3.   Allah ﷻ states,

ان الله اشترى من المؤمنين انفسهم واموالهم بأن لهم الجنة

'Surely Allah ﷺ has purchased from the believers their lives and

their properties in return that for them is Paradise.'
– Surah Tauba (9), Verse 111

Allah ﷻ is the buyer of the lives & properties of the believers and the Muslims are the sellers. This transaction occurred by the recognition (معرفة) of the Holy Messenger ﷺ, and he through whose recognition a transaction occurs must see the stock and its compensation. So, it was said, "O Beloved ﷺ, you've seen the properties and lives of the Believers, now come and see your slaves; in fact, come and see the buyer Himself (i.e. Allah ﷻ)." The recitation of the Imam in Salaah serves as the recitation for his followers. Similarly, the Holy Prophet ﷺ seeing something is seeing for us all.

4. Through Allah's ﷻ bestowal, Rasoolullah ﷺ is the *Malik* (owner, king) of the entire dominion of creation. This is why 'Laa ilaaha illalaahu Muhammad'ur-Rasoolullah' is written on every leaf of Jannah, on the eyes of its Maidens, and everywhere else. It signifies that these things have been created by Allah ﷻ and given to Rasoolullah ﷺ. So, on the night of Mi'rāj, it was the wish of the Almighty ﷻ to show the king his dominion.

When and how did the Mi'rāj occur? Mi'rāj occurred from the home of Sayyidah Umme-Haani ؓ (the daughter of Abu Talib) on Monday the 27th of Rajab at night, 11 years, 5 months after the proclamation of prophethood. It didn't occur from the home of Rasoolullah ﷺ because, in this way, Sayyiduna Jibrael عليه السلام could've gained access to him without requiring his permission. Had it occurred in his home, the angel would've either had to call out from the door and enter after gaining permission, or enter without any permission whatsoever. Indeed, both of these things were impossible. The Holy Quran states,

ان الذين ينادونك من وراء الحجرت اكثرهم لا يعلمون
'Certainly many of those who call you from behind your private apartments have no understanding.'
– Surah Hujarāt (49), Verse 4

يايها الذين آمنوا لا تدخلوا بيوت النبى الا ان يؤذن لكم
'O Believers, do not enter the homes of the Prophet ﷺ unless you gain permission.'
– Surah Ahzāb (33), Verse 53

Neither is it permissible to call the Prophet ﷺ from outside nor are we allowed to enter his home without permission. Bear in mind that the angels are also believers (and Rasoolullah ﷺ is the prophet of all).

The period of prophethood totals 23 years, half of which is 11½. Likewise, Rajab is in the exact centre of the Hijri calendar. Monday is also in the middle of the week. The Ummah is spoken of in the following manner,

وكذلك جعلنكم امة وسطا

'And so We made you a central, intermediate nation.'
– Surah Baqarah (2), Verse 143

So, Mi'rāj occurred in the month which is in the middle of the year, and the day which is in the middle of the week.

The Holy Prophet's ﷺ birth, migration, entrance into Madina, receiving of the first revelation, Ascension (Mi'rāj) and demise all occurred on Monday, because in Arabic, 'Monday' is *Yaumul-Ithnain* (the second day). In the words of the Scholars and Mashaaikh,

*'After Allah ﷻ, the Holy Prophet ﷺ is the most elevated
(i.e. he's second in respect and honor).'*

So, he who's second in rank has been blessed with every blessing on the second day. – *Roohul-Bayaan (under this verse)*

This is why, in Urdu, Monday is also known as *Pīr* (i.e. the leader of all days).

Now comes the last question: what occurred in the Mi'rāj? Its concise account mentioned in Bukhari, Muslim and other works of Ahadith is that in the last part of the 27th night of Rajab, while Rasoolullah ﷺ was resting in the house of his sister, Sayyidah Umme-Haani bint Abi Talib ؓ, Sayyiduna Jibrael السلام عليه presented himself with a procession of angels. The Burāq, which was to be the ride of the Holy Beloved ﷺ, was also part of it. Sayyiduna Jibrael السلام عليه came with a message from Allah ﷻ and woke up the Holy Prophet ﷺ to deliver it. He opened his chest, washed his blessed heart with Zum-Zum, and filled his chest (which is a citadel of Noor and guidance) with Noor and wisdom. The angel then presented the water of Kauthar to the Holy Messenger ﷺ for his usage, and thereafter Rasoolullah ﷺ was dressed in a Heavenly garb. The Burāq was brought forward after this. It's called the

'Burāq' due to either its speed being like lightning (known as 'barq' in Arabic) or due to it being completely white. – *Tafseer Roohul-Bayaan*

The body of the Burāq is bigger than a mule but smaller than a horse. Its one step can reach the end of where it sees!

Sayyiduna Jibrael ﷻ took hold of the Burāq's reins while Sayyiduna Israfil ﷻ stood behind. The angels surrounded the Burāq entirely, and the procession of the Holy Prophet ﷺ then left Makkah with this group and glory.

Almost immediately, Baitul-Muqaddas (Jerusalem) was reached. Here, all of the Prophets ﷻ were present to welcome Rasoolullah ﷺ, and preparations for Salaah were made as they awaited the Leader of Prophets ﷺ. When the Holy Prophet ﷺ arrived, the other Prophets ﷻ made salaam to him before they (along with the angels) stood as followers behind him in Salaah. Sayyiduna Jibrael ﷻ gave the Azaan and called out the Iqaamat. Subhanallah! What a Salaah this must have been! The Prophets ﷻ are the followers, their leader is the Imam, the first qiblah is the direction of prayer, and the highest-ranking angel is the Muazzin and Mukabbir! – *Shaami, Baabul-Azaan*

> Sayyiduna Esa ﷻ gave life to dead humans, but Rasoolullah ﷺ gave life to lifeless objects.

'The secret of the Salaah of the night-journey (i.e. Mi'rāj) is for the meaning of Awwal (First) and Aakhir (Last) to be revealed.'

'Those who were already kings are standing behind with folded hands.'

On that night, the meaning of 'First' and 'Last' was revealed (i.e. the last prophet leads the former kings).

After completing the Salaah, the journey towards the Heavens was to be made. Again, the Burāq and angelic procession undertook this journey with the Holy Prophet ﷺ, and with the same speed of travel, they continued past the Heavens, one after the other, while the Holy Prophet ﷺ met different prophets on each level. He met Sayyiduna Adam ﷻ, Yahya ﷻ, Esa ﷻ, Idris ﷻ, Hārūn ﷻ, Musa ﷻ and Ibrahim ﷻ on the first, second, third, fourth, fifth, sixth and seventh levels respectively, and after passing the seventh Heaven, Rasoolullah ﷺ came to the point of *Sidratul-Muntahā*, where his companionship with Sayyiduna Jibrael ﷻ on this journey came to an end.

The 'Sidrah' is a kind of berry tree. Its leaves are the size of elephants' ears and its fruits are like jugs. This is the final point which Sayyiduna Jibrael عليه السلام can travel to. When the angel reached this point, he apologized for not traveling further, to which the Holy Prophet ﷺ remarked, "Jibrael عليه السلام, etiquette requires that you not leave your companion." Sayyiduna Jibrael عليه السلام replied, "If I advance even a hair's length, the brilliance of its manifestation will burn my wings."

The angel explained that to proceed further is only the glory of the Holy Prophet ﷺ. Now, only Allah ﷻ and he who proceeded further know where he went. He went to where space and time end. "How," "when," and "where" do not apply in this region. Regarding what Allah ﷻ gave and what His Beloved ﷺ took, what Allah ﷻ spoke and what His Beloved ﷺ heard, and what secrets were shared here is known only between them. Even the Holy Quran didn't disclose this, but instead said,

فأوحى الى عبده ما اوحى
'And He revealed to His servant whatever He wished to reveal.'
– Surah Najm (53), Verse 10

Whatever private discussion occurred between Allah ﷻ and Sayyiduna Musa عليه السلام at the Mountain of Tūr was disclosed to the world in Surah Tāhā (20), but the secrets revealed to the Holy Messenger ﷺ on the night of Mi'rāj remained in the veil of obscurity.

Allah ﷻ revealed to His Beloved ﷺ whatever He wished – and why *should* He disclose it to others? Still, we know that Rasoolullah ﷺ brought 50 Salaah as a gift to us from there. While returning, Sayyiduna Musa عليه السلام suggested to him, "O Beloved of Allah ﷻ, this amount of Salaah is a lot. It should be lessened." The Holy Prophet ﷺ then returned to Allah's ﷻ court, and the amount was lessened to 45. When he came to Sayyiduna Musa عليه السلام a second time, the very same suggestion was made by him. The Holy Prophet ﷺ, in this way, traveled to the court of Allah ﷻ nine times on the advice of Sayyiduna Musa عليه السلام until Salaah was eventually reduced to five.

Sayyiduna Musa عليه السلام wished to see the Divine Splendor on the Mountain of Tūr, but he was stopped from such a desire. He must've thought, "Today I'm fortunate. The Holy Prophet ﷺ will see the Divine Splendor several times, and so I'll be able to see it to my heart's content through the radiance of the Prophet's ﷺ face."

Rasoolullah ﷺ also traveled through Jannah where he saw the mansions and estates of his slaves, and inspected Jahannam where he saw the punishments for sinners and the wicked revenge against his enemies. He saw a group of people who were eating hot, burning stones. Sayyiduna Jibrael عليه السلام informed him, "They're the people who never distributed the Zakaat of their wealth."

When Rasoolullah ﷺ saw a person standing in a river of blood eating stones, Sayyiduna Jibrael عليه السلام explained, "This is a person who consumes usury." When he saw a group of people whose tongues and lips were being cut with scissors of steel, he was told, "These are the learned who don't practice upon their knowledge." He also saw a group of people with nails of copper scratching their faces and injuring their bodies. Sayyiduna Jibrael عليه السلام said, "These are the people who would gossip about Muslims." In short, Rasoolullah ﷺ saw the condition and fate of all kinds of people. – *Roohul-Bayaan*

However, all of these observations were presented only as examples, because the eyes of the Prophets عليه السلام see past and future occurrences (the way we see the present) anyway. What was really being seen were things that will occur after Qiyaamat. In dreams, we sometimes see future occurrences, but these dreams of ours aren't absolute. On the other hand, the observations of the blessed Prophet ﷺ are certain in nature. Similarly, after death and before the Day of Judgment, the soul of the deceased travels through either Jannah or Jahannam. The souls of the martyrs also go to Jannah – but this entry is only spiritual, not physical. After the Last Day, however, the entry will be physical. In contrast to *barzakh* (one's time between death & resurrection), the world is like a dream; and in contrast to the Hereafter, barzakh is like a dream. – *Tafseer Roohul-Bayaan, Surah Baqarah, Verse 154*

After returning from this extensive journey, the bedstead of the Holy Prophet ﷺ was still warm and the chain on the house's door was still moving, i.e. a journey of approximately 80,000 years was completed in just a single moment. When the Prophet ﷺ informed people of his Ascension in the morning, Hadrat Abu Bakr رضي الله عنه immediately accepted it as the truth without hesitation. So, he became As-Siddique ('The Truthful'). Abu Jahl and others, on the other hand, rejected it and effectively branded themselves with the dishonor of heresy.

This was a brief account of the incident of Mi'rāj. We'll now discuss the points mentioned in the verse. The verse starts with 'Glory be to He…', and this is used on occasions of wonder. The Mi'rāj is an amazing and bewildering incident which is beyond the comprehension of man. So, 'Glory be to He' was used. In other words, this incident is through the wish of Allah ﷻ, the Being Who's free from helplessness, the All-Powerful. The blessed body of the Holy Prophet ﷺ ascending, passing swiftly beyond the atmospheric and empyrean region, entering other Heavens, traveling through Jannah and Jahannam, and thereafter returning so quickly may seem very difficult to carry out, but nothing is difficult for Allah ﷻ. The Noor of our vision travels to see the sky and returns from so far away immediately – the intense heat of the empyrean region and coldness of the atmospheric causes no harm to it. Yet this is merely the state of 'lightweight' Noor, while the Holy Prophet ﷺ is Noor from head to toe. His excellence is certainly far greater than the Noor of our vision.

In this verse, the Prophet ﷺ is addressed as 'His servant', not as 'the Messenger' or 'the Prophet', etc, because on that night, the creation was going towards the Creator to meet Him. So, this was not the time to demonstrate prophethood, but the time to demonstrate servanthood. A servant is someone annihilated in the desire of his master. The Holy Messenger ﷺ has the rank of *Fanā Fillah* (Annihilated in Allah ﷻ).

Servant (عبد) is he who waits for the Lord, such as Sayyiduna Musa عليه السلام in the valley of Sinai; 'Allah's ﷻ servant' (عبده) is he who's awaited by the Lord Himself.

'Servant' is he whose greatness is through affinity with the Lord; 'Allah's ﷻ servant' is that exalted slave through whose servitude the greatness of the Master is demonstrated.'

هو الذى ارسل رسوله

'It's He (Allah ﷻ) Who sent His Messenger ﷺ.'

– Surah Tauba (9), Verse 33

'It's he (the Prophet ﷺ) who's the first, it's he who's the last. It's he who's the manifest, it's he who's the hidden.

The proof of Allah ﷻ (i.e. Rasoolullah ﷺ) went to meet his Lord on the path leading to Him.'

– Alahadrat Imam Ahmed Raza رضي الله عنه

Dr. Iqbal eloquently says,

'Allah's ﷻ servant' is he who is the source of all other servants; Allah's ﷻ servant is he whose splendor is

found in all servants but loses no splendor himself.'

'Allah's ﷻ servant is he who's the confidant of the servants. None have reached the rank of 'Allah's ﷻ servant' until now.'

'The fate of all servants is connected to 'Allah's ﷻ servant'. I couldn't explain this term's meaning in these stanzas, so if you wish to know it, read the Quranic verse, "(O Beloved ﷺ), when you threw, you did not do so. It was Allah ﷻ who threw."'

The verse states 'by night', which means Mi'rāj occurred in a short part of the night, not during the day. In fact, it occurred in the latter part of the 27th night of Rajab when even the moon isn't seen and people are busy sleeping. This was because, on this night, the reality of the Holy Prophet ﷺ (حقيقة محمدية) was to come out of its veil, so which eye would've had the strength and ability to see it without hindrance? Although the close angels gave companionship, they too only reached points that they couldn't bear and had to eventually leave the Holy Prophet ﷺ. On that night, the Holy Prophet ﷺ was similar to the sun – the closer he got to his destination, the brighter he became.

The verse also states 'to the Aqsa Musjid', literally meaning 'until the furthest musjid.' Allah ﷻ Himself knows what was meant by this (was it to Baitul-Muqaddas in Jerusalem or to Baitul-Ma'moor, the musjid and qiblah of the angels?).

"He is the All-Hearing, All-Seeing," can have two meanings,

1. Either it refers to Allah ﷻ as the All-Hearing and All-Seeing,

2. Or it refers to the Holy Prophet ﷺ being able to see and hear all of creation – *Madaarijun-Nubuwwah, Roohul-Bayaan (under this verse)*

In other words, the Ascension of the Holy Messenger ﷺ occurred for it to be established that it's the Prophet ﷺ who has the ability and power to see the creation, directly see our plight, and hear our calls.

VERSE 46

وَمِنَ الَّيْلِ فَتَهَجَّدْ بِهِ نَافِلَةً لَّكَ ، عَسَى أَن يَبْعَثَكَ رَبُّكَ مَقَامًا مَّحْمُودًا

'And offer Tahajjud in some portion of the night, this is particularly and additionally for you. It's near that your Lord

may make you stand at a place where all will praise you.'
– Surah Bani Israel (17), Verse 79

This verse is explicit praise of the Holy Prophet ﷺ. Two unique excellences of his are mentioned within – one in the world and one in the Hereafter.

The Prophet's ﷺ uniqueness in the world is Tahajjud Salaah, and his distinctiveness in the Hereafter is his standing on the Station of Praise (المقام المحمود). Tahajjud being compulsory (فرض) on Rasoolullah ﷺ is unique to him. Neither did any prophet before him receive this Salaah nor did any of his followers within the Ummah. For us, it's *Sunnat'e-Kifaayah* (i.e. if only one person in a locality performs it, everyone else is absolved. On the other hand, if nobody performs it, all will be guilty of forsaking the Sunnah).

The minimum amount of rakaats in Tahajjud Salaah is two, while the maximum amount is twelve. After performing Esha Salaah and sleeping, whenever a person wakes up during the night, it becomes the time for Tahajjud Salaah. However, as soon as Subah Saadiq begins, the time for Tahajjud ends. This is a very blessed Salaah, and to perform it in the last quarter of the night is best.

> When the Prophet ﷺ was lowered into his blessed qabr, Hadrat Abdullah ibn Abbas ؓ noticed that his lips were moving. When he paid attention to it, he heard the Holy Prophet ﷺ interceding for his Ummah.

Actually, other nations didn't even receive five daily Salaah. This is a uniqueness of the Holy Prophet's ﷺ Ummah (i.e. the Muslims). Yes, the five daily Salaah were individually performed by former Prophets عليهم السلام.

Fajr Salaah was performed by Sayyiduna Adam عليه السلام in thanks of the coming of daytime. This was because he experienced no nightfall in Jannah. – *Shaami, Vol. 1, Kitaabus-Salaah*

Zohr Salaah was performed by Sayyiduna Ibrahim عليه السلام in thanks of his son's life (Sayyiduna Ismail عليه السلام) being saved and the ram sacrificed in his place. Asr Salaah was performed by Sayyiduna Uzair عليه السلام when he became animate again after 100 years, and Maghrib Salaah was performed by Sayyiduna Dawud عليه السلام in thanks of his repentance being accepted (at the time of Maghrib). He intended reading four rakaats but made salaam on the third.

Finally, Esha Salaah was performed by our Beloved Prophet ﷺ. – *Tahaawi, Baabu Salaatil-Wustaa*

So, Esha and the other daily Salaah is unique to the Holy Prophet's ﷺ Ummah, while the obligation of Tahajjud is unique to him alone.

Rasoolullah's ﷺ standing on the Station of Praise on the Day of Judgment is his distinction in the Hereafter. This is the place where he will be present and intercede for all. All former and latter people will search tirelessly for an intercessor, yet everyone they approach will say, "Go to somebody else." Eventually, they'll find the Holy Prophet ﷺ at this Station. After seeing this honor and greatness of his, all of his friends (and even enemies) will begin to praise him. This is why it's called the 'Station of Praise'. The caller of the Azaan and those who listen to it are commanded to supplicate for the Prophet ﷺ to receive the Station of Praise because the Prophet ﷺ himself states, "I'll intercede for he who makes this supplication for me." Likewise, when a person hears, 'I bear witness that Muhammad ﷺ is the Messenger of Allah ﷻ,' he should kiss his thumbnails and place them on his eyes. Several excellences have been mentioned about this. Refer to *Shaami, Vol. 1, Chapter of Azaan* and *Tafseer Roohul-Bayaan, Surah Māida (5), Verse 58*.

Although these narrations are classified as *hasan* or *daeef* (weak), they are nevertheless credible in matters of proving excellence. The worldly benefits of kissing the thumbnails are that the person who does so will never be blind and his vision will not decrease, Insha-Allah ﷻ. The benefit in the Hereafter will be that the Prophet ﷺ himself will intercede for him or her; and out of his mercy, he will personally make him stand within the rows of the inmates of Jannah. The method of gaining this blessing is to say,

صَلَّى اللهُ عَلَيْكَ يَا رَسُولَ الله

'Sallalaahu Alaika Ya Rasoolallah ﷺ'

The salutations of Allah ﷻ be upon you, O Messenger of Allah ﷺ.

when you hear the first *Ash'hadu anna Muhammadar-Rasoolulllah* ﷺ [during the Azaan] and say,

قُرَّةُ عَيْنِيْ بِكَ يَا رَسُولَ الله

'Qurratu Aini bika Ya Rasoolallah ﷺ'

The coolness of my eyes is through you, O Messenger of Allah ﷺ.

when you hear the second. Kiss both thumbs, place them on the eyes and say,

اَللّٰهُمَّ مَتِّعْنِیْ بِالسَّمْعِ وَالْبَصَرِ

'Allahumma Matti'nī bis-Sam'i wal-Basri'

O Allah ﷻ, bless me with hearing and sight.

– Shaami, Vol. 1, Baabul-Azaan

Allama Shaami ؓ didn't refute this issue, but merely said regarding the *marfū* narrations quoted in the excellence of this practice, "No *marfū* Hadith is sound (صحیح)." This clearly proves that the *mauqūf* narrations regarding this practice *are* sound. Upon close inspection, we see that he also didn't say that the marfū narrations are *weak* – just that they aren't sound. It's apparent that not being sound doesn't necessitate a Hadith being weak (e.g. it can be hasan, etc). If you wish to know more on this subject, refer to the treatise *Munīrul-Ain fi Hukmi Taqbīlil-Ibhāmain* by Alahadrat Imam Ahmed Raza ؓ. In it, he has proven through narrations that kissing the thumbnails during the Azaan isn't just the practice (sunnah) of Hadrat Abu Bakr Siddique ؓ, it's even the practice of Sayyiduna Adam ﷺ.

VERSE 47

قُلْ لَّوْ كَانَ الْبَحْرُ مِدَادًا لِّكَلِمٰتِ رَبِّیْ لَنَفِدَ الْبَحْرُ قَبْلَ اَنْ تَنْفَدَ كَلِمٰتُ رَبِّیْ وَلَوْ جِئْنَا بِمِثْلِهٖ مَدَدًا

'Say (O Beloved ﷺ), "If the sea was the ink for the words of my Lord, then necessarily the sea would be exhausted while the words of my Lord would not come to an end, though We may bring the like of it for help."'

– Surah Kahf (18), Verse 109

This verse is also the praise of the Holy Prophet ﷺ. The reason for its revelation is that once, the Jews came to the Prophet ﷺ and said, "You claim that the Holy Quran contains wisdom and that you've been granted it. The Holy Quran says,

ومن يؤت الحكمة فقد اوتی خیرا کثیرا

'And whoever has been given wisdom has certainly been given abundant good.'

– Surah Baqarah (2), Verse 269

"Why then do you say that you've been given only a small amount of knowledge?" The above verse was revealed in reply to this. – *Tafseer Khazaainul-Irfaan*

It states, "Indeed, the knowledge of everything is found in the Holy Quran, and this knowledge is truly vast. In contrast to the knowledge of Allah ﷻ,

however, it's like a drop in the ocean. The knowledge of the Holy Prophet ﷺ has an end while the knowledge of Allah ﷻ doesn't."

In other words, the verse is saying that if the water of the oceans was turned into ink and the words of Allah ﷻ were written using it, the ink would run out but the words wouldn't. Commentators of the Holy Quran have several opinions as to what is meant by 'the words of my Lord.' Some say that it means the enlightenment of Allah ﷻ, some say it refers to the plannings of Allah ﷻ, and some say it's the wisdom of Allah ﷻ. – *Roohul-Bayaan*

In short, there's no end to Allah's ﷻ knowledge, power, wisdom and qualities. In *Madaarijun-Nubuwwah*, Vol. 1, Chapter 3, Shaikh Abdul-Haqq Muhaddith Dehlwi ؓ states, "According to the scholars of extensive research, 'words of the Lord' refers to the excellence, knowledge and greatness of the Holy Prophet ﷺ." Effectively, the verse will mean that if the water of the oceans was used as ink to write the praise and qualities of the Holy Messenger ﷺ, the 'ink' would end but his praise and qualities wouldn't. In this verse, two oceans have been mentioned, though in another verse, more than two have been spoken about. The Holy Quran states,

ولو انما فى الارض من شجرة اقلم والبحر يمده من بعده سبعة ابحر ما نفدت كلمت الله

'And even if all the trees on the Earth were pens, and the sea, with seven more seas to help it (were ink), the words of Allah ﷻ would not be exhausted.'
– Surah Luqmān (31), Verse 27

"The words of Allah ﷻ would not be exhausted," again refers to the qualities of the Holy Prophet ﷺ.

Marvel at He who has granted greatness and he who attained it! This commentary by Shaikh Abdul-Haqq ؓ is also corroborated by other verses. Regarding the blessings of the world, we are told that we cannot count them. Without doubt, this is the truth, because we don't know the amount of strands of hair and veins found in our bodies. When each strand of hair has thousands of blessings, how then can a record of these blessings be known? Also, this is only the condition of blessings found within us. What about those found *around* us? What about the sun, moon, and stars, etc? Still, the Holy Quran states,

قل متاع الدنيا قليل

'Say, "The enjoyment of this world is little."'
– Surah Nisā (4), Verse 77

On the contrary, the Holy Prophet's ﷺ every excellence has been referred to as 'great' (عظیم) by the Holy Quran. Think! Not only has Allah ﷻ referred to His own qualities as 'great', He has also referred to the Holy Prophet's ﷺ as 'great'. Allah ﷻ says about Himself,

وهو العلى العظيم
'And He is the Most Exalted, the Great.'
– Surah Baqarah (2), Verse 255

Regarding His Beloved ﷺ, He says,

وانك لعلى خلق عظيم
'And indeed you are upon great manners.'
– Surah Qalam (68), Verse 4

Allah ﷻ has used the word 'great' here for the manners of the Holy Prophet ﷺ. At another juncture, He states,

وكان فضل الله عليك عظيما
'And great is the grace of Allah ﷻ upon you.'
– Surah Nisā (4), Verse 113

All of the qualities of Rasoolullah ﷺ are encompassed in this 'great grace.' We come to know then that every quality of the Holy Prophet ﷺ is great.

Regarding the Prophet ﷺ, Allah ﷻ also states,

الرحمن ، علم القران
'The Most Affectionate, taught the Quran (to His Beloved ﷺ).'
– Surah Rahmān (55), Verses 1-2

Subhanallah! The teacher is The Most Affectionate and the student is His Most Beloved ﷺ! Also, the text used is the Holy Quran! Can anyone even imagine the knowledge possessed by Rasoolullah ﷺ?! In short, every quality of the Holy Prophet ﷺ (his every attribute) is great. Which human, angel or jinn now has the ability to completely demonstrate his praise?

'After Allah ﷻ, you are the most cherished.'

'The intellect is unable to understand the secrets of Allah ﷻ and Mustapha ﷺ. Only Allah ﷻ knows Mustapha ﷺ, and

only Mustapha ﷺ knows the Supreme Being.'

This is why Imam Sharfuddin Busairi رحمة الله عليه states (as previously mentioned),

دع ما ادعته النصارى في نبيهم ، واحكم بما شئت مدحا فيه واحتكم

فان فضل رسول الله ليس له ، حد فيعرب عنه ناطق بفم

*'Besides calling the Holy Prophet ﷺ 'god' or 'the son of
god', ascribe whatever honor and greatness as praise to him,
because the excellence of the Holy Prophet ﷺ has no limit
that can be emplaced by a person's utterance.'*
– Qasida Burda Sharif

Sayyiduna Musa عليه السلام was granted the honor of conversing with Allah عزّوجلّ at the Mountain of Tūr, Sayyiduna Esa عليه السلام was elevated to the fourth Heaven, while Sayyiduna Idris عليه السلام was raised to Jannah. Our Beloved Prophet ﷺ was blessed with the Mi'rāj, and on this journey, he conversed with Allah عزّوجلّ, traveled the Heavens *and* inspected Jannah and Jahannam! In short, the excellences of the other Prophets عليهم السلام mentioned earlier were all encompassed on that single journey.

We don't even *know* the amount of praise written and proclaimed for the Prophet ﷺ! His praise is found in every language, amongst every species – even jinns!

A Hadith states that every morning and evening, 70,000 angels present themselves at the Rauda Sharif of Rasoolullah ﷺ and present their Salutations & Salaam. Those angels who come in the morning leave in the evening, and those who come in the evening leave in the morning. No angel will have the fortune of coming a second time. – *Mishkaat, Vol. 2, Baabul-Karaamaat*

This praise of the angels is separate from the praise of the rest of creation. Now, estimate how much praise has been made of the Holy Prophet ﷺ! Yet Allah عزّوجلّ is my Witness that in spite of all this, not even a dot from the volumes of the Prophet's ﷺ praise has been articulated.

The praise of the Holy Prophet ﷺ made by previous Prophets عليهم السلام is also separate from this. The Station of Praise too, which he will attain in the Hereafter when all of his friends (and even foes) will praise him, is besides this.

Also, the praise of Rasoolullah ﷺ made by Allah ﷻ is infinite. Who now claims that his praise can be encompassed entirely? The true praise of Allah ﷻ can be made by Rasoolullah ﷺ himself, and the Prophet's ﷺ praise can be made by Allah ﷻ alone!

The Qasidas we pen and recite aren't done while thinking that we have fulfilled the right of Rasoolullah's ﷺ praise. They are only a means of listing our names among those who praise him. An old woman once came to the marketplace with a bag of cotton, intending to buy Sayyiduna Yusuf عليه السلام (while he was being sold as a slave). People said to her, "Treasures are to be exhausted to purchase the beauty and splendor of Yusuf عليه السلام! What chance do you have with your bag of cotton?" She replied, "I know this, but I desire to be included among those who intended to purchase him." This is our likeness with regards to Sayyiduna Rasoolullah ﷺ.

VERSE 48

قُلْ إِنَّمَا أَنَا بَشَرٌ مِّثْلُكُمْ يُوحَى إِلَيَّ أَنَّمَا إِلَهُكُمْ إِلَهٌ وَاحِدٌ

'Say (O Beloved ﷺ), 'I'm a man like you. I receive revelation that your God is one God.''
– Surah Kahf (18), Verse 110

Those with no insight use this verse as proof that the Holy Prophet ﷺ is an ordinary human like us, since he *seems* to be like us when it comes to eating, drinking, living, and in his demise. If this verse is read with the sight of Imaan, however, it's seen as the praise of Rasoolullah ﷺ. We'll therefore discuss the following four things,

1. What's intended by the verse?

2. According to Islamic Law, is it permissible or impermissible (حرام) to address the Prophet ﷺ as a mere, mortal man (بشر) or by other general terms?

3. According to Islamic Law and the intellect, is the Prophet ﷺ truly a mere mortal like us? If he isn't, why was he told to say he was?

4. What do we learn from the second part of the verse (i.e. 'I receive revelation...')?

Discussion 1 – All Muslims and non-Muslims know that the Holy Prophet's ﷺ advent occurred amongst humanity. The non-Muslims used to say,

قالوا ما انتم الا بشر مثلنا

'You are nothing but a man like us.'
– Surah Yaseen (36), Verse 15

The Muslim belief is that Rasoolullah ﷺ is a prophet (نبي), and a prophet is a human being who has been sent by Allah ﷻ to propagate the commands of Islamic Law. In short, the entire world knows and accepts this. So, what's the intent of this verse?

The reason is simple. Christians saw just three miracles of Sayyiduna Esa عليه السلام (i.e. him being born without a father, giving life to the dead, and curing the sick) before calling him the son of Allah ﷻ. Jews too witnessed just one miracle of Sayyiduna Uzair عليه السلام (him returning to life after 100 years) before calling him the son of Allah ﷻ. Some polytheists accepted angels to be the daughters of Allah ﷻ while others regarded jinns to be His relatives. So, after seeing the miracles, power and strength of these personalities, these ignorant people started to exaggerate their status. Conversely, some tried to diminish the glory of the Prophets عليهم السلام by referring to them as men like themselves.

Islam wishes that Muslims be protected from both extremities. Previous nations saw only a few miracles and began calling these Prophets عليهم السلام the 'sons of God', etc, while the Holy Prophet ﷺ performed more exquisite and greater miracles than what was seen before. He split the moon in two, brought back the set sun by dua and a gesture, commanded clouds to form and water the lands, instructed trees apart to come together, had pebbles recite his Kalima, had a bark cry due to being separated from him, had an entire army's hunger satisfied with only a little amount of food, had fountains of water emerge from his blessed fingers, had those who were dead return to life on his gesture, etc. In short, an infinite amount of miracles were performed by Rasoolullah ﷺ. So, there was an apprehension that people may also begin calling him 'God' or 'the son of God'. This is why the Messenger ﷺ displayed his servitude to Allah ﷻ in his every action and deed, to the point of even making us say, "Muhammad ﷺ is the servant and Messenger of Allah ﷻ," in the Kalima. This is also why the Holy Quran commands him, "Say, 'I'm a man like you.'"

Discussion 2 – Every Muslim believes that the Prophets عليهم السلام are the servants of Allah ﷻ, and that their advent occurred amongst humans. However, to address them as '*bashr*' (the word used in the verse), 'brother', 'human' or 'man' is haraam, and if they are called so with the intent of disrespect, the caller becomes a non-Muslim. – *Alamghiri, etc.*

The Holy Quran states,

لا تجعلوا دعاء الرسول بينكم كدعاء بعضكم بعضا

'Make not the summoning of the Messenger 🕌 among yourselves
the way one calls the other amongst you.'
– Surah Noor (24), Verse 63

This verse proves that the common titles we generally use to address one another are not to be used for the Holy Prophet 🕌. Another verse states,

ولا تجهروا له بالقول كجهر بعضكم لبعض ان تحبط اعمالكم وانتم لا تشعرون

'And do not speak in his presence as you speak aloud to one another
lest your deeds become in vain while you are unaware.'
– Surah Hujarāt (49), Verse 2

If we regard the Holy Prophet 🕌 to be ordinary, our deeds will be ruined, because deeds are ruined through disbelief (كفر). So, the verse begins with the word 'Say' (i.e. O Beloved 🕌, *you* say in humility, 'I'm a man like you.'). We, however, will not address the Holy Messenger 🕌 with the term 'bashr' (i.e. a mortal man) used in the verse, and no one has permission to do so. This is why nowhere in the Holy Quran has the Beloved Messenger 🕌 been addressed with the word 'bashr', 'man', 'brother of believers', etc. Whenever he *was* addressed in the Holy Quran, it was as, "O Prophet 🕌," "O Messenger 🕌," "O you enwrapped one," "O you who has enfolded yourself within your mantle," etc. So, when Allah ﷻ Himself didn't address the Holy Prophet 🕌 with ordinary terms, what right do we slaves have to call him so?

Another point to remember is that to address a person of worldly rank with an ordinary title is tantamount to a refusal of his status. So, addressing those Prophets علیہم السلام who have attained lofty titles and ranks from the court of Allah ﷻ with ordinary and general callings is something that has no part in the deen. If a person calls his mother "O wife of my father," or calls his father, "O man," he'll be regarded as someone insolent and disrespectful. Therefore, how can the person who uses these words for Rasoolullah 🕌 not be disrespectful?

This is why the opinion of Scholars of deep research (محققین) is that the Holy Prophet 🕌 isn't included in the address of, "O you who believe," in the Holy Quran due to the following reasons,

1. Rasoolullah ﷺ is not to be addressed with general and common callings, and this is a general calling.

2. Believers attain Imaan (faith) from Rasoolullah ﷺ, and he's the giver of Imaan. 'Those who believe' then, refers to those who acquire Imaan.

3. 'Those who believe' refers to those who became Muslims while in the world, whereas the Holy Prophet ﷺ came into the world already as a Muslim. In fact, he came as a *prophet* to the world.

4. Commands of Islamic Law (احكام) became obligatory (فرض) on other believers after the revelation of the Quranic verses articulating them. The Holy Prophet ﷺ, however, was already a worshipper, performer of Salaah, and one abstinent from worldly pleasures (زاهد), practicing these commands even before the Quran was revealed! These verses were revealed not for the practice of the Holy Messenger ﷺ, but for the propagation of these laws. On the night of Mi'rāj, Rasoolullah ﷺ led Salaah, and prior to his proclamation of prophethood, he would perform Salaah in the cave of Hira (whereas laws weren't revealed regarding Salaah yet).

5. After calling out to 'those who believe', certain laws which cannot be enjoined on the Holy Prophet ﷺ were revealed. The Holy Quran states,

يايها الذين آمنوا لا تقدموا بين يدى الله ورسوله
'O Believers! Exceed not over Allah ﷻ and His Messenger ﷺ.'
– Surah Hujarāt (49), Verse 1

يايها الذين آمنوا لا ترفعوا اصوتكم فوق صوت النبى
'O Believers, do not raise your voice above the voice of the Prophet ﷺ.'
– Surah Hujarāt (49), Verse 2

The actions completed by the Holy Prophet ﷺ were to teach us. A passenger sits in an airplane to reach his destination, but the captain sits in the plane to make the passenger reach it. This is why the passenger pays for his seat while the captain *gets paid*.

Discussion 3 – Rasoolullah ﷺ is not like us, according to both Islamic Law and the intellect. He's not like us according to Islamic Law because we don't have any similitude with him, be it in Imaan, actions, laws or even in common things (معاملات). His Kalima is 'I'm the Messenger of Allah ﷺ.' If we had to say this, we would become non-Muslims. This is the difference between us and him with regards to only *one* thing!

Salaah five times a day is obligatory on us, but it was obligatory on Rasoolullah ﷺ six times a day. – *Holy Quran*

Five pillars of Islam are obligatory upon us, but only four are obligatory upon the Holy Prophet ﷺ. Zakaat wasn't. – *Shaami Kitaabuz-Zakaat*

Likewise, keeping four wives at one time is allowed for us, but Rasoolullah ﷺ could keep as many as he wished. Also, after we pass away, our wives can marry whoever they want, but the Holy Prophet's ﷺ wives were not allowed to marry again. – *Holy Quran*

After our demise, our estate is distributed, but after the Holy Prophet's ﷺ demise, his estate wasn't. – *Hadith Sharif*

We are compelled by the laws of Islam, but Divine Law awaits the movement of Rasoolullah's ﷺ blessed lips. He makes halaal whatever he wishes and makes haraam whatever he wishes. There is an infinite amount of proof for this. The Prophet ﷺ made the testimony of Hadrat Abu Khuzaima ؓ equal to two testimonies. He prohibited Hadrat Ali ؓ from marrying another woman in the presence of Sayyidah Fathima ؓ. He even fed a person his own *kaffarah* (compensation for not fasting).

The Prophet ﷺ himself said (after performing perpetual fast),

ایکم مثلی یطعمنی ربی ویسقینی
'Who of you is like me?! My Lord gives me to eat and drink.'
– Bukhari Sharif

When it came to sitting and performing optional Salaah, the Holy Prophet ﷺ said,

لکنی لست کاحد منکم
'I'm not like any of you.'
– Hadith Sharif

In short, in all of these issues, we are not like Rasoolullah ﷺ. This is the Islamic decision.

Likewise, we are not like the Messenger ﷺ even according to the intellect, because the Imaan of Rasoolullah ﷺ is faith after seeing (he saw Allah ﷻ, Jannah, Jahannam, etc). The Holy Prophet ﷺ went for Mi'rāj while we didn't. Whatever we eat and drink creates urine and excreta, etc. (i.e. impure things), yet Divine Light is created from whatever the Holy Prophet ﷺ consumes – honey comes from a bee while poison comes from a wasp (even though they eat the very same thing). Rasoolullah ﷺ is the Mercy unto Creation (رحمة للعلمين) but we are not; he is Imaan (faith itself) while we are believers (people of faith); his blessed body possessed no shadow while ours do; clouds used to form and shade him in heat yet no cloud does this for us. In short, we are not like Rasoolullah ﷺ even from an intellectual point of view.

> The praise of Rasoolullah ﷺ made by Allah ﷻ is infinite. Who now claims that his praise can be encompassed entirely? The true praise of Allah ﷻ can be made by Rasoolullah ﷺ himself, and the Prophet's ﷺ praise can be made by Allah ﷻ alone!

Maulwi Abdul-Hayy records the following Hadith in his *Fatāwa Abdul-Hayy*, "The Holy Prophet ﷺ states, "While I was in the womb of my mother, I used to listen to the sound of the Divine Pen's movement." Who else is like this? The Holy Messenger ﷺ was born as an *Aarif Billah* (one with the recognition of Allah ﷻ). Even after being born and attaining knowledge, we still don't reach this stage and rank. Therefore, what likeness or similitude with him can ever be claimed?

Now, what does the verse in question mean? It means, "O Beloved ﷺ, say to them, 'Only in physical appearance and outer-form do you seem similar to me.'" However, there is truly a major difference here. The verse also means, "In some outer human qualities and conditions, I'm a man like you (i.e. with regards to eating, drinking, walking, sitting, falling, outward sicknesses, etc)." However, the Prophet ﷺ is actually completely different to us in these conditions too.

'Like you' in the verse means, "Just as how you, O people, are mere servants (neither are you Allah ﷻ nor do you possess His attributes), so too am I a servant of Allah ﷻ. There is no divinity in me. I am not Allah ﷻ. I'm not His son, but His servant and the master of servants." Likeness is only in this, not in everything.

Discussion 4 – 'I receive revelation' removes any further doubt that may arise from 'I'm like you.' Someone could say, "The Holy Prophet ﷺ is like us in everything," but the Quran itself answers, "No! Say, O Beloved ﷺ, "I'm a receiver of Divine revelation while you are a follower of me (Ummati). How can the receiver of revelation be like the follower?"

The quality of 'I receive revelation' shows a difference between prophet and follower in the same way speech shows a difference between humans and animals. 'Zaid' is an anthropoid like other animals but he possesses the ability of comprehensive speech. The quality of having the ability to speak proves the difference in reality between Zaid and animals.

Huzoor Qibla'e-Aalam Pīr Sayed Jamāt Ali Shah Sahib Muhaddith Alipuri ؓ states that there are five stages of difference between matter and humans but there are 27 stages of difference between man and the Holy Prophet ﷺ. In other words, the station of being the Chosen Messenger ﷺ is 27 times greater than the station of humanity. Only the station of Divinity remains beyond it. How then can we be equal to Rasoolullah ﷺ when there's a difference of 27 stages between him and us?

Once, someone recited a Qasida in the presence of Dr. Iqbal. It stated, "Both the worlds are brightened by he whose name is Muhammad ﷺ." Dr. Iqbal replied, "Add two verses of this to it." He dictated,

> *'He becomes the form of power. He was not taught by anyone yet his words are the essence of speech. He creates the means of forgiveness yet he is ever so humble.'*

> *'Within a second, he reaches the Heavens. He opens his eyes and is back on the Earth. Call him the illuminant sun of Makkah, the light and radiance of the world.'*

Allama Ismail Haqqi ؓ states that there are three forms of the Holy Prophet ﷺ. – *Tafseer Roohul-Bayaan, Surah Maryam (19), Verse 1*

The first is human (بشرى) which is spoken about in this verse. The second is his rightful form (حقى) regarding which the Holy Prophet ﷺ said,

من رانى فقد راى الحق

'He who has seen me has seen the Truth (i.e. Allah ﷻ).'
– Bukhari Sharif

The third form is angelic (ملکی) as the Holy Prophet ﷺ states,

لى مع الله وقت لا يسعنى فيه ملك مقرب ولا نبى مرسل

*'On some occasions, I gain such proximity to Allah ﷻ that neither is it gained
by close angels nor by cherished Prophets علیهم السلام.'*

Nevertheless, this verse is a treasure of praise for the Holy Prophet ﷺ if it's
carefully studied with Imaan.

Hadrat Shaikh Abdul-Haqq Muhaddith Dehlwi رحمۃ اللہ علیہ states that this type of
verse (by which equality with Rasoolullah ﷺ is seemingly made) falls under
the category of *mutashābihāt* verses (i.e. verses which can be understood
literally, though their actual meanings aren't represented by their literal
wording). – *Madaarijun-Nubuwwah, Chapter 3*

An example of such a verse is when Allah ﷻ likened His Noor to a lamp,

مثل نوره كمشكوة

'The similitude of His light is as a niche wherein is a lamp.'
– Surah Noor (24), Verse 35

Nobody can now say that Divine Light is like the light of a lamp. Likewise,
no one can say that Rasoolullah ﷺ is a human like us.

The founder of Darul Uloom Deoband, Maulwi Qasim Nanotwi, writes,

رہا جمال پہ تیرے حجاب بشریت
نہ جانا کون ہے کچھ بھی کس نے بجز ستار

*'The veil of humanity remained on your beauty and splendor.
Besides the Almighty, no one truly knew you.'*

In other words, Rasoolullah ﷺ is Noor, and it's not within the power of man
to see resplendent Noor. An eye cannot see the sun except when assisted by a
slight cloud covering it. Similarly, to display his Noor, the veil and clothing of
humanity was given to the Holy Prophet ﷺ. After receiving this veil, none
then saw his true beauty except Allah ﷻ.

According to the terminology of the Sufiya, the word *bashr* in the verse is
the praise of Rasoolullah ﷺ because it means 'Created by the Hands of Allah's
ﷻ Power specifically.' Allah ﷻ created the entire creation via angels, but He

created Sayyiduna Adam عليه السلام with His own Hands. So, humanity (بشريت) is a great quality of man. Addressing Shaitaan, Allah ﷻ said,

ما منعك ان تسجد لما خلقت بيدى

'Why don't you prostrate to that which I've created by My hands?'
– Surah Saad (38), Verse 75

It has also been said,

لقد خلقنا الانسن فى احسن تقويم

'Undoubtedly We've created men in the best form.'
– Surah Tīn (95), Verse 4

This is why Allah ﷻ made the heart of man His centre of concentration,

*'The Holy Ka'ba is the construction of the pure
Khalil (i.e. Sayyiduna Ibrahim عليه السلام), while the heart
is the centre of the Almighty's ﷻ concentration.'*

'A single heart is better than a thousand Ka'bas.'

We have defiled our humanity with sin. So, this word ('man') has become offensive, and we've therefore become prohibited from remembering the Prophets عليهم السلام with it.

The method of teaching a parrot to speak is to place a mirror equal to the length of a man in front of it and speak from behind the mirror. Thinking that this is the speech of its own species, the parrot will begin repeating what was said. Rasoolullah ﷺ is the mirror of the Almighty ﷻ. If this mirror wasn't located between us, the servants wouldn't have been able to attain guidance from the Lord. This mirror also has two sides, one facing the servants and the other towards the Creator. The side facing the creation states, "Don't run away from me because I'm your kind," while the side facing the Creator says,

وما ينطق عن الهوى ، ان هو الا وحى يوحى

*'And he (the Prophet ﷺ) doesn't speak of his own desire.
It is not but revelation revealed to him.'*
– Surah Najm (53), Verses 3-4

VERSE 49

فَإِنَّمَا يَسَّرْنٰهُ بِلِسَانِكَ لِتُبَشِّرَ بِهِ الْمُتَّقِيْنَ وَتُنْذِرَ بِهِ قَوْمًا لُّدًّا

'So We made this Quran easy on your tongue so that you may give glad-tidings to the God-fearing and warn thereby a contentious people.'
– Surah Maryam (19), Verse 97

This verse is also the praise of the Holy Prophet 🌺. It states, "We've made the Quran easy on your tongue (or 'in' your tongue) so that you can give glad-tidings and warn people." We come to know that the Holy Quran is very difficult [in some aspects]. It's the speech of Allah 🕌 while we are only humans, weak in speech. However, this Quran has been made easy on the blessed tongue of Rasoolullah 🌺. So, his blessed tongue is greater in strength than a mountain because it endured it.

In the commentary of this verse, *Tafseer Roohul-Bayaan* states that the Holy Quran is a pre-existent (قديم), unlimited Divine attribute which our words of speech cannot encompass since they are new (حادث) and finite. However, Allah 🕌 has given the blessed heart and tongue of the Holy Messenger 🌺 the power to know it as per its right of being known.

> When Allah 🕌 Himself didn't address the Holy Prophet 🌺 with ordinary terms, what right do we slaves have to call him so?

A point which arises is that those who claim, "The Holy Quran is absolutely simple and encompassing to the extent that there's no need for the Hadith in its presence," are in clear deception and delusion. Indeed the Holy Quran is easy, but not for every tongue. It's easy for the tongue of the Holy Messenger 🌺 or for those who attain guidance from his blessed court. Indeed the Holy Quran is complete, but there's a great need for a complete person to extract pearls from its wholesomeness. Extracting pearls from the ocean isn't everyone's job.

Another point which is understood from this is that only that meaning and recitation of the Holy Quran which is related from the Holy Prophet 🌺 must be made. If a person's annotation on a verse is contrary to the Holy Prophet's 🌺 commentary, or if a person chooses a type of recitation which isn't established from him, it will be rejected. An example of this is the meaning of 'Seal of Prophets' (خاتم النبيين). The Holy Prophet 🌺 said, "There's no prophet after me," and, "I'm the last prophet." Now, regarding one who says that this meaning (i.e. the Final Messenger 🌺) is simply the thinking of the general public and thereafter ascribes the meaning of *direct prophet* or *original prophet* to 'Seal of Prophets', or he accepts a new prophet to come after our Beloved Rasoolullah 🌺 as permissible or possible, is an apostate.

Likewise, pronouncing Quranic letters with their source (مخارج) according to the method of recitation proven by Rasoolullah صلى الله عليه وسلم is necessary.

This verse can also mean, "O Beloved صلى الله عليه وسلم, We've made this Quran easy through the blessings of your tongue." Here, the letter ب in Bismillah stands for "means of obtaining". So, the verse will mean, "If this Quran wasn't articulated by your blessed tongue, who would've had the ability of attaining it? This Quran was in the Protected Tablet (لوح محفوظ) which no human intellect can reach. Your blessed tongue brought this secret treasure to the creation." If the Holy Prophet's صلى الله عليه وسلم medium was non-existent, the creation wouldn't have attained a connection with the Creator. In fact, it's the blessed *tongue* of the Holy Messenger صلى الله عليه وسلم which made the Quran the Quran! A loudspeaker has two sides, one towards the speaker (i.e. the microphone) and the other towards the audience. The loudspeaker conveys the message of the speaker to the audience. Similarly, the heart and mind of the Holy Messenger صلى الله عليه وسلم receives Allah's عز وجل speech and makes it reach the creation. Bear in mind that the words of the Holy Quran were revealed to Rasoolullah's صلى الله عليه وسلم blessed ears, its meaning to his blessed mind and its secrets to his blessed heart. Whoever attained anything from the Holy Quran received it from the Holy Prophet صلى الله عليه وسلم.

VERSE 50

طه ، مَا أَنْزَلْنَا عَلَيْكَ الْقُرْآنَ لِتَشْقَى

"Tāhā. O Beloved صلى الله عليه وسلم, We didn't send this Quran upon you that you may be troubled."
– Surah Tāhā (20), Verses 1-2

This verse is also the praise of Rasoolullah صلى الله عليه وسلم, and in it Allah عز وجل demonstrates His infinite mercy on His Beloved صلى الله عليه وسلم.

There are two opinions among the Commentators of the Quran regarding the reason for the revelation of this verse. The first is that Rasoolullah صلى الله عليه وسلم used to endure much for the sake of Allah's عز وجل worship to the extent that his blessed feet became *swollen* after lengthy periods of standing at night. (Blood would also flow from the swelling.) Allah عز وجل didn't desire this strict diligence of His Beloved صلى الله عليه وسلم, so He said, "O Beloved صلى الله عليه وسلم, this Quran was not sent for you to be put in hardship."

The second opinion is that the heartfelt desire of the Holy Prophet صلى الله عليه وسلم was for no servant of Allah عز وجل to be astray from His path. His heart grieved over even the stubbornness of the disbelievers. So, this verse was revealed wherein the Prophet ﷺ is told, "Propagating laws is your responsibility, which you have fulfilled. If these unfortunate wretches don't wish to benefit from it, why do you endure grief for them?"

Rasoolullah's ﷺ praise is found twice in these verses, first by the word 'Tāhā' and second by the rest of the verse.

According to some, Tāhā is from the *mutashābihāt* (verses which can be understood literally, though their actual meanings aren't represented by their literal wording). – *Roohul-Bayaan*

Some Scholars state that Tāhā is a name of the Holy Prophet ﷺ, while others say that it's his title. There are also opinions that it's the name of the Surah or the name of the Holy Quran. – *Roohul-Bayaan, Madaarijun-Nubuwwah*

Some even say that it's the name of Allah ﷻ, but preference is given to the opinion that it is from the *mutashābihāt*, or that it's the title of the Holy Prophet ﷺ. Shaikh Saadi Shiraazi ؏ states,

'The calling of Tāhā and Yaseen is sufficient praise of you.'

There are various opinions regarding what it means and which prophetic qualities are being gestured towards by it if it is the title of Rasoolullah ﷺ. Some say that it refers to the Holy Prophet ﷺ being the intecessor, the guide for those who are astray, the being pure of sin, the Seal of Prophets, etc. Some say that it means 'the moon on the 14th night', because the numerical value of the letters Tā and Hā is 9 and 5 respectively. The sum of these values is 14, which is the night of the full, bright moon. This is an apt description of the Holy Prophet's ﷺ blessed face. But, this similitude is merely for purposes of understanding. Otherwise, the moon has absolutely no likeness to even the blessed shoes of the Holy Messenger ﷺ. It experiences change while the Prophet's ﷺ greatness is fixed within the hearts of creation. Although at night the moon shines bright, during the day its brightness is removed. Nothing, however, can remove the Holy Prophet's ﷺ Noor.

'I'm not a poet who calls his face the moon.
I sacrifice the moon on the imprints of his blessed feet.'

The second part of the verse informs us of the great mercy and kindness of Allah ﷻ upon the Holy Prophet ﷺ. Everyone in the world has strongly been warned to perform the worship of Allah ﷻ and not abandon it. However, it's only the blessed personality of the Holy Prophet ﷺ who's commanded, "You shouldn't endure yourself with so much worship and hardship." An example without comparison is when a teacher strongly warns his or her students to work hard (except one). The teacher says to this student, "Don't work so hard." Just as how the kindness of the teacher upon the student is known from this, so too is the striving and good nature of the student apparent from it. Rasoolullah ﷺ is so engrossed in Allah's ﷻ obedience that his Lord commands him to lesson his strife!

VERSE 51

وَمَا أَرْسَلْنَاكَ إِلَّا رَحْمَةً لِّلْعَلَمِينَ

'And We didn't send you but as a Mercy for the Worlds.'
– Surah Ambiya (21), Verse 107

This verse is grand praise for the Holy Prophet ﷺ. Allah ﷻ blessed the Holy Prophet ﷺ with several qualities, and one of them is 'Mercy for the Worlds.' This verse speaks of this specific and unique quality of his. After paying attention to its tone and expression, the abundance and extent of Rasoolullah's ﷺ mercy is understood. The following discussions on this verse will be made,

1. Who is the mercy?

2. Upon whom is the mercy?

3. From when is the mercy?

4. Until when is the mercy?

Who is the mercy?

The verse states that being the mercy for the entire creation is only the Holy Prophet's ﷺ quality. None besides him has been bestowed with this rank. Regarding Sayyiduna Esa عليه السلام, the Holy Quran states, "He's mercy from Us," yet it doesn't mention who he is a mercy for, and until when. In reference to the Prophets عليهم السلام, the Holy Quran states,

وما كنا معذبين حتى نبعث رسولا

'And We don't torment until We have sent Our messenger.'
– Surah Bani Israel (17), Verse 15

From this, we come to know that the other Prophets ﷺ were mercy for the believers, and being disobedient to them was a means of attaining Allah's ﷻ anger. See how the nation of Sayyiduna Lut ﷺ was destroyed, how Firaun was drowned, and how the nation of Sayyiduna Nuh ﷺ was destroyed in the flood. Regarding the Holy Beloved ﷺ, however, Allah ﷻ says,

وما كان الله ليعذبهم وانت فيهم

'And Allah ﷻ isn't one to punish them while
(O Beloved ﷺ) you are in their midst.'
– Surah Anfāl (8), Verse 33

In short, this extensive mercy is the Holy Prophet ﷺ.

Upon whom is the mercy?

This question is answered by the words 'a Mercy for the Worlds.' Allah ﷻ is Lord of the Worlds and Rasoolullah ﷺ is Mercy to the Worlds. In other words, he's mercy for everything and everyone that Allah ﷻ is the Lord of. In fact, we should say, "Whoever attained any guidance from the Lordship of Allah ﷻ gained it through the means (صدقة) of the Holy Prophet ﷺ."

The word 'world' encompasses everything besides Allah ﷻ. It's divided into several categories: the world of angels, jinns, physical bodies, possibilities, etc. Furthermore, the world of physical bodies is also divided into various categories, such as the world of humans, animals, plants, stones, etc. From the word 'worlds', we come to know that the Holy Prophet ﷺ is mercy for every world. He is mercy for angels, jinns, humans, animals, Muslims and even non-Muslims!

Once, the Holy Prophet ﷺ asked Sayyiduna Jibrael ﷺ, "I'm the Mercy to the Worlds, and you are also part of the creation. Tell me, what mercy have you attained from me?" He answered, "O Beloved of Allah ﷺ, I had not known whether my ultimate end would be on goodness or opposite to it (Sayyiduna Jibrael ﷺ witnessed the fate of individuals such as Iblis and Harut & Marut). But, I've gained security through you and even peace of mind, because the Holy Quran says about me,

ذى قوة عند ذى العرش مكين ، مطاع ثم امين

'Who is powerfully established in the presence of the Owner of the
Highest Authority. He is obeyed and is the trustworthy.'
– Surah Takwīr (81), Verses 20-1

– *Tafseer Roohul-Bayaan, Surah Ambiya (21), Verse 107*

The Prophets ﷺ, Messengers ﷺ and close servants of the Almighty ﷻ all attained mercy from the Holy Messenger ﷺ. Even non-Muslims attained his mercy. Prior to the coming of Rasoolullah ﷺ, Allah's ﷻ punishment would descend upon the world. Now, it has stopped. People were ruined in the world due to their sins, yet even this has ceased. In the Hereafter, gaining salvation and accounting for one's actions (حساب), etc. will commence through the means of the Holy Prophet ﷺ. Abu Lahab's punishment is lightened on Mondays due to the happiness he demonstrated on the birth of the Noble Messenger ﷺ, and punishment was also lessened on Abu Talib through the Prophet's ﷺ blessings. *Sharah Qasida Burda* states that the intercession of Rasoolullah ﷺ will be of seven types. Non-Muslims will benefit from three while the remaining four are exclusive for Muslims, the virtuous and the sinful.

From when is the mercy?

This has also been answered by the word 'worlds.' In other words, the Holy Prophet ﷺ was mercy from the time worlds existed. His mercy has been descending from the time the Lordship of Allah ﷻ had been declared. The universe came into existence through the Prophet's ﷺ means. The Father of Humanity, Sayyiduna Adam ﷺ, attained all honor and respect through him; his mistake was forgiven through him; Sayyiduna Nuh's ﷺ ark came ashore through his blessing, etc. Refer to my discussion of Verse 37, Surah Baqarah (2) [Verse 5 in book]. In fact, the fire of Namrud becoming cool for Sayyiduna Ibrahim ﷺ and a ram bearing the slaughter for Sayyiduna Ismail ﷺ were both also through the means (صدقة) of the Holy Prophet ﷺ.

Until when is the mercy?

The word 'worlds' answers this too. The mercy of the Holy Prophet ﷺ is present for as long as creation exists. In other words, his mercy is present in this world, the Hereafter, the Scale of Deeds, the Fountain of Kauthar, Jannah, on the sinful Muslims in Jahannam…in short, every place until the end of time! I've already discussed this in the Hadith of intercession. Under this verse, *Roohul-Bayaan* quotes a Hadith wherein the Noble Messenger ﷺ said, "My life is good for you and my demise is also good for you." The Companions asked, "O Prophet of Allah ﷺ, your life being good for us is apparent, but how is your demise good for us?" He replied, "Your deeds will be presented to me in my grave every Monday and Friday. When seeing good deeds, I'll show gratitude to Allah ﷻ, and when seeing bad deeds, I'll supplicate for your forgiveness."

This verse states, "And We did not send you but as a Mercy to the Worlds," yet another verse states,

بالمؤمنين رءوف رحيم

'To the believers he is most kind and merciful.'
– Surah Tauba (9), Verse 128

Sayyiduna Sulaiman عليه السلام heard the voice of the ant from a distance of 3 miles, yet marvel at the hearing power of the Holy Prophet ﷺ – he heard the sound of the Pen being used on the Protected Tablet (لوح محفوظ) while he was in his blessed mother's womb!

What is the congruence between them? The answer is that all of creation attaining general blessings of sustenance, worldly comfort & ease, respite in the Hereafter, etc. are all through the generosity of the Holy Prophet ﷺ, but his speech and specific mercy & blessings in this world and in the Hereafter (such as attaining Imaan, sins being forgiven, rank increased, attaining acceptance in Allah's ﷻ court, etc.) are reserved solely for Muslims.

Without comparison, Allah's ﷻ quality is *Rahmān*, meaning 'He Who's merciful on all in the world." *Raheem* is also His quality, meaning 'He Who shows mercy to only the believers on the Day of Judgment.' The demonstration of Allah's ﷻ quality of *Raheem* is exclusively for Muslims, while His general mercy is for everything.

Some people ask, "If the Holy Prophet ﷺ is mercy for all in the world, why did he fight non-Muslims in Jihad? Why did he order their killing?" The answer to this is that mercy doesn't simply mean 'distributing sweets to everyone all the time.' Killing a venomous snake to prevent it from attacking someone, cutting off a part of the body affected by gangrene, extracting unfavorable blood through cupping, etc. are all also defined as merciful acts. Similarly, the government punishing thieves & bandits and protecting the country from them is also regarded as mercy and wisdom. So, to cut the power of non-Muslims and raise the word of Allah ﷻ is an act of mercy on the slaves of Allah ﷻ. Without comparison, Allah ﷻ is *Rahmān* and *Raheem*, yet He still keeps some people poor, makes others rich, grants some knowledge, and grants others less. All of this planning is from His wisdom and not contrary to mercy.

اَللهُ نُورُ السَّمٰوٰتِ وَالْأَرْضِ ، مَثَلُ نُورِهٖ كَمِشْكٰوةٍ فِيْهَا مِصْبَاحٌ ، الْمِصْبَاحُ فِىْ زُجَاجَةٍ

'Allah ﷻ is the light (Noor) of the Heavens and the Earth. The likeness of His Light is a niche wherein is a lamp. The lamp is in a chandelier (of glass).'
– Surah Noor (24), Verse 35

This verse is also the praise of the Holy Prophet ﷺ. It states that Allah ﷻ is the Light of the Heavens and Earth. *Noor*, which is a name from the names of Allah ﷻ, means 'that which brightens.' So, the meaning of the verse is, "Allah ﷻ is He Who brightens the Heavens and Earth." There are three ways He may brighten something,

1. He brings them from non-existence (adm) into existence/reality (wujood), because *adm* is darkness and *wujood* is Noor. In other words, Allah ﷻ is their Creator.

2. He brightens things through stars (such as our sun) and moons.

3. He spreads within them brightness from the Noor of Sayyiduna Muhammad Mustapha ﷺ, just as how another verse states,

قد جاءكم من الله نور

'Surely Noor has come to you from Allah ﷻ.'
– Surah Māida (5), Verse 15

The Holy Prophet ﷺ has been declared Noor in this verse. – *Tafseer Roohul-Bayaan (under the commentary of this verse)*

Just as how Allah ﷻ created the stars, our sun, the moon, etc. in the Heavens, so too has He spread the Noor of the Prophets علیہم السلام, Messengers علیہم السلام, and thereafter the scholars and spiritual leaders on the Earth. So, He illuminates the Heavens with specific creations and illuminates the Earth with exemplary beings. In this context, this part of the verse is the praise of the Holy Prophet ﷺ.

Commentators of the Holy Quran have several opinions regarding the word *Noor* found in the words 'Allah's ﷻ Noor',

1. It refers to the faith of the believers, while 'niche' refers to their chests and 'lamp' refers to their hearts.

2.   It refers to the Holy Prophet ﷺ.

– Roohul-Bayaan & Madaarijun-Nubuwwah, Chapter 3

The *entire verse* is now the praise of the Holy Prophet ﷺ! The faith of the Beloved ﷺ is the Noor, the niche is his blessed chest, and the lamp is his magnanimous heart. *Tafseer Roohul-Bayaan* states that the light is Rasoolullah ﷺ, the niche is Sayyiduna Adam عليه السلام, the chandelier is Sayyiduna Nuh عليه السلام, the olive tree (mentioned later in the verse) is Sayyiduna Ibrahim عليه السلام, and that 'neither East nor West' (also in the verse) means Sayyiduna Ibrahim عليه السلام was neither a Jew nor a Christian. Many other interpretations of this verse have been made. We come to know that if we wish to attain the Noor of Allah ﷻ, we must search for it in the generous and noble heart of the Beloved Messenger ﷺ, but we cannot attain that too without the mediation of the Saints and Scholars. So, the Holy Prophet ﷺ is the Light of Allah ﷻ, the niche is his blessed chest, and the lamp of this light is made up of the Saints and Scholars. He who's detached from these means is deprived of Allah's ﷻ Noor.

We also come to know that none can extinguish the Noor of Rasoolullah ﷺ because it is protected. It's in a lamp, and the lamp is preserved in a niche. Just as how the glass of a lamp protects the flame from wind, so too is this light guarded completely by the chandelier. Another verse clearly states that none can extinguish the Prophet's ﷺ Noor,

يريدون ليطفئوا نور الله بأفواههم والله متم نوره ولو كره الكفرون
'They desire to extinguish the Noor of Allah ﷻ with their mouths, but Allah ﷻ will perfect His Light even though the infidels may hate it.'
– Surah Saff (61), Verse 8

VERSE 53

لَا تَجْعَلُوا دُعَاءَ الرَّسُولِ بَيْنَكُمْ كَدُعَاءِ بَعْضِكُمْ بَعْضًا
'Make not the summoning of the Messenger ﷺ among yourselves the way one calls the other among you.'
– Surah Noor (24), Verse 63

This verse is also the praise of the Holy Prophet ﷺ. In it, the Sahaabah (in fact, all Muslims until Qiyaamat) are taught the etiquette of Rasoolullah's ﷺ blessed court. His praise is established through the following,

1. Allah ﷻ Himself taught the servants of the His Beloved ﷺ the manner of talking and interacting with him.

2. Allah ﷻ declares that the Prophet's ﷺ status and standing isn't like ordinary Muslims, that you may simply address him in whatever manner you wish. He has a prestigious court, and its respect is astonishing.

There are two interpretations of this verse: it either refers to 'calling the Messenger ﷺ', or 'the calling of the Messenger ﷺ'.

Based on the first interpretation, the verse will mean, "Do not call the Messenger ﷺ the way you call one another." We come to know that to call Rasoolullah ﷺ with, "O Muhammad ﷺ, O Ahmed ﷺ, O Son of Abdullah ﷺ, O Brother, O Father," etc. is impermissible (حرام). Rather, "O Rasoolullah ﷺ, O Beloved of Allah ﷺ, O Intercessor of the Sinful," etc. and other titles like these should be used.

We also come to know that to call the Holy Prophet ﷺ from any place and any time is permissible, but once again, it is necessary that admirable titles be used. Due to a need to rhyme their stanzas, poets sometimes do write "O Muhammad ﷺ," but the reader must say 'Sallalaahu Alaihi Wasallam' when coming across these words.

The second interpretation would lead the verse to mean, "Don't regard the calling of the Noble Messenger ﷺ to be like any other ordinary calling. Present yourselves immediately when he calls you." I've already discussed this in Verse 24 of Surah Anfāl (8) [Verse 34 in book].

A third interpretation of the verse could also be, "Don't regard the dua (supplication) the Holy Messenger ﷺ makes in My (Allah's ﷻ) court to be like your duas. Supplication from others can be accepted or declined, but his supplication is accepted in the Divine court." The movement of Rasoolullah's ﷺ blessed lips is the key to blessings. This is why, if the Prophets عليهم السلام wish to make dua for something which is contrary to Allah's ﷻ will, they are stopped from such a supplication (because it can't be that they make dua and it remains unaccepted). Their great esteem is in fact *established* by them being stopped from making these duas. When the Prophets عليهم السلام are stopped from supplicating for certain things, the reasoning behind it is, "We (Allah ﷻ) don't wish for your supplication to not be granted. So, don't plead over this matter." Allah ﷻ said to Sayyiduna Ibrahim عليه السلام when he wished to intercede in the matter of Sayyiduna Lut's عليه السلام nation,

يابرهيم اعرض عن هذا

'O Ibrahim ﷺ, don't plunge in this thought.'
– Surah Hūd (11), Verse 76

Those who study the Ahadith know that whenever Rasoolullah ﷺ
supplicated for something for any person, it was immediately accepted. Many
examples confirming this can be cited, but for the sake of brevity, I'll present
only a few.

In *Madaarijun-Nubuwwah*, chapter on Miracles, Shaikh Abdul-Haqq
Muhaddith Dehlwi ﷺ has dedicated an entire section dealing with how many
people came back to life through the supplication of the Holy Prophet ﷺ. The
incident of Hadrat Jabir's ﷺ children has been mentioned here. Refer to the
discussion on verse 24 of Surah Anfāl (8) [Verse 34 in book] to learn more of
it.

Once, during a severe drought in Madina, the Holy Prophet ﷺ was
delivering the Friday lecture when a Companion of his submitted, "It doesn't
rain!" In that state, the Holy Prophet ﷺ lifted his hands for dua. Allah ﷻ
surely knows whether his hands were merely ordinary hands or in fact a
channel to demonstrate the power of the Hands (i.e. power) of Allah ﷻ –
because when the Prophet ﷺ lifted his blessed hands, clouds immediately
formed and it began to rain! It rained so much that water even began to drip
from the roof of the musjid and onto the blessed face of Rasoolullah ﷺ.
When the Companions came out of the musjid after the Salaah, they found
every road and alley of the city experiencing rainfall, to the extent that some
of them even had difficulty returning to their homes. It continuously rained
until the next Friday. On that day, when the Holy Prophet ﷺ stood on the
pulpit to deliver the lecture, the same Companion of his who asked for rain
the week before (or possibly another Companion) said, "Roads cannot be
used, and foundations of houses are giving way! The rain is too extensive!"
So, Rasoolullah ﷺ said,

حوالينا ولا علينا

'O Allah ﷻ, let it rain around us, not on us.'

Previously (in Makkah), the Holy Messenger ﷺ gestured to the moon with
his finger and split it into two pieces. Using these very fingers, he then
pointed to these clouds, and they moved in the direction he gestured towards!
– *Bukhari Sharif & Muslim Sharif, Chapter of Miracles*

'Merely by his gesture, all gained safety.
O Rasoolullah ﷺ*! Whatever you uttered became a reality.'*

Rasoolullah ﷺ made various supplications for different people. He supplicated for the extension of a person's life (and his life was extended). If he supplicated for a person to attain knowledge, he became knowledgeable. If he supplicated for a person to attain wealth, he became wealthy, etc.

Hadrat Ali ؓ states, "The Holy Prophet ﷺ appointed me as the judge of Yemen. I said to him, "O Prophet of Allah ﷺ, I'm still very young and I don't have knowledge with regards to giving decisions." He replied, "Allah ﷻ grant salvation to your heart and tongue. Go to Yemen." Hadrat Ali ؓ states, "Through the blessings of this dua, I never hesitated since in giving any decision." – *Mishkat, Kitaabul-Imaaraat, Baabul-Amal fil-Qadhaa*

If I didn't fear the lengthening of this book, I would've quoted a few remarkable decisions of Hadrat Ali ؓ. His judgment and knowledge is extensively reported in the books of Jurisprudence (فقہ) even today. Which madrassah did he attend to gain this knowledge? What were the books he studied? No, dear readers. It was all due to the blessings of that prophetic dua.

VERSE 54

تَبَارَكَ الَّذِیْ نَزَّلَ الْفُرْقَانَ عَلٰی عَبْدِہٖ لِیَكُوْنَ لِلْعٰلَمِیْنَ نَذِیْرًا

'Immensely Great is He Who sent down the Quran
to His bondsmen that he may warn the worlds.'
– Surah Furqān (25), Verse 1

This verse is also the praise of the Holy Prophet ﷺ, and it mentions the generality of his prophethood. It has already been discussed that the Holy Messenger ﷺ is the Mercy to the Worlds. Meaning, he's the messenger of the entire creation of Allah ﷻ. Angels, jinns, humans, animals, plant-life…in short, all earthly and heavenly creatures are included in the word 'worlds'. *None* are excluded from being a follower in his Ummah. Sayyiduna Nuh الیہ السلام was the prophet of all humans during his time on the Earth, but the generality of his prophethood doesn't remain (it was abrogated later). Sayyiduna Sulaiman الیہ السلام was also the king of all humans and jinns, but the generality of his prophethood was also annulled. – *Roohul-Bayaan, under this verse*

The commentary of this verse is the following Hadith wherein the Holy Prophet ﷺ said,

وارسلت الى الخلق كافة
'I've been sent to the entire creation.'
– Mishkaat, Baabu Fadhaaili Sayyidil-Mursaleen, Section 1
(with ref. to Muslim)

In the explanation of this Hadith, Mulla Ali Qaari ﷺ states, "In other words, Rasoolullah ﷺ is saying, 'I have been made a prophet and sent to everything that exists, whether it's amongst humans, angels, animals, or even stones.' Imam Qastalaani ﷺ has presented excellent research on this in the book *Mawaahibul-Ladunya.*" – *Mirqaatul-Mafaateeh*

This verse states that those who gained an understanding of their servitude to Allah ﷻ attained it through the prophethood of the Holy Messenger ﷺ. Allah ﷻ is the Creator of everything, and the Holy Beloved ﷺ is the prophet of every creation. *Tafseer Jalaalain, Kabeer,* and *Roohul-Bayaan* have separated the angels from this generalization, but this exclusion is unsubstantiated and contrary to this Hadith. The senior and distinguished Scholars of the Ummah have also refuted this.

The fatherhood of Sayyiduna Adam عليه السلام and Rasoolullah's ﷺ prophethood is common to all humans. Rasoolullah's ﷺ prophethood however, is more general than the fatherhood of Sayyiduna Adam عليه السلام, because Sayyiduna Adam's عليه السلام fatherhood is only for humans while Rasoolullah's ﷺ prophethood is for all of creation.

Some claim that a prophet is sent to those who are obligated by the commands of Allah ﷻ while animals and stones are under no such obligation. Likewise, commands such as Salaah, fasting, etc. are not obligatory on angels. So, how can the Holy Prophet ﷺ be their messenger? Warning is given about punishment, and again, angels and stones face no such retribution.

The answer to this is that Divine commands are emplaced on all, but they differ within categories of creation. They aren't equal on everyone and everything.

A Hadith Sharif states, "On the Day of Judgment, the compensation of an animal without its horn will be given for the animal that has its horn. Thereafter, they'll be turned to dust." From this, we come to know that being oppressive is haraam, and this is a command even upon animals. Otherwise, what meaning would 'compensation' have?

That being said, the commands upon animals (and their punishment) is different. Salaah and fasting, etc. isn't compulsory upon them. Similarly, their mutual disagreements are not taken to a judge for a ruling. They are to only fulfill commands which are befittingly emplaced on them.

Likewise, grass, trees, etc. carry out the worship of Allah ﷻ,

وان من شىء الا يسبح بحمده ولكن لا تفقهون تسبيحهم

'And there is nothing that doesn't celebrate His praise.
Yes, you don't understand their glorification.'
– Surah Bani Israel (17), Verse 44

We come to know that every blade of grass and tree makes the *tasbeeh* of Allah ﷻ. This is why the punishment of the deceased is lessened in the grave (i.e. through their blessings). Similarly, stones and mountains also have perception and sense. The Holy Prophet ﷺ said, "The mountain of Uhud loves us and we love it." – *Muslim Sharif*

The pillar of Hanānah and the mountain of Uhud cried because of being separated from Rasoolullah ﷺ. Once, the Prophet ﷺ ascended the mountain of Uhud with Hadrat Abu Bakr ؓ, Hadrat Umar ؓ and Hadrat Uthman ؓ. Out of joy, the mountain began to move. In short, stones and mountains too have feelings and perception, along with recognition of the Holy Prophet ﷺ.

Likewise, some stones will also enter Jahannam, either for the idol-worshippers to see or for punishment.

In the end, Rasoolullah ﷺ is the prophet of all, and each type of creation attains the obligations and commands of Allah ﷻ from him. Jinns pledged allegiance to him and said, "O Prophet of Allah ﷻ, stop your Ummah from using bones and coal for *istinja* because they are our sustenance." – *Mishkaat, Baabu Adaabil-Khulaa*

Angels also attained blessings from the Holy Prophet ﷺ, and we've already mentioned this in the discussion of Verse 107 of Surah Ambiya (21) [Verse 51 in book]. This proves that Rasoolullah ﷺ is the prophet of all creation, and everything has commands enjoined on them, along with punishment should they go against these orders.

The verse mentions the word 'warner' (نذير), not 'bearer of glad-tidings' (بشير), because Jannah is only for humans. Virtuous jinns, animals and stones will not enter it. Evil jinns will be punished, and the virtuous will be annihilated. In other words, virtuous jinns will be saved from punishment. – *Roohul-Bayaan, under the commentary of this verse*

So, 'bearer of glad-tidings' wasn't used here because of the word 'worlds'. Angels will also be found in Jannah, but they will either be there for the servitude of its inmates or for the purpose of regulation; not because of the *thawaab* that they attained. The angels in Jannah are there for regulation just as how the angels in Jahannam are there for management (not because they are being punished). This is similar to how we find guards in prisons.

VERSE 55

وَتَوَكَّلْ عَلَى الْعَزِيْزِ الرَّحِيْمِ ، الَّذِى يَرٰكَ حِيْنَ تَقُوْمُ ، وَتَقَلُّبَكَ فِى السّٰجِدِيْنَ

'And rely upon Him Who's the Mighty, the Most Merciful; Who sees you when you stand and your movements amongst those who offer prayer.'
– Surah Shuarā (26), Verses 217-9

This verse is exceptional praise of the Holy Prophet ﷺ, and it even mentions a few of his grand qualities. It shows him to have trust only in his Lord, since Allah ﷻ sees his graceful manner. Even though Allah ﷻ sees the entire creation, he still singles out His Beloved ﷺ by saying, "I keep in My sight your performance of Salaah, your standing and your movement." We come to know that every grace of the Holy Prophet ﷺ is beloved, and it's viewed with mercy by the Supreme Lord.

> The words of the Holy Quran were revealed to Rasoolullah's ﷺ blessed ears, its meaning to his blessed mind and its secrets to his blessed heart. Whoever attained anything from the Holy Quran received it from the Holy Prophet ﷺ.

Commentators of the Holy Quran have a few interpretations of the words 'when you stand'. Some say it means, "We see you when you awaken from your bedstead for Tahajjud Salaah," while others say it means, "We see you when you stand at any place for whatever task."

Similarly, there are several opinions regarding '...and your movements amongst those who offer prayer.' What is meant by 'movements' and who's being referred to in 'those who offer prayer'? Some Commentators say that the Holy Prophet ﷺ would move about in the streets of Madina at the time of Tahajjud to gain awareness of the condition of his Companions. He wished to know how his loyal Sahaabah were spending this time and would hear the sweet sound of Quranic recitals and intense *zikrs* (acts of remembering Allah ﷻ) from their homes. – *Roohul-Bayaan*

So, the verse gestures to this 'movement' and is saying, "O Beloved ﷺ, We see well your movement to know the condition of your Sahaabah." This effectively means, "O Beloved ﷺ, you look at those who remember Me and I'll focus on your blessed action of looking." Some say that the verse means, "We see your standing to perform Salaah and your zeal to perform ruku and sajda," while according to others, "We see the movement of your eyes because you can see behind you in Salaah just as how you see in front." The blessed eyes of the Holy Prophet ﷺ could clearly see whatever happened behind him in the exact way he saw ahead!

Hadrat Ibn Abbas ؓ states that '…those who offer prayer' refers to the believers, and 'your movement' refers to generation after generation (i.e. the movement of the Holy Prophet ﷺ from blessed spines to pure wombs). – *Roohul-Bayaan*

From this, we come to know that all the ascendants of Rasoolullah ﷺ, from Sayyiduna Adam ﷺ to Hadrat Abdullah ؓ & Sayyidah Amina ؓ (his father and mother) were believers, and none of them were polytheists. This has already been discussed under verse 128 of Surah Tauba (9) [Verse 40 in book]. The name of Sayyiduna Ibrahim's ﷺ father was Tārikh, not Aazar. Refer to the abovementioned verse for an explanation of this.

VERSE 56

حَتَّى إِذَا أَتَوْا عَلَى وَادِ النَّمْلِ قَالَتْ نَمْلَةٌ يَأَيُّهَا النَّمْلُ ادْخُلُوا مَسَكِنَكُمْ لَا يَحْطِمَنَّكُمْ سُلَيْمنُ وَجُنُودُه وَهُمْ لَا يَشْعُرُونَ ، فَتَبَسَّمَ ضَاحِكًا مِّن قَوْلِهَا

'Until they came to the valley of the ants, and one ant said, "O Ants! Enter your homes lest Sulaiman ﷺ and his armies crush you unknowingly." Thereupon he smilingly laughed at her proclamation.'
– Surah Naml (27), Verses 18-9

This verse, as well as the verses before and after it, narrate the incident of a journey made by Sayyiduna Sulaiman ﷺ. I'll first briefly present this narrative, then present the points derived from it, including the point of the greatness of the Prophets ﷺ. Finally, I will explain how it is also the praise of our Beloved ﷺ.

The incident is that once, Sayyiduna Sulaiman ﷺ set out towards Yemen from Syria. His habit when traveling was to make the armies of all jinns, humans, animals and birds accompany him, and so all were with him on this occasion. *Tafseer Roohul-Bayaan* also states that this army was spread across 12,500 square metres and included all of the forms of creation mentioned above. It was during this journey that Sayyiduna Sulaiman ﷺ passed a jungle in Syria which had an extensive amount of ants. When these ants saw the approaching army, their leader (whose name was either *Munzirah* or *Tākhiya*) proclaimed to the others, "O Ants! Go into your homes before Sulaiman ﷺ crushes you unknowingly!" This was said when Sayyiduna Sulaiman's ﷺ army was 3 miles away. The prophet heard this discreet proclamation from this distance and understood it! He was so amazed by the ant's insight that he smiled and also showed gratitude to Allah ﷻ in appreciation of his dominion and knowledge.

The following points arise from this,

1. We see the generality of Sayyiduna Sulaiman's ﷺ authority. Let alone humans, even other forms of creation were under his power!

2. Sayyiduna Sulaiman's ﷺ knowledge is greater than the knowledge of ordinary humans, because he understood the speech of animals and insects.

3. Sayyiduna Sulaiman ﷺ had the ability to hear from far, since he was able to hear the proclamation of the ant from a distance of 3 miles.

4. Sayyiduna Sulaiman ﷺ is innocent (ma'sūm) from the sin of oppression, because even the ant knew that the prophet wouldn't crush them intentionally due to the prophet's greatness. Also, by the blessings of his companionship attained by the army, they too would not do so. This is why the ant said, "...lest Sulaiman ﷺ and his armies crush you *unknowingly*."

5. The ant recognized Sayyiduna Sulaiman ﷺ because he was its ruler, and it's necessary on subjects to recognize their king.

This was a description of Sayyiduna Sulaiman's ﷺ dominion. Now read the description of the dominion of my Beloved ﷺ, the king of all kings, the Imam of both qiblas, the Prophet of Prophets, Sayyiduna Muhammad Mustapha ﷺ! I've already explained that all the excellences of the previous Prophets ﷺ

(with added brilliance) is concentrated and found within our Holy Prophet ﷺ. Maulana Jaami ؓ states,

> *'The beauty of Yusuf ؑ, the spirit of Esa ؑ and*
> *the shining hand of Musa ؑ are possessed by you. Whatever*
> *excellences we individually possess are all found in you.'*

The dominion of Sayyiduna Sulaiman ؑ was also an excellence. So, this dominion was also bestowed to Rasoolullah ﷺ, along with all of the miracles of previous Prophets ؑ. It's necessary to understand this to be a unique quality of Rasoolullah ﷺ and that these excellences were demonstrated by him in different ways. The miracle of Sayyiduna Esa ؑ being born without a father was demonstrated by our Beloved Prophet ﷺ when his Noor gained existence without any source at all. He said, "I'm Noor by the Noor of Allah ﷻ." Sayyiduna Musa ؑ became *Kalīmullah* (the Communicator with Allah ﷻ) on the Mountain of Tūr, while the Holy Prophet ﷺ became the Communicator with Allah ﷻ on the night of the Ascension (Mi'rāj). Sayyiduna Musa ؑ made water flow from a stone, whereas Rasoolullah ﷺ made fountains of water gush out from his blessed fingers. Rasoolullah ﷺ gave life to the dead just like Sayyiduna Esa ؑ – in fact, he even made lifeless sticks and stones recite the Kalima! Similarly, all of the animate forms of creation were the subjects of Sayyiduna Sulaiman ؑ, yet animate and even *in*animate things, from the Heavens to the Earth (truly everything created by Allah ﷻ) is in the Ummah of Rasoolullah ﷺ. This has been discussed under verse 1 of Surah Furqān (25) [Verse 54 in book]. The truth is that the Holy Prophet ﷺ has dominion over everything, even if he didn't overtly disclose this.

Rasoolullah ﷺ once said, "Tonight, while I was in Salaah, Shaitaan came to me. I wanted to apprehend him and tie him up, and if I did so, even the children of Madina would've been able to play with him, but then I remembered the supplication of Sulaiman ؑ. He said, 'O Allah ﷻ, grant me a dominion like no other.' So I left him." – *Mishkaat Sharif*

This clearly proves that Rasoolullah ﷺ has control over Shaitaan, but he didn't display it. Another Hadith states that Hadrat Abu Hurairah ؓ was appointed as the guardian over the monies of Zakaat. Shaitaan once came to steal it and Hadrat Abu Hurairah ؓ imprisoned him. The devil was unable to escape. – *Mishkaat Sharif*

When this is the power of a servant of the Holy Prophet ﷺ over Shaitaan, what is the extent of *the Holy Prophet's* ﷺ authority and power?!

The set sun returned on the Prophet's ﷺ gesture, the moon split in two, trees were obedient to him, etc. If he didn't have power over these things, why were they obeying him?

> 'Salaam upon he who assisted the helpers,
> Salaam upon he who adopted humility in kingship.'

Sayyiduna Sulaiman السلام عليه knew and understood the language of animals. The Holy Prophet ﷺ understood not just the language of animals, but even that of sticks and stones! It's well known that a deer once complained to Rasoolullah ﷺ that it had been captured. – *Dalaailul-Khairaat*

A camel complained to the Prophet ﷺ that its master gives it little food and extracts lots of work from it. – *Mishkaat, with ref. to Abu Dawud*

Even the pillar of Hanānah cried due to being separated from the Holy Prophet ﷺ. The pillar was then consoled by his embrace.

Sayyiduna Sulaiman السلام عليه heard the voice of the ant from a distance of 3 miles, yet marvel at the hearing power of the Holy Prophet ﷺ – he heard the sound of the Pen being used on the Protected Tablet (لوح محفوظ) while he was in his blessed mother's womb! Refer to my book, *Ja'al-Haqq*, for a complete discussion on this.

While in Madina, Hadrat Umar ﷺ called out to Hadrat Sariyah ﷺ (who heard his voice in Nawāhind). The ant regarded Sayyiduna Sulaiman ﷺ to be free from the sin of oppression, yet *everything* in creation believes that our Beloved Prophet ﷺ is free of sin! This is why even hardened enemies of Islam (such as Jews & Christians) would come to Rasoolullah ﷺ to settle their disputes. They knew that he was the most just and fair person, his decisions never amounted to oppression, and that in fact, his court protects the oppressed from oppressors. Many examples of this have been presented.

The ant recognized Sayyiduna Sulaiman ﷺ, but even the sun, the moon and the stars recognized the Holy Prophet ﷺ. We present a couple of narrations regarding this below,

On the occasion of the Final Hajj, a few camels were presented to the Holy Prophet ﷺ for slaughter. The habit of animals is to become afraid and reluctant at the time of sacrifice, yet each of these camels yearned for the Holy

Prophet 🌸 to perform qurbaani on them first. They quarreled with each other and rushed towards him! – *Mishkaat, Kitaabul-Hajj, Baabul-Hadyi*

Animals recognize even the laws of Rasoolullah 🌸. Hadrat Safeenah ⚶, the freed slave of the Prophet 🌸, was once captured by Romans. During the Caliphate of Hadrat Umar ⚶, the Muslim army reached Roman territory, and this information came to Hadrat Safeenah ⚶ while he was still in prison. He thought that this would be a good time to escape imprisonment. So, he fled at night. The Companion didn't know how to get to the Muslim army, but as he was escaping in the jungle, he came across a lion and said to it, "O Abul-Haarith (a title of the lion), do you know that I'm the slave of the Holy Prophet 🌸? I've lost my path." Hearing this, the lion began to wag its tail and came in front of Hadrat Safeenah ⚶. It then led him to the Muslim army. – *Mishkaat, Baabul-Karaamaat*

Two points emerge from this Hadith,

1. The lion recognized Hadrat Safeenah ⚶.

2. The faithful scent of the Muslim army was sensed by the lion from afar. Through this, it came to know where the army was situated.

This proves that animals recognize not just the Holy Prophet 🌸, but even his servants.

VERSE 57

وَمَا كُنْتَ تَتْلُوا مِن قَبْلِهِ مِن كِتَبٍ وَّلَا تَخُطُّهُ بِيَمِينِكَ ، إِذًا لَّارْتَابَ الْمُبْطِلُونَ

'And you did not recite any Book before, nor did you write anything with your hand. In that case, the followers of falsehood would've doubted.'
– Surah Ankabūt (29), Verse 48

This verse is also clear praise of the Holy Prophet 🌸. It states, "O Beloved 🌸, the Arabs were well aware of your upbringing and condition prior to the proclamation of prophethood. You didn't write or read anything before that announcement. In fact, you didn't even sit in any gathering of the learned. So, witnessing the unrivalled revelation of Allah 🕮 being uttered by your blessed tongue and your disseminating of wisdom (that is unequaled in the world) should be sufficient for them to accept you as a true prophet. The Holy Quran is the speech of Allah 🕮, not the invention of the Messenger of Allah 🌸."

If Rasoolullah ﷺ chose to read or write before proclaiming prophethood, he could've been doubted in two ways. The first is that the People of the Book could've said, "The recognition of the Final Messenger in our books is that he will be someone who doesn't read and write (أُمِّي), and Muhammad reads and writes. How can he be the Final Messenger?" The second possible objection is that the polytheist Arabs could've said, "Muhammad acquainted himself with the knowledgeable sciences during his childhood. He read the works of the learned, studied history, and attended gatherings of scholars. Now he merely narrates the historical incidents and wise anecdotes which he saw in the books or heard from their scholars and calls it the Quran."

> Allah ﷻ is Lord of the Worlds and Rasoolullah ﷺ is the Mercy to the Worlds. In other words, he's mercy for everything and everyone that Allah ﷻ is the Lord of.

Since the Prophet ﷺ chose not to read or write, no doubt or objection can now be leveled against him. In other words, Rasoolullah ﷺ relating the Holy Quran and conveying it to people is a proof of his truthfulness and prophethood. However, the reality is that he is the knower (عارف) of all Divine Revelation and is knowledgeable of both their original and altered texts. Allah ﷻ states in the Holy Quran,

يا أهل الكتب قد جاءكم رسولنا يبين لكم كثيرا مما كنتم تخفون من الكتب ويعفوا عن كثير

'O People of the Book, there has come to you Our
Messenger ﷺ who makes clear to you much of that which
you had hidden in the Book and pardons much.'
– Surah Māida (5), Verse 15

We come to know that Rasoolullah ﷺ knew all the commands and verses understood by the People of the Book, but he hid some of their faults because this was the desire of Allah ﷻ.

Tafseer Roohul-Bayaan mentioned two interesting points in the commentary of this verse. The first is that writing is a human excellence, as per the Holy Quran,

الذى علم بالقلم

'(It's Allah ﷻ) Who teaches writing by the pen.'
– Surah Alaq (96), Verse 4

146

So, why wasn't the Holy Prophet ﷺ bestowed with this excellence? In fact, why is it that *not writing* has been declared an excellence of his? There are two replies to this,

1. Writing has been made a human excellence because humans forget and make mistakes. Through the pen, humans will be safe from forgetfulness and errs. A famous saying goes, "The pen doesn't forget knowledge." The glory of Rasoolullah ﷺ, however, is that although he doesn't write, he doesn't forget either. He's the most eminent and learned of the entire creation. He safeguards this great knowledge of his in his blessed chest, not in journals and books. The Holy Quran states,

2.

ان علينا جمعه وقرءانه

'The collecting of it (the Holy Quran) and the reciting
of it is certainly on Us.'
– Surah Qiyaamat (75), Verse 17

In other words, "O Beloved ﷺ, don't think that you'll forget the verses that have been revealed to you. Collecting them in your chest and making you convey them through your blessed tongue is Our responsibility." Again, if Rasoolullah ﷺ read and wrote, someone could object and say, "Muhammad has memorized the works of previous times, and he now conveys them as the Quran."

3. The shadow of the pen falls on the letters it writes, and Rasoolullah ﷺ must have not desired the shadow of his pen being cast on the remembrance of Allah ﷻ. In other words, his pen is on top while the name of his Lord is below. The reward he attained for this was, "O Beloved ﷺ, you don't wish for the shadow of your pen to fall on My name, and I too don't desire your shadow to be trampled on by anyone's feet. So, I've prevented you from having a shadow so that no one may walk on it." Allah ﷻ also doesn't wish for the Prophet's ﷺ voice to be overpowered by anyone else's (be it the voice of a human, angel, jinn, or anything else). – *Surah Hujarāt (49), Verse 2*

Roohul-Bayaan further states in the commentary of this verse that the Holy Prophet ﷺ was made of Noor (نورى) in human form, which is why he possessed no shadow. Sayyiduna Jibrael عليه السلام never cast a shadow whenever he descended in human form (because he was truly an angel).

*'[The Holy Prophet ﷺ has] a human form, angelic qualities,
the shadow of Allah's ﷻ Light.'*

According to deep research, Allah 🕮 granted the Holy Prophet 🕮 the knowledge of writing, so he definitely knew how to write. There are narrations that confirm this. *Tafseer Roohul-Bayaan* mentions such a narration in the commentary of this verse. Allama Karputi 🕮, an annotator of Qasida Burda Sharif, also narrates that Hadrat Ameer Muawiyah 🕮, the scribe of Divine Revelation, said, "The Holy Prophet 🕮 taught me how to hold a pen, where to position the inkpot, and how to write letters. He instructed me to write the letter 'م' in [a certain] manner, and other letters in a certain manner."

Hadrat Ali 🕮 was the scribe on behalf of the Holy Prophet 🕮 during the Treaty of Hudaibiyah. 'Muhammad is the Prophet of Allah' was written in the treaty, but the non-Muslims rejected this and said, "Write 'Muhammad the son of Abdullah' instead." In reply, Rasoolullah 🕮 instructed Hadrat Ali 🕮 to strike out 'Prophet of Allah' with his pen, but the Companion refused to do so and said, "My pen will not cross it out." So, the Holy Prophet 🕮 himself drew a line across it. – *Bukhari, Vol. 1, Kitaabus-Sulh*

The following was said by Rasoolullah 🕮 during his final illness,

ايتوني بكتب اكتب لكم بكتب لن تضلوا بعده ابدا

'Bring some paper to me so that I may write something by which you will not be astray afterwards.'
– Bukhari Sharif

Now, the negation by the Holy Quran of the Holy Prophet 🕮 having the knowledge of writing is with regards to the time prior to the proclamation of prophethood. Rasoolullah 🕮 didn't know the science of writing before this. When other branches of knowledge were bestowed on him afterwards, the knowledge of writing was also given. Yes, he still didn't adopt the habit of writing. And why should he have, when the Protected Tablet is his journal and the Divine Pen is his pen? What need was there for him to write with the pens and papers of this mundane world? – *Roohul-Bayaan, under the commentary of this verse*

The first person to write was Sayyiduna Adam 🕮 when he wrote Arabic, Farsi, Hebrew, Latin, Hindi, Chinese, etc. on sand. These languages were then passed on to his children. Sayyiduna Ismail 🕮 wrote in Arabic because the Arab nation is his progeny. The writing mentioned in the narration which states that Sayyiduna Idris 🕮 was the first person to write by pen refers to the letters of *Ilm'ul-Jafar*, not the writing of languages. – *Roohul-Bayaan*

In short, this verse is the praise of the Holy Prophet ﷺ and doesn't negate his knowledge of writing.

VERSE 58

اَلنَّبِيُّ أَوْلَى بِالْمُؤْمِنِيْنَ مِنْ اَنْفُسِهِم ، وَأَزْوَاجُهُ أُمَّهَتُهُمْ

'The Prophet (Muhammad ﷺ) is more worthy of the believers
than their own selves, and his wives are their mothers.'
– Surah Ahzāb (33), Verse 6

This verse is explicit praise of our Holy Prophet ﷺ. The reason for its revelation is as follows: when Rasoolullah ﷺ instructed his Companions to proceed for the expedition of Tabuk, some of them said, "We'll seek advice from our parents in this matter." This reply of theirs, and the act of deferring from the obedience of the Holy Prophet ﷺ, was disliked by Allah ﷻ. The abovementioned verse was then revealed. – *Roohul-Bayaan*

The verse states, "The Holy Prophet ﷺ has more nearness and right over your lives than you have over yourselves. Seeking counsel from someone else when he has given you a command is disliked. When he has commanded you to do something, obedience to him is compulsory on you, whether your parents agree to it or not, or whether your heart accepts it or not."

The word *Aulā* ('more worthy') in the verse has a few meanings ascribed to it,

1. It means 'more rightful'. So, the meaning of the verse will be, "Rasoolullah's ﷺ right and dominion over you is more than the right your life has over your body." Life has so much dominion over the body that no part of the body moves without it. Hands, legs, eyes, nose, ears, etc. are completely powerless and are under its control. However, the Holy Prophet's ﷺ authority and dominion is much greater than this because every movement must be in accordance with his declaration. Hadrat Sahl ؓ said, "He who doesn't regard his life, wealth, children – in fact, everything he possesses – to be the possession and in the control of the Holy Prophet ﷺ can never attain the pleasure of the prophetic ways (sunnahs)." – *Roohul-Bayaan*

2. The second meaning is 'more worthy'. Therefore, the verse would mean, "The Holy Prophet ﷺ is worthier of being obeyed than life itself." In winter, our lives and hearts don't wish to touch water, but if

ghusl became obligatory, Rasoolullah ﷺ has commanded us that cleanliness is necessary for performing Salaah. So, we don't complete the desire of our beings and hearts but obey the command of the Prophet ﷺ instead (by performing ghusl before Fajr Salaah). The reality is that no one has shown us kindness to the amount the Holy Prophet ﷺ has. After we pass away, our hands and feet become useless. In fact, they and other body parts will even testify *against* us on the Day of Judgment! The Holy Prophet's ﷺ mercy, however, encompasses our existence. It is with us in our demise, our graves, the Hereafter – *everywhere*. Similarly, the love of close relatives and family members will end and none of them will want to recognize us on the Last Day, but the Noble Messenger ﷺ will never forsake us anywhere.

3. The third meaning is 'more close'. Shaikh Abdul-Haqq Muhaddith Dehlwi ؓ has accepted this meaning in *Madaarijun-Nubuwwah*, Vol. 1, Chapter 3, and it has been agreed upon by even Maulwi Qasim Nanotwi in his book *Tahzeerun-Naas*. So, the meaning of the verse in this context will be, "The Holy Prophet ﷺ is closer to Muslims than their own lives." It's evident that our life is the closest thing to us in the world. This is why, if our bodies undergo even the slightest hardship, our souls become aware of it. Still, the Holy Prophet ﷺ is closer to us than this!

The issue of the Prophet ﷺ being present and aware (حاضر وناظر) has been clearly solved by this. Life is present and aware in every body part of ours, and so is the Holy Prophet ﷺ present by and aware of every Muslim. Muslims are spread over all parts of the Heavens and the Earth (because even angels and jinns are Muslims). So, the Holy Prophet ﷺ is present and aware everywhere.

Allah ﷻ stated the following regarding Himself,

نحن اقرب اليه من حبل الوريد
'We are nearer to him (mankind) than even his jugular vein.'
– Surah Qāf (50), Verse 16

And, regarding the Holy Prophet ﷺ, Allah ﷻ states,

النبی اولی بالمؤمنین من انفسهم
'The Prophet (Muhammad ﷺ) is closer

to the believers than their own lives.'
– Surah Ahzāb (33), Verse 6

If the jugular vein is severed, death follows immediately. If life is removed, death comes. The point is that if a person doesn't bring himself close to Allah ﷻ, his Imaan will be destroyed. So too if a person doesn't bring himself close to the Holy Prophet ﷺ, he'll lose his religion. Shaikh Abdul-Haqq Muhaddith Dehlwi ؒ states that although many sects became existent amongst Muslims and had severe differences between them, all of them still agreed that the Holy Prophet ﷺ is present and aware everywhere. This is why every person recites the following in the At-Tahiyaat of Salaah,

السلام عليك ايها النبى
'Peace be upon you, O Prophet ﷺ.'

Every person will gain the vision of the Holy Messenger ﷺ in the grave, irrespective of where he or she may die or be buried. When you enter a house and there's no one present inside, you say the following,

السلام عليك ايها ورحمة الله وبركاته
'Peace be upon you, O Beloved Prophet ﷺ, and Allah's ﷻ mercy and blessings.'

Several verses, ahadith and rulings of the Jurists prove that the Holy Prophet ﷺ is present and aware. There are many Islamic rules based on this quality of his. Refer to my book *Ja'al-Haqq* for a complete discussion on this.

The verse also states, "The wives of the Prophet ﷺ are the mothers of the faithful." This is also joined to the Holy Prophet's ﷺ quality of being 'Aulā' (more worthy/close, etc). We have the bloodline of our fathers, and the effect of this is that they've been declared the owners of our lives and wealth. Obedience to the father has been made obligatory. Any woman who enters into marriage with the father is prohibited for the son (and she's also considered the mother of the son). We came into existence through the Noor of the Holy Prophet ﷺ, and he is the source of everything. So, the fortunate lady whom the Holy Prophet ﷺ marries (and who stays in his marriage) is to be respected by us as a mother, although this is in respect to certain commands, not in all. Marriage with them is prohibited and they are to be respected like our mothers – in fact, more than that – but to see them without a covering or to travel alone with them is not permissible.

Also, the relatives of the blessed wives (i.e. their brothers, sisters, etc) aren't the uncles or aunts of Muslims, so it's permissible to marry them. For example, Sayyidah Aisha 🕮 is the mother of the believers, but her brother, Hadrat Abdur-Rahman ibn Abu Bakr 🕮, isn't the uncle of the Muslims. Sayyidah Aisha's 🕮 sister, Sayyidah Asmā bint Abu Bakr 🕮, is also not the aunt of the believers. Muslims married the relatives of the Blessed Wives of the Holy Prophet 🕮.

> Hadrat Ali's 🕮 judgment and knowledge is extensively reported in the books of Jurisprudence even today. Which madrassah did he attend to gain this knowledge? What were the books he studied? No, dear readers. It was all due to the blessings of that prophetic dua.

Just as how respect for the Blessed Wives is necessary, so too is respect necessary for all believing relatives of the Holy Prophet 🕮. In fact, respect for even his descendants (سادات) is necessary. Honoring them is imperative on Muslims, and speaking ill of them or causing them grief is totally forbidden (haraam) and necessitates Rasoolullah's 🕮 anger. Interestingly, why is utilizing Zakaat haraam upon all descendants of the Prophet 🕮? Simply because Zakaat is the impurity of wealth. How then can impurity be given to them?

Similarly, to keep the descendants of the Holy Prophet 🕮 as meager servants, giving them abhorred tasks, or using offensive language on them is severely prohibited. Dedicate respectful vocations to them and make them knowledgeable. From their home, we attained the Kalima, Islam, Imaan, the Quran, and even Allah 🕮 Himself. So, it's necessary for us to confer kindness upon this beneficial and august family. Ponder upon this verse,

قل لا اسئلكم عليه اجرا الا المودة فى القربى

'(O Beloved 🕮,) Say, "I don't demand any compensation for this propagation except that you have love for relations."'
– Surah Shūrā (42), Verse 23

Under the commentary of the verse in discussion, the author of *Tafseer Roohul-Bayaan* states, "It's not befitting for a spiritual disciple (مريد) to marry the divorced wife of his spiritual master (مرشد). Likewise, it's not befitting for a student to marry the divorced wife of his teacher. Even though marriage with her is totally permissible as per the Islamic verdict, it's contrary to piety, and piety (taqwā) takes priority over the verdict (fatwā). If these marriages do occur, the individual will not see goodness in this world nor in the Hereafter.

لَقَدْ كَانَ لَكُمْ فِى رَسُوْلِ اللهِ أُسْوَةٌ حَسَنَةٌ لِّمَن كَانَ يَرْجُوا اللهَ وَالْيَوْمَ الْاٰخِرَ وَذَكَرَ اللهَ كَثِيْرًا

'Certainly you have an excellent model in the following of the Messenger of Allah ﷺ for him who hopes in Allah ﷺ and the Last Day and (who) remembers Allah ﷺ in abundance.'
– Surah Ahzāb (33), Verse 21

This verse is also the praise of the Holy Prophet ﷺ. Here, Muslims are told, "If you hope for blessings from Allah ﷺ and success in the Hereafter, make the blessed life of Rasoolullah ﷺ a model to follow." This verse mentions the blessings of the Holy Prophet ﷺ in two ways,

Firstly, making his blessed life the model for our lives is the means of success (and this is the very meaning of *wasīlah*, i.e. medium/intermediary). The Holy Beloved ﷺ is the greatest intermediary for Muslims.

Secondly, this command applies to all Muslims, regardless of what country or era they're from. The meaning will then be, "All Muslims until the Day of Judgment should make their lives adhere to the Holy Prophet ﷺ."

It's apparent that there are some Muslims who are kings, some who are subjects, some who are wealthy, some who are poor, some who have palatial homes, and some who have no homes at all. Now, everyone desires for his or her life to be in accordance to the Holy Messenger's ﷺ life, but with so much difference and contrast, how can he be an example for all of us?

The verse therefore states, "The life of My Beloved ﷺ is so unique and matchless that everyone can make it an example to follow." Nobody led a life like Rasoolullah ﷺ. Sayyiduna Esa عليه السلام spent his life in abstinence from the world, to the extent that he didn't even build a home for himself! One who practices abstinence *can* make this prophet's life a model to follow, but a king or ruler cannot. The life of Sayyiduna Sulaiman عليه السلام, on the other hand, was spent in kingship and rule. So, kings and rulers can make his life an example to follow, but his life isn't an example for the mendicant. There are other examples of this. *Subhanallah!* It's only the glory of our Beloved Prophet ﷺ that *all people* - king *and* subjects, the wealthy *and* the beggars - are told, "Come! See the life of My Beloved ﷺ and follow him."

The being of the Beloved Messenger ﷺ is an example for every category and level of humans. His trust in Allah ﷺ (توكل) was so magnificent that for two months, no fire to prepare food was lit in his blessed home. The Holy Prophet ﷺ and his family made do with only dates and water!

The poor and needy of the Ummah should look at this condition and also demonstrate patience. Those who wish to lead their lives with kingship and dominion, however, should keep the following example of the Prophet's ﷺ life in mind: Makkah was eventually conquered and all those non-Muslims who'd wreaked havoc and hardship on the Prophet ﷺ and his followers were standing before him as the city's conqueror. This was the day for revenge, yet what did our Beloved ﷺ choose? As soon as the city was conquered, he made a grand proclamation of safety in the following manner, "Safety is for those who enter the homes of Abu Sufyan, for those who close the door of their home, or for those who throw down their weapons." The ten brothers of Sayyiduna Yusuf عليه السلام oppressed him for a couple of hours. When they came to him for grain during his rule in Egypt, he said,

لا تثريب عليكم اليوم ، يغفر الله لكم

'There's no reproach today on you today. May Allah ﷻ forgive you.'
– Surah Yusuf (12), Verse 92

However, for *13 years*, the Prophet ﷺ, his Companions, the household of Rasoolullah ﷺ, and even their family members endured oppression and difficulties at the hands of Makkah's disbelievers. Their lives, wealth and honor were all threatened by them, to the extent that they eventually had to leave their city and move to another area. Yet, the day Makkah was conquered, the Prophet ﷺ forgave all of them. Kings and rulers until the Day of Qiyaamat should make this an example for themselves.

Those who wish for leadership and wealth should consider the following incidents of Rasoolullah's ﷺ life: The farm of a person once produced a very big cucumber. The owner presented it to the Holy Prophet ﷺ as a gift, yet in return, the Prophet ﷺ gave him a handful of gold. Once, an entire valley of goats came into the ownership of Rasoolullah ﷺ. Someone said to him, "Allah ﷻ has now made you very wealthy." Rasoolullah ﷺ asked, "What makes you say so?" The man replied, "All of these goats are now yours." The Holy Prophet ﷺ then said, "I've given all of these goats to you." This person then went to his community with the goats and said, "O People, bring faith! Oath on the Lord, Muhammad the Messenger of Allah ﷺ gives so much that he doesn't even fear poverty."

The Holy Messenger ﷺ once bestowed so much to Hadrat Abbas ؓ that he was unable to carry what was given! All of these incidents are recorded in the

Ahadith, and Allama Karputi ﷺ has compiled them in a single work (i.e. his commentary of *Dalāilul-Khairāt*). Those with wealth and luxury should remember these incidents and spend even their *lives* for the pleasure of Allah ﷻ.

When it comes to domestic life with family and spouse, a person can have a maximum of four wives. The Holy Prophet ﷺ, however, had 9 at one stage of his blessed life. He also interacted with many people daily, such as his children, grandchildren, son-in-laws, slaves, guests and supporters. Still, none of these interactions deterred him from the worship and remembrance of Allah ﷻ.

A person who wishes to lead a life of abstinence from the world should refer to Rasoolullah's ﷺ worship, abstinence and spiritual strife in the cave of Hira. The *Kitaabur-Riqāq* found in compilations of Ahadith have recorded this here. Indeed, if his life was made the ideal by every nation of the world, all would be able to live in peace and satisfaction.

The strength and courage of the Noble Messenger ﷺ is apparent from the following incidents: During the Battle of Hunain, Rasoolullah ﷺ was alone on his ride and the non-Muslims found a chance to surround him (while the Muslim army was dispersed). When he noticed this, he descended from his ride and proclaimed, "I'm not a false prophet. I am the grandson of Abdul-Muttalib ﷺ." No non-Muslim had the courage to face him after this. Rasoolullah ﷺ came down from his ride even though Hadrat Abbas ﷺ and Hadrat Sufyan ﷺ held its reins!

Abu Rukana was a famous and undefeated wrestler, yet Rasoolullah ﷺ brought him to the ground thrice! He even praised Rasoolullah ﷺ for this. Yet even though Rasoolullah ﷺ possessed such strength and might, his mercy was that he never hurt anyone, nor did he hit his blessed servants or wives.

In short, the blessed life of the Holy Prophet ﷺ was an example of splendor and grace for all of us. This is why the verse makes a general proclamation, "*All people* should make his blessed life an example."

Another meaning of the verse is that the being and life of the Holy Prophet ﷺ is the ideal example from Allah ﷻ to lead our lives. The author of *Tafseer Roohul-Bayaan* expressed another point in this discussion: Following the Prophet ﷺ as an example refers to our lives. However, another meaning that can be ascribed to the verse is that 'coming after Rasoolullah ﷺ is most excellent for you'. In other words, the Prophet ﷺ is the ideal example in the

Realm of Souls – in fact, every realm – and we are his followers. His Noor was created first and we were created from it afterwards. His soul was the first to receive Divine guidance while we received it afterwards. It was the soul of the Holy Prophet ﷺ who answered, "Indeed, You are," when Allah ﷻ asked, "Am I not your Lord?" We then answered afterwards. Rasoolullah's ﷺ soul was the first to exit Sayyiduna Adam عليه السلام for the covenant with Allah ﷻ, and our souls followed him. So, it's now necessary on us to follow him in our lives, just as how we followed him in everything else!

VERSE 60

يَٰنِسَاءَ النَّبِيِّ لَسْتُنَّ كَأَحَدٍ مِّنَ النِّسَاءِ

'O Wives of the Prophet ﷺ, you are not like other women.'
– Surah Ahzāb (33), Verse 32

The verses preceding and following this verse outwardly offer guidance to the Holy Prophet's ﷺ blessed wives and proclaims their excellence, yet in reality they are truly the praise of the Prophet ﷺ himself. The verse proclaims, "O Wives of the Prophet ﷺ, you are not like other women. Your rank and commands are different from others." However, this rank and excellence is due to the fact that they *are* the wives of the Holy Prophet ﷺ. When this is the greatness of simply being associated with Rasoolullah ﷺ, imagine how intense is the honor of the Prophet ﷺ himself!

The following points emerge from this verse,

1. The wives of the Holy Prophet ﷺ are more excellent than the womenfolk of the entire world. There's no restriction on the word 'women' in this verse. Sayyidah Maryam ﷞ and Sayyidah Āsiya ﷞ (who's the wife of Firoun and the foster mother of Sayyiduna Musa عليه السلام) were the most excellent of womenfolk during their respective times on Earth. The blessed wives of the Holy Prophet ﷺ, however, are the most excellent of womenfolk of every era. Allah ﷻ states about the Bani Israel,

أني فضلتكم على العلمين

'And I exalted you over the entire world.'
– Surah Bani Israel (17), Verse 47

So, the Bani Israel were truly exalted over the people of that time. Now, however, the Ummah of the Holy Prophet ﷺ is the most excellent and exalted of nations.

2. There's a debate over whether Sayyidah Fathima ﷺ is more excellent than Sayyidah Aisha ﷺ. Some Scholars say that Sayyidah Aisha Siddiqah ﷺ was more excellent based on this verse, and that the blessed wives were more excellent than all the blessed daughters of the Holy Prophet ﷺ (because there's no restriction in the verse). Daughters are children while wives are mothers, and a mother is served by children. Sayyidah Aisha ﷺ and the other blessed wives will be with Rasoolullah ﷺ in Jannah, while Sayyidah Fathima ﷺ will be with Hadrat Ali ﷺ. Based on these reasons, we come to know that the blessed wives are more excellent than the daughters.

Still, some scholars maintain that Sayyidah Fathima Zahra ﷺ is more excellent than the blessed wives. The pure blood of Rasoolullah ﷺ flows in her veins. In other words, her purity is inherent while the others' is extraneous.

> 'Muhammad' can also mean *he who's praised by everyone*. In other words, the entire creation praises him…in fact, even the Creator praises him! Rasoolullah ﷺ has always been praised. Praise for him began before the creation of the world and it will last to the Day of Judgment (and even beyond it). The Beloved Messenger ﷺ will also always *be* praised. His praise is found everywhere – on the Earth, in the Heavens, in the depths of the ocean…every place imaginable!

Sayyidah Fathima ﷺ is the leader of the womenfolk of Jannah (hence her title, *Sayyidatun-Nisā*, 'the Leader of Womenfolk'). This is a notable point because the blessed wives of the Prophet ﷺ are *also* women of Jannah. Furthermore, Sayyidah Fathima ﷺ resembled the Holy Prophet ﷺ and was free from *haiz & nifās*. – *Madaarijun-Nubuwwah*

This is also why she's called *Zahra* (a fragrant flower of Paradise), *Fathima* and *Batool* (both meaning 'to abstain from the world even though one lives in it').

The Holy Prophet ﷺ would smell Sayyidah Fathima ﷺ and say, "I attain the fragrance of Jannah from her." – *Mabsūt Sarkashi, Kitaabul-Karaahiyat, Baabul-Lams*

However, we shouldn't even discuss such matters. (*Shaami, Baabul-Kafn* has advised the same.) Both Sayyidahs are our masters. If one is the beloved of the Messenger 🕊, then the other is the "coolness of his eyes". If we attain the honor of even carrying their sandals on our heads on the Day of Judgment, success is surely destined for us. Still, if one wishes that a decision be made, I submit, "In certain aspects, Sayyidah Fathima 🌸 is more excellent, and in other aspects, Sayyidah Aisha 🌸 is."

3. The wives of Rasoolullah 🕊 aren't like other women even with regards to the commands of Islam. A female can marry again after divorce or the death of her husband, but the Blessed Wives are the *Mothers* of the Faithful. A wife inherits from the estate of her late husband, but the Blessed Wives didn't inherit anything from the estate of the Noble Messenger 🕊. Women experience *ihtilām* (nocturnal dreaming) while the Blessed Wives didn't. Ihtilām is caused by the effect of Shaitaan, so how can the cursed wretch effect the Blessed Wives of Rasoolullah 🕊? Sayyidah Umme-Salma 🌸 heard of the ihtilām of women and was surprised by it. – *Mishkaat, Baabul-Ghusl*

After the demise of the Noble Messenger 🕊, the Blessed Wives also cut the hair from their heads. – *Muslim, Discussion on the Amount of Water for Ghusl*

They did this because they didn't have any need for beautification anymore. However, it's impermissible (حرام) for other women to cut their hair. The Holy Prophet 🕊 was also buried in the room of one of his blessed wives, while the husbands of other women cannot be buried in their homes. In short, there are major differences with regards to Islamic commands when speaking of the Blessed Wives.

Indeed, the Mothers of the Faithful are the most excellent of all womenfolk, yet there's a contrast of excellence amongst them. Sayyidah Khadija 🌸 and Sayyidah Aisha 🌸 are more excellent than the other Blessed Wives. Sayyidah Aisha 🌸 was a very young lady when Rasoolullah 🕊 made nikah with her, while Sayyidah Khadija 🌸 was the first person he married. The Messenger 🕊 also didn't perform any other nikah while Sayyidah Khadija 🌸 was alive (and his progeny spread from her). He always performed *udhiya* (qurbani, sacrifice) on her behalf.

On the other hand, the knowledge and wisdom of Sayyidah Aisha ؓ was unrivalled amongst womenfolk. She'd regularly resolve the knowledgeable differences of the Sahaabah. Her title is 'The Beloved of Allah's Beloved ﷺ.' Revelation came to the Prophet ﷺ while he was in her bedstead, Sayyiduna Jibrael ؑ made salaam to her, the Holy Prophet ﷺ passed away on her chest and lap, and her room will be visited by angels, believing humans and jinns until Qiyaamat (because it's the sacred burial place of Rasoolullah ﷺ). Even the Holy Quran (in Surah Noor) proclaimed her chastity and modesty when she was being accused by some. So, Muslims will recite the Holy Quran and testify to her purity until the end of days.

'She whose witness is Surah Noor,
May thousands of salutations be on her countenance of Noor.'

VERSE 61

وَمَا كَانَ لِمُؤْمِنٍ ٥ وَلَا مُؤْمِنَةٍ إِذَا قَضَى اللهُ وَرَسُوْلُهُ أَمْرًا أَنْ يَكُوْنَ لَهُمُ الْخِيَرَةُ مِنْ أَمْرِهِمْ

'And it's not befitting for a Muslim man and a Muslim
woman when Allah ﷻ and His Messenger ﷺ have decreed something
that they should have any choice in their matters.'
– Surah Ahzāb (33), Verse 36

This verse is explicit praise of the Holy Prophet ﷺ *and* it discusses his power granted to him by Allah ﷻ. The reason for its revelation is that Hadrat Zaid ibn Haaritha ؓ was emancipated by the Holy Prophet ﷺ yet he remained in his service. Rasoolullah ﷺ made a proposal of marriage for him to Sayyidah Zainub bint Jahsh ؓ, the daughter of the Prophet's ﷺ maternal aunt, Ameema bint Abdul-Muttalib ؓ. The proposal wasn't accepted by Sayyidah Zainab ؓ and her brother Hadrat Abdullah ibn Jahsh ؓ because she was from a lofty family of the Quraish tribe while Hadrat Zaid ؓ didn't have such a background. This verse was therefore revealed, proclaiming, "O Muslims, when Allah ﷻ and His Messenger ﷺ give a command regarding your lives, wealth or anything else, you don't have a right to interject. It's necessary on you to humbly accept the command."

Sayyidah Zainab ؓ and her brother agreed to the marriage after hearing this verse and the nikah was made. The mehr (dowry) given to Sayyidah Zainab ؓ was 10 dinars, 60 dirhams, a set of clothing, 50 *mudd* (a measurement) of food items, and 3 *sā'* (another measurement) of dates – all provided by Rasoolullah ﷺ.

The following points are understood by this incident,

1. The command of Allah ﷻ and Rasoolullah ﷺ are equally necessary to be fulfilled (i.e. commands found in the Holy Quran and Ahadith). Allah ﷻ says in this verse, "...when Allah ﷻ and His Messenger ﷺ have decreed something." In fact, Allah's ﷻ proclamations reached us solely through the Holy Prophet ﷺ. The difference between the Holy Quran and the Ahadith is that the Holy Quran's subject matter and wording have both been revealed as revelation. The Ahadith's subject matter is also sourced from revelation, but its wording is the Holy Prophet's ﷺ. This is why the Ahadith are not recited in Salaah. If it's conclusively established and proven that a Hadith is *Sahih* (correct in transmission), it necessitates our respect almost the same as the Holy Quran. Also, if the Hadith is successively proven as correct, it can even abrogate the Holy Quran – and to refute it is infidelity (کفر). However, if there is credible doubt regarding the authenticity of a Hadith, rejecting it will not be an act of infidelity (due to the doubt) and it won't abrogate the Holy Quran. Salaah, fasting, Zakaat, Hajj, etc. are all proven by the Holy Quran but the times of Salaah, its number and rakaats, the amount for Zakaat, the procedure of dispensing it, the compulsory acts of fasting, the conditions and procedure of Hajj, etc. are all proven from the Ahadith. In fact, the classification of all thirty parts of the Holy Quran, whether its 114 Surahs are Makki or Madani, and the place where a particular verse was revealed are all established by the Ahadith. So, we *have* to conclude that it is necessary in the deen.

2. The Holy Messenger ﷺ is the *Malik* (owner/master) of the lives, wealth, children...in fact, *everything* belonging to the Muslims. Just as how no slave has the right to reject the command of a master, so too does no believer have the right to refute Rasoolullah's ﷺ command. Marriage proposals are generally presented to a girl and her family (and they either accept or reject them). But look at this marriage proposal, that neither Hadrat Abdullah ibn Jahsh ؓ nor Sayyidah Zainab ؓ had the right to reject it! This wasn't a mere marriage proposal but the command of the Holy Prophet ﷺ. Likewise, permission is taken from the girl to make her nikah to a certain person (and again, she has the right to accept or reject it) but Sayyidah Zainab ؓ didn't have this right. This is the extent of the Prophet's ﷺ dominion.

No believer has the right to refute a proclamation made by Rasoolullah ﷺ as a prophetic command. Accepting whatever he utters as advice is better, but a person has a right to not accept it. Therefore, the verse refers to the former by using the word *qadā* (i.e. decree).

Sayyidah Barirah's ﷺ nikah had been made with Hadrat Mughith ﷺ before she could be emancipated. She attained the right to annul the marriage after she was freed (and desired annulling it). The Holy Prophet ﷺ interceded on behalf of Hadrat Mughith ﷺ for her not to annul the marriage. She asked Rasoolullah ﷺ whether it was a command from him or just advice. He replied that it was just advice. Sayyidah Barīrah ﷺ then said, "If this is advice, indeed I'm not content with Mughīth ﷺ," and she then terminated the nikah.

3. If a prophetic announcement conforms to our nature, we should praise Allah ﷻ and thank Him for this; but if the command is contrary to our disposition, opinion or intelligence, we should regard it to be in fact a fault of our own nature or intelligence and compel ourselves to obey the command as we'll see goodness in doing so, Insha-Allah ﷻ. Objecting to the command is a sign of misfortune. *Kufu* (compatibility) is taken into account in nikah. Hadrat Zaid ﷺ was outwardly not compatible with Sayyidah Zainab ﷺ, but when a prophetic command was given, it took precedence over everything else.

The respected author of *Tafseer Roohul-Bayaan* states in the commentary of this verse that it's befitting for a spiritual disciple (مرید) to accept the command of his spiritual master (مرشد) without any objections or reasoning. Maulana Jalaaluddin Rumi ﷺ states,

> *'Choose a spiritual guide for the journey on the spiritual path because there's no danger if one does so.'*

> *'After choosing him, become the personification of acceptance and pleasure. Sayyiduna Khidr عليه السلام said to Sayyiduna Musa عليه السلام, 'Don't object to anything about me."*

Maulana Rumi ﷺ then says,

> *'If he destroys a ship, don't question him.*
> *If he kills a child, don't object.'*

However, this is the respect to be displayed to an *accomplished* spiritual master. An incomplete one is a means of destruction. Pledging allegiance to a misguided or sinful "spiritual guide" is a severe form of oppression. Who then is an accomplished spiritual master? Insha-Allah ﷻ, this discussion will follow later in the book.

VERSE 62

مَا كَانَ مُحَمَّدٌ اَبَا اَحَدٍ مِّنْ رِّجَالِكُمْ وَلٰكِن رَّسُوْلَ الله وَخَاتَمَ النَّبِيِّيْنَ

'Muhammad ﷺ isn't the father of any of your men, but he's the
Messenger of Allah ﷻ and the Seal of the Prophets.'
– Surah Ahzāb (33), Verse 40

This verse is explicit praise of the Holy Prophet ﷺ. The following points will be discussed regarding it,

1. The reason for its revelation.

2. The knowledgeable points which emerge from it.

3. The meaning of 'Seal of the Prophets'.

The connection this verse shares with the verses preceding it is that, after the nikah of Sayyidah Zainub ؓ was made with Hadrat Zaid ؓ, it was the planning of Allah ﷻ that some discord took place between them (and Hadrat Zaid ؓ divorced Sayyidah Zainub ؓ). The Prophet ﷺ then entered into the nikah of Sayyidah Zainub ؓ, as mentioned in the verse,

فلما فضى زيد منها وطرا زوجنكها

'When Zaid ؓ severed relations with her, We gave her in marriage to you.'
– Surah Ahzāb (33), Verse 37

Sayyidah Zainub ؓ would proudly say, "The marriages of people are made by their family members, but my nikah was made by the Lord in the Heavens."

The Prophet ﷺ had previously adopted Hadrat Zaid ibn Haaritha ؓ as his son, so some disbelievers objected to the marriage and said, "Muhammad married the wife of his son!" Allah ﷻ *Himself* answered their objection in this verse, saying, "The command of prohibition is related to biological sons, and My Beloved ﷺ isn't the father of any of you. So how can he have a son? And since My Beloved ﷺ doesn't have one, how can the ex-wife of Zaid ؓ be impermissible for him?"

This verse proves to be the praise of the Holy Prophet ﷺ for the following reasons,

1. An objection is made against the Holy Prophet ﷺ yet it's Allah ﷻ Who answers it. Allah ﷻ didn't say to His Messenger ﷺ, "O My Beloved ﷺ, *you* say to them…" This means that objecting to the Holy Messenger ﷺ is actually an objection against Allah ﷻ. Look carefully: the verse before this said, "*We* gave her in marriage to you." Now who can object to this?

2. The Holy Quran never spoke of the Holy Prophet ﷺ by name except in four places. They are,

وما محمد الا رسول
'And Muhammad ﷺ is but a Messenger.'
– Surah Ale-Imran (3), Verse 144

ما كان محمد ابا احد من رجالكم
'Muhammad ﷺ isn't the father of any of your men.'
– Surah Ahzāb (33), Verse 40

بما نزل على محمد
'…what has been revealed upon Muhammad ﷺ.'
– Surah Muhammad (47), Verse 2

محمد رسول الله
'Muhammad ﷺ is the Messenger of Allah ﷻ.'
– Surah Fat'h (48), Verse 29

There's great wisdom in Rasoolullah's ﷺ blessed name being mentioned in only four places. The name of Muhammad ﷺ is also made up of four letters (in Arabic). Allah ﷻ knows well the significance of four.

'Muhammad' is the actual name (اسم ذاتی) of the Holy Prophet ﷺ while his other blessed names are descriptive (اسماء الصفات), just as how 'Allah' is the Almighty's true name while His other blessed names are descriptive. This word, Muhammad, has great affinity with the word Allah. Muhammad is made up of four letters and Allah too consists of four. Muhammad has a *tashdīd* (doubling of a consonant) and Allah also has a tashdīd. However, there's an alif on the tashdeed of Allah ﷻ while there's no alif on the tashdeed of Muhammad ﷺ. The wisdom behind this is that the Almighty is the Supreme King and Master, and Muhammad ﷺ is His greatest viceroy. When we say the word 'Allah', our lips are separated, and when we say the word 'Muhammad', our lips are joined. This is for us to understand that Allah's ﷻ being is so grand that we as His servants are unable to reach Him while Muhammad'ur-Rasoolullah ﷺ makes us lower beings reach the Supreme Being.

There are eleven letters in 'Laa ilaaha illallaah' and eleven letters in 'Muhammad'ur-Rasoolullah ﷺ'. Likewise, 'Abu Bakr Siddique', 'Umar ibn Khattab', 'Uthman ibn Affan', and 'Ali ibn Abi Taalib' all comprise of eleven letters each. The word 'Muhammad' has an efficacious nature. If a person who has only daughters wishes for a son, he should write with his finger on the stomach of his pregnant wife,

من كان فى هذا البطن فاسمه محمد

"Whoever's in this stomach will be named 'Muhammad'."

This practice should be done for forty days from the inception of the pregnancy and, Insha-Allah ﷻ, a son will be born to him. – *Roohul-Bayaan*

I've already explained a few distinctions of the word 'Muhammad' in verse 174 of Surah Nisā (4) [Verse 22 in book]. At this point, the meaning of 'Muhammad' has to be understood. 'Muhammad' means *he who's worthy of every kind of praise* (since there's no defect or imperfection in him). He who calls the Holy Prophet ﷺ 'Muhammad' but finds faults with him is a person proven to be a liar by his own utterance. This is why the disbelievers used to call Rasoolullah ﷺ 'Muzammim' (reprehensible) and slander him. The Prophet ﷺ, however, said, "Allah ﷻ has saved me from their slander. They call me Muzammim but I am Muhammad ﷺ." The word 'Muhammad' can also mean *he who's praised by everyone*. In other words, the entire creation praises him...in fact, even the Creator praises him! Rasoolullah ﷺ has always been praised. Praise for him began before the creation of the world and it will last to the Day of Judgment (and even beyond it). The Beloved Messenger ﷺ will also always be praised. His praise is found everywhere – on the Earth, in the Heavens, in the depths of the ocean…every place imaginable!

'Muhammad' is also comprised of two *meems*, one *haa* and one *daal*. The two *meems* refer to the dominions (ملكية) of this world and the Hereafter, the *haa* refers to mercy (رحمة) and the *daal* is indicative of being constant (دائمى). In other words, the Holy Prophet ﷺ is the constant mercy to both this world and the Hereafter! – *Dalaailul-Khairaat Sharif*

"Muhammad ﷺ isn't the father of any of your men," means he's the father of [his daughters] Sayyidah Fathima, Ruqayya, Umme-Kulthum and Zainub ؏, not the father of any male. His male children (Hadrat Ibrahim, Tayyib, Tahir and Qasim ؏) all passed away during infancy. So, they cannot be classified as men. Another point which emerges is that when no one has the right to even call the Holy Prophet ﷺ 'father', calling him 'brother' is firmly established as haraam.

Khātam'un-Nabiyeen (The Seal of the Prophets) means that Rasoolullah ﷺ is the Prophet of Allah ﷻ and Last of the Prophets. Khātam is derived from 'khatm' which means *seal* or *last*. In fact, a seal is called 'khatm' in Arabic because it comes at the end, or is called 'khātam' because once an envelope is sealed, nothing can be added to or removed from it. So too has the progression of prophethood been sealed – the last rose in the garden of prophethood has bloomed. Rasoolullah ﷺ himself explained the meaning of 'Seal of Prophets' when he said,

لا نبى بعدى
'There's no prophet after me.'

Therefore, to believe that someone can be a shadow of a prophet, or a temporary prophet, or any other imaginary type of prophet after the Holy Messenger ﷺ is apostasy. Likewise, the person who interprets 'Seal of the Prophets' to mean *a prophet by being* or believes that it's possible for a new prophet to emerge is also an apostate. Indeed, Sayyiduna Esa عليه السلام will return to the world yet he will not be a new prophet after our Beloved ﷺ. He will in fact return as a follower (امتى) of the Islamic Law laid down by Rasoolullah ﷺ. 'Last son' refers to the son after whom no other son was born. It doesn't mean that the sons born before him don't exist. So, although

Sayyiduna Esa ﷺ, Khidr ﷺ, Idris ﷺ and Ilyas ﷺ existed with worldly life during the Holy Prophet's ﷺ time (and are alive even now), they attained prophethood before him, and their respective commands were annulled with the advent of Rasoolullah ﷺ. When the sun appears, the stars become hidden wherever they may be. Similarly, Sayyiduna Khidr ﷺ and Sayyiduna Ilyas ﷺ are alive on the Earth while Sayyiduna Esa ﷺ and Sayyiduna Idris ﷺ are alive in the Heavens. With the advent of Rasoolullah ﷺ however, their respective orders are no longer applicable. When a judge goes to the courtroom of another judge to give testimony, although the former is a judge in his own right, he has come to the latter's solely as a witness. Like this, Sayyiduna Esa ﷺ was the prophet of his time, but he will return in the reign of the Holy Prophet ﷺ. So, his prophethood will not be propagated.

Another point to keep in mind is that prophethood has a relation to the Creator as well as to the creation. Grand rank, esteem, and proximity with Allah ﷻ is the dimension of prophethood related to the Creator. This magnitude of prophethood can never be diminished or removed. Propagation (تبلیغ) to people is the dimension of prophethood related to the creation. Sayyiduna Esa ﷺ isn't obligated to this responsibility when he returns (he won't propagate the commands of his former Law). When Sayyiduna Musa ﷺ went to meet Sayyiduna Khidr ﷺ, Sayyiduna Khidr ﷺ said to him, "O Musa ﷺ, you are the prophet of the Bani Israel! Don't object to any of my actions." – *Surah Kahf (18), Verse 70*

In other words, Sayyiduna Musa's ﷺ religious laws weren't binding on Sayyiduna Khidr ﷺ. Whatever Sayyiduna Khidr ﷺ did were all actions contrary to the Law of Sayyiduna Musa ﷺ (he killed a child before the child became sinful, etc.). Still, Sayyiduna Musa ﷺ couldn't enforce his laws on him. Why? Did he lose his prophethood? No! He was *still* a prophet, but propagating his Law at this instance wasn't his duty. The condition of Sayyiduna Esa ﷺ in the reign of the Holy Prophet ﷺ can be understood similarly.

VERSE 63

يَا أَيُّهَا النَّبِيُّ إِنَّا أَرْسَلْنَاكَ شَهِدًا وَّمُبَشِّرًا وَّنَذِيْرًا ، وَدَاعِيًا إِلَى الله بِإِذْنِه وَسِرَاجًا مُّنِيْرًا

'O Prophet (the communicator of unseen news), surely We
have sent you as a witness, a bearer of glad tidings, a warner, an inviter
towards Allah ﷻ by His command and an illuminating lamp.'
– Surah Ahzāb (33), Verses 45-46

This verse is a collection of praise for the Holy Prophet ﷺ, and it mentions many of his unique qualities. The 8 points of discussion emerging from this verse are (1) the usage of 'O', (2) the words 'Prophet/Nabi', (3) 'We have sent you', (4) 'Witness', (5) 'Bearer of glad tidings, (6) 'Warner', (7) 'An Inviter towards Allah ﷻ', and (8) 'An Illuminating Lamp'. Indeed, if a complete discussion on each point had to be made, volumes could be written. We therefore present only a select amount of secrets from these words.

1. 'O' is a call, or vocative particle. A calling is made for the following reasons: to make someone who is negligent attentive, to demonstrate rebuke: 'O wretch!'; to demonstrate grandeur: 'O Muzammil!', i.e. the enwrapped one – Surah Muzammil (73); to demonstrate love: 'O Beloved ﷺ!', etc. Here, the vocative particle has been used to demonstrate love. The Holy Messenger ﷺ was never negligent of Allah ﷻ even for a moment. He is addressed with only the best of titles.

2. There are two meanings to the word 'Nabi': *one who gives news* or *one with good rank*. Although both meanings are applicable here, to apply the first is more appropriate because *information* is implied in the words 'witness' and 'inviter', etc. further in the verse. The Holy Prophet ﷺ is a Prophet, a Messenger, *Muzammil, Mudath'thir*, etc. His quality of 'Nabi' (i.e. Prophet) has been mentioned here, and his title of 'Rasool' (i.e. Messenger) has also been gestured to by '…We have sent you…' (ارسلنك). So here, both his prophethood and messengership have been mentioned.

   If the meaning of 'prophet' is adopted as *he who communicates Our news to the bondsmen* and the meaning of 'witness' is adopted as *he who communicates news of the creation to Us on the Day of Resurrection*, it would be appropriate according to the Scholars of insight. Similarly, 'prophet' and 'witness' can be understood as *the communicator of news* and *the witness of Jannah & Jahannam* respectively.

3. "…We have sent you…" indicates that respect or disrespect to the Holy Prophet ﷺ is actually respect or disrespect to Allah ﷻ Himself, because it's He Who sent His Beloved ﷺ. So, the taunts against the Messenger ﷺ were all answered by Allah ﷻ on behalf of Muhammad'ur-Rasoolullah ﷺ.

4. 'Shaahid' actually has three meanings: (1) Witness, (2) someone present (حاضر), and (3) someone beloved. However, it's literally used for someone who is present. The Holy Quran states,

5.

علم الغيب والشهدة

'(Allah ﷻ) is the Knower of everything absent and present.'
– Surah An'ām (6), Verse 73

'Shaahid' is used both for a witness and a beloved because a witness is present at an occurrence and a beloved is someone always present in the heart of the lover. All the meanings of 'shaahid' are applicable here. 'Witness' is applicable because the Holy Prophet ﷺ will give testimony on the Day of Qiyaamat. Allah ﷻ states,

وجئنا بك على هؤلاء شهيدا

'(O Beloved ﷺ,) We will bring you as a witness against all of them.'
– Surah Nisā (4), Verse 41

All the other Prophets عليهم السلام gave testimony of Jannah and Jahannam based on their hearing, but the Holy Prophet ﷺ did so based on his seeing (on the night of Mi'rāj). So, he's the true witness. It isn't possible for the faith or disbelief of a person attested to by the Holy Messenger ﷺ to change, so he who doubts the Imaan of Hadrat Abu Bakr رضي الله عنه and Hadrat Umar رضي الله عنه is himself a person without deen, because he actually doubts the validity of Rasoolullah's ﷺ attestation. The Holy Prophet ﷺ himself has confirmed their Imaan.

Rasoolullah ﷺ is also the official witness in the dominion of Allah ﷻ, and the testimony of an official witness is accepted without any criticism. In fact, he who challenges his testimony becomes a criminal. The testimony of Imaan or disbelief by the Prophet ﷺ is accepted by Allah ﷻ without any invalidation. This is similar to when an engineer passes or fails a particular building and his ruling is accepted without question, when a university attests to a person's ability by passing or failing him, or when a specialist examines a patient to be healthy or unhealthy. In a court case, the loss or win of either the plaintiff or the defendant is based on witnesses. If the witness is dependable, the lawyer becomes effective and the judgment in the case will be made quickly. If the witness isn't dependable, all hope is lost.

The proof of *tauheed* (the Oneness of Allah ﷻ) in this world is dependent on the Holy Prophet ﷺ, and the entire creation being either inmates of Jannah or Jahannam in the Hereafter also hinges on him. In the Hereafter, all will look towards the Holy Messenger ﷺ because he's the Creator's witness on Earth and the witness of the creation in the Hereafter.

There are many qualities found in a witness, but three are of utmost importance,

1. The witness should be present both at the time of the occurrence and before the judge when giving testimony. This is why a witness is called a 'shaahid' (i.e. someone who's present).

2. A plaintiff wishes for the witness to succeed so that he wins the case. The defendant aims to make the witness fail by attacking his character. So, the defendant objects to the knowledge of the witness and regards him to be unaware.

3. An objection against the witness is actually a remonstration against the plaintiff.

Rasoolullah ﷺ is the witness of Allah ﷻ, Jannah, Jahannam, and all other unseen things for people of this world. So, while remaining in the distinguished proximity of Allah ﷻ before his advent in the world, he witnessed all things and then arrived. The Holy Prophet ﷺ is also the witness of the creation before Allah ﷻ in the Hereafter. So, it's necessary for him to be aware of every condition of the entire creation. Otherwise, what relevance would his testimony have? Today, the knowledge of the Holy Messenger ﷺ is challenged and ridiculed. Regard these challengers and ridiculers as those whom the Holy Prophet ﷺ will testify against. They are defendants, because only those who are testified against attempt to vilify the knowledge of the witness.

Defaming the knowledge and excellence of the Holy Prophet ﷺ is actually opposition to Allah ﷻ (because Rasoolullah ﷺ is His witness).

The Holy Prophet's ﷺ testimony is of four categories,

1. Witness of the Creator before the creation.

2.	Witness of the creation before the Creator.

3.	Witness of the Creator before the Creator.

4.	Witness of the creation before the creation.

Whoever Rasoolullah ﷺ attests to as an inmate of Jannah is truly an inmate of Jannah, and whoever and whatever he declares as good, bad, halaal or haraam is good, bad, halaal or haraam. This is because 'witness' is absolute (مطلق). Whatever is uttered from the blessed mouth of Allah's ﷻ witness is the truth (حق). Just as how a goldmine cannot produce steel, so too can Allah's ﷻ witness not utter falsehood with his blessed tongue.

I've discussed the issue of the Prophet ﷺ being present and aware (حاضر وناظر) in *Tafseer Naeemi, Part 2* comprehensively, and have proven this belief from the Quran, Hadith, and statements of the scholars in *Ja'al-Haqq*. Insha-Allah ﷻ, dissenters will not be able to reply to this.

Doctors say that the strength of a medicine should be more than the illness so that it can fight it. If this isn't the case, the medicine will be overcome by the sickness. Shaitaan is sickness and Rasoolullah ﷺ is the cure. The Holy Quran speaks about Shaitaan,

انه يراكم هو وقبيله من حيث لا ترونهم

'Certainly he and his tribe see you where you see them not.'
– Surah A'rāf (7), Verse 27

Shaitaan and his kin see us at all times. He keeps his eye on the entire creation, and when someone intends doing good, he leads that person astray. If the Holy Prophet ﷺ is regarded as unaware and unable, Allah ﷻ could then be slandered as creating the illness strong and the cure weak. So, it's necessary for Rasoolullah ﷺ to be aware of everyone at all times for the purpose of offering salvation.

According to Arabic grammar, 'shaahid' here is in the present tense (حال). So, the meaning of the verse is, "We have sent you in the state of you being present and aware (حاضر وناظر)." Meaning, the Holy Prophet ﷺ was already present and aware before being sent. We have to therefore conclude that before coming to the world, Rasoolullah was present amongst the creation and is present amongst the creation even after his demise.

Under the commentary of Verse 8 of Surah Fat'h (48), the respected author of *Tafseer Roohul-Bayaan* says that the Holy Prophet ﷺ was witnessing the Oneness and Lordship of Allah ﷻ even before the creation of the world. He also witnessed the creation of the souls, physical bodies, animals, plant-life, jinns, devils, angels, and human beings. Likewise, every action, doing and effort of all of creation was viewed by Rasoolullah ﷺ. He saw how Shaitaan was first a worshipper and then became rejected, he saw the mistake of Sayyiduna Adam عليه السلام, his repentence being accepted, the time he stayed in Jannah, his advent in this world, the advents of the other Prophets عليهم السلام, their efforts of propagation, the conduct of their nations (good and bad), etc. In short, all occurrences were witnessed by the Noble Messenger ﷺ. This is why a Hadith states, "I know whatever was and whatever will come to pass." This is definitely true, because the world exists through the blessed being of the Beloved Prophet ﷺ. The knowledge of all the Prophets عليهم السلام is only a part of his knowledge. The *sahīfa* of Sayyiduna Adam عليه السلام and the Book of Sayyiduna Musa عليه السلام are only chapters in his volumes of knowledge.

The respected author then states that every fortunate and pious person is under the Holy Prophet's ﷺ blessed gaze of mercy, and it's he who is Raqeeb (a guardian) over them. When the blessed gaze moves away from people, they become unfortunate and commit sin. The error of Sayyiduna Adam عليه السلام was due to this. A Hadith gestures to this too, "When a fornicator commits fornication, his faith is removed from him, and when he steps away from it, it returns." Imaan (faith) is the attention of Rasoolullah ﷺ. Based on this interpretation, the meaning of 'shaahid' (witness) as being present and aware (حاضر وناظر) for the Prophet ﷺ, him possessing knowledge of the unseen, and his ability to assist is clearly established.

'Shaahid' (witness) can also mean *beloved*, and indeed, the Prophet ﷺ is the beloved of the entire creation. Human beings, jinns, angels, trees, stones, etc. have love for him. Even the mountain of Uhud has love for him, and pieces of wood cry out of separation from him. When animals saw him, they embraced him and complained to him, deers implored his kindness, etc. In short, every heart beats with the love of Rasoolullah ﷺ.

Affection for the Prophets عليهم السلام is one of their miracles. Allah ﷻ said to Sayyiduna Musa عليه السلام,

والقيت عليك محبة مني

'And I cast on you the love from Me.'
– Surah Tāhā (20), Verse 39

He who sees Sayyiduna Musa عليه السلام loves him. When Hadrat Asiya رضي الله عنها saw him, she said to Pharaoh,

قرة عين لي ولك

'This child is comfort for you and me.'
– Surah Qasas (28), Verse 9

The beauty of Sayyiduna Yusuf عليه السلام and the sweet melody of Sayyiduna Dawud's عليه السلام voice were bestowed for the same purpose [generating affection in the hearts of people towards them]. Also, just as how all of the Holy Prophet's ﷺ miracles are most sublime, so too is affection for him not restricted to time or place. Today, there's nobody infatuated with Sayyiduna Yusuf's عليه السلام beauty or Sayyiduna Dawud's عليه السلام sweet voice. No person is a lover of someone in absence today, yet the extent of love for Rasoolullah ﷺ is that there are millions sacrificing their lives on his name even though they have not physically seen him. Those who had affection for Sayyiduna Yusuf's عليه السلام beauty spent their wealth to attain a glance of his splendor, but lives continue to be sacrificed for Muhammad Mustapha ﷺ! Gatherings, marches, lectures, Madrassahs, etc. are all for his sake. Another point to note is that not only human beings become his lovers – even dry wood cried due to being separated from him, and stones recited his Kalima, etc. In short, the Holy Messenger ﷺ is the beloved of both Allah ﷻ and the creation.

5. The verse further mentions three qualities of the Holy Prophet ﷺ: 'a bearer of glad tidings', 'a warner', and 'an inviter towards Allah ﷻ.'

Although the previous Prophets عليهم السلام also possessed these qualities, there are three differences between their propagation and the Holy Prophet's ﷺ. Firstly, the other Prophets عليهم السلام completed these tasks due to their hearing whereas Rasoolullah ﷺ completed them due to his witnessing. Secondly, the other Prophets عليهم السلام were bearers of glad tidings and warners for specific nations whereas the Prophet ﷺ was these things for the entire creation. Thirdly, the Prophets عليهم السلام were bearers of glad tidings and warners for a specific time while Rasoolullah ﷺ is these things until the Day of Judgment. The propagation made by the Scholars and Mashaaikh today is actually the propagation of the Holy Prophet ﷺ. Based on this distinction, these three qualities have been mentioned in this verse. In the commentary of Verse 8 of Surah Fat'h (48), the author of *Tafseer Roohul-Bayaan* says that on the Day of Judgment, the nations of all other Prophets عليهم السلام will number only 40 rows while the Ummah of Rasoolullah ﷺ will number 80!

6. Allah ﷻ describes Rasoolullah ﷺ as an illuminating lamp in this verse. The Holy Quran also called the sun a lamp,

وجعل الشمس سراجا

'And He made the sun a lamp.'
– Surah Nuh (71), Verse 16

If 'sirāj' is interpreted as *sun*, Rasoolullah ﷺ is indeed the sun of the Heaven of salvation. Everything is illuminated by the sun, yet the sun isn't illuminated by anything. Similarly, everyone is illuminated by the Prophet ﷺ but he isn't illuminated by anyone. The word *lamp* can also be taken as the meaning of 'sirāj'. Darkness is removed by the brightness of a lamp, and the dismay and darkness of ignorance and disbelief were definitely removed by Rasoolullah ﷺ. Lost objects and possessions are found with lamps, and the path of salvation was found through Rasoolullah ﷺ. A lamp is a favor for the household and an inconvenience for a criminal. Similarly, the Prophet ﷺ is the guardian of believers and banishes the reprehensible Shaitaan. Thousands of lamps can be lit by a single one yet its brightness and light will not be diminished in any way. All are illuminated by the Noor of Rasoolullah ﷺ but his Noor did not diminish in the least. A lamp spreads its light in all directions, and the Holy Messenger ﷺ disseminates his Noor in all orientations. Rasoolullah ﷺ has brightened the Earth and even the Heavens with his radiance. The flame of a lamp flickers upwards, and on the night of Mi'rāj, the Prophet ﷺ traveled upwards to where even angels cannot tread. A lamp can be moved from one place to another, and after illuminating Makkah, the Prophet ﷺ migrated and illuminated Madina.

'Munīr' (illuminating) has also been used to describe the Prophet ﷺ in this verse. Darkness is found at the bottom of a lamp, but Rasoolullah ﷺ is such a lamp that he emits brightness above, below, and in all other directions. A lamp only brightens the outer surroundings, but our Beloved ﷺ illuminates both the outer and inner being. A lamp is also sometimes extinguished by wind, but he who tries to extinguish this prophetic lamp will himself be ruined. A lamp serves no purpose during the day, yet this prophetic lamp is always illuminating others. Several lamps are used to attain light in homes and streets at night but they are extinguished as soon as the sun rises. Before, every nation, tribe and area had Prophets عليهم السلام, but now only the prophethood of Rasoolullah ﷺ is prevalent throughout the world. Robbery usually occurs at night. Similarly, before Rasoolullah ﷺ, Divine books were altered and devils would steal the conversations of angels. All of this ended as soon as this sun of salvation shone – now, robbing the Holy Quran (in the form of tampering with it) has become impossible, and devils have been stopped from entering the Heavens. If they even attempt going there, they are stoned. All of this is because the sun of salvation has emerged – a new dawn and era has come.

Some Mashaaikh point out that the Holy Quran has described both Rasoolullah ﷺ and the sun as 'sirāj', so the sun has some resemblance with the Holy Prophet ﷺ. The sun is the lamp of the sky while Rasoolullah ﷺ is the lamp of the Heavens & the Earth. The sun is the lamp of the world and Rasoolullah ﷺ is the lamp of the deen. The sun shines on towers, and Rasoolullah ﷺ shines upon gatherings. The sun is the lamp of physical bodies and Rasoolullah ﷺ is the lamp of Imaan. People awake from sleep when the sun emerges, and people came into existence from non-existence after the Holy Prophet ﷺ was created.

VERSE 64

يَا أَيُّهَا الَّذِينَ اٰمَنُوا لَا تَدْخُلُوا بُيُوتَ النَّبِيِّ إِلَّا أَن يُؤْذَنَ لَكُمْ اِلٰى طَعَامٍ غَيْرَ نَاظِرِينَ اِنٰهُ

'O Believers, don't enter the houses of the Prophet ﷺ unless you receive permission for a meal, not that you wait for its preparation.'
– Surah Ahzāb (33), Verse 53

This verse is also the praise of the Holy Prophet ﷺ, and it teaches us Muslims the respect and honor of the home wherein the Holy Messenger ﷺ resided.

The reason for its revelation is as follows: When the Holy Prophet ﷺ married Sayyidah Zainub ؓ, he extended a general invitation for the walimah. The Companions came in groups, ate and then left. Eventually, three people remained seated after completing their meal and their conversation became lengthy. The blessed house was small, and so, the household members (especially the Holy Prophet ﷺ) began to feel inconvenienced. Rasoolullah ﷺ walked to the other rooms, but when he returned, the guests were still seated there. Seeing this, he left again. The guests then realized their mistake and moved away.

Muslims have been taught the following from this verse,

1. Don't enter the blessed household without permission.

2. If you are invited to the Prophet's ﷺ home, don't arrive before the food is prepared and sit waiting there.

3. After eating, don't remain seated unnecessarily, but return to your homes.

Marvel at the glory of this blessed home and its master! The Lord of the Universe Himself teaches the respect of it! Even if angels are included in the meaning of "O Believers," it would be correct because they also maintain its respect. Angels too don't enter the Prophet's ﷺ home without permission.

At the time of the Holy Prophet's ﷺ demise, the Angel of Death sought permission from the Prophet's ﷺ household (Ahle-Bait) to enter. Even though Sayyidah Fathima ؓ stopped the angel from entering, he couldn't comply because it was Allah ﷻ who sent him. But, he entered the home only after he was given permission to do so.

'Even Jibrael ﷺ doesn't enter the home without permission.
Those of honor know the esteem and glory of the household (Ahle-Bait).'
– Maulana Hasan Raza Khan ؓ

This verse also conveys Rasoolullah's ﷺ mannerisms and modesty, that even when he is inconvenienced by someone, he still doesn't rebuke that person. However, Allah ﷻ is the Lord and it's He Who speaks out against such inconveniences. We also learn that we shouldn't present ourselves at a place where we aren't invited or become a guest for someone unnecessarily (since the host will have to endure difficulty).

VERSE 65

إِنَّ اللهَ وَمَلٰئِكَتَهٗ يُصَلُّوْنَ عَلَى النَّبِيِّ ، يٰٓأَيُّهَا الَّذِيْنَ اٰمَنُوْا صَلُّوْا عَلَيْهِ وَسَلِّمُوْا تَسْلِيْمًا

'Undoubtedly Allah ﷻ and His angels send blessings on the Prophet ﷺ. O Believers, send blessings upon him and salute him fairly well in abundance.'
– Surah Ahzāb (33), Verse 56

This verse is clear praise of the Holy Beloved ﷺ, wherein Muslims are commanded to send Durood Sharif on him. The Holy Quran commands many things. It commands Salaah, fasting, Hajj, Imaan, etc, but never does it say, "Allah ﷻ and His angels complete these actions, so, O believers, you too complete it." This unique proclamation has only been made with regards to Durood Sharif. The reason for this is clear. There's no action that can be shared by both Allah ﷻ and the creation. We cannot do what He does, and He is pure and exalted from our actions. Allah ﷻ creates, gives sustenance, orders death, etc, and we cannot. Our responsibility is to worship Him and show obedience, etc, and Allah ﷻ is free of this. It's only Durood Sharif upon the Holy Prophet ﷺ that is the practice of Allah ﷻ, His angels, as well as Muslims. Just as how the moon becomes the focal point of every vision, so too is the radiant moon of Madina the focal point of the entire creation (as well as the Creator Himself).

> The set sun returned on the Prophet's ﷺ gesture, the moon split in two, trees were obedient to him, etc. If he didn't have power over these things, why were they obeying him?

Even though the context of Allah's ﷻ Durood is the sending of mercy (and the Durood of the angels refers to the supplication of mercy), respect for the Holy Prophet ﷺ is common in both.

The verse first informs us that Allah ﷻ sends rains of mercy on His Beloved ﷺ in every moment of time, then it commands us to send Durood upon him too. (In other words, we too must ask Allah ﷻ to send mercy on him.) Only that which isn't already attained is asked for. So, if mercy is already descending upon Rasoolullah ﷺ even without our supplications, why then are we ordered to supplicate for it?

The answer to this can be understood from the following example: When a beggar goes to beg at a person's home, he first supplicates for the goodness of the owner's family and wealth, e.g. "May your children be blessed," "May your wealth not perish," etc. The owner understands that this is a cultured beggar. He begs, but he also desires goodness for the owner's children. Similarly, we are commanded in this verse, "O Muslims, when you come to ask Me (Allah ﷻ) for anything, then even though I have no children, I do have a Beloved, Muhammad'ur-Rasoolullah ﷺ. Come to me supplicating goodness for him, his Ahle-Bait (Family) and his blessed Sahaabah

(Companions). If you do, you'll be worthy of attaining a drizzle of the rain of mercy constantly descending on him." So, Durood Sharif is actually a method of supplication to Allah ﷻ.

'(O Beloved ﷺ!) It's He, the Lord, Who has made your entire existence mercy.
He has directed us mendicant individuals to your blessed court for alms.'
– Alahadrat Imam Ahmed Raza ؓ

This verse also cautions Muslims by saying, "O Reciters of Durood, don't think that the falling of My mercy on My Beloved ﷺ is dependant on your supplication. Don't think that My Beloved ﷺ is needy of your Durood. Whether you recite Durood or not, My mercy continuously descends upon him. You and your Durood have just gained existence while mercy has been descending upon him from before this. Commanding you to supplicate is actually only for your benefit." Allah ﷻ isn't needy of our praise and glorification, and neither is the Holy Prophet ﷺ needy of anyone's praise. Rasoolullah ﷺ is sufficient for Allah's ﷻ praise and Allah ﷻ is sufficient for his.

This is why reciting Durood at the beginning and end of every dua is necessary. If a person forgets to make dua and only recites Durood Sharif, if Allah ﷻ wills there will be no need for any further supplication and all of his needs will be fulfilled.

Once, Hadrat Ubai ibn Ka'ab ؓ asked the Holy Prophet ﷺ, "How much Durood should I send on you?" Rasoolullah ﷺ answered, "Whatever amount you wish." The Companion replied, "A quarter?" (In other words, he would spend three quarters of his time in other recitations and one quarter of his time in the recitation of Durood.) The Prophet ﷺ answered, "Whatever amount you wish, but if you increase its recitation, it would be better." Hadrat Ubai ؓ then asked, "Half of my time?" and the Prophet ﷺ replied the same. The Companion eventually submitted, "My entire time then will be dedicated to the recitation of Durood! (i.e. "I'll recite only Durood instead of other recitations and duas.")" To this, Rasoolullah ﷺ replied,

اذا يكفى همك ويكفر لك ذنبك

'This will be sufficient for all of your sadness and grief and it will erase your sin.'
– Mishkaat, Baabus-Salaat alan-Nabi ﷺ

I will discuss three issues with regards to Durood Sharif,

1. What is the excellence of Durood?

2. Which Durood is best to recite (or necessary)? Is the recitation of Durood Sharif *waajib*, *fardh* or *sunnah*?

3. What is the ruling on reciting Durood on someone besides the Holy Prophet ﷺ?

1. The excellence of Durood Sharif is too extensive to ever cover completely. Indeed, journals would be required for this task. Those who wish to view a comprehensive discussion on its benefits should refer to *Tafseer Roohul-Bayaan* (under this verse), *Madaarijun-Nubuwwah*, *Naseemur-Riyadh Sharah Shifaa Qaadhi Ayaad* ؓ, and *Mawaahibul-Ladunya*. Only a brief discussion on its excellence will be presented here.

Rasoolullah ﷺ said, "Allah ﷻ sends 10 mercies, forgives 10 sins and extends 10 times the rank of he who recites one Durood upon me." – *Ibid*

In other words, if a person recites Durood Sharif 1,000 times daily, 10,000 sins will be forgiven, 10,000 mercies will descend upon him, and his rank will be elevated 10,000 times. Imagine the benefit should this be practiced throughout one's life!

The Prophet ﷺ also said, "He who recites the most amount of Durood upon me will be closest to me on the Day of Judgment." – *Ibid*

Hadrat Umar ؓ states, "Your duas remain stagnant between the Heavens and Earth until you recite Durood Sharif." – *Ibid*

In fact, our duas should always be between two Durood Sharifs, because it's Durood that is accepted, and so it's hoped that Allah's ﷻ mercy doesn't reject something that's surrounded by it. Insha-Allah ﷻ, through the blessings of Durood Sharif, the dua will also be accepted.

Another Hadith states that the angels travel in search of reciters of Durood. "When a person recites Durood, the angels present it in my court." – *Ibid*

Subhanallah! Marvel at the excellence of Durood Sharif! Through its blessings, names of sinners like us are taken in the Holy Prophet's ﷺ august court. However, this doesn't mean that he doesn't hear our Durood from afar. Angels too present deeds in Allah's ﷻ court. So, does Allah ﷻ too not hear or know what we do?

Even rationally speaking, the recitation of Durood is extremely necessary. If a person shows favor to us, he should ideally be fully compensated, and, if compensation cannot be granted, we should at least make dua for him. When invited to a meal, we supplicate for the host. Similarly, the favors of the Prophet ﷺ are beyond our estimation – how then can we compensate him? We should therefore at least supplicate for him, just as how beggars supplicate for their benefactors.

Once, Sultan Mahmūd ordered the attendants of his court to take whatever they wished from his palace. Everyone hurried to its treasures except Hadrat Ayaaz ﷺ, who came and stood by the king. When the king asked him why he wasn't taking anything, Hadrat Ayaaz ﷺ explained, "Everyone has concerned themselves with wealth and possessions, but I'm taking the king who grants them these things." Sultan Mahmūd then said, "If you have taken me, I've taken you. You are mine and I am yours."

Likewise, the world is attained through duas, but Muhammad Mustapha ﷺ is attained through the recitation of Durood. And, when he is attained, what else is required? It's through his blessings that the world came into existence in the first place!

Durood Sharif is the label on our duas and acts of worship. Just as how goods reach their intended destination after being labeled, so too are good deeds accepted through the blessings of Durood Sharif. This is why it's recited in every dua.

Maulana Jalaaluddin Rumi ﷺ states that once, Rasoolullah ﷺ asked a bee how it makes honey. The bee submitted, "O Beloved of Allah ﷻ, we suck the nectar of different types of flowers in the garden, then carry it in our mouths to our hives. There we spit it out, and this is how we make honey." The Prophet ﷺ then asked, "The nectar from flowers is bland whereas honey is sweet. How does the honey attain its sweetness?" The bee explained, "We've been taught to recite Durood upon you from the garden to our hives. The flavor and sweetness of honey comes from the blessings of Durood!" – *Mathnawi Sharif*

We too hope that through the blessings of Durood Sharif, our flavourless worship becomes set with the sweetness of acceptance. Just as how many nectars become one honey through its blessings, so too will all Arabs and non-Arabs, rich and poor, become united through the Prophet's ﷺ teachings. The name given to this nation is 'Muslim'. Honey has become a cure through the blessings of Durood Sharif. Similarly, through the blessings of Rasoolullah's ﷺ name, every supplication becomes a cure for the sickness of sin.

2. Depending on circumstances, to recite Durood Sharif is sometimes *fardh, waajib, sunnah, mustahab*, even *haraam*. The details of this follow.

To recite Durood Sharif at least once in a lifetime is fardh (compulsory). – *Durre-Mukhtaar, Kitaabus-Salaah*

According to the respected author of *Durre-Mukhtaar*, if the name of the Holy Messenger ﷺ is mentioned in a gathering continuously, it's still waajib to recite Durood each time it's heard. Some however state that doing so is only *mustahab* (preferred).

The author of *Shaami* has mentioned several instances wherein the recital of Durood Sharif is mustahab. They are as follows: The night before Jumua, during the day of Jumua, Saturdays, Sundays and Mondays, mornings and evenings daily, at the time of entering or leaving the Musjid, when visiting the Rauda Sharif of the Holy Prophet ﷺ, near Saffa & Marwa, during the khutba of Jumua (at this time, the listener of the khutba should only recite it in his heart), after the Azaan, at the beginning and end of every dua, at the time of wudhu, when unseen voices are heard, when something is lost, at the time of delivering a religious discourse, teaching or learning, when issuing a verdict (fatwa), at the time of nikah, whenever faced with hardship, etc.

It's disliked (makrooh) to recite Durood in seven instances. They are: At the time of copulation, when answering the call of nature, to announce trade goods for awareness, at the time of slipping, when becoming surprised, at the time of slaughtering, and when sneezing.

It's impermissible (haraam) to recite Durood in three instances: When a trader shows his goods to a customer and he recites Durood to convey their nicety, if a respected person enters a gathering and Durood is recited to inform of his arrival (*Shaami*), and to recite Durood when hearing the name of the Holy Prophet ﷺ during the At-Tahiyaat of Salaah. Bear in mind that if the name of Rasoolullah ﷺ is mentioned during the recital of the Holy Quran, it's better not to recite Durood Sharif so that the progression of the Holy Quran isn't affected. – *Shaami*

It's sunnah to recite Durood after the At-Tahiyaat in Salaah (this applies to the second At-Tahiyaat of fardh and waajib Salaah). To recite Durood after the first At-Tahiyaat of a fardh or waajib Salaah is not allowed, while reciting Durood after both At-Tahiyaats in optional (nafl) Salaah is sunnah. In other words, Durood should be recited in the first sitting of a nafl Salaah as well. To recite it and then stand for the third and fourth rakaat is permissible.

Which Durood Sharif should be recited? Hadrat Abu Hameed Saa'idi ﷺ narrates, "We asked the Holy Prophet ﷺ how we should recite Durood on him. He answered: the Durood we recite after At-Tahiyaat in Salaah." – *Mishkaat, Kitaabus-Salaah, Baabus-Salaah alan-Nabi* ﷺ

In other words, the Prophet ﷺ told them to recite Durood'e-Ibrahim. Based on this Hadith, some maintain that to recite any Durood other than Durood'e-Ibrahim is prohibited, but this is incorrect. When Commentators of the Hadith take the blessed name of the Holy Prophet ﷺ, they merely say, "Sallalaahu Alaihi Wasallam (Allah ﷻ send Durood & Salaam upon him)." This then necessitates the use of 'Sallalaahu Alaihi Wasallam' alone to also be permissible. If reciting only transmitted Duroods was permissible, then only those foods and medicines which have been conveyed should also be consumed. Yet, just as how eating any type of food which isn't haraam in Islamic Law is permissible, reciting any Durood which isn't contrary to Islamic Law is also permissible. The Holy Quran states,

كلوا واشربوا

'Eat and drink.'
– Surah A'rāf (7), Verse 31

The command of "Eat and drink" is absolute (مطلق). So too is the command of sending blessings on the Prophet ﷺ. Whichever Durood is recited, reward will be attained. Yes, transmitted Duroods are better than others.

There are many Duroods mentioned in *Dalaailul-Khairaat*. The author of *Tafseer Roohul-Bayaan* has also explained the great merit and benefit of the following,

> *As-Salaatu was-Salaamu Alaika Ya Rasoolallah,*
> *As-Salaatu was-Salaamu Alaika Ya Habeeballah,*
> *As-Salaatu was-Salaamu Alaika Ya Khaleelallah.*

This is a very lengthy Durood. This beggar [the respected author] has experienced the following Durood to be extremely beneficial. After Jumua Salaah, recite the following 100 times facing Madina Sharif with folded hands,

> *Salallaahu alan-Nabiyyil-Ummiyi wa Aalihi, Salallaahu Alaihi*
> *wa-Sallam. Salaataw-was-Salaamu Alaika Ya Rasoolallah.*
> 'Salutations of Allah ﷻ be upon the Prophet of the unlettered & his
> family, peace & salutations of his Lord be upon him. Peace &
> salutations be upon you, O Messenger of Allah ﷺ!'

In some areas of the world, people loudly recite Durood Sharif after their fardh Salaah. This is regarded as an act of infidelity (کفر) and polytheism (شرك) by some, but their view is absolutely wrong. Durood can be recited in any appropriate manner. Its command is absolute (مطلق) – there's no specification in reading it silently or loudly. When regarding something as even disliked (makrooh) without a prohibition in Islamic Law isn't allowed, how can we regard something as an act of infidelity or polytheism without an Islamic prohibition? The Holy Prophet ﷺ would perform the remembrance (ذکر) of Allah ﷻ so loudly after Salaah that the residents in homes would come to know in this way that the Salaah had ended. – *Mishkaat Sharif*

I've comprehensively discussed the issue of loud zikr in my book, *Ja'al-Haqq*. Refer to it there.

3. As for the final question: What is the ruling on reciting Durood on someone besides the Holy Prophet ﷺ? The Jurists (فقهاء) have stated

that to send Durood independently (مستقل) on those who are not Prophets علیہ السلام is prohibited, e.g. saying, "Imam Husain, Alaihis-Salaam," or, "Imam Hussain, Sallalaahu Alaihi Wasallam." Yes, to adjoin their names to the Holy Prophet's ﷺ and *then* send Durood is permitted. The intent is Durood on the Holy Prophet ﷺ, and through his means, their names are also included, e.g. "O Allah ﷻ, send peace *&* blessings upon the Prophet ﷺ, his Family, Companions, Wives, and upon the Saints of the Ummah."

VERSE 66

وَمَا أَرْسَلْنٰكَ إِلَّا كَآفَّةً لِّلنَّاسِ بَشِيْرًا وَّنَذِيْرًا وَّلٰكِنَّ أَكْثَرَ النَّاسِ لَا يَعْلَمُوْنَ

'And (O Beloved ﷺ), We have not sent you but for the entire mankind as a bearer of good news and a warner, but most of the people don't know.'
– Surah Saba (34), Verse 28

This verse is the clear praise of the Holy Prophet ﷺ, and three prophetic qualities have been mentioned within: Rasoolullah ﷺ is a prophet to all, he's a bringer of good news to all, and he is also a warner to all. I've already discussed these three qualities in detail under Surah Furqān (25) and Ahzāb (33). The point behind this verse is to demonstrate the Holy Messenger's ﷺ prophethood as general and inclusive (عام). Prophets علیہم السلام, Saints ﷺ, human beings as well as non-human beings are all included in his prophethood.

Rasoolullah ﷺ said, "I've been bestowed five things which have never been granted to anyone before me,

1. I've been blessed with awe to the area of a month's travel,

2. The entire Earth has been purified and made a Musjid for me so that whenever the time of Salaah arrives, it can be performed,

3. If water cannot be attained, tayammum (dry ablution) can be made,

4. War-booty has been made permissible for me. It was never halaal for anyone before this,

5. And, I've been bestowed with major intercession."

He further said, "Prophets علیہم السلام were sent to specific nations and tribes, but I've been sent to all of humanity."

So, this verse proves that Rasoolullah's ﷺ prophethood is general and inclusive of all.

VERSE 67

إِنَّا أَرْسَلْنَاكَ بِالْحَقِّ بَشِيرًا وَنَذِيرًا ، وَإِنْ مِّنْ أُمَّةٍ إِلَّا خَلَا فِيهَا نَذِيرٌ

'(O Beloved Prophet ﷺ) Surely We have sent you
with truth, as a bearer of good news and as a warner. And
for every nation a warner has been appointed.'
– Surah Fātir (35), Verse 24

Like the previous verse, this verse also mentions three prophetic qualities: that Rasoolullah ﷺ is a prophet to all, that he is a bringer of glad-tidings, and that he is a warner. At the end of the verse, Allah ﷻ speaks about warners coming to the previous nations, and that every nation had a warner. So *what relevance does this have with the Holy Beloved's ﷺ prophethood?* This is something to ponder on. Actually, the verse states, "O Beloved ﷺ, you have been sent to all nations and your prophethood is inclusive of all of them, but every group and nation before you had a different warner that came to them." The praise of Rasoolullah ﷺ is clearly proven by this (that he is a warner to *all* nations).

By misinterpreting this verse, some people incorrectly claim that the religious leaders and personalities of other religions should always be revered and that no negativity should be ascribed to them. They claim that Krishna, Raam, Buddah, etc. should be respected because they were all prophets, but that their teachings were distorted by people who then began to commit idolatry and infidelity (just as how the Christians and Jews distorted the true teachings of Sayyiduna Esa علیہ السلام and Sayyiduna Musa علیہ السلام, the former by implementing the trinity into their religion).

Others claim that Prophets علیہ السلام were also sent to other creations besides human beings (i.e. Jinns also had a prophet, and that people with a 'low caste' had a prophet who also hailed from a low caste).

However, both of these arguments are wrong and baseless. Firstly, what proof is there of Krishna, Raam and Buddah's existence in this world? What proof is there that they were actually humans or something else? According to the stories of the polytheists, Hanuman had a tail, Ganesha had an elephant's trunk for a nose, and Kali Ma had several hands and feet, etc. These narratives grossly contradict Allah's ﷻ natural planning, the intellect of a man, and the Holy Quran. Allah ﷻ states,

184

لقد خلقنا الانسان فى احسن تقويم

'Undoubtedly We have created man in the best stature.'
– Surah Tīn (95), Verse 4

These personalities are not even human in appearance, yet we are to accept them as prophets? They resemble monkeys and elephants and are deprived of human appearance, which is the best nature according to Allah ﷻ, the Creator Himself. So, we will have to conclude that these fables are either all fabricated or that these 'people' were actually animals who were worshipped, just as how the cow and snake are worshipped today. To say that they were humans and righteous but that people distorted their appearances into looking differently is an unsubstantiated deduction and a useless defense for the polytheists. When their devotees themselves don't regard them as humans and ascribe them as animals (e.g. monkeys are known as Hanuman's kin), which verse will then tell us that they were humans and righteous? Should Muslims stop speaking ill of the idols worshipped by the Arab polytheists when the Quran personified (Rasoolullah ﷺ) himself censored them? So, just as how the Arabs had Laat & Uzza, so does the Indian sub-continent have Hanuman and others.

> People are on truth, but the Holy Prophet ﷺ *is* truth personified. He who has seen him has seen truth. People are those with Imaan (Mu'mins), but the Holy Prophet ﷺ is Imaan itself; people are scholars, but he is knowledge personified – being aware of his qualities and epithets *is* knowledge.

It's also wrong to claim that a prophet emerged from every type of genealogical heritage, including one of low-caste. The Prophets عليهم السلام always came from noble backgrounds, from both their paternal and maternal side. Just as how each prophet's character was impeccable and his appearance radiant, so too was his family background exceptional.

When Hiraqal, the king of the Roman Empire, summoned Abu Sufyan (who was not a Muslim then) and some other residents of Makkah to ask them about the Holy Prophet ﷺ, one of the questions he asked pertained to his genealogy. All of the Makkans answered that Rasoolullah ﷺ hailed from a prestigious and noble family, and when Hiraqal heard this, he replied, "Prophets عليهم السلام only come from prestigious and noble families." – *Bukhari Sharif, Vol. 1*

How then is it possible that 'low-caste' prophets were also found in the world? May Allah ﷻ protect us!

Where in this verse does it say that a prophet emerged from every kind of people? Definitely, a Nabi to guide was sent to every nation, but they were always of noble descent. The Holy Prophet ﷺ is the Messenger to all nations of the world, Arabs and non-Arabs equally. This doesn't mean that he has non-Arab genealogy.

These two discussions should be kept in mind. Also, to claim that Prophets عليهم السلام came in non-human form to non-human creation is also totally incorrect. The Holy Quran states,

وما ارسلنا من قبلك الا رجالا نوحى اليهم من اهل القرى

'And all those who were sent as Messengers before
you were men upon whom We revealed.'
– Surah Yusuf (12), Verse 109

We come to know that Prophets عليهم السلام were ever only humans and males. Refer to my book, *Ja'al-Haqq*, for a comprehensive discussion on this matter. [This book constantly being referred to by the author has also been translated into English (by a different publisher). Please contact us for further information. – *Translator*]. Actually, the correct interpretation of the verse is that there have been warners to every nation – not just in the form of Prophets عليهم السلام, but in scholars and virtuous personalities too.

The author of *Roohul-Bayaan* states that the nations referred to here are those who were punished in the world. So, the verse means, "Indeed Prophets عليهم السلام, Scholars and Saints were sent to those nations who were punished. They warned them of Allah's ﷻ punishment, but when they didn't take heed, Allah's ﷻ retribution was swift." This commentary is supported by the following verse,

وما كنا معذبين حتى نبعث رسولا

'And We don't torment until We have sent a Messenger.'
– Surah Bani Israel (17), Verse 15

Otherwise, there were some nations who didn't attain any prophet. Allah ﷻ also states,

وما ارسلنا اليهم قبلك من نذير

'Nor did We send any warner to them before you (O Beloved ﷺ).'
– Surah Saba (34), Verse 44

It's common knowledge that there's a distance of approximately 600 years between our Holy Prophet ﷺ and Sayyiduna Esa عليه السلام. – *Bukhari, Vol. 1*

No prophet came to the world in this time. So, explanation is necessary in face of clear evidence.

VERSE 68

يس ، وَالْقُرْاٰنِ الْحَكِيْمِ ، إِنَّكَ لَمِنَ الْمُرْسَلِيْنَ

'*Yaseen, by the wise Quran, Undoutedly you are of the sent ones.*'
– Surah Yaseen (36), Verses 1-3

This verse is also the praise of the Holy Prophet ﷺ. The non-Muslims of Makkah used to say that Rasoolullah ﷺ wasn't the Messenger of Allah ﷻ, yet in answering them, Allah ﷻ said, "O Beloved ﷺ, oath on the Quran, you are My messenger!"

'Yaseen' is a *mutashābihāt* verse. Its correct meaning is known only by Allah ﷻ and His Messenger ﷺ. However, Commentators have made some interpretations of this word. They are as follows,

1. Yaseen is a name of the Holy Prophet ﷺ, and the vocative noun of 'Ya' (i.e. "O") is hidden. So, the intention of the verse is, "O Yaseen!"

2. The letter yaa (ي) in Yaseen is actually the vocative noun, with 'Yaseen' therefore meaning 'O master of the worlds (يا سيد العالمين)!'.

3. It's the name of the Surah.

The grandeur of the Holy Quran is also later demonstrated by Allah ﷻ taking an oath on it. Here, Allah ﷻ wishes to demonstrate the glory of His Beloved's ﷺ prophethood by taking an oath on the Holy Quran! A great claim requires a grand oath. By Allah ﷻ taking an oath on the Holy Quran regarding Rasoolullah's ﷺ prophethood, Rasoolullah ﷺ becomes unique in this quality, since it wasn't taken for any other prophet.

VERSE 69

قُلْ يِعِبَادِىَ الَّذِيْنَ اَسْرَفُوْا عَلٰى اَنْفُسِهِمْ لَا تَقْنَطُوْا مِنْ رَّحْمَةِ الله

'(O My Beloved ﷺ), Say, 'O my slaves who have committed excesses against their own souls, don't despair of the mercy of Allah ﷻ."
– Surah Zumar (39), Verse 53

This verse is also explicit praise of the Holy Messenger ﷺ. The reason for its revelation is that a group of people said to the Holy Prophet ﷺ, "We can bring Imaan but we are very sinful. Will our sins be forgiven?" The above verse was then revealed, wherein Allah ﷻ states, "O My Beloved ﷺ, say to them, "O my slaves who have committed errors, don't despair of Allah's ﷻ mercy. Enter entirely into Islam and submerge yourselves in its ocean of mercy. You will be purified of every impurity and defilement."

The verse states, "O my slaves…" If anyone says that this refers to Allah's ﷻ devotees [and that none is also a devotee to the Holy Prophet ﷺ], certain restrictions would have to be emplaced,

1.   Instead of, "Say (O Prophet ﷺ), 'O my slaves…,'" the verse should've forgone the word 'Say' and Allah ﷻ should've spoken directly to His devotees. Had this been the case, the word 'Say' would've had no relevance.

2.   "[Those] who have committed excesses against their own souls…" will also have to be restricted, because polytheists and non-Muslims don't fall under this category. Only Muslims are meant by this. Although all are Allah's ﷻ servants, the polytheism of a non-Muslim cannot be forgiven. The Holy Quran states,

ان الله لا يغفر ان يشرك به

'Surely Allah ﷻ does not forgive association with Him as partner.'
– Surah Nisā (4), Verse 116

The part "O my slaves…" is then accepted to refer to the devotees of Rasoolullah ﷺ (i.e. his servants). 'Abd' (عبد) can mean worshipper and servant. So, the verse will now mean, "(O My Prophet ﷺ), Say [to them], 'O my servants…" The polytheists and non-Muslims are instantly ruled out by this, because only Muslims are the servants of Rasoolullah ﷺ. There would also be no need to shorten the verse.

The interpretation that 'my devotees' refers to the servants of Rasoolullah ﷺ has also been accepted by Maulwi Ashraf Ali Thanwi. Alahadrat Imam Ahmed Raza Khan Bareilwi ﷺ states,

*'By saying, 'O my devotees,' our king and master (i.e. Rasoolullah ﷺ)
made us his servants. What has this to do with you?!'*

Rule – This is why, to keep the name Abdun-Nabi (servant of the Prophet ﷺ),
Abdur-Rasool (servant of the Messenger ﷺ), etc. is totally permissible and
established from the Holy Quran. Allah ﷻ states,

وانكحوا الايمى منكم والصلحين من عبادكم وإمائكم

*'And marry those among you who have not been married, and
of your suitable servants and handmaids.'*
– Surah Noor (24), Verse 32

Arabs generally say, 'Abdi' (my servant). The grand teacher of the author of
Durre-Mukhtaar was Hadrat **Abdun-Nabi** Khalili ؓ. – *Introduction to
Durre-Mukhtaar*

The Hadith which states that 'Abdi' (my servant) and 'Ummati' (my
Ummah) should not be said is a desirable (استحبابى) command, just as how
another Hadith states, "Don't refer to grapes as *karam* (noble-natured)
because a Muslim is *karam*. – *Bukhari, etc.*

Rasoolullah's ﷺ blessed Companions are reported to have said several times,
"I was his (i.e. the Holy Prophet's ﷺ) servant and attendant." Refer to my
book, *Ja'al-Haqq*, wherein I have submitted evidence which the dissenters
will be unable to answer.

'Don't despair' informs us that to be despondent of Allah's ﷻ mercy isn't the
character of believers. In fact, we must both fear Allah ﷻ (bearing in mind
our transgressions) and be aspirant of His mercy.

*'What is the extent of Raza's ؓ sins? Even if they are thousands,
O Merciful, there's no limit or end to Your benevolence.'*
– Alahadrat Imam Ahmed Raza ؓ

Allah ﷻ will forgive all sins (Insha-Allah ﷻ), but He will also make those
who have rights on us (حقوق العباد) forgive our excesses against them. This is
mentioned in books of *Kalām* (scholastic theology), etc.

VERSE 70

إِنَّا فَتَحْنَا لَكَ فَتْحًا مُّبِينًا ، لِيَغْفِرَ لَكَ اللّٰه مَا تَقَدَّمَ مِنْ ذَنْبِكَ وَمَا تَأَخَّرَ

'Undoubtedly We have granted you a clear victory [so] that Allah ﷻ

may forgive sins of your formers and of your latters.'
– Surah Fat'h (48), Verses 1-2

This verse is a collection of praise for the Holy Prophet ﷺ. The reason for its revelation is as follows: Once, Rasoolullah ﷺ witnessed a dream in which he entered the holy city of Makkah with his Companions, took the key of the Ka'ba, made tawaaf and performed Umrah. When the Sahaabah were informed of this, they became happy. The Prophet ﷺ later did intend performing Umrah, and on the 1ˢᵗ of Zul-Qa'dah 6 AH, he set out for this journey accompanied by 1,400 of his Companions. Everyone put on their ihram in Zul-Haleefa along the way, but when they reached a place called Asfaan, they were informed that the disbelievers of Makkah were extensively prepared for war.

This verse also conveys Rasoolullah's ﷺ mannerisms and modesty, that even when he is inconvenienced by someone, he still doesn't rebuke that person. However, Allah ﷻ is the Lord and it's He Who speaks out against such inconveniences.

So, in a place called Hudaibiyah, several people were sent on behalf of the Muslims to the disbelivers, saying to them, "The Holy Prophet ﷺ has come with the intention of performing Umrah. He has no intention of fighting." Still, the non-Muslims didn't believe this and decided to send Urwa ibn Mas'ood Thaqafi to the Messenger ﷺ to investigate the situation. After seeing the respect the Sahaabah demonstrated in the blessed court of Rasoolullah ﷺ, Urwa could do nohing but stare in awe and amazement. He saw that whenever the Prophet ﷺ washed his blessed hands, the Companions would rush to attain the water which fell to the ground. When Rasoolullah ﷺ would spit, they would attempt to attain it, and the one who did would rub it over his face and body for blessings. Not a strand of Rasoolullah's ﷺ blessed hair fell to the ground. If any strand did separate from his body, the Sahaabah would take it with respect and keep it closer to them than their very own lives. When the Prophet ﷺ spoke, everyone would remain silent and none would look up. Rasoolullah's ﷺ gathering wasn't just a concentration, it was a gathering that personified knowledge, wisdom, respect and veneration. It was a gathering on Earth attended by angelic-natured humans. Urwa reported this to the non-Muslims of Makkah and said, "I've seen many grand courts of great kings, but I've never even *heard* of a court like the court of Muhammad. You won't be successful against him."

The Quraish replied, "Don't say that. We'll turn them away this year. They can come next year." Hadrat Uthman ؓ was one of the people who went to the people of Makkah on behalf of Rasoolullah ﷺ. Accompanied by a group of 10 Companions, he implored the non-Muslims not to stop the Prophet ﷺ from performing Umrah, yet they didn't accede and distracted Hadrat Uthman ؓ for a period of three days, saying to him, "If you wish, you can make tawaaf of the Ka'ba." Hadrat Uthman ؓ replied, "I cannot stand to make tawaaf before the Messenger ﷺ."

However, in the Muslim camp, news was received that Hadrat Uthman ؓ was martyred by the disbelivers. Based on this, the Holy Prophet ﷺ took a pledge of allegiance from all of the Muslims, wishing to confirm that if they were faced with war, they wouldn't turn their backs. The name of this pledge (bai'at) was the Bai'atur-Ridwaan (which occurred under a thorny tree). This incident is mentioned at the end of the Surah.

It was ultimately settled between the Muslims and non-Muslims that Rasoolullah ﷺ would return to Madina and perform his Umrah the following year. The above verse was revealed when the treaty was prepared. Allah ﷻ says to the Holy Prophet ﷺ in it, "O My Beloved ﷺ! We have granted you a clear victory." This settlement was actually the means through which Makkah was eventually conquered (and through which many other conquests were successful).

The above is the reason for the verse's revelation in brief. Two points, then, need to be discussed,

1. What is meant by *fat'h* (victory)?

2. What is meant by '...that Allah ﷻ may forgive sins of your formers and of your latters.'

    1.1 *Fat'h* may refer to the *Fat'he-Makkah* (victorious conquest of Makkah). However, this interpretation is weak because it seemingly contradicts what actually happened. The people of Makkah didn't allow the Muslims to perform their Umrah and sent them back. Actually, 'granted you' in the verse is in the past tense. So, it's befitting to say that the occurring of the treaty of Hudaibiyah *was* the actual victory. The non-Muslims of Makkah didn't want it to occur, yet Rasoolullah ﷺ wished for an agreement. So, what the disbelievers wanted didn't happen, but what the Holy Prophet ﷺ desired did! This was the great victory.

1.2 The treaty was the means of victory. So, it has been figuratively called *fat'h* (a victory).

1.3 Makkah would certainly be conquered and Arabs speak about inevitability in the past tense. This is why 'granted victory' was used.

1.4 It was due to this treaty that disbelievers began interacting with Muslims, resulting in many of them embracing Islam that year.

1.5 *Fat'h* also means 'to open'. So, the verse means, "O Beloved ﷺ, We have opened doors for you." Doors of what, then, have been opened? The answer is the doors of knowledge, salvation, wisdom, etc. In other words, "O Beloved ﷺ, We have opened for you the doors which were closed for others. The doors of intercession, the vision of Allah ﷻ, Jannah, the Station of Praise (المقام المحمود), the Fountain of Kauthar – i.e. all the doors of Divine mercy – have been opened for you."

The following interpretation can also be made. The Holy Quran states,

وعنده مفاتيح الغيب
'And with Him (Allah ﷻ) are the keys to the unseen.'
– Surah An'ām (6), Verse 59

None besides Allah ﷻ know them. The question is, "Have the doors of the unseen been opened for anyone with these keys?" This is then answered here in the verse, "We have opened for you..."

2. Now follows the discussion on 'sins of your formers and of your latters'. What is meant by this? All Muslims unanimously believe that the Prophets عليهم السلام are free (معصوم) from sin. Under the commentary of verse 124 of Surah Baqarah (2), *Tafseeraat'e-Ahmadia* states that the Holy Prophet ﷺ never intended sin even for a moment prior to his proclamation of prophethood or even after. This is why the Commentators of the Quran and Hadith have made several interpretations of this verse.

Shaikh Abdul-Haqq Muhaddith Dehlwi ﷺ states that the mistake of Sayyiduna Adam عليه السلام and the sins of the Ummah are what are meant by 'formers' and 'latters' respectively. – *Madaarijun-Nubuwwah*

Under the commentary of this verse, the respected author of *Tafseer Roohul-Bayaan* says that Sayyiduna Adam عليه السلام made dua through the medium of Rasoolullah ﷺ and it was accepted. Some scholars say that an error in Juristic Reasoning (اجتهاد) is meant here.

Some say it means, 'Allah ﷻ protected you from sins in the past and will also safeguard you in future.' In other words, "O Beloved ﷺ, you are protected from sins." Some Scholars say that the sins of the Ummah have been related to the Holy Prophet's ﷺ intercession, and the sins of the Ummahs have always been connected to the mercy of the Prophets عليهم السلام.

In other words, sin and transgression are sometimes related to the sinner himself and sometimes to the person responsible for the forgiveness. A criminal refers to a court case as 'his case', while the judge and lawyer too call it theirs. 'My case,' in reference to the criminal, means that he was arrested in connection to it, while 'my case' to the lawyer and judge means that they are responsible for its proceedings. So, the sins of the sinful who are apprehended in these transgressions have been related to the benevolent mercy of the Prophet ﷺ. In this context, he is somewhat responsible for their intercession. 'Your sins' can also refer to those acts which have been classified as sin by Rasoolullah ﷺ, since if it wasn't for his advent, no action would formally be regarded as a sin. So, an interpretation of this verse could also be, "...things which you have declared to be sins." – *Roohul-Bayaan*

This is why some say that Sayyiduna Adam عليه السلام didn't err. Rather, the reprehensible humans present in his spine were the cause of the mistake. Allah ﷻ didn't wish for these wicked individuals to be born in Jannah. So, it was declared, "O Adam عليه السلام, go to Earth, leave them in the world, and then return to your rightful abode (Jannah)." – *Tafseer Roohul-Bayaan, under the commentary of this verse; Mirqaat, Sharah Mishkaat*

I've discussed in detail the infallibility (عصمة) of the Prophets الصلوة in my treatise *Qahr'e-Kibriya bar Munkireen'e-Ismat'e-Ambiya* (found in the book *Ja'al-Haqq*). In it, I've presented proofs for our belief and answered objections against it. Refer to it there.

The author of *Tafseer Roohul-Bayaan* further writes in the commentary of this verse that the Holy Messenger ﷺ was blessed with three *fat'hs* (victories):

1. **Fat'he-Qareeb** – The opening of the heart's door, and being made aware of its secrets.

2. **Fat'he-Mubeen** – The opening of the Prophet's ﷺ soul.

3. **Fat'he-Mutlaq** – Allah ﷻ opening the door of His assistance for the Holy Prophet ﷺ. This is gestured to by the first verse of Surah Nasr (110).

VERSE 71

إِنَّا أَرْسَلْنَاكَ شَهِدًا وَمُبَشِّرًا وَنَذِيرًا ، لِتُؤْمِنُوا بِاللهِ وَرَسُوْلِهِ وَتُعَزِّرُوْهُ وَتُوَقِّرُوْهُ وَتُسَبِّحُوهُ بُكْرَةً وَأَصِيْلًا

'Certainly We have sent you as a witness, a bearer of glad-tidings and a warner so that people should believe in Allah ﷻ and His Messenger ﷺ and honor him, and that you may glorify Him morning and evening.'
– Surah Fat'h (48), Verses 8-9

This verse is clear praise for the Holy Prophet ﷺ and mentions several qualities of his. Muslims have also been commanded in it to respect and revere the prophetic court.

I've already explained 'witness' in Surah Ahzāb (33) to mean *someone who is present and observes*. Refer to it there to understand how this meaning and other interpretations of the word are applicable to it. However, I'll present another point below that is deduced from this word.

The Holy Prophet ﷺ said, "I bear witness that there's no being worthy of worship except Allah ﷻ." This testimony negates divinity of everything besides Allah ﷻ. The Holy Prophet's ﷺ testimony is an actual and faultless declaration which he made after witnessing (not by merely hearing from someone else). Testifying to prove is simple, but testifying to negate is difficult. If someone says, "A certain verse is found in the book *Gulistaan*," he has to only show the verse to be proven correct. However, saying, "A certain verse isn't in *Gulistaan*," is difficult, and only he whose knowledge encompasses the entire work could claim such a thing. Likewise, only he who sees the entire creation from the beginning until the end and has tested every minute particle for divinity can finally say, "There's no being worthy of worship besides Allah ﷻ. I've studied all and therefore conclude that only He is worthy of it."

Muslims have been commanded in this verse to respect and revere the Holy Beloved ﷺ. There's no restriction for a specific form of respect. So, any act that is allowed in Islamic Law may be performed. On the other hand, those prohibited forms of respect (e.g. sajda out of respect, etc.) cannot be performed for him. Respect him by speech, take his name with reverence, but don't call him 'Allah ﷻ' or His son. Respect everything associated to him: his blessed hair, his sacred relics, his magnificent city of residence, etc. Likewise, express his greatness and honor through every movement of your hand, feet, heart, etc.

The Jurists have even gone to the extent of writing that when one presents himself at the sacred Rauda of the Holy Prophet ﷺ to send salaam, he should stand with folded hands just as how one stands in Salaah. – *Fataawa Alamghiri, Kitaabul-Hajj, Baabu Ziyaaraati-Qabrin-Nabi* ﷺ

Similarly, to stand in respect for Rasoolullah ﷺ and kiss his blessed hands & feet, which was the habit and custom of the Sahaabah, is preferable (mustahab). – *Mishkaat, Kitaabul-Adab, Baabul-Qiyaam, Baabul-Musaafaha & Muaanaqah*

The standing in respect prohibited in some Ahadith refers to when a noble person is seated while others stand before him with folded hands. This is why the Hadith states,

لا تقوموا كما تقوم الاعاجم

'Don't stand the way the non-Arabs stand.'

Refer to my book, *Ja'al-Haqq*, for a detailed explanation on this. Once, when Hadrat Sa'ad ibn Muaaz ؓ came to a gathering of the Holy Prophet ﷺ, the Prophet ﷺ said to the Ansaar, "Stand (in respect) for your leader." In short, standing in respect is permissible and proven from the Sunnah. Likewise, coordinating gatherings of Meelad (i.e. celebrating the birth of Rasoolullah ﷺ) and standing when the blessed birth of the Holy Prophet ﷺ is mentioned is also respect for him. Whatever and in whichever form respect is shown, it's permissible, as long as Islamic Law doesn't prohibit it. There's no need to prove the form of respect.

Imam Malik ﷺ never rode a horse in the blessed city of Madina, and some other revered personalities would never even answer the call of nature within its precincts. Proof of these actions isn't established from the Sahaabah or those after them. It was in fact the emotion of Imam Malik's ﷺ heart, and no one objected to it. Respect and reverence is absolute (مطلق) in this verse. So, it's wrong to emplace a restriction on it.

Whatever and in whichever form respect is shown, it's permissible, as long as Islamic Law doesn't prohibit it. There's no need to prove the form of respect.

Under the commentary of Surah Ahzāb (33), Verse 40, *Tafseer Roohul-Bayaan* mentions the following incident: The son of Hadrat Ayaaz ﷺ was named Muhammad, and the king of the time used to take the name of this son with much respect. Once however, the king didn't call him by his name, but instead said, "O son of Ayaaz ﷺ! Come here." Hadrat Ayaaz ﷺ submitted to the king, "My honorable king, what mistake has my son committed that made you not call him by his name?" The king explained, "Ayaaz ﷺ, at that time I wasn't with wudhu, and I don't call out this name without ablution."

Now then, where's the proof of establishing this act of respect?

Similarly, coordinating gatherings of Meelad is also a form of respect for the Holy Prophet ﷺ. Refer to my book, *Ja'al-Haqq*, for a complete discussion on this, where Meelad is proven from the Holy Quran, Hadith, Consensus of the Ummah, and the practice of the previous Prophets التلقة.

Rule – Respect and reverence for the Holy Messenger ﷺ is included in Imaan (faith), to the extent that disrespect shown to even his blessed sandals is an act of disbelief (كفر).

VERSE 72

إِنَّ الَّذِينَ يُبَايِعُونَكَ إِنَّمَا يُبَايِعُونَ اللهَ يَدُ اللهِ فَوْقَ أَيْدِيهِمْ

'Surely those who swear allegiance to you indeed swear allegiance to Allah ﷺ. The hand of Allah ﷺ is above their hands.'
– Surah Fat'h (48), Verse 10

This verse is clearly the praise of the Holy Prophet ﷺ. It refers to the incident of the 'Bai'atur-Ridwaan'. I've already mentioned in a previous verse [Verse

70 in book] that when rumors were heard of Hadrat Uthman ؓ being martyred, the Holy Prophet ﷺ took a pledge of allegiance from people to perform Jihad. All of the blessed Companions gave their hands in the hands of the Holy Beloved ﷺ and pledged so. Thereafter, Rasoolullah ﷺ pointed to his left hand and said, "This hand is Uthman's ؓ." He then said about his right hand, "This hand is the Prophet of Allah's ﷺ, and I myself pledge allegiance on behalf of Uthman ؓ on my own hand."

Subhanallah! How fortunate is Hadrat Uthman ؓ?!

> *'The hand of the Holy Beloved ﷺ (which was Allah's ﷻ hand)*
> *became yours, O Uthman ؓ! That is the glory you occupy!*
> – Maulana Hasan Raza Khan ؒ

Metaphorically, the hand of the Holy Prophet ﷺ is Hadrat Uthman's ؓ hand *and* the hand of Allah ﷻ! The result of this is that Hadrat Uthman's ؓ hand is also Allah's ﷻ hand. Indeed the Holy Quran is the speech of Allah ﷻ, and this Divine speech was compiled and propagated by Allah's ﷻ hand (i.e. Hadrat Uthman ؓ). This is why one of the titles of Hadrat Uthman ؓ is 'the Compiler of the Quran' (جامع القرآن). The verse mentions this very pledge and thus proclaims the greatness of its participants.

The following points emerge from it,

1. Rasoolullah ﷺ has such an esteemed rank in Allah's ﷻ court that obedience and pledges of allegiance to him are actually obedience and pledges of allegiance to Allah ﷻ. His hand is Allah's ﷻ hand. I've already discussed this under Surah Anfāl (8), Verse 17 [Verse 33 in book].

   Tafseer Roohul-Bayaan states under this verse that Allah ﷻ blessed the Holy Messenger ﷺ with great rank unattained by anyone else. The Holy Prophet ﷺ forsook everything for Allah ﷻ. So, Allah ﷻ is for the Holy Prophet ﷺ and he is Allah's ﷻ Beloved ﷺ. The Messenger ﷺ is the complete manifestation of Allah's ﷻ power. It's Rasoolullah's ﷺ existence, but Allah's ﷻ power is projected through it. If you wish to view the splendor of Allah's ﷻ Divine attributes, look at the Holy Prophet ﷺ. This is why Rasoolullah ﷺ said in a Hadith,

   > *'He who has seen me has seen the Truth (i.e. Allah ﷻ).'*

However, the discipline of the Holy Prophet ﷺ was such that he demonstrated his servitude in every grace. Some Saints also attain a passing glimpse of this greatness, and when they do, Hadrat Mansoor Hallaj ؓ begins to say,

انا الحق

'I am the Truth (i.e. I am Allah).'

And Hadrat Bā-Yazīd Bustaami ؓ begins to say,

'Glory be to me! How grand is my adoration?!'

When the Holy Prophet's ﷺ hand is Allah's ﷻ hand, then his blessed tongue – in fact, all of his body parts – also project Divine power. This is the station known as Annihilation in Allah ﷻ (*fanā fillah*). When human beings enter this station, miraculous qualities are gained by them. One is that the servant begins to demonstrate Divine workings, e.g. Hadrat Asif Barkhiya ؓ brought the throne of Bilqees to Sayyiduna Sulaiman عليه السلام within a moment; Sayyiduna Yaqub عليه السلام attained the fragrance of Sayyiduna Yusuf عليه السلام from Egypt; after constructing the Holy Ka'ba, Sayyiduna Ibrahim عليه السلام invited all of the people of the world to perform Hajj (and every person to be born until Qiyaamat heard this call); the set sun returned, the moon split in two, and clouds rained all on the gesture of the Holy Prophet ﷺ. These incidents are the workings of Allah ﷻ demonstrated by His beloveds.

Another miraculous quality is that the servant says about Divine workings, "I can do this," or, "The entire creation is my dominion." Sayyiduna Jibrael عليه السلام said to Sayyidah Maryam ؓ, "*I* will give you a son," and Sayyiduna Esa عليه السلام said, "*I* can give life to the dead; cure the blind and lepers," etc. – *The Holy Quran*

These statements of theirs are based on their trust in Allah's ﷻ favor upon them. Namrud said in opposition to Allah ﷻ, "I give life to the dead," yet he was rejected. Sayyiduna Esa عليه السلام, on the other hand, said, "I give life to the dead," but he remained a beloved of Allah ﷻ. This is because there's a major difference in context between both statements. If a robber threatens, "I can kill you," he'll be censored as a criminal, yet if a prime minister says, "I can cause you to die by hanging," he's regarded as truthful.

2. We come to know that to pledge allegiance (bai'at) is necessary. Rather, it's sunnah. In fact, people made *bai'at* on the Day of Covenant (يوم الميثاق) as per the Holy Quran,

الست بربكم ، قالوا بلى

"Am I not your Lord?' They answered, 'Yes."
– Surah A'rāf (7), Verse 172

The Sahaabah pledged allegiance on the hands of the Prophet ﷺ, and anyone who came to accept Islam did so too. However, this pledge was for Islam, whereas the pledge in Hudaibiyah was for Jihad. At times Rasoolullah ﷺ would take specific pledges from people (e.g. he took pledges from some not to beg from anyone).

Thereafter, pledges were made on the hands of the Four Khalifas, but this was an affirmation of power and succession as well as a pledge of loyalty (i.e. an allegiance by a spiritual seeker). This is why the tradition of *bai'at* with spiritual guides wasn't habitual at that time (Hadrat Abu Bakr ؓ and Umar ؓ, etc were spiritual masters themselves). The pledging of allegiance was also an affirmation of succession (khilāfat). So, it had to be made at the hands of every Khalifa who gained it.

When the era of the Khalifas ended, power remained with kings. For this reason, a pledge as an affirmation of power and rule was made with Muslim kings while the pledge of spirituality was made with the Shaikhs. The word murīd (the title of the one who pledges allegiance) means 'someone who seeks.' A murīd is a seeker of Allah's ﷻ pleasure. So, he has been given this identity. The word has been deduced from the following Quranic verse,

يريدون وجه الله ، واولئك هم المفلحون

'Those who seek the pleasure of Allah ﷻ, and it's they who are prosperous.'
– Surah Rūm (30), Verse 38

Rule – To pledge allegiance to a spiritual master (مرشد) is important. Maulana Jalaaluddin Rumi ؓ states,

'Select a guide, for without him the path of this journey is littered with hardship, fear and risk.'
– Mathnawi Sharif

It's stated in *Karpūti Sharah Qasida Burda* that Shaitaan is the guide of a person who doesn't take the guidance of the accomplished. The Holy Quran states,

يوم ندعوا كل اناس بامهم

'On the day of Qiyaamat when We will call every people with their leaders.'
– Surah Bani Israel (17), Verse 71

In other words, the call will be given, "O Chishtis, O Qadris, O Suharwardis, O Naqshbandis," or, "O Hanafis, O Shafis, O Maalikis, O Hambalis!" Those who don't accept the guidance of the accomplished will be called with, "O Shaitaans," for as I've just submitted, Shaitaan is the guide of he who doesn't take the guidance of the accomplished. – *Tafseer Roohul-Bayaan (under the commentary of Surah Bani Israel, Verse 71)*

A narration found in Muslim Sharif states that the death of a person who doesn't have the rope of someone around his neck (i.e. he who doesn't have the guidance of someone) is the death of ignorance.

The inner-debase/carnal self (nafs) is a dog. Put the collar of someone around it so that it doesn't stray. The progression (شجرة) of the spiritual masters is like the chain of the collar whose first link is around the neck of the disciple (murīd) while the last is in the blessed hands of Rasoolullah ﷺ. Also, if you are far from the lamp of prophethood, have a connection with those mirrors by which its light is reflected. Rasoolullah ﷺ is the rain of mercy while the Scholars and Mashaaikh are its ponds. He who can't access the rain should satisfy his field of Imaan with these alternatives.

We also come to know from this verse that it's sunnah to place the hands in the hands of the spiritual master (مرشد) when making *bai'at* because joining hands indicates strong affirmation for the allegiance. Also, we use our hands to take in the world. This is why we lift them when making dua, because it's as if we are taking from Allah ﷻ. The Holy Prophet ﷺ himself gestured to holding a handful of knowledge and bestowed it to Hadrat Abu Hurairah ؓ.

Still, it's not permissible for foreign (ghair-mahram) males to touch the hands of females as this is against *hijāb*. Yes, a Shaikh can hold the hands of his female *mahram* relatives in *bai'at*. Womenfolk cannot be made spiritual masters because being one is a type of leadership. Neither can a woman become the leader of a male nor is her leadership correct.

Rule – There are four types of *bai'ats* (pledges of allegiance), and the *bai'ats* prevalent today is the *bai'at of Iraadat* (spiritual pledge). Refer to *Fataawa Africa* by Alahadrat Imam Ahmad Raza ﷾ for a detailed study on this.

Important note – Four qualities must be sought in a spiritual master before pledging allegiance to him,

1. He must be Sahihul-Aqeedah (i.e. his beliefs must be in accordance to the Ahle-Sunnah wal-Jamaat).

2. He must have sufficient knowledge to guide people.

3. He must not be an open sinner. Rather, he should be pious in nature.

4. His spiritual chain must correctly reach the Holy Prophet ﷺ.

If a 'spiritual master' lacks in *even one* of these qualities, *bai'at* must not be made on his hands.

3. At the time of pledging allegiance, the disciple should give his hands into the hands of the spiritual master. The verse states, "Allah's ﷾ hand is above their hands." So, we come to know that Rasoolullah ﷺ took their hands during the pledge. However, when *bai'at* is taken from females, it must only be a verbal allegiance. Foreign males may not touch the hands of foreign womenfolk.

Sayyidah Aisha Siddiqah ﷾ states, "Never did the Holy Prophet ﷺ touch the hand of any female when making *bai'at*." – *Mishkaat*

In fact, womenfolk should observe covering before their Shaikhs if they are foreign.

The disciple touching the hands of the master is for the Noor attained from Rasoolullah ﷺ and transmitted through the Mashaaikh to manifest its blessings within the disciple. It's permissible for a

Shaikh to hold one end of a shawl and extend the other end to a female foreign woman in *bai'at* so that the Noor is conveyed to her as well.

The successor (*sajjādah-nashīn*) of a Shaikh must also possess the four qualities of a spiritual guide mentioned above. This is the command of the Shariah. A successor can be selected in the following ways,

1. The Shaikh himself chooses his successor during his lifetime, just as how Hadrat Abu Bakr Siddique ؓ chose Hadrat Umar ؓ as the Khalifa during his lifetime.

2. After the demise of the Shaikh, the general body of the Shaikh's disciples chooses someone as his successor. The caliphate of Hadrat Abu Bakr ؓ is an example of this. The Holy Prophet ﷺ didn't declare it; it was after the consultation of the general body of Muslims that Hadrat Abu Bakr Siddique ؓ was chosen as the leader.

3. Selected, trusted individuals from amongst the disciples make someone the Khalifa. The caliphates of Hadrat Uthman ؓ and Hadrat Ali ؓ are examples of this. Their caliphates were established by the consultation of authorities amongst the Companions.

These Khilaafats are proof of the Khilaafats prevalent today. Sadly, in our current era, people say that the son of the master should also be a Shaikh, irrespective of whether his father granted him successor-ship (خلافت) or not, whether he is worthy of being a spiritual master or not, or whether the disciples are content with him or not. This is completely wrong. The annotator of Qasida Burda Sharif, Allama Karputi ؓ, has strongly refuted this notion. He writes, "Today, becoming the successor has become a form of amusement, that the minor son of the Shaikh is also made a Shaikh even though he doesn't fulfill the criteria of one nor is he worthy of being made so. May Allah ﷻ grant us the ability to travel on the path of righteousness. The offspring of Shaikhs also regard being Shaikhs as their inheritance. If succession was inheritance, the children of the Four Khalifas alone would've been their successors!"

VERSE 73

لَقَدْ رَضِيَ اللهُ عَنِ الْمُؤْمِنِيْنَ إِذْ يُبَايِعُوْنَكَ تَحْتَ الشَّجَرَةِ فَعَلِمَ مَا فِيْ قُلُوبِهِمْ فَأَنْزَلَ السَّكِيْنَةَ عَلَيْهِمْ وَأَثَابَهُمْ فَتْحًا قَرِيْبًا

'Certainly Allah ﷻ was pleased with the believers when they were pledging allegiance to you under the tree, and He knew what was in their hearts. So, He sent down on them tranquility and rewarded them with an expedition's victory.'
– Surah Fat'h (48), Verse 18

This verse also proclaims the honor of the Holy Prophet ﷺ, and mentions within it the excellence of those fortunate people who pledged allegiance on his blessed hands (in the *Bai'atur-Ridwaan*). The Companions who made this pledge received four distinctions in this verse,

1. Certainty of Allah's ﷻ pleasure.

2. Glad-tidings of victory and aid soon.

3. Descent of tranquility.

4. Great spoils of victory.

When this is the amount of favors bestowed upon those who only made *bai'at*, who then can fathom the greatness and excellence of he through whose blessings these favors were attained (i.e. Rasoolullah ﷺ)?!

> The Holy Prophet's ﷺ comfort is so pivotal that even commands of Islamic Law are relaxed for it.

1,400 Sahaabah took part in the Bai'atur-Ridwaan. It's called 'Ridwaan' because the participants were informed that Allah ﷻ is pleased with them (*Ridwaan* means contentment). However, this doesn't mean that Allah ﷻ isn't pleased with others besides these Companions. Indeed He is pleased with all of the Sahaabah and has promised Jannah to each and every one of them. Allah ﷻ says in the Holy Quran,

و كلا وعد الله الحسنى
'And Allah ﷻ has promised all the reward of Paradise.'
– Surah Hadīd (57), Verse 10

رضى الله عنهم ورضوا عنه ، ذلك لمن خشى ربه

'Allah ﷻ is well pleased with them and they are well pleased
with Him. This is for him who fears his Lord.'
– Surah Bayyinah (98), Verse 8

This is why it's permissible to say 'Radiyallahu Anhum' (Allah ﷻ is pleased with them) and 'Rahmatullah Alaihi' (May the mercy of Allah ﷻ be upon them) for all of the Prophet's ﷺ Ahle-Bait (Family), Companions, Saints and Scholars. – *Raddul-Muhtaar, Kitaabul-Karaahiyat*

Those who speak ill of the Sahaabah, especially the participants of the Bai'atur-Ridwaan (Allah ﷻ forbid) or calls them Hypocrites, or says that Hadrat Abu Bakr Siddique ﷺ, Hadrat Umar ﷺ, or Hadrat Uthman ﷺ became apostates are themselves apostates and non-Muslims. Their claim would necessitate that Allah ﷻ had no knowledge of the Companions' end result, whereas Allah ﷻ has verified His contentment with them. Indeed, Allah ﷻ is All-Knowing. When He is content with someone, that person is truly an inmate of Jannah. In fact, he becomes the leader of its inmates!

This pledge occurred either under an acacia tree or a berry tree (narrations found in *Tafseer Roohul-Bayaan* substantiate the former). Divine power caused this tree to disappear, and people later began visiting (زيارة) another tree (thinking it to be the original). They even performed Salaah there for the sake of blessings. Hadrat Umar ﷺ initially stopped them because it wasn't the original tree, but when he came to know that the people were misled into believing the second tree to be the actual one, he cut it down to save them from committing this mistake. – *Muslim, Kitaabul-Imaaraat, Baabu Bai'atur-Ridwaan; Bukhari, Kitaabul-Maghaazi; Tafseer Roohul-Bayaan, under the commentary of this verse*

Some people use this action of Hadrat Umar ﷺ to justify demolishing the graves of the Saints and disrespecting them. They say, "Hadrat Umar ﷺ cut the tree down, so we'll destroy these relics."

Under the commentary of this verse, the author of *Tafseer Roohul-Bayaan* states that such people are totally bereft of the deen and this action of theirs is an act of infidelity (كفر). Pharaoh said the very same thing,

ذروني اقتل موسى وليدع ربه
"'Leave me alone that I may kill Musa, and let him call his lord.'"
– Surah Mu'min (40), Verse 26

If Hadrat Umar ﷠ opposed the respect of sacred relics, why did he spare the other prophetic relics, such as Rasoolullah's ﷺ blessed hair and clothes, etc. which the Sahaabah also visited? Why did he himself construct the Rauda of the Holy Messenger ﷺ? Scholars of the Ummah have visited Madina Sharif throughout the ages, yet none of them objected to the building of the blessed Rauda. Refer to my book, *Ja'al-Haqq*, for proof from the Holy Quran, Hadith, and verdicts of the Jurists regarding the construction of buildings and domes, etc. for the Saints.

Roohul-Bayaan mentions a Hadith wherein Rasoolullah ﷺ is reported to have said to the Sahaabah who made this pledge, "You are the most excellent of people on Earth." It was further said, "Sayyiduna Khidr ﷜ also made this pledge." The proof of this is that Sayyiduna Khidr ﷜ is a prophet, and the Sahaabah are not superior to Prophets ﷜. So, we have to conclude that Sayyiduna Khidr ﷜ also made this pledge since he was alive on Earth.

VERSE 74

هُوَ الَّذِى أَرْسَلَ رَسُولَه بِالْهُدى وَدِينِ الْحَقِّ لِيُظْهِرَه عَلَى الدِّينِ كُلِّه ، وَكَفى بِاللهِ شَهِيْدًا ، مُحَمَّدٌ رَّسُوْلُ اللهِ ، وَالَّذِيْنَ مَعَه أَشِدَّاءُ عَلَى الْكُفَّارِ رَحَمَاءُ بَيْنَهُمْ ، تَرَاهُمْ رُكَّعًا سُجَّدًا يَّبْتَغُوْنَ فَضْلًا مِّنَ اللهِ وَرِضْوَنًا

'It's He Who sent His Messenger ﷺ with guidance and the religion of truth so that He may make it present over all other religions; and Allah ﷻ suffices as a witness. Muhammad ﷺ is the Messenger of Allah ﷻ, and those with him are severe against the infidels but compassionately tender among themselves. You will see them bowing and prostrating themselves (in power) seeking grace from Allah ﷻ and His pleasures.'
– Surah Fat'h (48), Verses 28-9

This verse is the praise of the Holy Prophet ﷺ as well as praise for his Companions.

There are a few points to discuss regarding it,

1. In 'It's He', Allah ﷻ presented Himself.

2. In 'Muhammad ﷺ is the Messenger of Allah ﷻ', Allah ﷻ presented the Holy Prophet ﷺ.

3. In 'Those with him', Allah ﷻ presented the Sahaabah.

In other words, one can say that Allah ﷻ presented Himself through the Holy Beloved ﷺ, and introduced His Holy Beloved ﷺ through the Sahaabah.

In "It's He Who has sent His Messenger ﷺ", Allah ﷻ is saying, "O humanity, if you wish to identify the Lord, know that it's He who has made and sent such a Messenger ﷺ to you." A good example of this is when a skillful teacher says, "I'm the one who has made this certain student accomplished. If you wish to see my prowess in knowledge, look at this student, because he's the example of my knowledge and skill." The power of Allah ﷻ too has affinity for this unique masterpiece of creation (i.e. the Holy Prophet ﷺ). If you wish to view the manifestation of Allah's ﷻ mercy, benevolence, wisdom – in fact, *all* of the Divine attributes – look no further than the Holy Messenger ﷺ of Allah ﷻ. Indeed, Rasoolullah ﷺ is the manifestation of Allah's ﷻ Qualities. Discussion on this is very lengthy.

Another example to further clarify this is that no naked eye can view the sun directly, but if the sun's reflection is captured on a glass screen, its brilliance may then be witnessed through it. Prophets ﷺ are similar to this screen – they help us view the Qualities of Allah ﷻ.

There are two interpretations of 'guidance',

1. Allah ﷻ sent His Beloved ﷺ as someone already possessing guidance. In other words, people are guided by their parents, teachers, elders, friends, etc. by accepting their advice, but there's no need for the Holy Prophet ﷺ to be so. Allah ﷻ bestowed him every type of guidance (this is why Rasoolullah ﷺ performed sajda as soon as he was born). – *Roohul-Bayaan (under this verse)*

   The Prophet ﷺ always drank from one side of the nurse, Sayyidah Halima ؓ, and left the other for his brothers. He performed Salaah even before proclaiming his prophethood!

2. It can also mean, "O people! Your guidance has been granted to the Holy Messenger ﷺ," meaning whoever will attain any guidance will acquire it from him. Allah ﷻ made His Beloved ﷺ the fountain-head of guidance and salvation.

Also, 'Religion of truth' may either mean 'true religion' or 'mighty religion'. In other words, although the deens of previous Prophets ﷺ were true, they weren't permanent (so they were abrogated). The deen of Rasoolullah ﷺ, however, is true as well as strong. So, it can never be annulled.

The verse states, "Muhammad ﷺ is the Messenger of Allah ﷻ". Other Prophets عليهم السلام were also messengers, but the Holy Prophet ﷺ was mentioned here specifically. *Tafseer Roohul-Bayaan* lists the following reasons for this,

1. Other Prophets عليهم السلام came into this world and *thereafter* became Messengers عليهم السلام (after attaiing the distinction of *risālat*, i.e. messengership). The Holy Prophet ﷺ, however, was Allah's ﷻ Messenger ﷺ even in the Realm of Souls! His proclamation of being a messenger begins from the time Allah's ﷻ worship was perceptible.

2. The Messengership and prophethood of others remained on Earth for a certain period of time, but the messengership of Rasoolullah ﷺ remains until the Day of Judgment. In fact, it's found even in Jannah. Every leaf of Paradise has written on it, "لا اله الا الله محمد رسول الله" There's none worthy of worship but Allah ﷻ, Muhammad ﷺ is the Messenger of Allah ﷻ."

3. All the Prophets عليهم السلام had unique and distinct miracles, but Rasoolullah ﷺ possessed *all* of these extraordinary miracles!

I've already presented secrets of the word 'Muhammad' in Surah Ahzāb (33).

There are two personal (ذاتی) names of the Holy Prophet ﷺ,

1. **Ahmad**, meaning he who praises the Lord as He deserves.

2. **Muhammad**, meaning he who has been praised by Allah ﷻ Himself, and Allah ﷻ further commanded the entire creation to also praise him.

Under the commentary of this verse, *Tafseer Roohul-Bayaan* states that the gathering of Meelad (i.e. celebration of the birth of the Holy Prophet ﷺ) is a demonstration of sincere respect to the Holy Messenger ﷺ, and it's practiced by the entire Ummah.

Although Rasoolullah ﷺ possesses many qualities, Allah ﷻ mentions the quality of his messengership (رسالۃ) here, which is also the quality found in the Kalima. There are two displays of wisdom behind this,

1. The Holy Prophet ﷺ has bonds with both the Creator as well as the creation, and his quality of being the Messenger mentions both of these relationships. In other words, he is sent by the Creator, and is sent to the creation. Even though this meaning is also explained when mentioning his prophethood, the quality of a prophet is only to convey Allah's ﷻ message, whereas the quality of a Messenger is to transmit both messages of salvation *and* the blessings of Allah ﷻ.

2. A messenger is responsible for joining two separated beings. Affinity between these two would end if it were not for a messenger between them. Similarly, Rasoolullah ﷺ is the individual sent to create a relationship between the Creator and the creation. If he is removed from the equation, there wouldn't be affinity between Allah ﷻ and us. The Holy Prophet ﷺ is the Messenger of Allah ﷻ and relays His blessings to us. He is also our Messenger ﷺ and presents our requests in the court of Allah ﷻ. He even forgives our sins after presenting them there.

The person who says that he will reach Allah's ﷻ court himself is actually refuting the messengership of Rasoolullah ﷺ. If we *could* reach Allah's ﷻ court ourselves, what need was there for a messenger? How could we, the sinful, even think that we can have an affinity with Allah ﷻ without the means of a messenger?! This is why Allah ﷻ states,

ولو انهم اذ ظلموا انفسهم جاءوك فاستغفروا الله واستغفر لهم الرسول لوجدوا الله توابا رحيما

'And when they do injustice unto their souls (O Beloved ﷺ), they should come to you and beg forgiveness of Allah ﷻ, and the Messenger ﷺ should intercede for them. Then surely they would find Allah ﷻ Most Relenting, Most Merciful."
– Surah Nisā (4), Verse 64

'Those with him' speaks of four qualities,

1. Companionship with the Holy Prophet ﷺ,

2. Believers being tough against non-Muslims…

3. While being kind and merciful amongst themselves,

4. Performing *ruku* and *sajda* extensively, i.e. being dedicated worshippers (عابدين).

Through the grace of Allah ﷻ, all the Companions were blessed with these qualities, but each Khalifa, in order of their Caliphate, were the epitomes of the above.

Companionship with the Holy Prophet ﷺ (1) was made famous by Hadrat Abu Bakr Siddique ؓ, harshness against non-Muslims (2) by Hadrat Umar ؓ, kindness and mercy towards believers (3) by Hadrat Uthman ؓ, and extensive worship (4) by Hadrat Ali ؓ. These Khalifas are similar to four sides of a glass case surrounding the light of prophethood. If you wish to see the prophetic light, look no further than towards them. He who is far from these personalities is actually far from the Noor of Rasoolullah ﷺ. Could Allah ﷻ choose for His Beloved ﷺ the companionship of those who, Allah ﷻ forbid, didn't possess Imaan?! Definitely not! If dust remains near a flower, it also begins to emit a fragrance, and if the sun focuses its light on an impure piece of land, the land becomes pure. So, how can those who remained with the Holy Messenger ﷺ not become scented themselves? How can those who sat in the Prophet's ﷺ companionship ever remain impure while he is the true sun of both the worlds? Indeed, those who transmitted the Holy Quran and Ahadith, those who propagated the deen and its teachings – in fact, those who were ultimately the *custodians* of the fragrant garden of Rasoolullah ﷺ – were the Sahaabah. If they weren't people of Islam, then Allah ﷻ forbid, it would mean that the Holy Quran and religious teachings were disseminated by heretics and contemptible people! *Astaghfirullah!*

The rank of a person who saw the splendor of Rasoolullah's ﷺ being with their naked eye of Imaan is more excellent than all of the Saints of the world. What then is the rank of those who continuously remained with the Holy Prophet ﷺ and followed him everywhere?!

Hadrat Abu Bakr Siddique ؓ accompanied Rasoolullah ﷺ so devotedly that he remained with him in the Realm of Souls prior to their advent in this world and also remained with him in this world throughout his infancy, childhood, adulthood, in journey and in residence. He was the Prophet's ﷺ loyal companion during the migration and even in the cave. Allah ﷻ states,

اذ هما فى الغار اذ يقول لصحبه لا تحزن ان الله معنا

'When they were both in the cave and when he said to his companion, 'Grieve not. Surely Allah ﷻ is with us."
– Surah Tauba (9), Verse 40

Here, the Holy Quran has conclusively declared the companionship of Hadrat Abu Bakr ؓ and has proclaimed him the 'companion' of the Cave. Hadrat Abu Bakr ؓ truly did fulfil the rights of companionship while in the Cave of Thūr.

His companionship with Rasoolullah ﷺ in demise is that they both passed away at the same age (63). The manner of his demise is also similar to the Holy Prophet's ﷺ. Poison given by a Jewish woman to the Prophet ﷺ at Khaibar was the cause of his demise, while the venom of the snake-bite in the Cave of Thūr was the reason for Hadrat Abu Bakr's ؓ. In both cases, the poison's effect returned to be the reason for their departure.

Authentic narrations state that there was no oil for the lamp in Rasoolullah's ﷺ home on the night of his demise, and at the time of Hadrat Abu Bakr's ؓ passing, there wasn't any kafn for him (or even money to buy it)! So, he was buried in the same clothes he kept in use. – *Books of Asmaa'ur-Rijaal*

After his demise, Hadrat Abu Bakr ؓ was also fortunate to attain the proximity of the Holy Prophet's ﷺ blessed grave until the Day of Qiyaamat.

> Allah ﷻ promised His Beloved ﷺ, "The *collecting* of the Holy Quran is on Us (i.e. We will make you a Hafiz of it), the *reciting* of it is on Us (i.e. We will make you a Qari), and on Us is also the *explaining of its minute detail* (i.e. We will grant you its knowledge)."
>
> So, these three things which people endure so much hardship to achieve were given to the Holy Messenger ﷺ without him having to come into any difficulty! Also, these sciences are acquired from different teachers, yet Rasoolullah ﷺ was taught by his Lord alone! *Allahu Akbar!* How great is the glory of Rasoolullah ﷺ?!

Concerning Hadrat Umar ؓ, what was the intensity of his harshness against the disbelievers?! A Hadith Sharif states, "O Umar ؓ, Shaitaan runs away from the path which he sees you walking upon." Hadrat Umar ؓ was of the opinion that Muslims shouldn't go to the grave of the Hypocrite Abdullah ibn Ubai and perform his Janaazah (and the Holy Quran later endorsed this opinion). Even today, if one writes, "Ya Umar ؓ (O Umar ؓ)!" across his chest and sleeps, he is protected from Shaitaanic-influenced dreams and nocturnal emissions.

Hadrat Uthman Ghani ﷺ granted a major favor to the Muslims by gathering the Holy Quran. There was also a shortage of water in Madina once with only one well of drinkable water. This well's owner would sell the water at an exorbitant rate, so Hadrat Uthman ﷺ purchased the well and donated it (وقف) to the Muslim Ummah. People performing Hajj will drink from this well until the Day of Judgment. So, the favor of Hadrat Uthman ﷺ will also remain for as long. Hadrat Uthman ﷺ was so merciful and benevolent that he never physically hit anyone by hand or allowed his workers to fight the rebels who would (eventually) martyr him in Madina. He only enriched the Muslims with wealth and means during his lifetime.

Hadrat Ali ﷺ too was such a devoted worshipper that he was literally *born* in the Holy Ka'ba!

'None have attained this honor except Ali ﷺ of being born
in the Ka'ba and martyred in the Musjid.'

'The Ka'ba was made the place of his birth because it was the
Ka'ba of Islam, and he the Ka'ba of Imaan.'
– Mufti Ahmed Yaar Khan Naeemi ﷺ

Hadrat Ali ﷺ is the convergence of Law and Spirituality (Shariah & Tariqah). He distributes sainthood (ولاية) amongst the Friends of Allah ﷺ and is the patriarch of the Holy Prophet's ﷺ Family (Ahle-Bait). The Prophet ﷺ was nurtured in Hadrat Ali's ﷺ home while Hadrat Ali ﷺ was nurtured in the Prophet's ﷺ home. All of the Saints humble themselves before Hadrat Ali ﷺ since they receive their validation of sainthood from him.

In short, the fragrance and appeal of each flower (i.e. the Four Khalifas) is different.

Later in this verse, Allah ﷺ used the likeness of farming to describe the Sahaabah, not a fruitful orchard. There are three reasons for this,

1. The existence of creation is dependent on farming, not on orchards bearing fruit. Fruits are eaten in luxury while items of grain and corn are among the provisions of life. Similarly, for us to lead a life of Imaan, the entire creation is dependent on the example of the Sahaabah.

2. The owner of an orchard isn't attentive to it at all times, only during the seasons when it bears its fruits. A farm owner, on the other hand,

is always observant of his farm. The Sahaabah are likewise those whom Allah's 🕮 mercy is always focused upon.

3. A farm is cut and harvested but crops are always planted again. Similarly, the Companions of the Prophet 🕮 were martyred in the initial stages of Islam yet they still increased in number. The army of Yazid destroyed the entire progression of the Prophet's 🕮 household (Ahle-Bait) except Imam Zainul-Ābideen 🕮, who was sick during the Battle of Karbala. From this, how many descendants of the Holy Prophet 🕮 are there in the world today?

VERSE 75

يَا أَيُّهَا الَّذِينَ امَنُوا لَا تُقَدِّمُوا بَيْنَ يَدَيِ اللهِ وَرَسُولِهِ ، وَاتَّقُوا اللهَ ، إِنَّ اللهَ سَمِيْعٌ عَلِيْمٌ ، يَا أَيُّهَا الَّذِينَ امَنُوا لَا تَرْفَعُوا أَصْوَاتَكُمْ فَوْقَ صَوْتِ النَّبِيِّ وَلَا تَجْهَرُوا لَهُ بِالْقَوْلِ كَجَهْرِ بَعْضِكُمْ لِبَعْضٍ أَنْ تَحْبَطَ أَعْمَالَكُمْ وَأَنْتُمْ لَا تَشْعُرُوْنَ

'O Believers! Don't commit any excess before Allah 🕮 and His Messenger 🕮, and fear Allah 🕮. Surely Allah 🕮 hears, knows. O Believers, don't raise your voices above the voice of the Prophet 🕮 and don't speak aloud in his presence as you speak to one another, lest your deeds become in vain while you are unaware.'
– Surah Hujarāt (49), Verses 1-2

This verse is also the praise of the Holy Prophet 🕮, and in it, Muslims have been taught the manner and conduct of being present in his prophetic court. We are unable to fully practice this today, but the verse is significant for two reasons,

1. Muslims must believe this conduct to be the respect of the Prophet's 🕮 court,

2. This respect is binding (even after the demise of Rasoolullah 🕮).

Whoever comes to Rasoolullah's 🕮 sacred presence must maintain this respect and not give preference to his or her own view on religious or worldly matters over the prophetic proclamation.

Believers have been commanded three things in this verse,

1. Not to commit any excess before Allah 🕮 & His Messenger 🕮.

2. Not to raise their voices above the voice of Rasoolullah 🕮.

3. Not to speak aloud in his presence.

There are two verses quoted above, and the reason for both of their revelations is different.

For the first, there are several opinions regarding the reason for its revelation. Hadrat Mujaahid ◈ and Hasan ◈ state that some people performed their qurbaani on the day of Eidul-Adha before the Prophet ﷺ. So, they were stopped from doing so and ordered not to surpass the Holy Messenger ﷺ [in any way].

Sayyidah Aisha ◈ is of the opinion that some people kept fast on the 'day of doubt' before the commencement of Ramadaan. This verse was then revealed to prohibit this. If the moon isn't sighted on the 29th of Shabaan (due to overcast conditions, etc) and there's a doubt as to whether it was seen or not, it's prohibited for general Muslims to fast on such a day. This is what is referred to as a 'day of doubt'.

Hadrat Qatāda ◈ states that some would say, "How nice if so-and-so verse was revealed", "How nice if so-and-so commands were revealed." This verse is also said to be prohibiting such wishes.

> The truth is that past, present and future tenses are used only for our understanding. Rasoolullah's ﷺ elevation was *already* enshrined before the history of time!

Hadrat Hasan ◈ states that people from afar would come to the Holy Prophet ﷺ and besiege him with questions. For this reason, this verse was revealed to stop them from doing this. – *Tafseer Roohul-Bayaan; Khazaainul-Irfaan*

Whatever the reason for the verse's revelation, its command is still applicable to all: to exceed Rasoolullah ﷺ in any action or matter is prohibited. If the Messenger ﷺ has to walk, it's unacceptable to walk in front of him (except as a servant or due to a need after seeking permission). It's also impermissible to commence eating if the meal is shared with Rasoolullah ﷺ. Likewise, to give preference to our intelligence or opinion over the Holy Messenger's ﷺ is haraam.

During his final illness, the Prophet ﷺ appointed Hadrat Abu Bakr Siddique ◈ the Imam of Salaah. One day, Rasoolullah ﷺ came to the musjid while Hadrat Abu Bakr ◈ was leading the Salaah, and immediately, the

Companion became the follower and the Prophet ﷺ the Imam. – *Mishkaat, Baabu Maa alal-Ma'moom*

We also come to know that no one has the power of becoming the Imam in the presence of Rasoolullah ﷺ. If he has to arrive while an Imam is leading, the latter's Imamat (leadership) is annulled (since this is also included in exceeding Rasoolullah ﷺ). Yes, if Rasoolullah ﷺ himself permits someone to be (or remain) the Imam, then to become or remain so is permissible. Such was the case with Hadrat Abdur-Rahman ibn Auf ؓ.

Another point we can deduce from this is that to think of the Holy Prophet ﷺ and honor him in the state of Salaah doesn't invalidate the prayer. On the contrary, it *enhances* its acceptance! This verse states that we mustn't exceed Allah ﷻ and His Rasool ﷺ, whereas surpassing Allah ﷻ is impossible, as He is free from time and space (the elements in which surpassing someone occurs). So, we ascertain the verse to refer to Rasoolullah ﷺ, and so by disrespecting him, we are also disrespecting Allah ﷻ.

'He who is rejected from his (i.e. the Holy Prophet's ﷺ) court is cursed too in the sight of Allah ﷻ!'

With reference to this verse, Allama Ismail Haqqi ؒ has proven that to walk in front of the spiritual elders and Islamic scholars, or to precede them in speech, is the outcome of deprivation. Hadrat Abu Darda ؓ narrates that he once walked in front of Hadrat Abu Bakr ؓ. Rasoolullah ﷺ saw this and said, "O Abu Darda ؓ! Do you walk before the person who's more excellent than you…in fact, the entire world?!" – *Tafseer Roohul-Bayaan*

There are also various incidents cited as the reason for the revelation of the second verse. Once, Hadrat Abu Bakr ؓ submitted to the Prophet ﷺ that Aqra ibn Haabis be appointed as the collector of Zakaat, while Hadrat Umar ؓ said that it should be Qa'qaa ibn Ma'bad. Their voices became loud in this discussion and the verse was then revealed. After this, they'd speak so softly to the Holy Messenger ﷺ that he would have to occasionally ask them what they were saying. – *Roohul-Bayaan*

Tafseer Khazaainul-Irfaan states that this verse was revealed concerning the Sahaabi Hadrat Thaabit ibn Qais ibn Shammas ؓ. He was hard of hearing. So, his voice would become loud at times.

Nevertheless, whatever the reason for this verse's revelation, the Holy Quran taught this act of respect for the prophetic court, that we are not allowed to raise our voices there. Even until today, Muslims performing Hajj and those fortunate to visit the sacred Rauda are commanded to send salaam & salutations softly and stand a small space away. In fact, some Jurists have said that if a Hadith of Rasoolullah ﷺ is being taught somewhere, other people must not speak loudly there because, even though the speaker is someone else, he's still transmitting the words of the Messenger ﷺ. – *Tafseer Roohul-Bayaan*

We are commanded in this verse not to speak in the Prophet's ﷺ court the same way we speak amongst one another. So, we understand that to address the Holy Prophet ﷺ by his name (i.e. to say, "O Muhammad!"), or to call him by proclaiming, "O man!", "O brother!", "O father!", etc. is haraam. Hadrat Abbas ؓ was the Holy Prophet's ﷺ uncle and Sayyidah Aisha ؓ was his wife. Furthermore, Hadrat Abu Bakr ؓ and Hadrat Umar ؓ were his father-in-laws, but whenever they narrated any Hadith, they didn't say, "My nephew said…", "My husband said…", or, "My son-in-law said…" They would *all* say, "The Messenger of Allah ﷺ said…" I've comprehensively discussed this under Surah Kahf (18). In short, these verses are the praise of Rasoolullah ﷺ.

VERSE 76

وَالنَّجْمِ إِذَا هَوٰى ، مَا ضَلَّ صَاحِبُكُمْ وَمَا غَوٰى ، وَمَا يَنْطِقُ عَنِ الْهَوٰى ، إِنْ هُوَ إِلَّا وَحْيٌ يُوْحٰى

'By the brightly shining star (i.e. the Holy Prophet ﷺ) when he descended from the Ascension (i.e. Mi'rāj). Your companion (the Holy Prophet ﷺ) has not strayed nor was he misled. And he does not speak of his own desire. It's no less than revelation revealed to him.'
– Surah Najm (53), Verses 1-4

These verses radiate the praise of Rasoolullah ﷺ, and three in particular have to be understood,

1. 'By the brightly shining star (i.e. the Holy Prophet ﷺ).'

2. 'Your companion (the Prophet ﷺ) has not strayed…'

3. 'And he doesn't speak of his own desire.'

A discussion on these verses follow,

1. Commentators of the Quran have differing opinions regarding what is meant by *najm* (the brightly shining star) and the true object of *hawā* (descension). Najm in Arabic refers to *a star* but can also mean *creeping plants that are spread covering the Earth* (e.g. the pumpkin

215

plant). Some say that najm refers to the Suraya (Pleiades) star in the Heavens and that *hawā* refers to *near-setting*. Just as how Allah ﷻ has taken an oath on worldly objects such as the fig, Mount Sinai, etc, so too does He take an oath on these things. Other Commentators state that najm refers to the blessed being of Rasoolullah ﷺ. They say this because the purpose of stars is to guide travelers at sea and land (as was the case in previous times) and the Holy Prophet's ﷺ being is the guide of the creation. They also say that hawā is the return from the Ascension (Mi'rāj). A return is only possible after going somewhere. So, physical ascension is proven from the Holy Quran.

Some are of the opinion that najm refers to either the Sahaabah, Islamic scholars, or the Mashaaikh, because a Hadith states, "My Sahaabah are like stars." Hawā refers to being buried in graves after demise. – *Tafseer Roohul-Bayaan*

So, an oath has been taken on the graves of the Sahaabah and Scholars of the deen. We may deduce from this that their graves are extremely sanctified. In fact, some have interpreted the following verse to refer to the graves of the Sahaabah, Scholars and Saints,

فلا اقسم بموقع النجوم

"Then I swear by the places where the stars set."
– Surah Wāqiah (56), Verse 75

2. In 'Your companion (the Holy Prophet ﷺ) has not strayed', the greatness of Rasoolullah ﷺ is proclaimed as well as his purity from sin and defective beliefs. I've comprehensively discussed this in my treatise about the Prophets عليهم السلام being unable to commit sin (معصوم). All Prophets عليهم السلام are pure from sin after prophethood, but our Beloved ﷺ was free from sin – in fact, free from even *intending* sin – both before his proclamation and afterwards. This verse establishes this belief. I'll discuss the issue of the sinlessness of the Prophets عليهم السلام under Surah Duha (93) in this book as well.

Bear in mind that '…has not strayed' is past indefinite and has no restriction of far or near. We come to know then that Rasoolullah ﷺ never strayed, either before announcing his prophethood or afterwards.

3. Regarding, 'And [the Prophet ﷺ] does not speak of his own desire. That isn't but the revelation that is revealed to him,' there are two explanations in understanding this,

1. Rasoolullah ﷺ has annihilated himself in the sea of the Oneness of Allah ﷻ to such an extent that when he speaks, although it's with his mouth, it's the speech of the Lord. I've already discussed this under Surah Anfāl (8).

2. Whatever Rasoolullah ﷺ speaks is either the Quran or Hadith, and both are regarded as revelation (wahi). The Holy Quran is Manifest Revelation (Wahi'e-Jali) and its recitation is permissible in Salaah, while the Hadith is Concealed Revelation (Wahi'e-Khafi), and although aspects of Allah's ﷻ law apply to it (e.g. respect to its credibility as a source of Islamic Law, etc.), it cannot be recited in Salaah. A comprehensive discussion on this has already been presented.

VERSE 77

مَا كَذَبَ الْفُؤَادُ مَا رَأَى ، أَفَتُمَٰرُونَهُ عَلَى مَا يَرَى ، وَلَقَدْ رَآهُ نَزْلَةً أُخْرَى ، عِنْدَ سِدْرَةِ الْمُنْتَهَى

'The heart lied not in what it saw. Do you then
dispute with him concerning what he has seen? And indeed,
he saw that splendid sight twice; near the farthest Lote-tree.'
– Surah Najm (53), Verses 11-14

This verse is also the praise of the Holy Prophet ﷺ, and it mentions him seeing something. The previous verses stated that he only communicates Allah's ﷻ speech while this verse states that he saw Allah ﷻ with his physical eyes. Rasoolullah's ﷺ Ascension (Mi'rāj) is being discussed here.

Commentators have different opinions regarding the verse's meaning. What is truly meant by '...that splendid sight'? Some say that it refers to the Prophet ﷺ seeing Sayyiduna Jibrael (no other prophet saw the archangel in his normal form, but Rasoolullah ﷺ saw him in that state twice!). Sayyiduna Jibrael would normally take the form of a human whenever he descended to the Prophets. So, this is what is meant by the verse according to some.

Others say that the verse refers to Rasoolullah ﷺ seeing Allah ﷻ. This viewpoint is then further divided into two opinions,

1. The Prophet ﷺ saw Allah ﷻ with his heart. This is the opinion of Hadrat Abbas ؓ. – *Muslim*

2. The Prophet ﷺ saw Allah ﷻ with his physical eye. This is the ruling of Hadrat Anas ibn Malik, Hasan and Ikramah ؓ. – *Tafseer Khazaainul-Irfaan*

Rasoolullah ﷺ said, "Allah ﷻ honored Musa عليه السلام with His communication and me with His vision." – *Tafseer Roohul-Bayaan*

The Ahle-Sunnah wal-Jamaat rules that the Holy Messenger ﷺ saw Allah ﷻ with his physical eyes. Imam Hasan Basri ؓ would even take an oath and say, "Rasoolullah ﷺ saw Allah ﷻ during the Mi'rāj." Imam Ahmed ibn Hambal ؓ also said, "The Prophet ﷺ saw Allah ﷻ, saw Allah ﷻ, saw Allah ﷻ…" until he ran out of breath. – *Ibid*

Rasoolullah ﷺ said,

رأيت ربى فى احسن صورة
'I've seen my Lord in a most splendid form.'
– Mishkaat, Baabul-Masaajid

Under the commentary of this Hadith, Mulla Ali Qaari ؓ states, "It's evident that the Prophet ﷺ saw Allah ﷻ with his physical eyes on the night of Mi'rāj while he was awake. This is the most correct ruling, and there's no proof that a vision in a dream is meant here." – *Mirqaatul-Mafateeh*

Hadrat Wakee ؓ narrates from Hadrat Ka'ab Ahbaar ؓ, "The Holy Prophet ﷺ saw Allah ﷻ twice." – *Tafseer Roohul-Bayaan*

Nevertheless, the preferred view is that Rasoolullah ﷺ saw Allah ﷻ. A detailed discussion on this may be found in *Shifa Sharif* and *Mawaahibul-Ladunya*.

Sayyidah Aisha ؓ strongly opposed this opinion and said, "When Allah ﷻ Himself states, '*Eyes cannot comprehend Him*' (Surah An'ām (6), Verse 103), how is Divine vision possible?"

However, the narrations of Hadrat Ibn Abbas ؓ and other senior Sahaabah have already been presented. The opinion of Sayyidah Aisha ؓ is of her own deduction (اجتهاد). She hasn't presented any narration. On the other hand, Hadrat Ibn Abbas's ؓ opinion *is* a narration, and a deduction (اجتهاد) isn't chosen when a narration is present. The meaning of the verse quoted by Sayyidah Aisha ؓ is evident: that no eye can encompass Allah ﷻ in this world. The realm of the Prophet's ﷺ Mi'rāj, however, was totally different. Won't Muslims see Allah ﷻ in the Hereafter and in Jannah?

Sayyidah Aisha ؓ also opposes the fact that Rasoolullah's ﷺ Ascension to the Heavens was physical. Her opinion isn't accepted by anyone because, again, it's based on her reasoning. She states, "The Prophet ﷺ was in my home on the night of Mi'rāj. His blessed body wasn't lost." Some believe after reading this that the Mi'rāj wasn't physical. However, when the physical Ascension did occur, it occurred from the home of Sayyidah Umme Haani bint Abu Talib ؓ [not in the house of Sayyidah Aisha ؓ].

Tafseer Roohul-Bayaan states that Rasoolullah ﷺ ascended 34 times, once physically and in a state of consciousness while the remaining times were in a dream and spiritual.

VERSE 78

اِقْتَرَبَتِ السَّاعَةُ وَانْشَقَّ الْقَمَرُ

'The Hour neared and the moon was split.'
– Surah Qamar (54), Verse 1

This verse is the praise of Rasoolullah ﷺ and it refers to two prophetic incidents,

1. The proximity of the Last Day,

2. The splitting of the moon.

1. Qiyaamat being near means that, in the respective eras of previous Prophets ﷺ, a new prophet was always awaited. Now though, the final Messenger ﷺ has come, and only Qiyaamat is expected. It can also be said that Rasoolullah's ﷺ dominion is until Qiyaamat (i.e. his deen and Quran can never be negated). He himself said,

> *'The Final Day and I are like two joined fingers.'*
> – Bukhari, Kitaabur-Riqaaq

In other words, there's no new prophet to come between Qiyaamat and Rasoolullah ﷺ. His epoch is until the end.

2. Allama Karputi ﷺ narrates the incident of the moon splitting in the following manner: Abu Jahl once wrote to the ruler of Yemen, Habib ibn Malik, saying, "Your religion is being eradicated! Come quick!" The ruler received this message and immediately came to Makkah, after which he was overwhelmed with lies about Rasoolullah ﷺ by Abu Jahl (whose motive was for the ruler, who had great influence over the Makkans, to dissuade them from accepting Islam). The ruler, however, wisely said, "A decision is given after hearing both parties. I wish to hear the case of Muhammad." So, he sent a message to Rasoolullah ﷺ stating, "I've come from Yemen and wish to meet with you."

The Holy Messenger ﷺ attended the meeting with Hadrat Abu Bakr Siddique ﷺ. When he entered, the entire gathering was awe-struck and none had the courage to say anything. Eventually, the Prophet ﷺ himself asked the ruler what he wished to enquire. After mustering up the courage, the ruler said, "You've claimed prophethood, and a miracle is necessary for prophethood." Rasoolullah ﷺ replied, "I'll demonstrate any miracle you ask for." The ruler then submitted, "I wish to see a miracle related to the heavenly abode, then I want you to tell me what the desire of my heart is." Hearing this, the Prophet ﷺ told him to proceed to the mountain of Safa to witness the miracle. There, he pointed to the full moon and the moon split into two pieces! This was seen on either side of the mountain.

> 'The set sun returned, the moon split
> on his gesture; O blind hypocrites! Marvel at
> the power of Allah's ﷻ Messenger ﷺ!'
> – Alahadrat Imam Ahmed Raza ﷺ

Rasoolullah ﷺ then said to him, "Listen to what the desire of your heart is. You have a daughter who is constantly ill. Her hands and feet are lifeless and you wish that she be cured." When Habib heard this, he immediately proclaimed the Kalima, *Laa Ilaaha Illalaahu Muhammad'ur-Rasoolullah* ﷺ! He then proceeded home and reached it at night. Outside the house, he called for the door to be opened, and his daughter, who previously couldn't even lift herself up, woke up and opened it for him! When she saw her father, she too recited the Kalima and was then asked by him where she heard this. She said, "I saw a bright personality in a dream saying to me, 'O my daughter, your father has come to Makkah and embraced Islam. You too recite the Kalima here and you'll be cured instantly.' So, in the morning, I recited the Kalima and was indeed cured from my disability." – *Allama Karputi's* ﷽ *commentary on Qasida Burda Sharif*

Approximately all the eminent Sahaabah and general body of Commentators of the Holy Quran state that the splitting of the moon already occurred (during the Prophet's ﷺ time). So, one who interprets the verse to mean that the moon will split near Qiyaamat is surely misguided. The sea was split for Sayyiduna Musa عليه السلام while the moon split on the command of the Prophet ﷺ. We come to know that Rasoolullah ﷺ has been bestowed miracles superior to those of other Prophets عليهم السلام.

VERSE 79

الرَّحْمٰنُ ، عَلَّمَ الْقُرْآنَ ، خَلَقَ الْإِنْسٰنَ ، عَلَّمَهُ الْبَيَانَ

'The Most Affectionate; Taught the Quran; He created
(the soul of) mankind; He taught him expression.'
– Surah Rahmān (55), Verses 1-4

These verses are manifest praise of the Holy Prophet ﷺ. There are two reasons cited as their reason for revelation,

1. When the verse, 'Prostrate to the Most Affectionate (al-Rahmān)' was revealed, the non-Muslims of Makkah said, "Who is this Most Affectionate? We don't know him." The verses above were then revealed wherein the Kuffaar are told, "You don't know Who's the Most Affectionate? It's He Who taught His Beloved ﷺ the Holy Quran!"

2. The non-Muslims of Makkah used to also say, "A man teaches Muhammad the Quran." So, the above verse was revealed, wherein they are being told, "It's the Creator of man that teaches the Quran."

– Tafseer Khaazin

We come to know that the teacher is Allah ﷻ the Most Affectionate (al-Rahmān), and that He taught the Holy Quran. What isn't known is who has been taught it. Upon this, the Commentators of the Quran state that the one whom the Quran was revealed upon is the one who was taught it.

So, the intensity of the Holy Prophet's ﷺ knowledge can be ascertained from this. A student's lack of knowledge can only be attributed to three reasons,

1. Either the teacher wasn't able to teach or was a miser in teaching,

2. The text that was taught was defective,

3. Or the student was incapable of learning.

Rasoolullah ﷺ has such great proximity in the Divine Court that there's no need for him to visit a doctor for treatment at the time of need. Allah ﷻ Himself sees to his needs! The Holy Prophet ﷺ is the curer of the entire creation. All of us require him, and he is dependent on Allah ﷻ alone.

There can't be a fourth reason. Here, the teacher is Allah ﷻ, the text is the Holy Quran, and the student is Rasoolullah ﷺ. If the Holy Quran contains all knowledge, when then was the Prophet's ﷺ knowledge not perfected? Who from these three are unable and imperfect? When Allah ﷻ is the perfect teacher, Rasoolullah ﷺ the perfect student, and the Holy Quran the perfect book, how can the Prophet's ﷺ knowledge ever be imperfect?

We also learn from this that Rasoolullah ﷺ is more excellent than all of the other Prophets عليهم السلام and even the entire creation. The Quran states that Sayyiduna Adam عليه السلام was taught the names of all things, Sayyiduna Dawud عليه السلام was taught how to maneuver steel, Sayyiduna Esa عليه السلام was taught the science of medicine, Sayyiduna Khidr عليه السلام was taught inspired knowledge (علم لدنی) and Sayyiduna Yusuf عليه السلام was taught the interpretation of dreams. Rasoolullah ﷺ, however, was taught *the Holy Quran* (which is far more superior than all of these things). He has also been taught all past and future occurrences. The Holy Quran states,

وعلمك ما لم تكن تعلم
'And He taught you whatever you didn't know.'
– Surah Nisā (4), Verse 113

Another point to understand is that Rasoolullah ﷺ is the direct student of Allah ﷻ, not a pupil of Sayyiduna Jibrael عليه السلام. The archangel Jibrael عليه السلام is only a messenger between Allah ﷻ & and His Beloved ﷺ. In fact, although Sayyiduna Jibrael عليه السلام used to descend with the Quran, he was unfamiliar with its secrets. Under the commentary of Surah Kahf (18), Verse 1, *Tafseer*

Roohul-Bayaan narrates that when Sayyiduna Jibrael صلى الله عليه وسلم said, "ك ('Kaaf', i.e. the first letter of Surah Maryam (19), Verse 1)," the Prophet ﷺ replied, "I've understood." The Prophet ﷺ also said the same when the other letters of the verse ('Haa', 'Yaa', 'Ain' and 'Sawd') were relayed to him. The angel was astounded regarding this since he didn't understand it while the Holy Prophet ﷺ did!

'There are secrets between Allah ﷻ & and the Beloved ﷺ which even the Kiraaman-Kaatibeen (the angels recording on our shoulders) have no idea of.'

So, when was Rasoolullah ﷺ taught? This isn't known, but it's apparent that he was taught before time, or that he was taught previously but this was the time the teaching was projected.

Mankind in 'He created mankind' refers to the blessed being of the Holy Prophet ﷺ because the perfect example is meant in absolute usage. '...Taught him expression' refers to whichever incidents occurred in the past and those that will take place afterwards. So, the verse means, "Allah ﷻ created Muhammad'ur-Rasoolullah ﷺ and taught him all branches of knowledge."

Each word of this verse is the Holy Prophet's ﷺ praise.

VERSE 80

يَا أَيُّهَا الَّذِينَ آمَنُوا اتَّقُوا اللهَ وَآمِنُوا بِرَسُولِهِ يُؤْتِكُمْ كِفْلَيْنِ مِن رَّحْمَتِهِ وَيَجْعَل لَّكُمْ نُورًا تَمْشُونَ بِهِ وَيَغْفِرْ لَكُمْ ، وَاللهُ غَفُورٌ رَّحِيمٌ

'O Believers! Fear Allah ﷻ and believe His Messenger ﷺ. He will give you a two-fold portion of His mercy, will provide a light by which you will walk, and will grant you forgiveness. And Allah ﷻ is Most Forgiving, Most Merciful.'
– Surah Hadīd (57), Verse 28

This verse is also the Prophet's ﷺ praise. 'O Believers' refers to the People of the Book (i.e. Jews and Christians) who believed in the previous Prophets صلى الله عليه وسلم. They are commanded here, "O People of the Book! Believe in this messenger of Mine! If you do, you'll attain twice the reward given to others – one for believing in your respective prophet and another for believing in the final one." Ahadith state that there are three people who'll receive twice the reward,

1. A person who owns a slave-girl, educates her, frees her, and then marries her,

2. A slave who serves his master and is obedient to Allah ﷻ,

3. The People of the Book (Ahle-Kitāb) who believed in their respective prophet *and* the Final Messenger ﷺ afterwards.

However, no one should think that if a Christian or Jew accepts Islam, he acquires more reward than the Sahaabah or Ahle-Bait, because while they are promised double the reward, a single good deed of a Companion outweighs *thousands* performed by one who isn't.

Ahadith state that if a Companion gives a small amount of barley in charity while another Muslim gives an entire mountain of gold, the reward attained by the Companion will be more than the Muslim's! Attaining reward and being high in rank are two different things. If a king handsomely pays a soldier but doesn't reward his prime-minister, the former attains wealth while the latter retains a higher rank.

VERSE 81

لَا تَجِدُ قَوْمًا يُؤْمِنُوْنَ بِاللهِ وَالْيَوْمِ الْآخِرِ يُوَآدُّوْنَ مَنْ حَآدَّ اللهَ وَرَسُوْلَه وَلَوْ كَانُوْا آبَاءَهُمْ أَوْ أَبْنَاءَهُمْ أَوْ إِخْوَانَهُمْ أَوْ عَشِيْرَتَهُمْ

'You will not find a people who believe in Allah ﷻ and the Last Day loving those who act in opposition to Allah ﷻ and His Messenger ﷺ, even though they may be their fathers, sons, brothers, or their kinsmen.'
– Surah Mujādalah (58), Verse 22

This verse is the praise of Rasoolullah ﷺ and also shows us the recognition of Muslims, which is that they don't possess love for the enemies of Allah ﷻ & His Messenger ﷺ even if these enemies are their own close relatives. We come to know that although our parents have great rights over us, the right of the Holy Prophet ﷺ outweighs the rights of others.

Rasoolullah ﷺ commanded us to keep beards. So, it's impermissible to shave it off completely, even if our parents, wives, friends or family members order us to do otherwise. Similarly, Allah ﷻ has commanded us to perform Salaah. So, if our parents or other family members tell us to forsake it, they won't be followed, because again, the rights of Allah ﷻ and His Messenger ﷺ take precedence over all others. Likewise, if someone's parents, children or relatives are non-Muslims or apostates (مرتدين), having love for and friendship with them is totally haraam.

The commentary of this verse reflects the lives of the Sahaabah,

1. In the Battle of Uhud, Hadrat Abu Ubaidah ibn Jarraah ؓ executed his father (Jarraah) due to his father's contempt for Rasoolullah ﷺ.

2. Once, Hadrat Abu Bakr Siddique ؓ called his son, Abdur-Rahman ؓ (who was a non-Muslim at the time), to fight against him. He said, "Come, Abdur-Rahman! Let a father and son do battle today." However, Rasoolullah ﷺ stopped him from doing so.

3. Hadrat Mus'ab ibn Umair ؓ killed his non-Muslim brother, Abdullah ibn Umair ؓ.

4. Hadrat Umar ؓ killed his non-Muslim uncle, 'As ibn Hisham,

5. And Hadrat Ali ؓ and Hadrat Hamza ؓ killed their close relatives, Utba and Shaiba, in the Battle of Badr.

– Tafseer Roohul-Bayaan, Khazaainul-Irfaan

Those who have Imaan on Allah ﷻ and His Rasool ﷺ honor believers and criticize non-believers.

This verse proves that it's haraam to love and have social interaction with those who swear Allah ﷻ and His Messenger ﷺ. Having affection for them and happily associating with them is a sign of being bereft of faith. A loyal son doesn't love his father's enemies. If someone has to swear and curse our parents, we refuse to interact with him. So, how can we intermingle and love those who ridicule and slander the Holy Prophet ﷺ, the one upon whom our parents, children, and even our lives, are sacrificed?!

A snake takes our life whereas 'friends' who are truly wolves in sheep clothing steal our Imaan. If a wealthy person maintains a friendly relationship with honorable thieves, he is soon parted with his wealth. Likewise, if believers have love and adoration for those deprived of Imaan, they'll soon be robbed of their own. There are many examples (even today) which prove that love for the astray causes one to also become astray.

VERSE 82

وَمَا اٰتٰكُمُ الرَّسُوْلَ فَخُذُوْهُ وَمَا نَهٰكُمْ عَنْهُ فَانْتَهُوْا

'And whatever the Messenger of Allah ﷺ gives you, take it; and stay away from that which he prohibits you from.'
– Surah Hashr (59), Verse 7

This verse is also the praise of Rasoolullah ﷺ. Indeed, the Holy Messenger ﷺ is the master of all believers and we are his destitute and needy slaves. We learn from this that a faithful believer is he who accepts every command of Rasoolullah ﷺ without question, whether it makes sense to him or not, and whether he finds any worldly benefit in it or not.

The Holy Prophet ﷺ prohibited interest. Even though there externally seems to be worldly benefit in it, Imaan demands that we forsake it. Only in obedience to Rasoolullah's ﷺ commands is there gain.

Whatever the Holy Prophet ﷺ did himself (Sunnat'e-Fe'li), commanded (Sunnat'e-Qawli), or saw and didn't prohibit (Sunnat'e-Sukooti) all fall under '…whatever the Messenger of Allah ﷺ gives you.' Also, bear in mind that it's only the status of Rasoolullah ﷺ that his every action and command is worthy of emulation and practice. None besides him possesses this distinction, because the Beloved Prophet's ﷺ every action and proclamation is from Allah ﷻ while our utterances and deeds are at times Shaitaani and from our carnal desires. Shaitaan and our impure desires (Nafs'e-Ammarah) cannot accept Rasoolullah ﷺ. Just as how only gold emanates from a gold mine, so too is only truth uttered by the Messenger ﷺ. So, practice upon his commands and actions without indecision and measure the proclamations and deeds of others by the yardstick of Islamic Law (Shariah).

VERSE 83

هُوَ الَّذِى أَرْسَلَ رَسُوْلَه بِالْهُدى وَدِيْنِ الْحَقِّ لِيُظْهِرَه عَلَى الدِّيْنِ كُلِّه وَلَوْ كَرِهَ الْمُشْرِكُوْنَ

'It's He Who sent His Messenger ﷺ with guidance and the true religion so that He may cause it to dominate over all religions, even though the polytheists may hate it.'
– Surah Saff (61), Verse 9

This verse is the praise of Rasoolullah ﷺ and also speaks of Islam's dominion. I've discussed the secrets of 'It's He…' at the end of Surah Fat'h (48). Here, I'd like to submit that Allah ﷻ has promised to make Islam dominant over all other religions. Naturally, Allah ﷻ fulfills His promises, and we can see this even today.

When the light of Islam first dawned in Makkah, its radiance was covered by dust and dark clouds, to the extent that the inviter towards Islam (Rasoolullah ﷺ) and the Muslims were forced to leave the city. Ultimately, Islam became dominant over the entire Arabian Peninsula (including

Makkah). Previously regarded as one of the most debased nations of the globe, the Arabs would eventually become the world's leaders through the blessing of the Holy Prophet's ﷺ 23 years of teaching. The ignorant became teachers, thieves became protectors, the uncouth taught manners, alcoholics broke the cases of intoxication and immersed themselves in the love of Allah ﷻ, and worshippers all over began to worship the One, True, Divine Being. Through the Prophet's ﷺ blessings, who could ever count the positive changes brought within humanity and the world?!

Rasoolullah's ﷺ reformation of the Arabs – rather, the *entire planet* – occurred within just a short space of time in the backdrop of impoverished means. No leader of any nation until today can boast any likeliness in this regard. The Prophet ﷺ even made his followers rulers and kings, who likewise dominated the world with awe and power. By the grace of Allah ﷻ, the Messenger's ﷺ slaves are still kings today, even though our state of affairs has become a plea of mercy.

Today, the Muslim Ummah is lagging behind other nations in respect to worldly wealth, honor, power and knowledge, etc. It's a reality that they have succeeded us in these matters, but if one pays careful attention, he'll realize that religious wonder is still only possessed by Muslims. Examples of this follow,

1. If musjids, churches and temples are compared with one another, we'd see that musjids are the ones that are the most frequented (5 times a day). Churches are visited only on Sundays, and even though temples are visited daily (in the evenings), only a few followers of the Hindu faith endeavor doing so.

2. The recitation, transcription and phonetics of the Holy Quran – in fact, its every letter – is protected, while the true Old Testament (Torah), the New Testament (Bible) and the Vedas are all lost. Bibles sold today are translations with interpolation, not the original record.

3. The commentaries and recitation modes of the Holy Quran outnumber any other 'religious text'.

4. A *hafiz* (one who memorizes the Quran) can be found in every city. If even one letter is incorrectly pronounced, the mistake will be rectified almost at once. No other religion can boast someone who has memorized their particular religious text.

5. The life of the Holy Messenger ﷺ (even before his birth), including his domestic life, public life, the manner in which he sat, walked, talked, smiled, etc. – in fact, his every physical countenance, *to the extent of how many of his blessed hairs were white!* – is comprehensively recorded. No other religious leader's life has been chronicled to this extent. What exactly is the Hadith? It's truly the biography of Rasoolullah ﷺ. No king or accomplished personality of this world has such a grand bio written about them.

Muslims consume the meat of only halaal animals such as sheep, goats and cows, etc. Pork is the staple diet of other nations of the world. How abhorred, then, is the animal which is its source? Truly where there's smoke, there's fire.

In fact, nations of the world are slowly beginning to accept Islamic rulings and law. Objectors were once against Islam's law of marrying more than one wife, but when we began to understand that men are outnumbered by women, the wisdom in this law becomes apparent.

I'll conclude this discussion for the sake of brevity. Otherwise, if we were to discuss the beauty and wisdom behind every Islamic ruling, this book would not end!

So, in short, Muslims still possess Islamic domination. Yes, if we *are* subdued in the world due to our negligence in practicing Islam, it would be solely due to our shortcomings, not Islam's. May Allah ﷻ grant us the ability to hold strong to the rope of Islam.

VERSE 84

وَلِلّٰهِ الْعِزَّةُ وَلِرَسُوْلِهٖ وَلِلْمُؤْمِنِيْنَ وَلٰكِنَّ الْمُنٰفِقِيْنَ لَا يَعْلَمُوْنَ

'And to Allah ﷻ belongs the dignity, and to His Messenger ﷺ
and the believers, but the Hypocrites don't know.'
– Surah Munafiqūn (63), Verse 8

Rasoolullah's ﷺ blessed praise is clearly expressed in this verse, his great honor and dignity is spoken in it, and the respectability possessed by Muslims through his blessed means is also mentioned.

The reason for this verse's revelation is as follows: After the Battle of Muraisee, the Prophet ﷺ set up camp near a well to rest. Here, a fight occurred between Jahjah Ghaffari (the servant of Hadrat Umar ؓ) and

Sinaam ibn Dehar Jhany (an ally of the Hypocrite, Abdullah ibn Ubai). Abdullah ibn Ubai seized this opportunity to malign the Holy Messenger ﷺ, saying, "On reaching Madina, we praiseworthy people will expel these dishonorable individuals out of the city (referring to the Muslims who migrated from Makkah)." He also said to his tribe, "If you withhold your leftovers from them, they won't be able to over-ride you. So, from now on, don't give them anything, and make them run away from Madina."

Hadrat Zaid ibn Arqam ؓ became impatient with this slander and said to him, "You're truly a dishonorable wretch! The crown of the Ascension (Mi'rāj) is on the blessed head of the Prophet ﷺ, and Allah ﷻ has granted him strength and honor." Abdullah ibn Ubai replied, "Keep quiet. I was only joking."

Hadrat Zaid ؓ then informed Rasoolullah ﷺ of this utterance, and when the Prophet ﷺ asked Abdullah ibn Ubai if he truly made such a comment, he denied it under oath. Even his people supported him by saying, "Abdullah ibn Ubai is a senior member of our tribe and cannot speak lies. Zaid ibn Arqam must be mistaken." Upon this, the above verse was revealed, confirming what was said by Hadrat Zaid ؓ and negating the denial of Abdullah ibn Ubai.

> From the narrations that have been transmitted, we know that the knowledge of every grain, particle, and drop from the inception of time until the Day of Judgment has been given to the Holy Prophet ﷺ. The very core of the Earth until the heights of the Heavens have been shown to him. He has even been given the knowledge of when a bird flaps its wings.

Allama Ismail Haqqi ؓ states under this verse that Abdullah ibn Ubai's son was an accomplished Companion named Hadrat Abdullah ؓ. When he was informed of his father's disgraceful utterance, he apprehended him at the gates of Madina and drew his sword from its scabbard, stopping him from entering the city and commanding, "Father! Attest that Allah ﷻ is All Glorified and that Muhammad'ur-Rasoolullah ﷺ is also honored! If not, I'll slay your neck!" Out of fear, Abdullah ibn Ubai was forced to make this statement. When Rasoolullah ﷺ heard about this incident, he supplicated for the Sahaabi, Hadrat Abdullah ؓ. – *Tafseer Roohul-Bayaan*

We come to know that to sacrifice one's parents, children, and even one's own dignity (i.e. everything) on the honor of the Holy Prophet ﷺ was the practice of the Sahaabah. Rasoolullah's ﷺ right truly overshadows the rights of anyone else.

This verse establishes dignity for Allah ﷻ, His Messenger ﷺ, and (through his blessings) Muslims as well. 'Izzat' (used in the verse) literally means *dominion* and *strength*, and indeed, it's only for these three until Qiyaamat.

Allah's ﷻ dignity is that nothing occurs in the world without His desire. He is truly the Most Powerful and Mighty. True power belongs to Him, and He is the Helper and Guardian of all. If He gives honor to someone, none can make that person dishonorable, and if He gives dishonor to someone, none can grant that person honor. His greatness was, and will eternally exist. Everyone is finite while He is Everlasting (Bāqī), and everything is dependent on Him.

Rasoolullah's ﷺ honor is that he has no fear for his ultimate fate. Allah ﷻ bestowed him with honor, intercession, and granted his religion dominion over all other religions. Allah ﷻ is Sufficient (Kāfī) for the Holy Prophet ﷺ, and so Rasoolullah ﷺ isn't needy of anyone from the creation. Rather, everyone created is needy of the Prophet's ﷺ benevolence. Respect for the Prophet ﷺ is respect for Allah ﷻ, and dishonor and disobedience towards him is also disobedience towards Allah ﷻ. Rasoolullah's ﷺ blessed being is the manifestation of Allah's ﷻ glory and splendor. Sinners like us are commanded to present ourselves at the Prophet's ﷺ blessed door. The Prophet ﷺ rules over everything in this world; animals, stones, trees, etc. all present Salaam to him; and jinns, humans and even angels invoke his supplication. The kings of the world are beggars at his door, Sayyiduna Jibrael عليه السلام is a servant of his court, the height of the Heavens is the point of his Ascension, the Earth is his throne, and eyes hopeful of mercy will be fixed on him on the Day of Judgment. In short, who am I to relate even a miniscule part of his honor? To summarize his dignity, one can only say, "Only his Lord Who bestowed him honor and he who received this honor know the intensity of this greatness." In the words of the esteemed Friends of Allah ﷺ,

'After the being of Allah ﷻ is the honor of Rasoolullah ﷺ.'

Mawaahibul-Ladunya states that when a Muslim performs a good deed, one reward is attained by the doer, two by his spiritual master (murshid/teacher), four by his master's master and eight by his master. Likewise, the higher you progress, the more the amount increases. When this reward arrives in the Holy Prophet's ﷺ court, it comes as infinite reward! Also, this is regarding *just one* deed of the Ummah. How many good deeds are performed by

Muslims daily?! Now think of the amount of reward presented in the Prophetic court! It's truly beyond our estimation. A Hadith states,

من دل على خير فله مثل اجر فاعله

*'He who guides someone to a good deed acquires
the reward similar to the doer.'*
– Mishkaat, Kitaabul-Ilm

Truly the greatest guide to humanity is the Holy Prophet ﷺ. Whoever performs (or will perform) any good deed until Qiyaamat does so through his guidance. So, how could we ever hope to count the reward that he receives?! Having faith on this isn't strange. Have you forgotten that it's Allah ﷻ the All-Powerful Lord Who grants reward? And what does His generosity lack? This, too, is a reflection of the Holy Prophet's ﷺ honor. Allah ﷻ states,

وإن لك لأجرا غير ممنون

'And surely for you (O Prophet ﷺ) is an endless reward.'
– Surah Qalam (68), Verse 3

The dignity of the believers is that they will not remain under eternal punishment in Jahannam, they are the true servants and loyal devotees of their Lord, and all other nations are subservient to them (from a religious point of view). The verse under discussion confirms this, and if believers remain true and sincere, dominion and kingship is promised for them. Allah ﷻ states,

وأنتم الأعلون إن كنتم مؤمنين

'And you will be superior if you have faith.'
– Surah Ale-Imran (3), Verse 139

The religion of the believers will remain until Qiyaamat, their Divine Book is protected, and Saints, Scholars & Aghwās (plural of *Ghaus*, i.e. high-ranking Friends of Allah ﷻ) are present amongst them everywhere. Through the effects of wudhu, their hands, faces and feet will be shining bright like the fourteenth moon on the Day of Judgment. They'll enter Paradise before all other nations, and half of it will belong to them (while the other half will facilitate the rest).

In the previous verse, I discussed the honor of Muslims and the dominion of our religion. Now I wish to present the following to reflect on: Baitul-Muqaddas is the qiblah of Jews, Christians and other People of the Book while the Ka'ba is the qiblah of only Muslims. However, Hajj is made only to the Ka'ba, not Baitul-Muqaddas, so the glory and splendor enjoyed by the Ka'ba isn't possessed by Baitul-Muqaddas. Jinns worked in building Baitul-Muqaddas and Sayyiduna Sulaiman عليه السلام was their commander. On the other hand, Allah ﷻ *Himself* commanded the construction of the Holy Ka'ba; Sayyiduna Jibrael عليه السلام, Sayyiduna Ibrahim عليه السلام and Sayyiduna Ismail عليه السلام all worked on it; and it was the Holy Messenger ﷺ who preserved its honor! There are thousands of Prophets عليهم السلام resting in Baitul-Muqaddas, but there's only Sayyiduna Muhammad'ur-Rasoolullah ﷺ present in Madina Munawwarah. Still, Baitul-Muqaddas doesn't receive even a tenth of the number of visitors Madina does!

In short, Allah ﷻ has blessed Muslims with every kind of religious and worldly honor. Indeed, honor isn't based on wealth or power. These are merely blessings we may or may not acquire.

Important Note – While this verse establishes dignity for three (Allah ﷻ, Rasoolullah ﷺ & the Believers), another verse states,

إن العزه لله جميعا

'Surely all honor belongs to Allah ﷻ.'
– Surah Yunus (10), Verse 65

The explanation for this is that true, inherent (ذاتی) and eternal honor is solely for Allah ﷻ while measurable honor Divinely bestowed by Him is also possessed by the Prophets عليهم السلام, Saints ﷺ & Muslims. Another interpretation could be that the honor possessed by all others is truly possessed by Allah ﷻ.

VERSE 85

ن ، وَالْقَلَمِ وَمَا يَسْطُرُوْنَ ، مَا أَنْتَ بِنِعْمَةِ رَبِّكَ بِمَجْنُوْنَ ، وَإِنَّ لَكَ لَأَجْرًا غَيْرَ مَمْنُوْنَ

'Nūn; By the Pen and what they write; By the grace of your Lord, you are not at all insane; and surely for you is an endless reward.'
– Surah Qalam (68), Verses 1-3

These first sixteen verses of this Surah are a treasure-chest of praise and prophetic greatness for Rasoolullah ﷺ! Truly every letter here is an expression of it! Let us then discuss the following aspects of these verses,

1. Why were they revealed?

2. What is meant by 'Nūn' and 'The Pen'?

3. How is the praise of Rasoolullah ﷺ proven in these verses?

1. The polytheists of Makkah (especially Waleed ibn Mugheera) would call the Prophet ﷺ insane. Because Rasoolullah's ﷺ merciful heart was hurt by this disturbing word, Allah ﷻ took an oath articulating the excellence of His Beloved ﷺ and exposing the faults and flaws of his slanderers, doing this so that the Prophet's ﷺ blessed heart could gain solace. So, Allah ﷻ states here, "Oath on Nūn, oath on the Pen, and oath on their writing, O My Beloved ﷺ, you are not insane. Your slanderers are disgraceful, disbelieving, contemptible, backbiters, the illegitimate product of illicit interaction, etc…"

2. There are several interpretations regarding what is meant by 'Nūn' in the verse. It's been said,

   2.1 It's the name of the Surah.

   2.2 It's the name of Allah ﷻ.

   2.3 It's the first letter of the words *Noor* (light) and *Nāsir* (helper).

   2.4 *Al-Rahm* (mercy) joins with the letter nūn and becomes *al-Rahmān* (The Most Merciful). So, Nūn is a part of the names of Allah ﷻ. By this interpretation, Allah ﷻ here takes an oath on Himself.

   2.5 Nūn is the blessed name of the Prophet ﷺ.

   2.6 It's the first letter of the word Noor, and Noor is the Holy Prophet's ﷺ quality,

   قد جاءكم من الله نور
   'Truly a splendid light (Noor) has come to you from Allah ﷻ.'
   – Surah Māida (5), Verse 15

   Based on this interpretation, the verse is an oath on the Holy Messenger ﷺ.

   2.7 'Nūn' means fish in Arabic. So, this could refer to the fish in whose stomach Sayyiduna Yunus عليه السلام remained, the fish which will be the first source of sustenance for the inmates of Jannah, or the fish on which the world rests.

– Roohul-Bayaan & Tafseer Azeezi

There are also several interpretations regarding what is meant by 'The Pen',

1. It refers to ordinary pens because knowledge is written by them. It's therefore revered by Allah ﷻ taking an oath on it.

2. It refers to the Pen which will scribe all occurrences on the Protected Tablet (لوح محفوظ).

3. It refers to the pen by which the angels write the fate of a child in the womb.

4. It refers to the pen by which the angels write the deeds of humans.

However, in these interpretations, there's no correspondence between 'Nūn' and 'The Pen'. So, some Commentators of the Quran say that 'The Pen' is also the name of the Holy Prophet ﷺ, based on the Hadith, "Allah ﷻ first created the Pen," while another states, "Allah ﷻ first created my Noor (i.e. the Noor of the Prophet ﷺ)." Congruity between these two narrations is that 'Nūn' and 'The Pen' both refer to the true reality of Rasoolullah ﷺ (الحقيقة المحمدية). The Holy Messenger ﷺ is called 'The Pen' because, just as how a pen exists before any of piece of writing, so too did Rasoolullah ﷺ exist before the rest of creation. Also, just as how the writing of the Divine Pen cannot be changed by anyone, so too can no one overrule the proclamation of the Beloved Prophet ﷺ in this world. It's as if Rasoolullah ﷺ is the Divine Pen himself.

Some have said that 'Nūn' and 'The Pen' refer to the Holy Prophet's ﷺ blessed lips and tongue respectively. Just as how a pen writes with assistance from an inkpot, so too did the blessed tongue of Rasoolullah ﷺ speak via his blessed lips. Although some letters are pronounced from the tongue while others from the lips, every letter uttered by the Prophet ﷺ is formed from Divine revelation. His blessed tongue and mouth is the key to Allah's ﷻ will,

وما ينطق عن الهوى ، ان هو الا وحى يوحى
'And he does not speak of his own desire. It isn't but revelation that is revealed to him.'
– Surah Najm (53), Verses 3-4

Bear in mind that the letter Nūn, the lips of a human being, and an inkpot all have something in common to one another. So, Rasoolullah's ﷺ blessed mouth is the vessel (or source) of Allah's ﷻ words, his tongue the pen of Allah ﷻ, and his speech the proclamation of Allah ﷻ! – *Tafseer Roohul-Bayaan*

Regarding the words, 'Oath on what they write,' it can be asked, who writes? The following interpretations answer this,

1. It refers to general people who record religious sciences. In other words, Allah ﷻ is saying, "O Beloved ﷺ! Oath on your blessed tongue and oath on your blessed speech which Muslims will read and write until Qiyaamat…" Kings inscribed their names on silver and gold coins but were still ultimately forgotten. Look at the glory of the King of Kings, however, who uttered merciful words in the desert of Arabia, yet until today his speech has neither been forgotten nor erased! No worldly force and power has been able to change his words and teachings. His blessed name has been transcribed in the aeons, in the hearts and minds of the creation, and even on the stones of this Earth – all to the extent that it cannot be wiped out.

2. Some say these words refer to the writing of the angels who record the Prophet's ﷺ blessed speech and actions.

Referring to, 'By the grace of your Lord, you are not at all *majnūn* (insane),' majnūn can be interpreted to mean either *insane* or *hidden*. Based on the first meaning, it becomes clear that Rasoolullah ﷺ could never have experienced insanity, because the minds of the Prophets ﷺ are superior to the entire creation, while the Holy Messenger's ﷺ rank of consciousness is greater than all of the other Prophets ﷺ! If the prime-minister of a king becomes insane, the complete workings of his country are disrupted. So, if madness had to come to the Holy Prophet ﷺ, how could the world have survived? Allah ﷻ Himself speaks to His Beloved ﷺ; angels, jinns, and humans present their plight to Rasoolullah ﷺ; the creation has hope in him; the Creator concentrates his mercy unto him; Rasoolullah ﷺ is the helper of those with sorrow; he conveys Allah's ﷻ mercy to the creation; he submits the needs of the world to Him, etc. How could a person with so many responsibilities ever be insane?!

Based on the second meaning (i.e. 'You are not at all hidden.'), the verse would mean, "O Beloved ﷺ, you are not kept hidden.' In other words, "The unseen, former and latter occurrences and every minute detail of creation are not kept hidden from you." – *Roohul-Bayaan*

It could also mean that Allah ﷻ isn't hidden from the Holy Prophet ﷺ, or that Rasoolullah ﷺ isn't hidden from the creation. Muslims believe in him, disbelievers recognize him, and even natural elements and Heavenly inmates accept him.

Regarding, 'And surely for you is an endless reward,' *reward* can be interpreted as intercession, according to *Tafseer Roohul-Bayaan*. In other words, the Prophet's ﷺ intercession will never end. From the beginning of time until the end, the hardships of all have been and will be removed by his blessed means. Through Rasoolullah ﷺ, the penance of Sayyiduna Adam عليه السلام was accepted, the ark of Sayyiduna Nuh عليه السلام reached land, the fire became cool for Sayyiduna Ibrahim عليه السلام, the lives of Sayyiduna Ismail عليه السلام and Hadrat Abdullah ؓ were saved due to him, and even today, mercy descends to the Earth and hardships are removed due to the Holy Prophet's ﷺ blessed means,

وما كان الله ليعذبهم وأنت فيهم

'And Allah ﷻ isn't one to punish them while
(O Beloved ﷺ) you are in their midst.'
– Surah Anfāl (8), Verse 33

O Beloved Prophet of Allah ﷺ! Your remembrance is tranquility at the time of sorrow, the success of the deceased during the questioning in the grave is dependent on your recognition, the right of intercession lies with you in the Hereafter, Jannah resonates with your glory, and sinful believers are saved from punishment in Jahannam due to your blessings!

Another interpretation of 'Surely for you is an endless reward' is, "O Beloved ﷺ! Your reward will never cease, because the good deeds of your Ummah will remain until Qiyaamat, and you will receive the rewards of these deeds many times over."

Yet another interpretation is, "O Beloved ﷺ, no servant has favor upon you when it comes to your reward." People acquire knowledge, faith, sustenance, children, etc. through the means of others. So, they are indebted to them. On the other hand, O Rasoolullah ﷺ, you are the only being through whom the entire creation has attained recognition of Allah ﷻ. All are needy of you, and you are needy of none but Allah ﷻ. Your favor is upon all while no one has favor upon you. It's said that Sayyidah Halima Saadiyah ؓ nurtured the

Prophet 🌸, but oath on Allah ﷻ, it was actually the Holy Prophet 🌸 taking care of *her*! By his arrival in her home, she experienced opulence in spiritual and worldly means.

> 'The barren desert-land of the Saad tribe is the envy of gardens, because
> Halima ؓ has brought with her the scented flower of the Hashmis.'

Some Sufiya state that even the *being* of Allah ﷻ is a reward for the Holy Messenger 🌸.

Regarding, 'And surely for you is an endless reward,' I'll present a complete explanation on this in the next discussion.

Allah ﷻ has related the excellence of the Holy Prophet 🌸 until here and comforted him. Now, Divine anger is focused on those wretches who made the abhorred statement, "Muhammad is a lunatic." Allah ﷻ therefore mentioned ten defects in Waleed ibn Aqba, the leader of those who called the Holy Prophet 🌸 mad,

فلا تطع المكذبين ، ودوا لو تدهن فيدهنون ، ولا تطع كل حلاف مهين ،
همّاز مشاء بنميم ، مناع للخير معتد أثيم ، عتل بعد ذلك زنيم

> 'O Beloved 🌸, don't yield to the rejecters, who would've
> had you compromise that they may compromise; neither obey
> each feeble oath-monger, detracter, spreader abroad of slanders,
> hinderer of the good, transgressor, wrongdoer, greedy, and
> after all that, of doubtful birth.'
> – Surah Qalam (68), Verses 8-13

When Waleed heard this, he rushed to his mother with a sword in hand and said to her, "Muhammad related ten faults of mine. I recognize nine of them but have no knowledge about the tenth. You do! Tell me, am I of legitimate birth or not? Tell me the truth or I'll slay your head, because Muhammad never lies!" She replied, "You're illegitimate. Your 'father' Aqba was rich but impotent. I was scared of others gaining his wealth, so I went to a shepherd and you are the product of that. You're the son of that shepherd." – *Roohul-Bayaan & other Commentaries*

We come to know that speaking ill of Rasoolullah 🌸 is a habit of the illegitimate.

وَإِنَّكَ لَعَلَى خُلُقٍ عَظِيمٍ

'And indeed, you are upon great manners.'
– Surah Qalam (68), Verse 4

This verse is clear praise of the Holy Prophet ﷺ. It describes the manners of Rasoolullah ﷺ as great (عظيم). The word translated as 'manners' (خلق) can be interpreted as a habit by which good works naturally transpire by the doer without exertion. So, the verse means, "O Beloved ﷺ, the good works that you do are your essence, and you are not exerting yourself when carrying them out."

This is gestured to in another verse of the Holy Quran,

وما انا من المتكلفين

'I don't resort to formal effort in my conduct.'
– Surah Saad (38), Verse 86

By using the word 'great' (عظيم), Allah ﷻ explains that if one wishes to estimate the beautiful mannerisms and qualities of Rasoolullah ﷺ, he will be unable to do so. The blessings of this world have been described as meager,

قل متاع الدنيا قليل

'Say, 'The possessions of this world are little.''
– Surah Nisā (4), Verse 77

Even though they are 'little', no one can count them. So, if the Holy Prophet's ﷺ mannerisms and qualities are described as great, who could ever estimate their greatness?

In the commentary of this verse, *Tafseer Roohul-Bayaan* states that Rasoolullah ﷺ has been blessed with the gratefulness of Sayyiduna Nuh عليه السلام, the proximity of Sayyiduna Ibrahim عليه السلام, the sincerity of Sayyiduna Musa عليه السلام, the truthfulness of Sayyiduna Ismail عليه السلام, the patience of Sayyiduna Yaqub عليه السلام and Sayyiduna Ayub عليه السلام, the delivery of Sayyiduna Dawud عليه السلام, and the humility of Sayyiduna Sulaiman عليه السلام and Sayyiduna Esa عليه السلام. Allama Ismail Haqqi ﷺ further states that the Holy Prophet ﷺ has been bestowed with the cherished mannerisms of all the Prophets عليهم السلام. This is why the Holy Quran states,

فبهدهم اقتده

'Then you follow their path.'
– Surah An'ām (6), Verse 90

In other words, "Become the convergence of all the Prophets' ﷺ great mannerisms."

Sayyidah Aisha ؓ was once asked about the character of Rasoolullah ﷺ and replied, "His character was the Holy Quran." – *Muslim, Kitaabus-Salaah*

There are two meanings to this answer,

1. Practicing upon the Holy Quran was the life of the Prophet ﷺ. For this reason, some Gnostics (عارفين) have said that he who yearns to be visited by the Holy Messenger ﷺ should look at the Holy Quran (since it's the silent representation of his blessed life). Or, it could just be said that Rasoolullah ﷺ is the Holy Quran personified.

2. Just as how the marvels of the Holy Quran are endless, so too is the exquisiteness of the Prophet's ﷺ character unbounded.

Tafseer Roohul-Bayaan summarizes the character of Rasoolullah ﷺ in the following words, "[It was] to choose Allah ﷻ and be segregated from the creation." The author further states that on the night of the Ascension (Mi'rāj), Allah ﷻ presented the keys to the treasures of creation to the Holy Prophet ﷺ, but he didn't accept them. He was shown all the angels, Jannah, and all of its blessings, yet he didn't pay attention to them. Rather, he chose Allah ﷻ. This is why the Quran states,

ما زاغ البصر وما طغى
'The eye (of Muhammad ﷺ) didn't deviate nor exceed the limit.'
– Surah Najm (53), Verse 17

In other words, the vision of the Holy Beloved ﷺ didn't stray from his Lord.

A Hadith states that Muslims should have excellent and pure conduct since this is the sign of the inmates of Jannah. They should also protect themselves from contemptible character because this leads to Jahannam. So, how should our conduct be? Simple! It should be merciful towards Muslims and hard against non-Muslims,

والذين معه اشداء على الكفار رحماء بينهم
'Those with Muhammad ﷺ are severe against

infidels but tender towards Muslims.'
– Surah Fat'h (48), Verse 29

If someone causes personal harm to you, forgive him. But if he wishes to harm Islam, don't spare him!

The Holy Prophet 🌸 went to Tāif for the purpose of propagating Islam and suffered much abuse from its residents, to the extent that they even physically injured him. Sayyiduna Jibrael عليه السلام then presented himself in the prophetic court and submitted, "If you supplicate, they'll be immediately ruined." Yet the Mercy unto the Creation said, "O Allah ﷻ, shower Your mercy on these people who shower stones on me." *Subhanallah!* Sayyiduna Jibrael عليه السلام then said, "O Beloved of Allah 🌸, these people will not believe now," yet Rasoolullah 🌸 explained, "I have hope that their children will."

> The Jurists (فقهاء) are agreed that the piece of earth of the Holy Prophet's 🌸 sanctified grave touching his blessed body is greater in excellence than the Holy Ka'ba and even the greatest Heaven.

This was an example of mercy in a personal incident. However, once a woman stole and the Holy Prophet 🌸 commanded that her hand be cut. People interceded for her forgiveness and exemption from this punishment but the Beloved Messenger 🌸 replied, "This is the order of Allah ﷻ and cannot be stopped."

This is the prophetic character, yet today Muslims think that to be soft with apostates and to have enmity with true Muslims is good conduct. No! It's Islamic conduct to be severe against apostates. Removing thorns from a garden is better than letting them spoil its beauty.

VERSE 87

عٰلِمُ الْغَيْبِ فَلَا يُظْهِرُ عَلٰى غَيْبِهٖ اَحَدًا ، اِلَّا مَنِ ارْتَضٰى مِن رَّسُوْلٍ
'He is the Knower of the unseen. He does not reveal His secrets to any except His chosen Messengers.'
– Surah Jinn (72), Verses 26-7

This verse is also the praise of the Holy Prophet 🌸 and demonstrates his knowledge of the unseen. The verse states (in other words), "Allah ﷻ is the Knower of the unseen and doesn't give a position to anyone regarding this unique knowledge except His chosen Messengers."

There are two things to bear in mind with regards to this verse,

1. The special knowledge of the unseen of Allah ﷻ,

2. Him granting a position over it.

The unseen (غیب) is defined as that which cannot be known by the senses and which cannot be immediately comprehended by the intellect, e.g. Jannah, Jahannam, etc. So, knowledge of Cape Town and London isn't regarded as knowledge of the unseen because we can go to these places and see them. Thousands of people have informed us that these are two cities in the world. So, these aren't unseen things.

There are two types of the unseen,

1. Something unseen which can be known through proof, evidence, etc, such as the existence of Allah ﷻ, His Qualities, etc.

2. Something unseen which cannot be known, even through proof, etc.

The first category is attained by the Messengers and others besides them, as per the Holy Quran,

يؤمنون بالغيب
'Those who believe without seeing.'
– Surah Baqarah (2), Verse 3

The second category is Allah's ﷻ knowledge of the unseen, and this will not be divulged to anyone besides the Holy Messenger ﷺ. Yes, if the Messenger ﷺ does inform one of this knowledge out of his mercy, it will then be known through his means. This is what's meant in the verse, that Allah ﷻ doesn't position anyone over His special knowledge of the unseen except Rasoolullah ﷺ. The verse establishes that he's been specially conferred with it. – *Tafseer Kabeer, Tafseer Baidawi, Roohul-Bayaan*

So, the verse that states that none besides Allah ﷻ knows the unseen means that actual and unbestowed knowledge is unique to Allah ﷻ. The Holy Quran refutes anyone possessing unbestowed knowledge of the unseen, but affirms bestowed knowledge (*Ilm'e-Ataa'i*). Allah ﷻ states,

ان العزة لله جميعا

'All honor belongs only to Allah ﷻ.'
– Surah Nisā (4), Verse 139

He then said,

والله العزة ولرسوله وللمؤمنين
'Honor is for Allah ﷻ, the Messenger ﷺ, and the believers.'
– Surah Munafiqūn (63), Verse 8

In another juncture, Allah ﷻ states,

ان الحكم الا لله
'There's no order but of Allah ﷻ.'
– Surah An'ām (6), Verse 57

However, He also states,

فابعثوا حكما من اهله وحكما من اهلها
*'(When there's discord between husband and wife) Appoint a
decider from his side and one from her side.'*
– Surah Nisā (4), Verse 35

Now, these verses mean that true honor and judgement is only for Allah ﷻ,
but Muslims also possess honor and power by His bestowal. Similarly is the
concept of the knowledge of the unseen. Exactly how much of it was given to
Rasoolullah ﷺ is known only by He who bestowed it and he who acquired it.
The Protected Tablet has the knowledge of what has happened and what will
(ما كان وما يكون) yet this is only a drop in the ocean of knowledge belonging to
our master, Sayyiduna Rasoolullah ﷺ. Imam Busairi ؓ states,

ومن علومك علم اللوح والقلم
'And from your knowledge is the knowledge of the Protected Tablet.'
– Qasida Burda Sharif

Yes, from the narrations that have been transmitted, we know that the
knowledge of every grain, particle, and drop from the inception of time until
the Day of Judgment has been given to the Holy Prophet ﷺ. The very core of
the Earth until the heights of the Heavens have been shown to him. He has
even been given the knowledge of when a bird flaps its wings. Refer to my
book, *Ja'al-Haqq*, for further research on this subject. Finding such a
comprehensive discussion elsewhere is difficult.

Another point we derive from this verse is that Rasoolullah ﷺ has been delegated over Allah's ﷻ knowledge of the unseen. So, should he cast his special favor on someone, the Earth to the Heavens will also become apparent to that individual. Shaikh Abdul-Qadir Jilani ؓ states,

نظرت الى بلاد الله جمعا ، كخردلة على حكم اتصال

'I've seen all the cities of Allah ﷻ like a few mustard seeds joined together.'
– Qasida Ghousia

Every quality of the Holy Prophet ﷺ is extraordinary.

VERSE 88

يَا أَيُّهَا الْمُزَّمِّلُ ، قُمِ الَّيْلَ إِلَّا قَلِيلًا

'O you enwrapped one! Stand praying at night except a small portion thereof.'
– Surah Muzammil (73), Verses 1-2

This verse is also the praise of the Holy Prophet ﷺ. It commands him to perform Tahajjud Salaah and recite the Holy Quran with a correct, rhythmic tone (ترتیل). However, the manner in which this command occurs is indeed unique. It firstly describes Rasoolullah's ﷺ clothing, proving that his every appearance is beloved.

Commentators have different views regarding the reason for these verses' revelation,

1. During the initial period of revelation, Rasoolullah ﷺ used to wrap himself up in his clothes due to the awe of Divine Revelation. The above calling was therefore made to him while he was in this condition.

2. This calling was made to the Messenger ﷺ while he was wrapped in a mantle and resting.

3. Some Scholars suggest that the verse means, "O he who wraps himself in the mantle of prophethood."

4. In the commentary of this verse, Allama Ismail Haqqi ؓ states that one night, while the Holy Prophet ﷺ was wrapped in a mantle and resting, Allah ﷻ desired that His Beloved ﷺ communicate with Him in submissive supplication. So, the calling was made, "O Beloved ﷺ who rests, communicate with Me at this time."

Whichever interpretation one chooses, the glory of Sayyiduna Rasoolullah ﷺ remains apparent.

Rule – Tahajjud Salaah was compulsory (waajib) in the initial period of Islam (some say it was fardh). Its obligation was annulled later by the following verse of this very Surah,

فَاقْرَءُوا مَا تَيَسَّرَ مِنَ الْقُرْآن

'Now recite from the Quran as much as is easy for you.'
– Surah Muzammil (73), Verse 20

Tahajjud Salaah is now regarded as *Sunnat'e-Muakkadah alal-Kifaayah*. Meaning, if just one person in an area performs it, all other residents will be absolved. However, if no one performs it, all will have neglected a sunnah.

Rule – The time of Tahajjud commences for a person when he wakes up from sleep after performing Esha Salaah. So, if a person performs Esha Salaah at 8 o'clock in winter and sleeps, the time of Tahajjud for him will begin whenever he wakes up, even if it's 9 o'clock. If a person stays awake the entire night, he will not attain the time for Tahajjud (since waking up from sleep is necessary for it). The preferred time for this Salaah is the last part of the night. Two rakaats is the minimum amount and twelve is the maximum. If Surah Ikhlās (112) is recited thrice in every rakaat, the reward for reading an entire Quran Sharif will be attained for every rakaat.

VERSE 89

إِنَّا أَرْسَلْنَا إِلَيْكُمْ رَسُوْلًا شَهِدًا عَلَيْكُمْ كَمَا أَرْسَلْنَا إِلَى فِرْعَوْنَ رَسُوْلًا

'Surely We have sent to you a Messenger ﷺ who is a witness against you, as We sent a Messenger towards Pharaoh.'
– Surah Muzammil (73), Verse 15

This verse is also the praise of the Holy Prophet ﷺ. Both Muslims and non-Muslims are addressed in it and are being told, "O People! This Prophet ﷺ who has come to you isn't unaware of you or your condition. Rather, he knows you and your belief & disbelief. He's aware of every state of all people until Qiyaamat. So, he'll testify about you in his Lord's court (i.e. he'll express the Imaan of a believer and the disbelief of a non-Muslim)." This proves the knowledge of the unseen for the Holy Prophet ﷺ, as well as him being present and seeing (حاضر وناظر) for every person (since testimony must be witnessed, i.e. by seeing). On the Day of Qiyaamat, when our Ummah will testify in favor of the previous Prophets الْعَلَيْهُم, our Prophet ﷺ will bear witness about us. I've discussed this in several places already. Refer also to my book, *Ja'al-Haqq*, for a researched study on the Prophet ﷺ being present and aware.

VERSE 90

إِنَّ رَبَّكَ يَعْلَمُ أَنَّكَ تَقُومُ أَدْنَى مِن ثُلُثَيِ الَّيْلِ وَنِصْفَهُ وَثُلُثَهُ وَطَائِفَةٌ مِّنَ الَّذِينَ مَعَكَ ،
وَاللهُ يُقَدِّرُ الَّيْلَ وَالنَّهَارَ ، عَلِمَ أَن لَّن تُحْصُوهُ فَتَابَ عَلَيْكُمْ ، فَاقْرَءُوا مَا تَيَسَّرَ مِنَ الْقُرْآنِ

'Surely your Lord knows that you remain standing in devotion nearly two-thirds of the night, sometimes half of it, and sometimes a third of it, along with a party of your Companions ﷺ with you. And Allah ﷻ measures the night and the day. He knows that you (O Muslims) are not able to calculate it. So, He has turned to you (mercifully). Therefore, recite how much is easy of the Quran.'
– Surah Muzammil (73), Verse 20

This verse is a sermon of glory for Rasoolullah ﷺ! The reason for its revelation is that when Tahajjud Salaah was obligatory on Muslims, Rasoolullah ﷺ (with the Sahaabah ﷺ) would stand in it so zealously that blisters would form on their feet and would eventually burst (causing blood to emerge). They stood with dedication because they wanted the obligation to be fulfilled, and if what they read was more than the required amount, there wouldn't be any harm. Watches didn't exist in that era. So, Muslims were unable to correctly ascertain whether it was night or morning, resulting in them standing

The life of the Holy Messenger ﷺ (even before his birth), including his domestic life, public life, the manner in which he sat, walked, talked, smiled, etc. – in fact, his every physical countenance, *to the extent of how many of his blessed hairs were white!* – is comprehensively recorded. No other religious leader's life has been chronicled to this extent. What exactly is the Hadith? It's truly the biography of Rasoolullah ﷺ. No king or accomplished personality of this world has such a grand bio written about them.

sometimes even until Subh-Saadiq. The command of Tahajjud Salaah remained for a year, after which the abovementioned verse was revealed (annulling the obligation). We come to know that the Holy Prophet's ﷺ comfort is so pivotal that even commands of Islamic Law are relaxed for it. The actual Tahajjud Salaah remained forever compulsory on Rasoolullah ﷺ, but there wasn't any compulsion to stand for a particular amount of night.

Whatever amount he wished to stand for was accepted. Yes, the obligation, however, isn't incumbent on us.

Rule – To perform *Shabīna* (قيام الليل), i.e. completing the recital of the entire Quran in one night during Tahajjud or Taraweeh Salaah, is permissible if the recital isn't a burden on the reciter.

Under the commentary of Verse 4, Surah Muzammil (73), *Tafseer Roohul-Bayaan* states that four individuals completed the entire Quran in one rakaat: Hadrat Uthman ﷺ, Hadrat Tameem Daari ﷺ, Hadrat Saeed ibn Jubair ﷺ, and Imam Abu Hanifa ﷺ. Hadrat Hamsa ibn Minhaal ﷺ would complete the Holy Quran 90 times a month, while Hadrat Abul-Hasan Ali ibn Abdullah ﷺ would complete four Qurans a day! It's also reported in *Tahaawi*, Vol. 1, Baabu-Jaamis-Suwar fir-Rak'aat that Hadrat Tameem Daari ﷺ, Abdullah ibn Zubair ﷺ, and Saeed ibn Jubair ﷺ would complete the entire Quran in just one rakaat. I recall reading in *Raddul-Muhtaar* that Imam Abu Hanifa ﷺ used to complete the Holy Quran 61 times in Ramadaan. Imam Nawawi ﷺ states, "Numerous individuals used to complete the Holy Quran in just one rakaat (Hadrat Uthman ibn Affan ﷺ, Hadrat Tameem Daari ﷺ, and Saeed ibn Jubair ﷺ)." – *Kitaabul-Azkaar, Baabu Tilaawatil-Quran*

These references prove Shabīna. However, two things must be observed in its performance,

1. The reciter must recite the Quran properly and clearly. The letters of the Quran must all be heard.

2. The listeners must listen attentively, not laze around and quickly join the congregation when the Imam goes into ruku.

Both of the above (i.e. not reciting clearly or listening attentively) are prohibited. The Hadith which prohibits the quick completion of the Holy Quran refers to the above two things. The personalities that completed the Holy Quran in one rakaat would recite it with understanding and correct articulation, even though the recitation was fast.

VERSE 91

يَأَيُّهَا الْمُدَّثِّرُ ، قُمْ فَأَنْذِرْ ، وَرَبَّكَ فَكَبِّرْ ، وَثِيَابَكَ فَطَهِّرْ

'O you who enfolded yourself in your mantle. Arise and warn; and glorify the dignity of your Lord; and purify your garments.'
– Surah Mudath'thir (74), Verses 1-4

This verse is also the praise of the Holy Prophet 🌸. The reason for its revelation is, as Rasoolullah 🌸 narrates, "I was once on the mountain of Hira when I heard an unseen voice proclaim, 'O Muhammad 🌸, indeed you are the Messenger of Allah 🌸.' I looked around and couldn't find the one who said it, but when I looked up, I saw the very angel who brought the verse, *'Read in the name of your Lord Who created,'* (Surah Alaq (96), Verse 1) in the cave. He was seated on a chair making this proclamation." In other words, it was Sayyiduna Jibrael عليه السلام. Sayyiduna Rasoolullah 🌸 further narrates, "Due to the awe of this incident, I came to Khadija 🌸 and ordered her to cover me in a mantle. When I was covered, the following was revealed to me, *'O you who enfolded yourself in your mantle. Arise and warn; and glorify the dignity of your Lord; and purify your garments.'"* Just as how the previously discussed word 'Muzammil' (the enwrapped one) demonstrates love and mercy, so too does this calling of 'Mudath'thir' (the one who enfolded himself in his mantle) demonstrate the same.

This verse also proves the action of *Takbeer Tahrīmah* as compulsory (فرض) in Salaah. Furthermore, 'purify your garments' means that if any impurity has to come into contact with your clothes, it should be washed off, since wearing unclean clothing without a just reason is prohibited. Human beings should keep themselves pure and clean even out of Salaah. It could also mean that one's clothing (i.e. pants, kurta, tahband (lungi), etc.) should not be worn so low that they drag over impurities and dirt (effectively becoming spoilt). Rather, it's sunnah for the lower-garment or pants to reach half the shin, although women are commanded to wear clothing low enough to cover their ankles.

VERSE 92

لَا تُحَرِّكْ بِهِ لِسَانَكَ لِتَعْجَلَ بِهِ ، إِنَّ عَلَيْنَا جَمْعَهُ وَقُرْآنَهُ ، فَإِذَا قَرَأْنَاهُ فَاتَّبِعْ قُرْآنَهُ ، ثُمَّ عَلَيْنَا بَيَانَهُ

'(O Beloved 🌸) Don't move your tongue with it (the Quran) that you may hasten to learn it. Undoubtedly, it's upon Us to preserve and recite it. Therefore, when We have recited it, follow the recitation. Then on Us is the explaining of its minute detail.'
– Surah Qiyaamat (75), Verses 16-9

This verse is also the praise of the Messenger 🌸. The reason for its revelation is that when Sayyiduna Jibrael عليه السلام would bring revelation, Rasoolullah 🌸 used to also recite it while listening to him. He did this to exceptionally remember the words. However, listening and reciting at the same time was difficult, and so this hardship was something Allah 🌸 didn't wish for His

Beloved 🌺. So, He said, "O Beloved 🌺, don't take on the difficulty of reciting while listening. We promise you that We will make you remember the Quran by just listening to it once."

The Holy Prophet's 🌺 praise is proven by the following,

1.   Allah ﷻ doesn't wish that His Beloved 🌺 be involved in even a small amount of difficulty.

2.   Today, there are three groups of people who endure great difficulty and sacrifice much to learn the Holy Quran,

    a.   The **Hafiz** – One who sacrifices much to completely memorize it.

    b.   The **Qari** – One who sacrifices much to learn its correct recitation.

    c.   The **Scholar** – One who sacrifices much to learns its laws (while acquiring knowledge from different teachers).

Allah ﷻ, on the other hand, promised His Beloved 🌺, "The *collecting* of it is on Us (i.e. We will make you the Hafiz of the Quran), the *reciting* of it is on Us (i.e. We will take the responsibility of teaching you its recitation), and on Us is also the *explaining of its minute detail* (i.e. We will grant you its knowledge)."

So, these three things which people endure so much hardship to achieve were given to the Holy Messenger 🌺 without him having to come into any difficulty! Also, these sciences are acquired from different teachers, yet Rasoolullah 🌺 was taught by his Lord alone! *Allahu Akbar!* How great is the glory of Rasoolullah 🌺?!

Rule – It's prohibited to recite the Holy Quran loudly when a few people are gathered together. – *Shaami*

All should either recite softly, or one should recite loudly while the others listen.

VERSE 93

عَبَسَ وَتَوَلَّى ، أَن جَاءَهُ الْأَعْمَى ، وَمَا يُدْرِيكَ لَعَلَّهُ يَزَّكَّى

248

*'He frowned and turned aside because the
blind man came to him; but what could convince you
that he may be seeking to purify himself?'*
– Surah Abasa (80), Verses 1-3

This verse is regarded by some to be revelation rebuking the Holy Prophet ﷺ, but if seen with the vision of Imaan, it demonstrates his grand splendor. First we need to know the reason for its revelation, and afterwards will we discuss its objective.

The reason for the verse's revelation was that the leaders of the Quraish, i.e. Abu Jahl, Utba, Shaiba, etc. wanted Rasoolullah ﷺ to co-ordinate a special gathering of admonition for them in which no poor Companion was present. Rasoolullah ﷺ accepted this (hoping that they attain salvation and so that Islam is explained to them). So, he arranged such a meeting, and all of the Quriash leaders attended. While Rasoolullah ﷺ was engaged in his speech, a blind Companion by the name of Hadrat Abdullah ibn Umme-Maktoom ؓ approached him (unable to see that the Prophet ﷺ was busy speaking to the Quraishi leaders) and loudly said, "O Prophet of Allah ﷺ, teach me too what Allah ﷻ taught you." At that moment, Hadrat Abdullah's ؓ loud speech and interruption wasn't appreciated by the Prophet ﷺ (it also led to the leaders of the Quraish leaving the meeting). The Prophet ﷺ then returned home without answering the Sahaabi. So, this verse was revealed on his return (which cautioned about the annoyance). Look at the manner of speech the Holy Quran used, though! It didn't say, "You frowned," but, "He frowned." In other words, "My Beloved ﷺ has become somewhat annoyed with one of his loyal slaves. O Beloved ﷺ! Why do you busy yourself in propagating Islam to such an extent that you are even troubled if one of your slaves approach you?!"

Some individuals conclude that Allah ﷻ rebuked Rasoolullah ﷺ because of this behavior and was angry with him. Displeasure and rebuke is directed to a fault. What fault, then, did the Holy Prophet ﷺ commit for Allah ﷻ to become displeased with him? He was engaged in the propagation of Islam (تبلیغ) which was his obligation as a prophet. Is displeasure incurred for completing an obligation? Definitely not! In fact, it was Hadrat Abdullah ؓ who faulted in three things – (1) he interjected while others spoke, (2) he addressed Rasoolullah ﷺ loudly, and (3) he interrupted what he was saying. If this verse *was* truly for rebuke, the Companion ؓ would've been worthy of it, not Rasoolullah ﷺ.

Shaikh Abdul-Haqq Muhaddith Dehlwi ⚘ and Maulana Rumi ⚘ in *Madaarijun-Nubuwwah* and *Mathnawi Sharif* respectively say that this verse is actually support for the Holy Beloved's ⚘ slave. Allah ﷻ is saying in it, "O My Beloved ﷺ! He's your destitute slave, so his mistakes are forgiven in My court."

The word used was A'maa (one who's blind), meaning, "O Beloved ﷺ, We implore you to also forgive those who love you to such an extent that they become unaware of worldly etiquette and speech." This is a recommendation for someone who has extreme love for Rasoolullah ﷺ, not rebuke for the Holy Prophet ﷺ.

This explanation illustrates Rasoolullah's ﷺ glory, that even the mistakes of his servants are forgiven through his blessings, and he is made pleased with them. *Allahu Akbar!* This is the Holy Prophet's ﷺ favor on his slaves, and his kindness on his enemies is expressed in the verse,

وما كان الله ليعذبهم وأنت فيهم

'And Allah ﷻ isn't one to punish them while (O Beloved ﷺ) you are in their midst.'
– Surah Anfāl (8), Verse 33

Rasoolullah ﷺ would always show Hadrat Abdullah ibn Umme-Maktoom ⚘ great respect after this verse was revealed. When seeing him, he would humbly say, "This is the person my Lord censored me for," (saying this only because the verse was seemingly a rebuke).

Bear in mind that there's a difference between a reprimand (عتاب), punishment (عذاب), and severe punishment (عقاب). The first is used for an obedient servant, the second for the disobedient, and the third for enemies. A complaint about the beloved can also be referred to as 'a reprimand'.

In the commentary of this verse, *Tafseer Roohul-Bayaan* states that during the time of Hadrat Umar ⚘, there was an Imam who would recite this Surah in every Salaah. When Hadrat Umar ⚘ was informed about this, he summoned this person to him and, after establishing that he was a Hypocrite, executed him. Reciting this Surah (which is seemingly a rebuke against the Holy Prophet ﷺ) in *every* Salaah is indicative of enmity towards him. So, Hadrat Umar ⚘ said, "He (i.e. the Imam) is a Hypocrite who has enmity towards Rasoolullah ﷺ in his heart. This is why he'd recite this Surah in every Salaah, a Surah which is seemingly a rebuke."

Two important lessons emerge from the above,

1. To recite the Holy Quran with a mischievous intention is disbelief (كُفر). The following verse is also recited by some whenever they go around speaking to others, *"Say (to them, O Beloved 🌸), 'I'm a man like you.'"* (Surah Kahf (18), Verse 110). Although they *are* reciting the Quran, their intention (i.e. the defamation of the Holy Messenger 🌸) is incorrect. Why don't they repeat to others the verses wherein the Holy Prophet's 🌸 lofty station has been explained? The Ahadith mention regarding the Khawārij (the oldest sect of dissidents against Islam), "A group will appear who will recite the Quran but it won't go down their throats," and, "The Quran itself will curse them." Such people mentioned above are from this group.

2. Certain verses are superior to others in excellence. A Companion 🌸 used to always recite Surah Ikhlās (112) in every Salaah. When the Prophet 🌸 asked him why he did this, he explained, "This Surah mentions the qualities of my Lord. This is why it's beloved to me." Rasoolullah 🌸 said (about this Companion 🌸), "Inform him that Allah 🌸 has love for him." – *Mishkaat, Kitaabu Fadhaa'ilil-Quran*

Under the commentary of Verse 82 of Surah Nisā (4), Allama Ismail Haqqi 🌸 states that the verses which speak about Allah's 🌸 Being *&* Qualities are more excellent than those which mention other things. – *Tafseer Roohul-Bayaan*

So, the verses of Surah Ikhlās (112) are more excellent than Surah Lahab (111), because the former's speech is good, and He whom it speaks about is also the Most Lofty. The latter Surah's speech is only good while he whom it speaks about (i.e. Abu Lahab) isn't. So, Surah Ikhlās has two reasons of excellences while Surah Lahab has just one.

Based on this study, we come to know that the verses expressing the praise of Rasoolullah 🌸 are more excellent than those which some have regarded as a rebuke against him.

VERSE 94

لَا أُقْسِمُ بِهَذَا الْبَلَدِ ، وَأَنْتَ حِلٌّ بِهَذَا الْبَلَدِ ، وَوَالِدٍ وَّمَا وَلَدَ

'I swear by this city (Makkah) as (O Beloved 🌸) you dwell in this city, and by your father (Sayyiduna Ibrahim عليه السلام) and his progeny (i.e. Rasoolullah 🌸).'
– Surah Balad (90), Verses 1-3

These verses are shining examples of Rasoolullah's ﷺ praise. The first verse explains that whatever is connected to the Holy Prophet ﷺ acquires immense greatness. It was revealed prior to the migration (هجرة) and states, "O Beloved ﷺ, oath on this city of Makkah." But what's the reason for Allah ﷻ taking an oath on this city? The verse that follows it explains, "As you dwell in this city." In other words, "O Beloved ﷺ, the city of Makkah acquired this honor due to the blessings of your presence in it."

Makkah is known for the following excellences,

1. Sayyiduna Ibrahim السلام عليه cultivated the city and even made dua for it.

2. Sayyiduna Ismail السلام عليه was raised and nurtured in it.

3. The House of Allah ﷻ (and qiblah of this world) is found in it. In fact, even Baitul-Ma'mūr (the qiblah of the Heavens) corresponds to it.

4. The Holy Prophet ﷺ was a resident of it.

The first three excellences of Makkah remained after the migration, but the forth was detached from it. So, the verses actually state, "The reason for swearing an oath on this city isn't because of the first three reasons, but because of the fourth (i.e. the Prophet ﷺ stayed in Makkah)."

Rule – The Jurists (فقهاء) are agreed that the piece of earth of the Holy Prophet's ﷺ sanctified grave touching his blessed body is greater in excellence than the Holy Ka'ba and even the greatest Heaven.

They also agree that the Holy Ka'ba is more excellent than the streets of Madina. But yes, there is some disagreement regarding whether the city of Makkah is more excellent than the city of Madina. Hajj occurs in the city of Makkah, Sayyiduna Ibrahim السلام عليه cultivated this city, and he even supplicated for it. One good deed in Makkah is equal to 100,000, whereas one good deed in Madina is equal to 50,000. Nonetheless, Imam Malik ؓ states, "The city of Madina is more excellent than Makkah." Refer to *Naseemur-Riyadh Sharah Shifa Qaadhi Ayaadh* ؓ for a complete discussion on this.

Imam Malik ؓ based his ruling on the following proofs,

1. The above verse of Surah Balad (90), "I swear by this city." In other words, the place where the Prophet ﷺ lives is the most excellent place on Earth. So, Makkah was more excellent before the migration and Madina became the most excellent after it.

2. Makkah is the place of pilgrimage for worldly creation while Madina is the place of pilgrimage for Heavenly creations, i.e. the angels. Every morning and evening, 70,000 angels descend to the Holy Prophet's ﷺ blessed grave and convey their Salaat & Salaam to the best of creation, Sayyiduna Muhammad Mustapha ﷺ. – *Mishkaat, Baabul-Karaamaat*

   Also, Hajj in Makkah occurs just once a year, but the pilgrimage of angels to Madina is continuous!

3. Yes, the reward of a single good deed in Makkah is equal to 100,000, but a single transgression there incurs 100,000 sins. In other words, Makkah is a place of mercy and anger, yet Madina is the concentration of only mercy. One good deed in Madina is equal to 50,000 while a single transgression there is equal to just one (that too, if it even remains, since it's hoped that through the Holy Prophet's ﷺ intercession, it will be forgiven). Also, while a good deed in Makkah is worth twice as much as a good deed in Madina (with regards to reward), single rakaats of Salaah in Madina are worth several thousand than in Makkah (with regards to acceptance).

4. Makkah was cultivated by Sayyiduna Ibrahim عليه السلام (the Friend of Allah عزّوجلّ), while Madina was inhabited by Rasoolullah ﷺ (the Beloved of Allah ﷺ). Sayyiduna Ibrahim عليه السلام made dua for Makkah while Rasoolullah ﷺ made dua for Madina, saying, "O Allah عزّوجلّ! Grant Madina double the blessings and mercy of Makkah." Undoubtedly, the Holy Ka'ba, Maqaam'e-Ibrahim عليه السلام, the well of Zum-Zum, Arafat, Mina, etc. are all found in Makkah, but Madina is blessed with the Beloved of Allah ﷺ, through whose blessings these places possess excellence. Alahadrat Imam Ahmad Raza رحمة الله عليه states,

'Where would Sayyiduna Ibrahim عليه السلام, the Ka'ba or Mina have gained existence from if it weren't for you, the reason of creation?!'

If it wasn't for the King of Madina, nothing would've come into being. This was the difference amongst the celebrated Imams of Islam [regarding whether Makkah or Madina is more excellent]. Who then can truly make a conclusive decision on this matter? How aptly did Alahadrat Imam Ahmad Raza ﷺ explain this in the following couplet,

'If superiority isn't for Taiba (i.e. Madina) and Makkah
is greater, then so be it! O You devoted to worship! We are the
slaves of love. What need is there for us to argue?'

Black is the dominant colour of the Ka'ba (in its covering, the Black Stone, etc.) while green surrounds Madina (i.e. its greenery found around the city, the blessed dome, the covering of the Rauda, etc.). Black is the colour of separation while green is for union. Madina Sharif has union with the Beloved ﷺ while the Ka'ba mourns separation from him.

Maulana Jalaaluddin Rumi ﷺ states,

'A lover was asked by the beloved, "You've traveled
extensively. In your opinion, which is the best city?" The reply he
received was, "The city which is home to my beloved."'
– Mathnawi Sharif

The eminent poet of the East, Dr. Iqbal, eloquently said,

'The earth of Madina is more excellent than both worlds,
because our Beloved ﷺ is found in this city.'

Although there are several places of natural beauty found in the world, it was Madina chosen by Allah ﷺ for His Beloved ﷺ to reside in. Indeed, the gardens of this world can be sacrificed on this city!

Alahadrat Imam Ahmad Raza ﷺ writes,

'O Raza ﷺ, listen carefully! There's a sound coming from the Ka'ba
saying, "Look at the Rauda of my Beloved ﷺ through my eyes!'

The Holy Ka'ba has a duct called the *Channel of Mercy* (ميزاب الرحمة) which directly points to the Rauda of Rasoolullah ﷺ. If a shop is found in an alley, a signboard is placed on the roadside informing people that it's there. Imam Ahmad Raza ﷺ states that this gutter of the Holy Ka'ba is also an information board saying, "Friends! You've completed the Hajj, now proceed to the court of the Intercessor of Sinners if you want your pilgrimage to be successful. He rests beneath the green dome of Madina."

Tafseer Roohul-Bayaan states that 'By your father' in the verse refers to Sayyiduna Ibrahim ☜ and 'his progeny' to the Holy Prophet ☺. In other words, it's saying, "Oath on that father and that son." Another opinion within the Commentaries is that 'By your father' refers to the Noble Messenger ☺ and 'his progeny' refers to his Ummah. A Hadith states, "O Muslims, I'm like a father to you." This is why Rasoolullah's ☺ blessed wives are known as the Mothers of the Faithful. It's also possible for 'By your father' to refer to Rasoolullah ☺ and 'his progeny' to refer to the blessed Ahle-Bait (i.e. the progeny of Rasoolullah ☺). This interpretation explains the grandeur of the Prophet's ☺ lineage. A Hadith states, "On the Day of Judgment, no lineage or affinity through marriage will be favorable except mine." – *Shaami, Vol. 1, Discussion on Ghusl for the Deceased*

> O Beloved Prophet of Allah ☺!
> Your rememberance is tranquility at the time of sorrow, the success of the deceased during the questioning in the grave is dependent on your recognition, the right of intercession lies with you in the Hereafter, Jannah resonates with your glory, and sinful believers are saved from punishment in Jahannam due to your blessings!

This is why Hadrat Umar ☝ married Sayyidah Umme-Kulthum ☝ (the daughter of Sayyidah Fathima ☝) – so that he could attain affinity with Rasoolullah ☺ in two ways: (1) by being his father-in-law (Sayyidah Hafsa ☝ was married to Rasoolullah ☺ and was Hadrat Umar's ☝ daughter) and (2) by being Sayyidah Fathima's ☝ son-in-law.

Refer to the collection of my Fatāwā if you wish to know who the family of the Prophet ☺ comprises of, the different categories of the word, and who the 'family' in Durood Sharif refers to.

VERSE 95

وَالضُّحٰى ، وَالَّيْلِ إِذَا سَجٰى ، مَا وَدَّعَكَ رَبُّكَ وَمَا قَلٰى ، وَلَلْاٰخِرَةُ خَيْرٌ لَّكَ مِنَ الْاُوْلٰى ، وَلَسَوْفَ يُعْطِيْكَ رَبُّكَ فَتَرْضٰى

'By the brightness of the morning, and by the night when it covers, your Lord has not forsaken you nor is He displeased. And undoubtedly the Hereafter is better for you than the former. And indeed soon your Lord will give you so much that you'll be satisfied.'
– Surah Duhā (93), Verses 1-5

Indeed, this entire Surah is a treasury of praise for Rasoolullah ﷺ. If it had to be explained in its entirety, it would take volumes. So, I'll only briefly discuss these verses here. May it be accepted in the Prophetic Court.

The reason for the revelation of this Surah is that revelation from Allah ﷻ once halted, resulting in the non-Muslims of Makkah taunting, "Muhammad's Lord has forsaken him and is angry with him!" This Surah was therefore revealed in reply to their mockery. Allah ﷻ took an oath in it and said, "I've neither deserted My Beloved ﷺ nor am I angry with him." The interesting point here is that it was the non-Muslims who made these taunts yet Allah ﷻ didn't reply to them. Instead, He replied to His Beloved ﷺ! He consoles Rasoolullah ﷺ by saying, "Oath on the brightness of the morning and the night when it's dark! Neither have I forsaken you nor am I angry with you." This itself is a great instance of praise.

Commentators of the Holy Quran have different opinions concerning what is meant by 'morning' and 'night'. One opinion is that 'morning' refers to the time in which Sayyiduna Musa السلام عليه vanquished the magicians with his miracles, causing them to make sajda. The Holy Quran states,

قال موعدكم يوم الزينة وأن يحشر الناس ضحى

'(Sayyiduna Musa السلام عليه asked,) 'Your promise is for the day of festival and that the people be assembled late after sunrise?'"
– Surah Tāhā (20), Verse 59

'Night' refers to the night of Ascension (Mi'rāj). So, the verse will mean, "By the morning and the night of Ascension."

Another opinion is that 'morning' and 'night' refer to the radiant face of the Holy Prophet ﷺ and his blessed locks of hair respectfully. If this is taken as the meaning, the verse will read, "Oath on your blessed face which shines bright like the sun, and oath on your locks of hair which sometimes fall over it like clouds of mercy." – *Tafseer Roohul-Bayaan & Khazaa'inul-Irfaan*

'O Beloved ﷺ, neither has your Lord forsaken you nor is he displeased with you. You are the Beloved ﷺ, and how can the Beloved ﷺ be forsaken?'

Rule – Salaat'ud-Duhā (Chāsht Salaah) is sunnah, and its time commences from when the sun rises and becomes warm until mid-day (زوال). Either two rakaats or four with one salaam are performed in this Salaah.

Two explanations have been given for 'the Hereafter is better for you than the former.' The first is that the actual Hereafter (الآخرة) is better for you than the world. There are some in the world who slander and have enmity for you (O Rasoolullah ﷺ), but there'll be no such thing in the Hereafter. Your honor will be manifest to all. The Fountains of Kauthar, intercession, the Station of Praise (المقام المحمود) and other excellences will all be demonstrated in next world.

The second explanation is that every coming moment is better for the Holy Prophet ﷺ than the one before it. Meaning, Rasoolullah ﷺ will experience advancement in every juncture, and his greatness will be constantly exalted!

The verse, 'And indeed soon your Lord will give you so much that you'll be satisfied,' refers to those blessings that were bestowed to the world and to Islam or those that will be. Victory over nations during the worldly prophetic time, success in conquests in the time of the Companions ﷺ, Islam spreading from the East to the West, the Muslim Ummah being the most excellent of nations, the manifestations of Rasoolullah's ﷺ miracles, and likewise, intercession in the Hereafter, the Fountain of Kauthar, etc. are all incorporated in this.

Once, the Holy Prophet ﷺ fervently supplicated for the Ummah with tears in his eyes. Sayyiduna Jibrael عليه السلام was commanded to enquire, "O Beloved ﷺ, what's the reason for your crying?" Rasoolullah ﷺ answered, "Grief over my Ummah makes me cry." Allah عزوجل then ordered Sayyiduna Jibrael عليه السلام to say to Rasoolullah ﷺ, "O Beloved ﷺ, We'll make you content regarding your Ummah." In other words, "We'll forgive them to the extent that you'll become pleased." – *Muslim Sharif*

Another Hadith states that when the Holy Prophet ﷺ heard this verse, he said, "I won't be pleased while even a single follower of mine undergoes the torment of Hell." – *Tafseer Khazaa'inul-Irfaan*

Everyone wishes for the pleasure of Allah عزوجل through thousands of attempts, but Rasoolullah's ﷺ glory is that Allah عزوجل Himself bestows to make him satisfied!

'Both worlds desire the pleasure of Allah عزوجل, and Allah عزوجل wishes for the contentment of Muhammad ﷺ.'
– Alahadrat Imam Ahmad Raza ﷺ

The forgiveness of Rasoolullah's ﷺ parents is also included in this verse. How can the son be in Jannah while his parents suffer the punishment of Hell-fire? I've already discussed this issue under Surah Tauba (9).

VERSE 96

وَوَجَدَكَ ضَالًّا فَهَدَى

'He (Allah ﷻ) saw you deeply immersed in your love, so He guided you.'
– Surah Duhā (93), Verse 7

In the verse prior to this, Allah ﷻ said, "Did He not find you (O Beloved ﷺ) an orphan, so He gave you shelter?" There are two interpretations ascribed to this. The first refers to the honored father of Rasoolullah ﷺ, Hadrat Abdullah ؓ, passing away before his blessed birth (after which Hadrat Abdul-Muttalib ؓ and Abu Talib, the Prophet's ﷺ grandfather and uncle, became responsible for his upbringing). The second interpretation is, "You were found to be the matchless pearl (among orphans). So, you were given place near Allah ﷻ, because precious gems are kept safe and close."

Now, in this verse, the word ضال has been used for the Holy Prophet ﷺ. Since it's usually understood to mean 'astray', many explanations about this exist, because the word can never mean astray here. Refer to my treatise on the Prophets عليهم السلام being unable to commit sin (معصوم) in my book, *Ja'al-Haqq*, for a thorough explanation on this.

Many meanings have been ascribed to this word. It could mean any of the following,

1. "O Beloved ﷺ, you were so infatuated with Our love that you didn't focus on your own elevation. So, We made you progress from this stage in the spiritual path (سلوك)." We come to know that this passion of love isn't greater than undergoing the spiritual journey. When Sayyiduna Yaqub عليه السلام said to Sayyiduna Yusuf's عليه السلام brothers, "I'm getting the fragrance of Yusuf عليه السلام," they replied,

قالوا تالله إنك لفي ضلالك القديم

'By Allah ﷻ, you are infatuated with the same old love?'
– Surah Yusuf (12), Verse 95

ضال here cannot mean 'astray'. In Sayyiduna Yaqub's عليه السلام case, it means 'obsessed'. The same can apply to the verse under discussion.

2. "You weren't adorned with such excellence in knowledge at one stage, but you were later given the knowledge of what was and what will be (ما كان وما يكون). Indeed, you were informed of all things unknown, and all the secrets of the unseen were revealed to you." – *Tafseer Roohul-Bayaan & Tafseer Khazaa'inul-Irfan*

3. Water that is mixed with milk is called ضال (dāl). So, the verse could mean, "O Beloved 🌸, you were among the disbelievers but were made dominant over them."

4. A tall, noticeable tree in a desolate area is also called ضال (dāl) in Arabic. People see it from afar and learn the direction to their destination. So, the verse would mean, "O Beloved 🌸, We found you to be matchless and uniquely possessing the qualities of honor. So, We guided people through you." The object (مفعول) of 'guided you' in the verse is the nation of people. – *Madaarijun-Nubuwwah, Vol. 1, Chapter 3*

5. Once, in his childhood, the Prophet 🌸 got lost while in the care of Sayyidah Halima 🌸. After much search and effort, Abu Jahl found him and took him to Hadrat Abdul-Muttalib 🌸. So, the verse could mean, "We found you lost once in your childhood, so We showed people the way to reach you."

6. The verse could also mean, "O Beloved 🌸, We found you among the astray." In other words, "The light of prophethood had not yet brightened anyone from the community you were raised in. We kept you on the path of salvation (هداية) among them. Otherwise, how can one be a knower (عالم) while with them (in other words, if We hadn't created you unable to sin, how would you have remained on the true path)?" – *Roohul-Bayaan, Madaarijun-Nubuwwah*

7. "On the Night of the Ascension (Mi'rāj), We found you unaware of Our Qualities. So, We informed you of them so that you may come to the Divine Court and praise Us through them." – *Madaarijun-Nubuwwah*

Several other meanings may also be ascribed to the word.

Rule – The Prophets عليه السلام are pure and safe from being astray and committing acts of infidelity (كفر). Those who regard them to have been non-Muslims or astray before or after prophethood (even for a moment) is one without deen.

As soon as Sayyiduna Adam عليه السلام was created, he read the Kalima on the pillars of the Throne of Allah جل جلاله (عرش). When Sayyiduna Esa عليه السلام was born, he immediately proclaimed that he was the servant of Allah جل جلاله, a prophet, a recipient of Divine revelation, one who is obedient to his mother, and one who establishes Salaah. Sayyiduna Ibrahim عليه السلام taught his mother, paternal uncle and nation the Oneness of Allah جل جلاله as soon as he could speak! When these Prophets عليه السلام were such great recognizers of Allah جل جلاله in their infancy and childhood, how could they ever be astray?!

Similarly, as soon as the Holy Prophet ﷺ was born, he made sajda and supplicated for his Ummah's forgiveness. By this action, he informed us that he was a prophet even before his advent in this world. How then could he *ever* be astray?!

Allah جل جلاله states,

ما ضل صاحبكم وما غوى

'Your companion (Muhammad ﷺ) has not strayed nor was he misled.'
– Surah Najm (53), Verse 2

In short, the entire Surah Duhā (93) is the praise of Rasoolullah ﷺ.

VERSE 97

أَلَمْ نَشْرَحْ لَكَ صَدْرَكَ ، وَوَضَعْنَا عَنكَ وِزْرَكَ ، الَّذِيْ أَنقَضَ ظَهْرَكَ

'Have We not expanded your chest for you? And removed your
burden from you? [That] which had broken your back?'
– Surah Sharh (94), Verses 1-3

This entire Surah is a treasure-chest of the Prophet's ﷺ praise. The first verse states, "Have We not expanded your chest for you?" Commentators of the Quran provide several explanations to this,

1. It refers to when the Holy Prophet's ﷺ blessed chest was opened by Sayyiduna Jibrael عليه السلام and his heart was removed and dipped in Zum-Zum water. This occurred three times, the first when Rasoolullah ﷺ was in the care of Sayyidah Halima رضى الله عنها, the second when he began to receive revelation, and the third on the night of Mi'rāj. In the third occurrence, Sayyiduna Jibrael عليه السلام opened his chest until his navel, Sayyiduna Mikaīl عليه السلام brought a tray of Zum-Zum water, and the archangel [Sayyiduna Jibrael عليه السلام] passed it over the blessed heart. Another tray with the Noor of recognition (معرفة),

wisdom (حكمة) and faith (ایمان) was brought, and its contents placed in the heart. No pain or discomfort was experienced in any of the openings of the chest.

2. 'The expansion of the chest' means that it was made to bear the intensity of Allah's ﷻ Secrets, knowledge of the unseen, and the Noor of prophethood. Other hearts don't have the strength and ability to bear these things.

3. The blessed chest of Rasoolullah ﷺ was expanded to such an extent that connection with the world didn't make him negligent of Allah ﷻ. Inversely, being in proximity with Allah ﷻ didn't make him inattentive to the world. In other words, Rasoolullah ﷺ was in complete nearness to Allah ﷻ and, at the same time, not unaware of the world. Generally those who involve themselves in the world become negligent of the deen while those who bring themselves closer to the deen lose focus of the world. The blessed chest of the Holy Messenger ﷺ is attentive to all.

Such amazing grace does the blessed grave of Rasoolullah ﷺ possess! Millions of Durood & Salaam are conveyed there daily, with even angels paying their respects – but with all this, Rasoolullah ﷺ is still attentive to *each* submission! Good and bad deeds are also presented in his court, he intercedes for his followers and distributes the bounties of Allah ﷻ amongst the creation – all while in complete commune with Allah ﷻ Himself! He is one being, but is always mindful of the creation's goodness.

'Removed your burden' means that the blessed heart of Rasoolullah ﷺ was always sorrowful about the sinful Muslim's plight until Allah ﷻ made a promise of forgiveness to him, bringing contentment to his heart. Some Commentators say that Rasoolullah's ﷺ blessed heart was troubled by the polytheism and idolatry committed in Makkah and that he had no power to stop this transgression outwardly. After some time, Allah ﷻ blessed His Messenger ﷺ with this power, by which he removed idolatry from the Arab nation, purified the Holy Ka'ba from the filth of idols, and transformed a nation of idolaters into worshippers of the One Lord, Allah ﷻ!

VERSE 98

وَرَفَعْنَا لَكَ ذِكْرَكَ

'And have We not elevated your remembrance?'
– Surah Sharh (94), Verse 4

Although this verse is brief, the pen and tongue are unable to articulate the great praise of Rasoolullah ﷺ found in each letter of it! I'll explain this praise based only on the following points of this verse,

What is meant by 'Have We not elevated your remembrance'?

1. The remembrance of all eminent individuals is made on Earth, but the Holy Prophet ﷺ is remembered on the Earth, in the Heavens, and even in Jannah,

    > *'What do these mortals know of the heights of your splendor?*
    > *O King, the flag of your eminence flies high even in the Heavens!'*
    > – Alahadrat Imam Ahmad Raza Bareilwi ﷺ

    The mind of a poet soars the highest, but the status of the Prophet ﷺ is a height not even a poet's mind can reach!

    > *'I've not praised Muhammad ﷺ by my utterances. Rather, my*
    > *utterances have become praiseworthy by praising him.'*
    > – Hadrat Hasan ibn Thaabit ﷺ

2. The Holy Prophet's ﷺ name is found wherever Allah's ﷻ is. Proof of this is the Kalima, the Azaan, Salaah, at-Tahiyyāt, the sermon (خطبة), etc.

3. The Quran mentioned other Prophets عليهم السلام by their names, yet it speaks of the Holy Messenger ﷺ and addresses him by his exquisite qualities alone.

4. Several prolific people have existed in this world but none remember them now. However, neither is Rasoolullah ﷺ neglected nor can his remembrance be forgotten. Many have tried to end his remembrance by terming it an innovation (بدعة) or polytheism (شرك) yet they themselves were ruined. The Prophet's ﷺ remembrance can never stop since Allah ﷻ Himself promised to elevate it.

5. All the Prophets عليهم السلام and angels were made to send Durood & Salaam upon him.

6. On the Day of Covenant (the Day wherein Allah ﷻ made the Prophets ﷺ promise their assistance to the Holy Messenger ﷺ), all of the Prophets ﷺ recited Rasoolullah's ﷺ Kalima.

There are several other points through which we can gauge how elevated is Rasoolullah's ﷺ remembrance, but we shall do with just the above.

Why did Allah ﷻ relate this act of elevating to Himself?

Generally, one attains honor due to being from a particular community, through wealth, being born on a particular day or time, or by another's favor. Our Beloved Prophet ﷺ, however, didn't attain honor from anyone. Every distinction was attained from him, and it was Allah ﷻ that blessed him with eminence. This is why Rasoolullah ﷺ wasn't born on a Friday, Saturday or Sunday (as they are already days of excellence in Islam, Judaism and Christianity respectively). He was born on a Monday for Monday to gain distinction by his birth!

Similarly, he wasn't born in any famous month like Ramadaan or Muharram, but in Rabiul-Awwal, for this month to also gain honor by his birth. He wasn't born in Baitul-Muqaddas because it could've been said, "He was born in Jerusalem, the city of the Prophets ﷺ, so his distinction has increased." No. It was

> Everyone wishes for the pleasure of Allah ﷻ through thousands of attempts, but Rasoolullah's ﷺ glory is that Allah ﷻ Himself bestows to make him satisfied!

the desert of Arabia (not even a place of greenery) that was chosen for the Messenger's ﷺ birthplace. In this way, none could make such remarks. Thereafter, Rasoolullah ﷺ wasn't kept in Makkah, but in Madina. The wisdom behind this was that people would have to undergo a special journey to visit him, not just casually visit the Rauda because they just so happened to be in Makkah for the Hajj. In fact, Salaah is offered in the direction of the Ka'ba solely *because* Rasoolullah ﷺ desired it to be the qiblah. I've already explained this in Surah Baqarah (2) [Verse 10 in book].

This is why Baitul-Muqaddas was initially made the qiblah. If the Ka'ba was made the qiblah first, the grandeur of the Holy Prophet ﷺ wouldn't have been demonstrated!

The reality is that the world and the Hereafter, Jannah, Jahannam, believers, non-believers, and even devils exist to elevate Rasoolullah's ﷺ remembrance through different means. Believers will praise him, non-Muslims will try to stop his remembrance but will inadvertently cause it to be publicized further, and those obedient to him will enter Paradise while his enemies will be cast into the Hell-fire. Allah ﷻ rejected Shaitaan just by his refusal to make one prostration in spite of having given him knowledge, wisdom, proximity and power. Shaitaan was granted loftiness but was later brought below Scholars, Saints, the pious elders (and even ourselves) so as to realize that even the slightest disrespect towards the Prophetic court ruins all our accomplishments. Sajda to Sayyiduna Adam عليه السلام was actually sajda towards the Noor of Rasoolullah ﷺ.

A product made by man can be disturbed by a human being, but something created by Allah ﷻ cannot be damaged or affected by anyone's interference. Lamps and furnaces can be extinguished by a human because they are lit by people, but the light of the sun and moon cannot be removed because it's Allah ﷻ Who brightened them. Allah ﷻ explained that Rasoolullah's ﷺ elevation isn't due to any human being by relating it to Himself! It's His bestowal upon Rasoolullah ﷺ. So, the verse is saying, "O Beloved ﷺ, none can lower your glory. Those who wish to do so will themselves be ruined, and those who praise you will be praised in the world."

By using the past tense (i.e. 'We have elevated…'), Allah ﷻ informs us that this elevation wasn't recently bestowed, but was from a long time back. The past indefinite tense (مطلق) also proves that this elevation is free from the bond of a past perfect or present perfect tense of verb. So, it's saying, "Your glory in every era and time." The truth is that past, present and future tenses are used only for our understanding. Rasoolullah's ﷺ elevation was *already* enshrined before the history of time!

Why was 'for you' included in the verse?

It was for us to realize that loftiness and grandeur has been placed in Rasoolullah's ﷺ property. Whoever he wishes to elevate becomes elevated and whoever earns his indifference cannot be helped in either world. Examples of this follow,

1. People undergo many journeys but none acquire honor in the process. When a person goes for Hajj, however, he immediately gains respect and is referred to as a Haaji.

2. Planes that carry people to far and exotic locations aren't seen off by crowds, while people leaving for Hajj are surrounded by multitudes.

3. The parents of Abu Lahab, Abu Jahl and Hadrat Abu Hurairah رضى الله عنه kept other names for their children, but it was the Holy Prophet ﷺ who addressed them with these words, making their original names secondary and the Prophet's ﷺ bestowed titles what these individuals will forever be remembered as.

4. There are thousands of names in the world, but the names related to the Holy Prophet ﷺ, his deen, Companions and Family رضى الله عنه are the most common on Earth.

5. There have also been thousands of Prophets السلام عليهم and Sahifas (Divine Books) to have come to this world, but only the names of those whom Rasoolullah ﷺ has divulged are remembered today.

6. The Jews maligned Sayyidah Maryam رضى الله عنها, but our Holy Prophet ﷺ professed her greatness and nobility. Effectively, the entire world now pronounces her chastity and praise!

In short, anyone who becomes the Holy Prophet's ﷺ attains greatness, while those who wish to stop his remembrance are actually challenging Allah عز وجل.

'If you had intelligence, you wouldn't pick a fight with Allah عز وجل. They want to tarnish the Prophet ﷺ, yet Allah عز وجل wishes to extend his majesty.'
– Alahadrat Imam Ahmed Raza رضى الله عنه

VERSE 99

وَالْعَصْرِ ، إِنَّ الْإِنْسَانَ لَفِي خُسْرٍ

'By the time (of My Beloved ﷺ), indeed man is in a state of loss.'
– Surah Asr (103), Verses 1-2

This verse is also the explicit praise of Rasoolullah ﷺ, and an oath on *Asr* (time) has been sworn in it. The Commentators have given several meanings to this word,

1. It either relates to the time of Asr. Meaning, Allah عز وجل took an oath on Asr Salaah or its time. We come to know that Asr Salaah is the most emphasized of all Salaahs. It's also called *Salaatul-Wustā* [according to Scholars of the Hanafi Madh'hab – *Translator*].

2. The word may also refer to the time of the Holy Prophet ﷺ. So, we can say that Allah ﷻ took an oath on Rasoolullah's ﷺ city of residence, his blessed age, and even his era!

Bear in mind that 'Rasoolullah's ﷺ time' may either refer to the era in which he physically lived in this world or the period of his prophethood. Indeed, the period of his prophethood is until the Day of Judgment because his deen cannot be annulled. This is why he said, "Qiyaamat and I are like these two fingers." – *Mishkaat*

Once, a Maulana was reciting Fatiha on some food when a person objected to this and said, "Making Fatiha on food items is a bad innovation (بدعة)." The Maulana asked him what he meant by 'a bad innovation', and the man explained, "An action not found in the era of the Holy Prophet ﷺ." The Maulana replied, "So is this your father's time? This is also the Holy Prophet's ﷺ time. In fact, his time is from the *beginning* of time until the end!"

VERSE 100

إِنَّا أَعْطَيْنَاكَ الْكَوْثَرَ

'(O Beloved ﷺ), undoubtedly We've bestowed upon you Kauthar (an abundance of good).'
– Surah Kauthar (108), Verse 1

This verse is also the praise of the Holy Prophet ﷺ. Its reason for revelation was that when the son of Rasoolullah ﷺ (either Hadrat Ibrahim ؏ or Hadrat Qasim ؏) passed away, Ās ibn Waa'il came to his tribe [after visiting the Prophet ﷺ] and said to them, "I come to you after visiting that *abtar* (i.e. someone whose surname won't live on due to not having any offspring)."

This offensive comment was hurtful to the Holy Prophet ﷺ, so this verse was revealed to remove his pain. The verse proclaims, "O Beloved ﷺ, why do you grieve over the nonsensical utterances of an enemy? I've blessed you with Kauthar (i.e. an abundance of good)." This proves that Rasoolullah ﷺ has such great eminence in the court of Allah ﷻ that if one attempts to cause distress to him, it's Allah ﷻ Himself Who safeguards His Beloved ﷺ from such an action.

Several meanings have been ascribed to 'Kauthar',

1. It could mean 'several excellences, virtues and a plentiful amount of remembrance'. So, the verse would mean, "This non-Muslim thinks that your name needs to be propagated by male descendents and that because you have no heirs, it won't be carried forth. He's wrong, because only he whose remembrance I choose to preserve remains, and I will make your remembrance remain until the Day of Judgment." Bear in mind again, that Allah ﷻ has described worldly goods as 'meager' while Rasoolullah ﷺ has been given Kauthar, meaning 'the greatest possible amount'. Allah ﷻ said even about Himself,

وهو العلى العظيم

'And He alone is the Most Exalted, the Great.'
– Surah Baqarah (2), Verse 255

Allah ﷻ said that His favor upon His Beloved ﷺ is great and that he possesses spectacular mannerisms. The word 'great' has been used in the verses explaining this. So, we come to know that none can comprehend the greatness possessed by Allah ﷻ and the loftiness bestowed upon Rasoolullah ﷺ. Indeed, no one can determine the magnitude of blessings Allah ﷻ gave him.

2. Kauthar can also mean 'many'. So, the verse will read, "O Beloved ﷺ, even though no son of yours has been kept alive, your progeny will continue through your daughter, Fathima Zahra ؓ, even to the last days of time." Indeed, the family of Rasoolullah ﷺ (سادات) is found everywhere in the world even today, and will be found until Qiyaamat, Insha-Allah ﷻ!

3. 'The Fountain of Kauthar' is another interpretation of Kauthar, and this is also a meaning found in the Hadith. Taking this meaning, the verse would read, "We have granted you the Fountain of Kauthar whose water is sweeter than honey and whiter than milk, and he who drinks from it once will never be thirsty again." Mulla Ali Qaari ؓ states, "Every prophet has been given a fountain from which he will provide his Ummah to drink from, but the fountain given to the Holy Prophet ﷺ is called Kauthar because it's the biggest of all of these fountains. Its water is the most excellent, the most enjoyable, and of the highest quality." – *Mirqaatul-Mafateeh*

4. Kauthar can also mean 'the creation in its entirety'. So, the verse will mean, "You've been given the entire creation." Our Beloved Prophet

👑 has right over everything Allah ﷻ is the Lord of. Refer to my book, *Sultanat'e-Mustapha* 👑, for a detailed study into this. [This book has been translated into English and is also available from the publisher – *Translator*].

5. Kauthar also refers to 'an extensive amount of followers in the Ummah', leading the verse to mean, "Even though your direct sons have passed away, you'll be blessed with an amount of spiritual sons (i.e. Muslim followers) like none before." As a result, Rasoolullah's 👑 Ummah will occupy *half* of Jannah while the other half will be occupied by the nations of all the other Prophets ﷺ combined!

Question – If Kauthar is interpreted here to mean 'the Fountain of Kauthar', how would this Surah censor the disbeliever who said that the Prophet 👑 would have no heir?

Answer – If this meaning is taken, the verse would mean, "O Beloved 👑, today, this disbeliever and others like him can mock and scorn you as much as they wish, but the day will come when you'll be the distributer at the Fountain of Kauthar. On that day, these people will begin to praise you, but at that time it won't be beneficial to them." So, if Kauthar here is interpreted as 'the Fountain of Kauthar', the Surah would still censor the non-Muslim who insulted the Messenger 👑.

> The Prophet's 👑 mercy in this world is that while sinners sleep the entire night, he is occupied in crying for their forgiveness.

Those who belittle the Holy Prophet 👑 today will surely pronounce his praise after witnessing his lofty status in the Hereafter!

Question – Surah Kauthar ends with, "Indeed your enemy himself is *abtar* (i.e. his progeny is no more)," yet the person who insulted Rasoolullah 👑 (Ās ibn Waa'il) had children that survived him. So, how is he 'one without progeny'?

Answer – Abtar has two meanings, and in relation to Ās ibn Waa'il both are applicable,

1. To be cut off from all goodness,

2. To have children acquire the salvation of faith, effectively causing a divide in religion between father and child. Having a different

religion is akin to death, this is why the inheritance, Janaazah, kafn, or burial of a Muslim cannot be acquired or completed by a father or child if he is a non-Muslim. Indeed, this is what happened to Ās ibn Waa'il. His son, Hadrat Amr ⬥, become an accomplished Sahaabi.

VERSE 101

قُلْ أَعُوذُ بِرَبِّ الْفَلَقِ

'(O Beloved ⬥), Say, 'I seek refuge with the Lord of the daybreak."
– Surah Falaq (113), Verse 1

قُلْ أَعُوذُ بِرَبِّ النَّاسِ

'(O Beloved ⬥), Say, 'I seek refuge with the Lord of mankind."
– Surah Naas (114), Verse 1

These Surahs also contain the praise of the Holy Prophet ⬥. The reason for their revelation was that a Jew named Labeed ibn As'am and his daughters cast black magic on the Prophet ⬥. Still, although the witchcraft was severe, only his physical and exterior body parts were affected by it, while Rasoolullah's ⬥ heart, mind and faith remained unaffected through the grace of Allah ⬥. After a few days, Sayyiduna Jibrael ⬥ came to him and said, "A Jew has practiced witchcraft on you, and the item for the magic is pressed beneath a rock [in a certain well]." Rasoolullah ⬥ then sent Hadrat Ali ⬥ to the well, who, after clearing the water, lifted the rock and found a leaf in a bud from a date tree. A few strands of the Prophet's ⬥ hair, some teeth of his comb, an effigy made from a candle with eleven needles pierced into it, and a cord with eleven knots were all found in the wrapping. This was brought before the Holy Prophet ⬥, at which time Allah ⬥ revealed Surah Falaq and Surah Naas, both of which have a sum of eleven verses (Surah Falaq has five while Surah Naas has six). When a verse was recited, a knot opened, and eventually, all eleven knots were opened by the recital of these two Surahs. The Prophet ⬥ regained complete health afterwards. – *Tafseer Khazaa'inul-Irfaan*

The following points are established from this,

1. Rasoolullah ⬥ has such great proximity in the Divine Court that there's no need for him to visit a doctor for treatment at the time of need. Allah ⬥ Himself sees to his needs! The Holy Prophet ⬥ is the curer of the entire creation. All of us require him, and he is dependent on Allah ⬥ alone.

2. Besides bestowing knowledge of religion, Allah ﷻ blessed the Holy Prophet ﷺ with the knowledge of medicine. In fact, Allah ﷻ blessed His Beloved ﷺ with the knowledge of all sciences. This is why there's no evidence of the Prophet ﷺ consulting any physician or doctor during any of his illnesses or acquiring the knowledge of medicine from anyone. The works of Hadith have chapters on duas, but they also have sections dedicated to medicine, including medicines and cures prescribed and narrated from the Noble Messenger ﷺ himself! Our Beloved Prophet ﷺ didn't learn medicine from anyone, yet the expertise he had in knowing the names of all medicines, their benefits and dosage, etc. would make even the modern science of medicine blush!

3. The hearts and intelligence of the Prophets عليهم السلام cannot be affected by witchcraft. Yes, their physical bodies can, and this isn't contrary to their rank of prophethood. Aren't their bodies affected by swords, poison and venomous animals? Don't food, water, and the elements benefit their bodies? Likewise is the effect of magic, which is a natural phenomenon. Magic affecting the Prophets عليهم السلام doesn't negate them being Prophets عليهم السلام.

Some say, "When magicians were defeated by the staff of Sayyiduna Musa عليه السلام, how could magic affect the Holy Prophet ﷺ when he's more excellent than Sayyiduna Musa عليه السلام?" The answer to this is that in the occurrence of the magicians and Sayyiduna Musa عليه السلام, there was a confrontation between magic and miracle. Here there was no challenge. Bear in mind, though, that the magic of the magicians *did* impact Sayyiduna Musa's عليه السلام sight,

فإذا حبالهم وعصيهم يخيل إليه من سحرهم أنها تسعى

'(When they cast their ropes and staffs), they looked to him as if they were running by the strength of their magic.'
– Surah Tāhā (20), Verse 66

4. To recite duas & quranic verses and blow (دم) to remove illnesses, magic, the evil-eye, etc. is correct. Likewise, the usage of an amulet with inscriptions of Imaan (تعويذ) is also permissible. – *Fataawa Shaami, Vol. 5*

Yes, it's haraam to use utterances of polytheism for this purpose, or to use utterances in a language which we don't know (since we will not be able to determine whether the wording is anti-Islamic or not). To write Quranic verses on amulets with blood, to write them upside-down, to stitch the amulet in a shoe or to stomp on it by foot is all impermissible due to the disrespect shown to respected wording.

Rule – Taking a compensation for writing an amulet or making dua is permissible even if Quranic verses are written or said in these actions, since they are forms of treatment.

VERSE 102

اَلْحَمْدُ لِلّٰهِ رَبِّ الْعٰلَمِيْنَ

'All praise be to Allah ﷻ, the Lord of the Worlds.'
– Surah Fatiha (1), Verse 1

This Surah contains the praise of Allah ﷻ and also teaches us servants the method of dua, but it too is a great example of the Holy Prophet's ﷺ praise. If the article 'ال' is taken as a comprehensive article (استغراقی), the meaning of the verse will be, "All praise absolutely is Allah's ﷻ." In other words, if one has to praise someone in the world at any time, or if one wishes to thank another for a favor, it will actually be the praise of Allah ﷻ. Whoever possesses any admirable trait has been blessed with it by Allah ﷻ. The praise of a product is in fact the praise of the maker.

> Yes, the Prophet ﷺ still didn't adopt the habit of writing. And why should he have, when the Protected Tablet is his journal and the Divine Pen is his pen? What need was there for him to write with the pens and papers of this mundane world?

If the article is take as اهدی, it'll mean, "That special praise is for Allah ﷻ." Which special praise then? The praise articulated from the blessed mouth of Rasoolullah ﷺ, or the praise of Allah ﷻ uttered by the Prophet's ﷺ teaching of it. So, the verse will mean, "No matter who praises Allah ﷻ, the accepted praise is the one made by the Holy Beloved ﷺ, or the praise made by his teaching of it." – *Roohul-Bayaan*

This is why the praise of the disbeliever will not be accepted (even if they spend their entire lives doing so), because they wouldn't have used the accepted praise taught by the Holy Messenger ﷺ. It's also based on this that the Flag of Praise (لواء الحمد) will be given to Rasoolullah ﷺ.

The Hadith of intercession states that Allah ﷻ will inform Rasoolullah ﷺ of His special, unique praises and the Holy Prophet ﷺ will begin to praise Him by them. In short, only praise made by the Prophet ﷺ is uniquely accepted in this world *and* in the Hereafter. This is why the Messenger's ﷺ name is *Ahmad*, meaning 'he who praises his Lord the most'. Allah ﷻ is also *Mahmūd*, 'One Who is praised by His Beloved ﷺ.'

The verse can also mean, "Perfect praise is only Allah's ﷻ appraisal." In other words, the entire creation can get together and praise the Holy Prophet ﷺ, but their praise will not equal the praise his glory deserves. The perfect praise of Rasoolullah ﷺ is only that which is expressed by Allah ﷻ. This is why Rasoolullah's ﷺ name is *Muhammad* (he who has been praised exceptionally). So, who has exceptionally praised him? Undoubtedly it was his Lord! Allah's ﷻ name is also *Hāmid* (The One Who praises). Who has He praised then? The answer is His Beloved ﷺ Mustapha ﷺ!

In short, the *entire* Surah Fatiha – its every verse – resonates the praise of Allah's ﷻ Beloved ﷺ.

VERSE 103

اِهْدِنَا الصِّرَاطَ الْمُسْتَقِيْمَ ، صِرَاطَ الَّذِيْنَ أَنْعَمْتَ عَلَيْهِمْ غَيْرِ الْمَغْضُوْبِ عَلَيْهِمْ وَلَا الضَّالِّيْنَ

'Guide us on the straight path, the path of those whom You have favored. Not those who have earned Your anger, nor of those who have gone astray.'
– Surah Fatiha (1), Verses 6-7

These verses are the clear praise of the Holy Prophet ﷺ. Muslims are taught in it to make the following supplication, "O Allah ﷻ, guide us on the straight path, the path of those whom You have favored."

The deen of Islam is the straight path, and the straight path *is* obedience and emulation of the Holy Prophet ﷺ! In fact, this Surah further explains that the straight path is the path that those who have been favored traveled upon, and undoubtedly Sayyiduna Muhammad'ur-Rasoolullah ﷺ is the one that has been favored the most by Allah ﷻ. So, Allah ﷻ has taught Muslims to supplicate, "O Allah ﷻ, grant us the ability to walk on the path of Your Beloved ﷺ, grant us steadfastness on it, and may our demise occur on it." *Ameen Ya Rabbal-Ālameen!*

We also come to know from this verse that it's compulsory on us to follow (تقليد) the Imams because they are also from among those whom Allah ﷻ has favored. The entire Ummah, Scholars, Saints, Commentators of both the

Quran & Hadith, and the Islamic Jurists all followed and follow the Imams. To now reject this or choose a path separate from it is a grave mistake and offence. Refer to my book, *Ja'al-Haqq*, for a complete discussion on following the four Imams. May Allah 🕮 grant us an end on goodness. Ameen!

LAST WORDS

This sinful servant, one who is aspirant of Allah's 🕮 Mercy, Ahmed Yaar, submits that others present their works and treatises in the courts of kings, noblemen and the wealthy hoping for favor. This *faqeer*, this mendicant beggar, presents these humble words in the court of his true king, the king of both worlds, the sympathizer of the deprived, the holy Beloved of Allah 🕮, the Intercessor of the Sinful, Ahmad'e-Mujtaba, Muhammad Mustapha 🕮, and I hopefully aspire that it be accepted.

'It is only you, O Rasoolullah 🕮, that is my hope!'

Readers, please don't think that only the verses I've discussed are praise for the Holy Prophet 🕮. As I explained in the introduction, *every verse* of the Holy Quran is the praise of Rasoolullah 🕮! There are several other verses which are explicitly his praise, but I make do with only these for the sake of brevity.

I commenced writing this book in the middle of Jamaadul-Ūla 1361 A.H, and it was completed on Monday the 3rd of Shabaan 1361 A.H.

May Allah 🕮 make this a blessing in the Hereafter for my respected elder, Haaji of the Haramain Shareefain, the union of Shariah and Tareeqah, Shaikhul-Mashaai'kh Turaab Iqdaam Ahmed and al-Haaj Muhammad Ali, as well as for me. May Allah 🕮 grant the Haajis the ability to serve the deen more. Ameen.

The insignificant *Ahmed Yaar Khan*
Ūjhyāwi Badayūni

I plan to end this book with the remembrance of Rasoolullah's ﷺ close servants (i.e. the glorious Saints of Islam) since the praise of the servants is in fact praise of the master. So, proclaiming the excellence of the Saints and Scholars is ultimately the praise of the Prophet ﷺ, because they attained their rank in his servitude. This is similar to how the excellence of Madina, its soil and its surroundings, etc. are all the praise of the Prophet ﷺ himself, because it was through him that the excellences of these things were attained.

The Holy Quran states,

أَلَا إِنَّ أَوْلِيَاءَ اللهِ لَا خَوْفٌ عَلَيْهِمْ وَلَا هُمْ يَحْزَنُوْنَ ، الَّذِيْنَ آمَنُوا وَ كَانُوا يَتَّقُونَ ، لَهُمُ الْبُشْرَى فِي الْحَيٰوةِ الدُّنْيَا وَفِي الْأَخِرَةِ ، لَا تَبْدِيلَ لِكَلِمٰتِ اللهِ ، ذٰلِكَ هُوَ الْفَوْزُ الْعَظِيْمُ

'Listen carefully; no doubt there is no fear nor any grief upon the friends of Allah ﷻ, those who believe and kept up their duty. For them are glad-tidings in the life of the world and in the Hereafter. The words of Allah ﷻ are not challenged. That indeed is their supreme triumph.'
– Surah Yunus (10), Verses 62-4

I'll present a few points as a preface before commentary on this verse.

What need is there in the world for the Friends of Allah ﷻ?

In the material world, some physical bodies are givers and some are takers, some attain guidance while others give guidance. The sun, moon and clouds give benefit while the Earth and its crops receive benefit. Similarly, in the realm of spirituality (روحانية), the Prophets عليهم السلام and, through their blessings, the Scholars, Mashaaikh and Friends of Allah ﷻ are the ones who bestow guidance while the entire creation is in need of them. Maulana Jalaaluddin Rumi ﷺ states,

> *'His blessed being (i.e. the Holy Prophet ﷺ) is the pivot of need. This is why it was said by Allah ﷻ, "Send Durood & Salaam upon him."'*

Just as how the world always has a need for the sun and rain, so too does it have a great need for the Saints and Scholars of Islam. Rasoolullah ﷺ addressed Islamic Scholars as the reservoirs of the merciful rain of prophethood. – *Mishkaat, Kitaabul-Ilm*

Note that the One Who bestows mercy is Allah ﷻ while the one who distributes it is His Beloved ﷺ,

والله يعطى وانما انا قاسم

'Indeed Allah ﷻ gives and I am the distributor.'
– Bukhari, Kitaabul-Ilm

The Saints and Scholars are the means of this distribution. A Hadith Sharif states that it rains, victory is attained, and punishment remains far from the people of Syria, all through the blessings of the 40 *Abdāls* (a category among Saints). – *Miskhaat*

The Prophet ﷺ also said that even the fish in the sea make dua for Scholars. – *Mishkaat, Kitaabul-Ilm*

Mulla Ali Qaari ؓ writes in the commentary of the above Hadith, "The fish know that rain and the flowing of rivers is through the blessings of the Scholars." – *Mirqaatul-Mafateeh*

> The presence of scholars in a sect isn't evidence of its truthfulness, but the existence of the Friends of Allah ؓ is indeed. This is because a scholar conveys the message after hearing the truth while the Saints convey the truth after seeing it!

Through the Holy Prophet ﷺ, we reach Allah ﷻ, and it's through the Saints and Scholars that we reach Rasoolullah ﷺ. The Sahaabah directly attained the prophetic Noor from the blessed chest of Rasoolullah ﷺ, and people after them attained it from the chests of the Sahaabah.

The chests of the Friends of Allah ﷻ (Auliya-Allah ﷻ), then, are like clear mirrors for us which reflect Noor that brightens the entire world. When a person stands in front of them, the Noor that they give off is cast on them. This is why a pledge of allegiance (bai'at) is made with them.

The Prophets ﷺ came to correct the inner and outer condition of the creation. Since the end of their progression, this task has been delegated to two groups: (1) Scholars have the duty of correcting the outer condition of creation, while (2) Saints have been made to rectify our inner condition. It's necessary for all of the duties of Rasoolullah ﷺ to be maintained since his prophethood lasts until Qiyaamat. This is only possible if these two groups are found in the world. To purify the body for Salaah and explain Salaah's acts and conditions, etc. is the task of the Islamic Scholars (Ulama), while instilling sincerity and concentration in the heart of the one reading Salaah and making it free from boast, etc. is the responsibility of the Saints (Auliya). So, the Scholars fulfill the conditions of performance while the Friends of Allah ﷻ complete the conditions of acceptance.

One who sees the Holy Quran or the Ka'ba is not a Companion of the Holy Prophet ﷺ (Sahaabi). He who sees the Holy Prophet ﷺ with sincerity is. We come to know, then, that *suhbat* (companionship) has more of an effect than deeds.

Once, a king invited Chinese and Roman artists to demonstrate their skill to him. He took them to a room with a covering in the middle and gave one wall to the Romans and one to the Chinese. The Chinese artists drew ornamentation on their wall and made it look like a beautiful garden, while the Roman artists rubbed their wall so carefully that they made it look like a clear mirror. After they had both completed their art, they called for the king to judge, and when the king saw their artwork, he remarked, "This covering is the cause of the dilemma. Bring it down and then I'll judge." When the covering was brought down and both walls faced each other, the garden of the Chinese artists displayed itself on both sides.

Similarly, a human being is like a room with two walls, a form and a heart. The Scholars of Islamic Law adorn the form with Shariah, and the Mashaaikh (plural of Shaikh) cleanse the heart with contemplation in Allah ﷻ (مراقبة) and spiritual strife. However, the cover of life is between these two walls, and Insha-Allah ﷻ, only when it's removed will the ornamentation of the form be visible in the clean heart. In the test of the grave, the unseen Beloved ﷺ will appear, and if the heart is clear, we'll be able to recognize him.

Imaan (faith) is attained through a Scholar, but the protection of one's Imaan is attained through the Friends of Allah ﷻ. This is why the Saints are the students of the Scholars while the Scholars pledge allegiance to the Saints. These two groups are similar to the two arms of deeds and Imaan. Just as how a bird cannot fly without wings, so too can deeds not reach the court of Allah ﷻ without the help of these two contingents of people. The Saints & Scholars are the two wheels of the vehicle of existence.

Similarly, just as how rust forms on steel and our bodies experience sickness, so too does the rust of negligence develop on our hearts. Doctors have been created to treat physical ailments, while spiritual luminaries have been created to treat our neglected spirituality of Imaan. Maulana Jalaaluddin Rumi ﷺ states,

> 'You've learnt some medical wisdom, [now] learn the wisdom of Imaan from us (i.e. the Friends of Allah ﷻ).'

Steel that is affected by rust needs a furnace, and the heart which has gathered the rust of negligence needs the companionship of the Saints, along with worship and spiritual strife. However, association with the Friends of Allah ﷻ is a faster cure.

Recitation of the Holy Quran slowly but surely removes the darkness of the heart (*Mishkaat*), but the vision of mercy of the beloved servants of Allah ﷻ *instantly* changes its condition! Maulana Rumi ﷺ further states,

> 'A single duration of time spent in the companionship of the Friends of Allah ﷻ is greater than the selfless obedience of hundreds of years.'

It's indeed true, 'Fates are changed by the vision of complete believers.'

Once, the home of the King of Baghdad, Shaikh Abdul-Qadir Jilani ﷺ, was infiltrated by a thief. The man searched the house thoroughly but found nothing for himself. At that time, Shaikh Abdul-Qadir ﷺ remarked to his servant, "A thief is leaving my home empty-handed, and this is an embarrassment to my generosity." When the servant enquired as to what should be given to the thief, the great Saint replied, "He should be given that which will be beneficial for him in both worlds! The *Qutub* (i.e. a high-ranking Saint) of a certain area has passed away. Make this thief, then, the Qutub of that area and send him (towards it)!"

Subhanallah! An individual comes as a thief and leaves as a Friend of Allah ﷻ! O King of Baghdad, cast your glance of benevolence on us criminals as well! Ameen.

Shaikh Abdul-Qadir Jilani ﷺ was once passing a jungle alone when a robber grabbed his expensive garment, intending to steal it. He commanded that Shaikh Abdul-Qadir ﷺ remove it, yet the Saint merely supplicated, "O Allah ﷻ, he has held the covering of Abdul-Qadir ﷺ. May it not leave his hand until Qiyaamat."

Hadrat Khwaja Bahauddin Naqshbandi ﷺ once passed by the furnace of a potter while clay-pots were being prepared in it. Through just a *glance* of his towards it, the fire turned into Noor and all the pots had 'Allah' ﷻ imprinted on them! The potter witnessed this and said,

> 'O King of Naqshband! Grant me the impression of your servitude.'

Just as how a traveler needs a guide in the world, so too will the traveler of the Hereafter need a guide in Tareeqah. Even in this world, one without a guide in a foreign place is lost.

Maulana Rumi ﷺ states,

> 'Choose a spiritual master (مرشد), because without him, this
> journey will be a path of hardship & grief.'
> – Mathnawi

Allah ﷻ states in the Holy Quran,

> 'And search for the means (wasīlah) towards Allah ﷻ.'
> – Surah Māida (5), Verse 35

Humanity exists in the world to work. Imaan (Faith) and deeds are the earnings which we send to the Hereafter. In the course of this, our carnal desires (نفوس) and Shaitaan attack us. So, it's necessary that these precious commodities are taken in someone's protection. The individuals of this group of protectors are known as the 'Friends of Allah ﷻ'. Precious belongings are safeguarded and protected by insurance companies. Similarly, through the favor of the blessed Mashaaikh, our Imaan will be protected, Insha-Allah ﷻ. Alahadrat Imam Ahmed Raza ﷺ states,

> 'Once Your name became etched on my heart,
> The thief of Imaan (i.e. Shaitaan) scampers.'

The lower-self (نفس) is a dog. Affix the collar from a Shaikh to it so that it doesn't become troublesome. Obedience to the Friends of Allah ﷻ is the collar, the Chain of Authority (شجرة) is the collar's chain, the chain's first link is the neck of our carnal desires (nafs), and the last link is in the hands of the Holy Prophet ﷺ. If this collar and chain remains fixed on one's desires, Insha-Allah ﷻ, it won't be misled. Alahadrat ﷺ states,

> '(O Shaikh Abdul-Qadir ﷺ!) Your court has a relation
> to you, and it's my honor to be connected to the dog of your court.
> My neck has fixed to it the most humble relation to you'

'The dog bearing your seal of servitude is never troubled. May your collar remain on my neck until the Day of Resurrection.'

A train doesn't look at the class of its passengers. It transports all, irrespective of status, on condition that the carriages are joined strongly together. So, Islam is like a train, we are the passengers on it, the Friends of Allah ﷻ are the links, and the Holy Prophet ﷺ is our destination. If our carriages are linked by the Saints, we can reach our goal. Otherwise, we won't be able to attain his happiness.

The Stations of Sainthood (ولاية)

There are different stations and several ranks of Sainthood. Some accomplished Saints who lose their reasoning in the intoxication of Divine love are known as *majzūbs*. Islamic law doesn't apply to them as they've lost their reasoning in the hue of Allah's ﷻ affection. Hadrat Mansoor Hallaj ﵀ said, "I am the Truth (i.e. I am Allah ﷻ.)," yet he remained a believer because he rid himself of his being. Pharaoh, on the other hand, said,

أنا ربكم الأعلى

'I am your lord, the most high.'
– Surah Nāziāt (79), Verse 24

and he became a disbeliever because he claimed Divinity while in his worldly senses. These majzūbs become the phenomenon of Allah's ﷻ Qualities. It's *their* tongue – but Allah's ﷻ words! Maulana Jalaaluddin Rumi ﵀ states,

'His (the servant's) utterance is actually the words of Allah ﷻ; even though it comes from the throats of the bondsman.'

'When 'I am Allah ﷻ' can emanate from a tree, why would it be impossible to hear it from a virtuous human?'

Note – Some Sufiya become annihilated (فنا) in Allah ﷻ, and in this condition of spiritual concentration (جذب) they say, "I am Allah ﷻ," yet no one can be annihilated in Rasoolullah ﷺ and say, "I am Muhammad ﷺ."

'Lose yourselves when it comes to Allah ﷻ, but be careful when dealing with Muhammad ﷺ.'

Dr. Iqbal states,

*'There's a place beneath the sky more exquisite than the
Heavens. Even spiritual greats like Junaid ☙ and Bā-Yazīd ☙ come
to offer their servitude in this court (i.e. the court of Rasoolullah ﷺ).'*

When a piece of coal is placed in a fire, it's so annihilated in it that it begins
to reflect the fire's qualities. This helps in understanding the station of
majzūbs.

However, there are some Saints who reach lofty stations in Sainthood but don't lose their senses and reasoning. The people of this group are known as *saaliks*. Bear in mind that the Prophets عليهم السلام are the manifestation of Allah's ﷻ Qualities while the Friends of Allah ☙ are the manifestation of the Prophets عليهم السلام. The Qualities of Allah ﷻ are different, and so are the conditions of the Prophets عليهم السلام diverse. This leads to the Sufiya also showing great diversity.

> To purify the body for Salaah and explain Salaah's acts and conditions, etc. is the task of the Islamic Scholars (Ulama), while instilling sincerity and concentration in the heart of the one reading Salaah and making it free from boast, etc. is the responsibility of the Saints (Auliya). So, the Scholars fulfill the conditions of performance while the Friends of Allah ﷻ complete the conditions of acceptance.

The Saints with Sainthood related to Sayyiduna Esa عليه السلام renounce the world, those related to Sayyiduna Sulaiman عليه السلام possess the awe of power and throne, those related to Sayyiduna Ibrahim عليه السلام are the phenomenon of Jamāl (attractive disposition) while those related to Rasoolullah ﷺ are the possessors of all qualities. This is why it's said that the majzūbs are on the path of Sayyiduna Musa عليه السلام (who lost his consciousness after the minutest glance of Allah's ﷻ magnificence),

وخر موسى صعقا

'And Musa عليه السلام fell down unconscious.'
– Surah A'rāf (7), Verse 143

The saaliks (سالكين), however, are on the path of Rasoolullah ﷺ,

*'By one glance of Divine splendor, Musa عليه السلام lost
his consciousness. (O Rasoolullah ﷺ!) You remained smiling
even while seeing His (Allah's ﷻ) actual Being.'*

This is the context of Shaikh Abdul-Qadir Jilani's ﷺ verse,

وكل ولى له قدم واني ، على قدم النبي بدر الكمال

'And every Saint has a path, and indeed I'm on the path
of the Prophet ﷺ who's the moon of excellence.'
– Qasida Ghousia

In the Battle of Badr, the Holy Prophet ﷺ said to Hadrat Abu Bakr ﷺ, "Your likeness is that of Sayyiduna Ibrahim ﷺ," and to Hadrat Umar ﷺ, "You likeness is that of Sayyiduna Nuh ﷺ." This Hadith is the source of categorization of Sainthood.

The Recognition of a Friend of Allah ﷻ

The truth is that it's difficult to identify a Saint. Hadrat Bā-Yazīd Bustaami ﷺ said, "The Friends of Allah ﷺ are the secret stations of Allah's ﷻ mercy, and only those with cognizance have knowledge of them." This is why it's also said,

'A Saint recognizes a Saint.'

Shaikh Abul-Abbas ﷺ states, "To identify Allah ﷻ is simple, but to recognize a Friend of Allah ﷻ is difficult. This is because Allah ﷻ is distinguishable from creation by His Being & Qualities, and every creation bears testimony to this. A Friend of Allah ﷻ, however, is like us in form, features, actions and practices. – *Tafseer Roohul-Bayaan under the commentary of this verse*
Shariah (Islamic Law) fosters demonstration (اظهار) and Tareeqah cultivates concealment (اخفا). At times, some Friends of Allah ﷺ pronounce their rank and station, and this pronouncement is the voice of their uncontrolled passion. The Holy Prophet ﷺ saying, "I'm a man like you," (Surah Kahf – 18) is a voice of this kind, while him saying, "Who is like me?" (Bukhari Sharif) is the intensity of Islamic Law.

The Beloved Messenger ﷺ said, "There are many in my Ummah whose hair is disheveled and who are in such a pitiful appearance that people chase them away from their doors; but if they take an oath in the name of Allah ﷻ, their oath is completed." – *Mishkaat, Baabu Fadhlil-Fuqarā*

'Don't look with contempt at those simple in appearance. What
do you know of the honor they might possess?'

People have formulated their own theories on the recognition of the Saints. Some say that those who demonstrate miracles (كرامات) are the Friends of Allah ﷻ, but this is incorrect because there are different categories of wondrous, miraculous occurrences (عجائبات). Below are three of them,

1. **Mu'jizah** – A miracle exhibited by a prophet in verification of his claim (of prophethood), e.g. the staff of Sayyiduna Musa عليه السلام, Sayyiduna Esa عليه السلام giving life to the deceased, etc.

2. **Karāmat** – A miracle demonstrated by someone in the Holy Prophet's ﷺ Ummah, e.g. the Sahaabah and Friends of Allah رضي الله عنهم, such as Shaikh Abdul-Qadir Jilani رحمة الله عليه, Hadrat Khwaja Ghareeb Nawaaz رحمة الله عليه, Hadrat Khwaja Naqshband رحمة الله عليه, etc.

3. **Istidrāj** – A wondrous feat by a non-Muslim.

Shaitaan demonstrates many astounding acts, jogis and magicians are able to display several wondrous feats while Dajjāl (the antichrist) will be able to give life to the dead, cause it to rain, etc. If Sainthood was based on miracles, Shaitaan and Dajjāl would be noted Saints! The Sufiya state, "If flying in the air is Sainthood, Shaitaan would be a great Saint."

Some say that a Friend of Allah ﷻ is an individual who divorces him- or herself from the world (تارك الدنيا) and who has no material possessions. They argue, "How can one who possesses wealth be a Saint?" Yet this too is a deception: Sayyiduna Sulaiman عليه السلام, Hadrat Uthman Ghani رضي الله عنه, Shaikh Abdul-Qadir Jilani رحمة الله عليه, Imam Abu Hanifa رحمة الله عليه, Maulana Rumi رحمة الله عليه were all distinguished in wealth and material means. Were they not also Friends of Allah ﷻ? In fact, they even nurtured others as Saints! There are many Hindu ascetics who divorce themselves from the world. Are they also Friends of Allah ﷻ? Definitely not!

Some say that a Saint is he who's insane, and in our time, people interpret those who have a twitch in their eyebrows to be Friends of Allah ﷻ. This too is incorrect. I've already explained that a saalik has a higher rank than a majzūb since the former passes on guidance while the latter's condition doesn't allow him to do so. A majzūb is he who was exposed to a single splendor but was unable to bear its magnitude while a saalik is stronger than that.

When a village-woman goes to fetch water, she has a clay-pot on her head and one under each arm, yet she manages to talk to her friends and still reach home with filled pots. Excellent (کامل) is he who carries the duties of Islamic Law while maintaining the responsibilities of Tareeqah and worldly interaction. He manages all of this and travels the path towards his destination (i.e. the path leading towards Allah ﷻ).

Some Jews claim that they possess Sainthood, but neither do they perform Salaah nor do they fast. Yet more peculiarly, some 'accomplished' practitioners of spiritualism claim that they perform Salaah in the Ka'ba when asked why they aren't seen performing Salaah with the local congregation. Subhanallah! They perform Salaah in the Ka'ba but eat in the homes of their disciples and even accept gifts from them! They are all deceivers – very much in their senses and therefore not exempt from the obligations of Islam. A Farsi stanza aptly sums up such devils,

> 'His name is Saint, but he does the work of Shaitaan,
> If a 'Saint' is he, cursed be upon him!'

The True Recognition of a Saint

We've already explained that the Friends of Allah ﷻ possess different ranks and are the manifestation of different Prophets ﷺ. To search for a single recognition in all of them is incorrect. A government has various departments with each one having a different uniform and method of conduct. The uniform of a policeman is different to the uniform of a soldier. They all belong to the same government yet they are uniquely distinguishable. Similarly, the Quran & Hadith have illustrated different identifications of the Friends of Allah ﷻ,

1. Hadrat Abdullah ibn Abbas ؓ states, "A Saint is he who reminds one of Allah ﷻ when seen." – *Tafseer Khaazin*

   It's narrated that some Friends of Allah ﷻ cause the animals (and even the walls and environment around them) to reverberate with the remembrance of Allah ﷻ (ذکر) wherever they sit.

2. Hadrat Ali ؓ said, "A Saint is an individual whose face is yellow in color (due to the fear of Allah ﷻ), whose eyes are moist and whose stomach is hungry." – *Tafseer Roohul-Bayaan*

3. Some Friends of Allah ﷻ state, "The recognition of a Saint is that the individual has no concern over the world and is engaged in the thought of the Lord." Others say, "A Saint is he who completes the obligatory (فرض) acts, occupies himself in Allah's ﷻ obedience, and whose heart is immersed in the recognition (معرفة) of the Noor of Allah's ﷻ grandeur. When he sees, the sees the signs of Allah's ﷻ omnipotence; when he hears, he hears the praise of Allah ﷻ; when he speaks, he utters the glory of Allah ﷻ; whatever movement he makes is in the obedience of Allah ﷻ; and he doesn't tire of Allah's ﷻ remembrance." – *Tafseer Khazaainul-Irfaan*

4. The Scholars of Theology (متكلمين) define a Friend of Allah ﷻ as one who possesses true beliefs while his actions adhere to Islamic Law. A Hadith states, "A Saint is he who loves for Allah ﷻ and displays enmity for His sake." The Holy Quran has explained the signs of their recognition,

والذين معه أشداء على الكفار رحماء بينهم تراهم ركعا سجدا يبتغون فضلا من الله
ورضوانا سيماهم في وجوههم من أثر السجود

"(The Saints with the Holy Prophet ﷺ) are severe against
the infidels but compassionately tender with their Muslim brothers.
You'll find them in ruku and sajda seeking the pleasure of their
Lord. Their faces have the glow of prostration (سجدة)."
– Surah Fat'h (48), Verse 29

This verse states that a Saint is one who brings Imaan and lives virtuously. At another juncture, we are told that a Friend of Allah ﷻ is he who performs Salaah and gives Zakaat. If all of these definitions are pondered upon, it becomes apparent that although the wording is different, the theme is the same. Each definition has explained a quality of the Saints, and these qualities are found in one who acquires the proximity of Allah ﷻ.

We also come to know from these signs of recognition that Imaan and piety (taqwa) are extremely necessary for a Saint. So, no astray person or adherent of a religion of false beliefs can be a Friend of Allah ﷻ, irrespective of how much worship he or she may perform. This is because they have no Imaan. After reflection, we even come to know that no group except the Ahle-Sunnah wal-Jamaat has produced the Friends of Allah ﷻ. Baghdad, Ajmer, Pāk Patan, etc. are all centers of the Ahle-Sunnah. The Friends of Allah ﷻ aren't found in other sects. Qadri, Chishti, Naqshbandi and Suharwardi are all Sunni appellations. Is any function held in the remembrance of a Saint in

Najd, Qadian, or Iran? Is spiritual guidance dispersed from these places? Definitely not!

Likewise, one who abhors good practice (عمل) or is a sinner (فاسق) is not a Saint (no matter how much he flies in the air). Obedience to the law of Islam is obligatory for as long as one is in his senses. So, Shariah (Islamic Law) is the benchmark for Tareeqah (spiritual training).

The Status of the Saints

The status of the Friends of Allah ﷻ is limitless. Some designation is by acquirement (کسب), e.g. Imaan, piety, etc. and some solely by the grace of Allah ﷻ, e.g. His recognition (عرفان), special proximity, acceptance, annihilation (فنا), etc.

A Hadith states, "A small measurement of barley given as charity by a Companion of mine is more excellent than a mountain of gold given by others." – *Mishkaat, Baabu Fadhaa'ilus-Sahaabah*

It's simple – acceptance is solely the grace of Allah ﷻ. No high-ranking Saint, whether he be a *Ghaus* or *Qutub*, can reach the status of a Companion of the Holy Prophet ﷺ.

There are three conditions of Sainthood – natural, bestowed and acquired. Those who are born Friends of Allah ﷻ are in the first category, e.g. Shaikh Abdul-Qadir Jilani ﷺ, Hadrat Mujaddid Alf Thaani ﷺ, etc. Shaikh Abdul-Qadir Jilani ﷺ would never drink his mother's milk during the days of Ramadaan. His drinking of milk (or abstinence from it) was confirmation of whether the crescent moon of Ramadaan was seen or not.

As soon as Sayyiduna Esa عليه السلام was born, he testified to the chastity of his mother (and even his own prophethood)! We come to know that he was a born Friend of Allah ﷻ (because every prophet definitely possesses Sainthood). This is **Natural Sainthood.**

Bestowed Sainthood is sainthood attained by the glance of mercy from a pious servant of Allah ﷻ. I've already explained how Shaikh Abdul-Qadir Jilani ﷺ turned thieves into Qutubs. This is the second form.

Those magicians who came to challenge Sayyiduna Musa عليه السلام came as people who were non-Muslims, sinners and transgressors. By the vision of guidance from Sayyiduna Musa عليه السلام, they became believers, companions of a prophet and distinguished creation. Base-metals are turned into gold through alchemy. The vision of Sayyiduna Musa ﷺ turned magicians into alchemists of Imaan. This is Bestowed Sainthood. In fact, Sayyiduna Hārūn's ﷺ prophethood is Bestowed Prophethood because he attained it through the dua of Sayyiduna Musa ﷺ.

Acquired Sainthood is sainthood attained through strife and worship, etc. However, the first two forms of Sainthood are of a higher rank than this distinction, just as how the sun and moon are both greater than a lamp. The sun and moon are greater because the action of the bondsman has no bearing on its brightness while the bondman's effort plays a part in the lighting of a lamp, etc.

The Holy Prophet ﷺ said, "There will always remain 40 Abdāls in Syria through whose blessings people will attain rain." – *Mishkaat, Baabu Zikril-Yemen wash-Shaam*

The commentary of this Hadith states that the Holy Prophet ﷺ said, "There will always be in my Ummah 300 Saints in the footsteps of Sayyiduna Adam ﷺ, 400 in Sayyiduna Musa's ﷺ and 7 in Sayyiduna Ibrahim's ﷺ. There will be 7 Friends of Allah ﷻ whose hearts will be like Sayyiduna Jibrael's ﷺ, 3 like Sayyiduna Mikaīl's ﷺ and 1 like Sayyiduna Israfil's ﷺ. When the individual (possessing a heart like Sayyiduna Israfil's ﷺ) passes away, he'll be replaced from someone of the 3, the place in the 3 will be filled by someone of the 5, the place in the 5 will be filled by someone of the 7, the place in the 7 will be filled by someone from the 40, the place in the 40 by someone from the 300, and the place in the 300 by someone from the general body of Muslims." – *Mirqaatul-Mafateeh*

Hadrat Abu Uthman Maghribi ؓ states, "There are 40 Abdāls, 7 Ameens, 3 Khulafa and 1 Qutb'e-Ālam. None recognizes the Qut'be-Ālam besides the three Khulafa." Shaikh'e-Akbar Muhiyyudin Ibn Arabi ؓ also states, "The creation of the Earth is steadfast by the Qutb, and he has two ministers – one on his left and the other on his right. The minister on the right safeguards all souls while the minister on the left protects the physical realm. Beneath them are four Autād who are the protectors of the North, South, East & West. There are also seven Abdāls who are the guardians of the Seven Territories."

In the commentary of Surah Māida (5), Verse 12, *Tafseer Roohul-Bayaan* states that after the demise of the Qutb, the minister on the right takes his place while the minister on the left takes his. Someone from below is then made to progress to become the minister on the left." In this chain, the right-hand minister is more excellent than the minister on the left. This is the point the Sufiya gesture towards in the verse,

فأصحاب الميمنة ما أصحاب الميمنة ، وأصحاب المشأمة ما أصحاب المشأمة

'Those of the right hand. (How happy) are the those of the right hand? And those of the left hand; how are they?
– Surah Wāqiah (56), Verses 8-9

The minister on the left is *Jalālī* and from the *Ahle-Fanā* (those who are annihilated) while the minister on the right is *Jamālī* and from the *Ahle-Baqā* (those with longevity).

This is the number of Saints who are *Ahle-Khidmāt* or *Takwīnī*, meaning they have the responsibility of worldly workings. Saints besides them are difficult to number. The Sahaabi Hadrat Abdullah ibn Abbas ؓ said, "Wherever 40 pious Muslims gather, there's definitely a Friend of Allah ﷻ among them." This is why the attendance of 40 Muslims is hoped for in a Janaazah Salaah. These are known as *Tashree'ī* Saints, and there are some among them who are unaware of even their own Sainthood.

Excellence of the Saints

The Friends of Allah ﷻ possess innumerable excellences. Only a few are presented below,

1. The continuance of the Heavens is through the moon and stars, and the Earth survives through the Friends of Allah ﷻ.

2. External light is projected by the sun & moon while internal light is from the Saints.

3. The Holy Quran proclaimed their great esteem. It states, "Don't call those slain by the Divine sword 'dead'", "Don't regard them to be dead", "They attain sustenance from their Lord", "They have no fear or grief", "There are glad-tidings for them in this world", etc.

4. A ship cannot be steered without a captain. Likewise, the ship of life travelling towards its destination without the Friends of Allah ﷻ is difficult.

5. Veins create a connection between various parts of a body. Body-parts would be disassociated from one another if these veins didn't

exist. Similarly, the Friends of Allah ﷻ serve as the link between the Holy Prophet ﷺ and the Ummah – the Ummah would be disconnected from Rasoolullah ﷺ without them.

6. The Saints are the existing miracle of the Holy Messenger ﷺ. Through their excellence, we can gain some perspective of the prophetic majesty. When the slaves of the king of the worlds possess such power and greatness, how grand will be the authority and intensity of the king himself?!

7. Electricity is created in a power-station but it reaches cities and homes through cables and poles. Thereafter, different colors of globes decide the color of light the electricity gives off. It's this very same electricity that powers big machinery, and people also use it for major projects. Bearing this similitude in mind, Madina is the power-station where the electricity of Imaan is produced. The spiritual chains (سلاسل) of Tareeqah (Qadri, Chishti, Naqshbandi & Suharwardi, etc.) are its cables, the Mashaaikh of these chains are its poles, and each Saint is its globe. Qadri, Chishti, Naqshbandi, Suharwardi, etc. are all powered by the same spark of Imaan, but the differences of these paths is akin to the assorted colors of the globes. Also, remember that some globes can be seen with our naked eye and some can't. Just as how those who steal electricity cables or uproot electricity poles are criminals in the sight of the government, so too are those who disregard the Friends of Allah ﷻ criminals in the sight of Allah ﷻ.

8. A dry leaf in a forest is easily blown away by a gust of wind, but if a heavy object (such as a rock) is placed over it, the leaf is protected. Similarly, the world is akin to the forest, the human heart to the dry leaf, and the trouble, hardship and bad company of this world to gusts of wind. We can't trust our hearts not to be blown away by the trials of the world (and effectively change its destination), so it's pivotal to place them in the protection of a Friend of Allah ﷻ. Alahadrat ﷺ states,

> 'This useless heart is wafted away like a petal due to fear,
> Even though the scale is light, heavy is hope in you!'
> – Hadaa'iq'e-Bakshish

9. The Earth is steady because of mountains. If they didn't exist, tremors would break out. Likewise, the constancy of the world is due

to the Friends of Allah ﷻ. They are its pegs. This is why some Saints are known as *Autād*, or 'the pegs of the world'.

10. As soon as one dies, all objects of this world leave his side. Link with the Friends of Allah ﷺ, however, is useful in this world, in the grave, *and* in the Hereafter. Allama Ismail Haqqi ﷺ states that on the Day of Resurrection, people will be called by the link of the Mashaaikh of their spiritual chain. – *Tafseer Roohul-Bayaan*

Allah ﷻ states in the Holy Quran,

يوم ندعو كل أناس بإمامهم

'The Day when We'll call every people with their leaders.'
– Surah Bani Israel (17), Verse 71

In other words, it will be proclaimed, "O Qadris!, O Chishtis!, O Naqshbandis!, O Suharwardis!", or, "O Hanafis!, O Shafis", etc. One who doesn't have a Shaikh (someone he turns to for guidance) is easily deceived by Shaitaan. The proclamation to them will be, "O Shaitaanis!" – *Roohul-Bayaan, Qasida Karputi*

Similarly, on the Day of Judgment, there will be different flags in the hands of various Imams, and every group will be under the banner of their Imam. For example, the flag of patience will be in the hand of Imam Husain ﷺ, and beneath it will be those who demonstrated patience. The flag of generosity will be in the hand of Amīrul-Mu'mineen Hadrat Uthman ﷺ, and beneath it will be those who were generous. Likewise, the flag of bravery will be given to Hadrat Ali ﷺ, and beneath it will be the courageous Mujahideen & Ghaazis. In short, the Day of Qiyaamat will be a day of awe and grandeur. May Allah ﷻ grant us an end with Imaan. Maulana Hasan Raza ﷺ states,

'The sole reason for the occurrence of the Day of Resurrection is for his (Rasoolullah's ﷺ) grandeur of belovedhood to be demonstrated.'

The Friends of Allah ﷺ are the living miracles of the Holy Prophet ﷺ and proof of Islam's truth. There are 73 sects in Islam but no sect besides the Ahle-Sunnah has a Saint among them. Qadianis, Wahabies, Shias, etc. can't produce Friends of Allah ﷻ because they are sects of falsehood. Many Saints were produced by the deen of Sayyiduna Musa ﷺ until it was annulled: the People of the Cave,

Hadrat Asif Barkhiya 🙵 and Sayyidah Maryam 🙵 were all examples of this. The presence of scholars in a sect isn't evidence of its truthfulness, but the existence of the Friends of Allah 🙵 is indeed. This is because a scholar conveys the message after hearing the truth while the Saints convey the truth after seeing it!

Commentary on the Verse regarding the Saints

All of the above was a preface. Now follows the commentary of the verse of the Holy Quran regarding the Friends of Allah 🙵. Read it and let your Imaan be rejuvenated,

أَلَا إِنَّ أَوْلِيَاءَ اللهِ لَا خَوْفٌ عَلَيْهِمْ وَلَا هُمْ يَحْزَنُونَ

'Listen carefully; No doubt there is no fear nor
any grief upon the Friends of Allah 🙵.'
– Surah Yunus (10), Verse 62

In Arabic, the article of reproof is used to warn and admonish when there's a possibility of a rejection of a statement. 'Ala' (أَلَا) (in the beginning of the verse) is from this category. Allah 🙵 knew that many people would be born who would reject the excellence, station and power of the Saints. So, He commenced this verse with two articles of reproof, i.e. أَلَا (*Listen carefully*); إِنَّ (*No doubt…*)'

Wali (i.e. 'friend', plural Auliya) has different meanings,

1. One who's close.

2. A friend.

3. A helper.

4. One with authority (والى).

In this verse, the word can mean 'one who's close', 'a helper', or even 'a friend' – i.e. one who's close to Allah 🙵, a helper of Allah's 🙵 deen or a friend of Allah 🙵. The Saints of Islam are thus known as the Friends of Allah 🙵. They are people He has selected. The friends of Shaitaan are known as the Friends of Shaitaan, friends besides Allah 🙵, or the army of Shaitaan. They are those chosen by either Shaitaan or our carnal desires. The Quran has strongly censored this group and has categorized those who follow them as non-Muslims. The Friends of Allah 🙵, however, have been praised tremendously by Allah ﷻ in the Quran. This verse is a verse about their excellence and merit. So, the term 'Friends of Allah ﷻ' has been used to remove 'friends of Shaitaan' from the minds of people.

Fear is described as 'concern for future harm', and grief is 'sorrow over the detriment of the past'. In other words, the Saints have no fear of the future nor sorrow about the past. They are far from these two trials.

OBJECTION Some people object to this by saying, "How can the Friends of Allah ﷻ be without fear whereas fear is part of Imaan? Don't you know that Imaan is dependent on fear and hope? We *must* have fear in Allah ﷻ and in the judgement of Qiyaamat. Everyone's concerned about a bad end. The wife of an oil-man asked Hadrat Bā-Yazīd Bustaami ﷺ, "Which is better – your beard or the tail of my ox?" He replied, "If I leave this world with goodness, my beard is certainly better than your ox's tail; but at the time of my death, if I lose my Imaan, then indeed the tail of your ox is far better than my beard, because Jahannam will be for me – not for your animal." See! Hadrat Bā-Yazīd Bustaami ﷺ was a king among the Saints (سلطان العارفين) yet he still had this level of fear."

Answer – Fear is of two types, (1) detrimental and (2) beneficial. Detrimental fear is negated in this verse, not beneficial fear. This is why عليهم was used and not لهم (as the preposition لا is used for detrimental fear). Also, the word generally used to express fear of Allah ﷻ is 'khashiyat'. The Holy Quran states,

لو أنزلنا هذا القرآن على جبل لرأيته **خاشعا** متصدعا من خشية الله

'Had We revealed this Quran upon a mountain, you would've certainly seen it humbled and split asunder out of the fear of Allah ﷻ.'
– Surah Hashr (59), Verse 21

إنما **يخشى** الله من عباده العلماء

'Only those of His devotees who possess knowledge fear Allah ﷻ.'
– Surah Fātir (35), Verse 28

Detrimental fear is that which makes one negligent of Allah ﷻ. If one doesn't perform Salaah due to fear of winter, doesn't give Zakaat fearing poverty, etc, this would be considered detrimental fear – the type that is being negated here. In other words, fear for such things isn't experienced by the Friends of Allah ﷺ. Why should they fear these worldly things when they truly fear Allah ﷻ? The Saints have lions as transport, and jinns and Shaitaans run away from even their names! Hadrat Safeenah ﷺ, a slave of the

Holy Prophet ﷺ, was shown the path leading towards the Muslim army by a lion who obediently walked in front of him, wagging its tail like a dog. When the objects of this world tremble in fear of the Friends of Allah ﷺ, how can the Saints be affected by them? The Friends of Allah ﷺ fear none in proclaiming the truth. Hadrat Mujaddid Alf Thaani ﷺ destroyed the fabricated 'Deen'e-Ilaahi' of Akbar, not fearing the king of the time. In fact, everyone eventually became obedient to him! The Saints don't commit an act in this world by which they are ultimately cast into sorrow. This is because their time is adjoined to the remembrance of Allah ﷺ – they have no time for impermissible and absurd things. So, what sorrow *will* they have?

Another interpretation is that the verse is speaking about the Day of Judgment. In other words, it's saying, "All will fear the reckoning, judgment, the Bridge of Sirāt, Divine anger, etc. and will grieve over their lives squandered in disobedience. The Friends of Allah ﷺ, however, are free from these things.

In addition, the Sufiya state that the verse used the words 'Friends of Allah ﷺ' and not 'Prophets of Allah ﷺ' because on that Day, all will have fear besides the Friends of Allah ﷺ. The general body of Muslims, as well as the Prophets ﷺ, will have fear on the Day of Judgment (people will fear for themselves while the Prophets ﷺ will fear for their nations). This is why the Prophets ﷺ will say, "O Allah ﷺ! Grant safety! Grant safety!" on the Bridge of Sirāt. The Friends of Allah ﷺ, however, will have no fear or grief over themselves nor fear about others (because they aren't obligated to intercede).
– *Tafseer Roohul-Bayaan (under the commentary of this verse)*

A Hadith states, "On the Day of Resurrection, the Prophets ﷺ will be envious of the Saints of my Ummah." This also means the same as above. Just as how a king with responsibilities is envious of the free life of a subject, so too will the Prophets ﷺ be envious of the Saints.

Furthermore, these Saints will have no fear in their account of deeds to Allah ﷺ because we will come to give account on that Day while they will come to receive it. When someone who is given a trust spends more than necessary in the protection of it, he receives compensation for his extra effort from the owner, while if someone given a trust spends the normal (or a lesser) amount protecting it, he has to give account either way. Those upon whom five Salaah was obligatory, 2½ % Zakaat was compulsory, etc. and who completed these obligatory acts precisely or a little less will give account to Allah ﷺ about their doings. However, Hadrat Abu Bakr Siddique ﷺ and Hadrat Umar ﷺ (as well as their followers) sacrificed everything in the path of Allah ﷺ. Every part of their life was engaged in His obedience. So, they will actually come to receive their *compensation* on the Day of Judgment! The Day of Account will be a day of immense happiness for them. This is why the verse states, "There's no fear or grief upon the Friends of Allah ﷻ." On that Day, they will enjoy the coolness of the Holy Prophet's ﷺ garment to such an extent that they'll be unaffected by the tribulations surrounding them.

The Holy Prophet ﷺ, on the other hand, will be concerned about the account of his Ummatis. Once, Ummul-Mu'mineen Sayyidah Aisha ﵁ asked the Messenger ﷺ, "Where should we search for you on the Day of Qiyaamat?" He replied, "At the Scale of Deeds, the [Bridge of] Sirāt, or at [the Fountain of] Kauthar." The Prophet ﷺ will at times intercede while crying in sajda, be saving those who will fall from the Sirāt, or be making heavy the light scales of his followers. People will cry out to him and beseech him saying, "Have mercy on us or we'll be ruined!" Some will even look to him in longing for him to save them from being taken to Jahannam. Rasoolullah ﷺ is one, but he has concern for all.

This is the scene of Qiyaamat. The Prophet's ﷺ mercy in this world is that while sinners sleep the entire night, he is occupied in crying for their forgiveness. Reciting the following verse, he performed Salaah until the early break of dawn,

إن تعذبهم فإنهم عبادك وإن تغفر لهم فإنك أنت العزيز الحكيم

'If you punish them, they are Your bondsmen, but if You forgive them, then surely You are the Mighty, the Wise.'
– Surah Māida (5), Verse 118

On the Day of Judgment, our parents, families and friends will all be concerned about themselves; but our master, the benefactor of the Ummah, upon whom our parents are sacrificed, Sayyiduna Muhammad Mustapha ﷺ, will be concerned about *us*. By linking the sinful to the merciful court, however, the Friends of Allah ﷻ will be left without any concern. This is why the verse states, "There is no fear nor grief upon the Friends of Allah ﷻ."

الذين آمنوا وكانوا يتقون

'They (the Friends of Allah ﷻ) are those who believe and keep up their duty.'
– Surah Yunus (10), Verse 63

In this verse, two signs of a Saint have been demonstrated. The first is that they are true Muslims, and the second is that they are pious. Imaan & piety both have three levels. So too does Sainthood,

1. Wilayah'e-Awām – Sainthood related to the general body of people.

2. Wilayah'e-Khawās – Sainthood related to those of distinction.

3. Wilayah'e-Akhasul-Khās – Sainthood related to those unique from those of distinction.

The reality of Imaan is to believe in the Holy Prophet ﷺ as required. All articles of faith are incorporated in this. One who believes in the Messenger ﷺ correctly has brought belief in the Quran, Qiyaamat, Jannah, Jahannam – everything.

There are also three levels of conviction (يقين),

1. Ilm'ul-Yaqeen – Conviction by hearing.

2. Ain'ul-Yaqeen – Conviction by seeing.

3. Haqq'ul-Yaqeen – To become annihilated in the conviction.

A person becomes convinced that fire is hot from hearing so (not by seeing it). This is the first type of conviction. Another person sits by the fire and is convinced of its heat after feeling it. This is the second type. The *third* person, however, jumped into the fire and annihilated himself in it. This is the third type.

The first level of conviction is possessed by every Muslim, and Imaan is dependent on it (this is also Imaan's first level). The second level of conviction is possessed by those of distinction. It was this very level Sayyiduna Ibrahim عليه السلام supplicated for to Allah ﷻ,

رب أرني كيف تحي الموتى
'O my Lord! Show me how You give life to the dead.'
– Surah Baqarah (2), Verse 260

The third level of conviction is acquired by one who's annihilated in Allah ﷻ or in Rasoolullah ﷺ. When a Saint reaches this level, his condition becomes such that he eats when Allah ﷻ feeds him, drinks when Allah ﷻ quenches his thirst, and speaks when Allah ﷻ makes him speak. Otherwise, he remains silent. A Hadith'e-Qudsi states that Allah ﷻ said, "I become the hand of My friend by which he touches, his mouth by which he speaks, and his eye by which he sees." – *Mishkaat, Baabuz-Zikr*

This is the state reached by some in which they proclaimed, "I'm the Truth (i.e. I am Allah ﷻ)", and, "Glory belongs to me! How great is my glory!" This is also why the Holy Quran states, "And you (O Messenger ﷺ) didn't throw when you did, but it was Allah ﷻ Who threw," regarding the incident during the Battle of Badr when Rasoolullah ﷺ took a handful of stones and threw it towards the non-Muslims.

Piety (تقوى) is 'to fear or save oneself'. It also has three levels,

1. **Taqwa'e-Awām** – To save oneself from impermissible things.

2. **Taqwa'e-Khawās** – To save oneself from doubtful things.

3. **Taqwa'e-Akhasul-Khās** – To be detached from everything besides Allah ﷻ.

To stay away from that which causes us to neglect Allah ﷻ, and to do away with it, is the conduct of the [distinguished] believers.

Hadrat Khwaja Mahboob'e-Ilaahi Nizamuddin Auliya ﷺ narrates, "There was a dervish who used to live on one side of the Jamuna river. He said to his servant, "There's another dervish on the other side of the river. Go give him food." The servant submitted, "Huzūr, I don't have a problem fulfilling your command, but it's night-time and the river lies in the path. No boat will be available for me to cross over to the other side, so how will I get there?" The master said, "Say to the river, 'I'm sent by one who hasn't been intimate with his wife for thirty years.'" The servant was troubled by this statement because the dervish had children! Nonetheless, he observed respect, didn't object and headed off with food to the river. When he reached it, he addressed it with the words taught to him and the river provided a path for him to the other side! The servant then crossed it and went to feed the second dervish. After the feeding, the dervish said, "Say to the river, 'I'm returning from someone who has never eaten food.'" The servant was now more confused than ever, because this dervish had just eaten right in front of him yet still says he never ate a morsel of food! Nevertheless, he remained silent and came to the river, and yet again, he uttered the words taught to him and the river made a path for him to cross. When he finally reached his master, he asked, "What secret existed in the words of that dervish and you?" The master explained, "We don't do anything for our desires. Whatever is carried out is only for Allah ﷻ. This is why, in relation to us, our actions are non-existent."

This is the reality of the third level of piety, and it's for this reason that the verse states, "The Friends of Allah ﷻ are those who believe and keep up their duty." The level of Imaan and piety determines the intensity of Sainthood,

لهم البشرى فى الحيوة الدنيا وفى الأخرة

'For them are glad-tidings in the life of this world and in the Hereafter.'
– Surah Yunus (10), Verse 64

Glad-tidings can mean 'things of happiness'. In other words, true happiness in both worlds is attained by the Friends of Allah ﷻ because their hearts aren't affected by worldly thoughts. For them, worldly thoughts are like the water of a river while their hearts are like boats on top of it. If the boat remains above the water, it's safe; but if the water dominates the boat, it's destroyed. We are subdued by the world whereas these personalities master it.

Love for Allah ﷻ and His Messenger ﷺ hasn't left a place for fear and grief in their hearts. A house unoccupied by its owner becomes the home of vagrants, but the house occupied by the owner (who also brightens it) cannot be overtaken by vagabonds. The vagrants see the light of the house, causing them to abort any plan of occupation.

Tafseer Roohul-Bayaan states that a person saw the Holy Prophet ﷺ in a dream and asked him, "I heard a Hadith which states that the soul of a believer is removed from his body the way a strand of hair is removed from flour. Is this a sound narration (صحيح)?" The Holy Messenger ﷺ replied, "Yes, it is." The Ummati then submitted, "The Quran mentioned severe hardship and pain at the time of the soul leaving the body,

كلا إذا بلغت التراقي ، وقيل من راق ، وظن أنه الفراق ، والتفت الساق بالساق ، إلى ربك يومئذ المساق

'But when the soul comes up to the throat and will say, "Who is a magician to restore him?" He will then realize that it's the hour of parting (death). And one leg will cling to the other. To your Lord on that Day will be the drive.'
– Surah Qiyaamat (75), Verses 26-30

"What's the conformity between these verses and the Hadith?" The Holy Prophet ﷺ explained, "Read Surah Yusuf. The answer to this is there." When the man awoke, he recited the Surah several times but couldn't find the answer. He then helplessly came to a noted scholar of his time and explained whatever transpired thus far. The scholar replied, "The answer to your question lies in this verse of Surah Yusuf,

فلما رأينه أكبرنه وقطعن أيديهن وقلن حاش لله ما هذا بشرا إن هذا إلا ملك كريم

'And when the women saw Yusuf عليه السلام, *they began to speak
of his greatness, cut their hands, and said, "Holy is Allah* جل جلاله!
He isn't from mankind! He is but a noble angel!"
– Surah Yusuf (12), Verse 31

These women cut their hands with knives, blood flowed, and even pain occurred, yet they were so engrossed in the beauty of Sayyiduna Yusuf عليه السلام that they didn't feel anything! In fact, their hands were being cut but they *remained* praising his beauty. Likewise, the beauty of the Holy Prophet ﷺ is displayed to a virtuous person at the time of *his* demise. While the soul is being removed from his body, the prophetic splendor will be before him, and he'll then appreciate the Holy Beloved ﷺ and not feel any pain at all! The Holy Quran has indeed mentioned hardship while the Hadith has negated feeling it. There's no contradiction here.

This is the state of life and death. With regards to the grave, however, it's definitely the place where we are able to see the Holy Prophet ﷺ. On the Day of Qiyaamat, the Friends of Allah جل جلاله will be under the shade of Rasoolullah's ﷺ garment with solace and tranquility. This is glad-tidings for them in that world.

Glad-tidings of this world can also mean 'good dreams' or 'inspiration' (كشف، الهام). A Hadith states, "Good dreams are a one-fortieth part of prophethood." The period of our Beloved's ﷺ prophethood is 23 years, but he used to see true dreams 6 months before his announcement. Glad-tidings of this world can even mean 'revered recognition'. Even after their demise, the Friends of Allah جل جلاله rule the hearts of people. Hadrat Qatāda رضي الله عنه states, "'Worldly glad-tidings' is the good news conveyed [to the Saints] by angels at the time of death, and 'glad-tidings of the Hereafter' is the good news spoken to them after their demise."

Rule – We come to know from this verse that the one who's regarded by Muslims as a Friend of Allah جل جلاله is considered by Allah جل جلاله to also be His friend. This is because 'worldly glad-tidings' is the sign of Sainthood, and Muslims calling someone a Saint is indeed a glad-tiding.

Once, in Makkah, the Imam of the Haram said to me, "We don't know for sure that the person you call a Friend of Allah جل جلاله passed away with goodness, so why do you respect anyone's grave? We can't even say if the inmate of the grave left the world with Imaan – what proof is there that he's a Saint?" I answered, "Muslims regarding him to be a Saint is proof of his Sainthood. The Holy Prophet ﷺ said, "You people are the witnesses of Allah ﷻ on Earth." Mulla Ali Qaari ؓ also says in the annotation of this Hadith, "The speech of the entire creation is the pen of the Creator."

The Imam replied, "This is unique to the Sahaabah, that whoever they testify for is indeed an inmate of Jannah, because the Hadith says 'You', meaning the Sahaabah." I said, "If that's the case, Salaah, Zakaat, Hajj, etc. is not obligatory upon you because the Sahaabah were addressed in these commands of worship. Only *they* were present at the time of the Quran's revelation, not us." Upon this, the poor Imam became silent.

In short, Muslims calling someone a Friend of Allah ﷻ is a glad-tiding in the world, and on the Day of Qiyaamat, the Book of Deeds being given in their right hand, their faces made bright, etc. will all be glad-tidings of the Hereafter.

THE MARTYRS

A martyr (shaheed / شهيد) is a type of Saint. The excellence of such individuals is like the excellence of the Friends of Allah ﷻ, and their praise is the praise of the Holy Prophet ﷺ.

Definition of a Martyr

Shaheed literally means 'witness' or 'someone present', and according to Islamic Law, it refers to someone who has been unjustly killed. There are a few reasons why the term 'witness' was used for the martyrs,

1. On the Day of Reckoning, the Ummah of Rasoolullah ﷺ will bear witness in favor of the past Prophets عليهم السلام: On that Day, previous disbelieving nations will claim, "O Allah ﷻ, we didn't receive Your commands, so how could we have brought Imaan?" Their Prophets عليهم السلام will reply, "We definitely propagated Your commands, O Allah ﷻ, but these wretches didn't accept them. The Ummah of the Prophet ﷺ will testify to this." There are two types of witnesses, one suggested by the claimant in a case, and the other an official one. So, it's as if those who make up the general Muslim body are the witnesses of the Prophets عليهم السلام while the martyrs are the official witnesses. Also, all Muslims attest to the Oneness of Allah ﷻ (توحيد), some through speech and others through action. Reciting the Kalima is a verbal testimony whereas performing Salaah, Hajj, etc. are practical testimonies. A martyr, however, testifies to the Oneness of Allah ﷻ with his blood. So, his testimony is more excellent than the other two, and he's therefore regarded as a perfect witness. This is why he's buried with his blood (for the evidence to remain with him).

2. Before Qiyaamat, none can enter Jannah as a reward. Sayyiduna Adam عليه السلام lived there and our Beloved Prophet ﷺ traveled there on the night of Ascension (Mi'rāj), but these instances weren't as a reward for any action. In the graves of virtuous servants, a window from Jannah is opened. Its breeze enters the grave via this window and the deceased even sees Paradise, but he can't enter it. It's only the martyrs (whose souls are in the bodies of green birds) that enter Jannah and eat from its provisions. – *Quran & Hadith*

This is why they are called *witnesses*, i.e. those who are present in Jannah before Qiyaamat.

3. A martyr will be brought in the court of Allah ﷻ and told by Him, "If you desire something, ask and it will be provided." The shaheed will reply, "I wish to be sent to the world again to experience the relish of injury and death in Your path." However, it will be said, "We don't test after having already tested someone." This is also why martyrs are called *witnesses* (i.e. they will experience the Divine court).

Types of Martyrdom

There are two types of martyrdom (شهادة),

1. Haqīqī

2. Hukmī

Haqīqī martyrdom is when someone is killed unjustly and blood-money isn't obligatory on the killer.

Hukmī martyrdom is when someone isn't killed unjustly but, on the Day of Judgment, Allah ﷻ will resurrect that person among the martyrs.

The Ahadith state that a woman who dies while giving birth, or one who dies by drowning, burning, in a plague, etc. are all considered martyrs according to the second definition (Hukmī). There are several further subdivisions within this category. Refer to part 2 of my commentary of the Holy Quran (*Tafseer'e-Na'eemi*) for information about this.

There are also two categories of Haqīqī martyrdom,

1. Shahādat'e-Fiq'hī

2. Shahādat'e-Ghair Fiq'hī

Shahādat'e-Fiq'hī is when a sane, mature Muslim is killed unjustly by wounds and his injuries cannot be treated. The Islamic command about such a martyr is that he shouldn't be given ghusl and kafn. Rather, he should be buried in the same blood-stained clothing.

Shahādat'e-Ghair Fiq'hī is also martyrdom but the above command doesn't apply here. The fighters of Karbala are all regarded as martyrs, but there *is* a difference in the martyrdoms of Imam Husain ☙, Hadrat Ali ☙ and Hadrat Ali Asghar ☙.

The Excellence of a Martyr

There are several excellences of a martyr. We'll mention only some of them below,

1. Other people serve the deen by sacrificing their wealth, time and other things, but a martyr sacrifices his *life* for Islam. A person's life is his most beloved possession. So, greater sacrifice belongs to a martyr, and he or she is therefore the greater servant of the deen.

2. Even today, governments are obliging to soldiers and servicemen killed in the line of duty because the powers that be know that they've sacrificed their life for their nations. Likewise, Allah ☙ has allotted much to one who's a martyr because he has served the deen by sacrificing his or her life for its upliftment.

3. A martyr has a very close relation to a prophet, in the same way martyrdom has much relation to prophethood.

   Rule – Sleep invalidates wudhu while death breaks ghusl. After waking up, one isn't allowed to perform Salaah without making wudhu first; and the deceased cannot be buried without being given ghusl. However, the wudhu of a prophet isn't invalidated by sleep and the ghusl of a martyr isn't broken by death. A prophet performs Salaah without wudhu after waking up and a martyr is buried without being bathed!

4. The natural discharges of the Holy Prophet ☙ (i.e. his urine, etc.) are pure for his Ummah. (*Shaami*) Likewise, if the blood-stained clothes of a martyr fall into a well, the water won't become impure.

   Also, the living existence of a prophet after demise is attested to by the Hadith, "The Prophet of Allah ☙ is alive and attains sustenance. (*Mishkaat, Baabul-Jumua*). And so does the Quran testify to the living existence of the martyrs. – *Surah Baqarah (2), Verse 154*

   A poet once passionately said,

'A non-Muslim is he who doesn't mourn Husain ﷺ (by beating).'

The reply to this by another poet was,

*'He who disbelieves in the martyrs being alive is a non-Muslim.
We don't mourn those who are alive!'*

5. No one wishes to return to the world and experience it after passing away except a martyr. He'll submit to Allah ﷻ, "I desire to return to the battlefield to experience its burning sand and injuries!" – *Mishkaat, Baabu Fazaa'ili-Jihad*

6. A Hadith states that martyrdom erases all sins except debt.

7. Three people will enter Jannah first: (1) a martyr, (2) one who has a family and is in need of begging but refrains himself, and (3) an obedient servant. – *ibid*

8. A martyr is forgiven instantly, he's shown his station in Jannah, doesn't experience hardship in the grave, won't experience restlessness on the Day of Judgment, will have a crown of honor placed on his head (one emerald of which is better than the entire world), maidens of Jannah will be given to him in marriage, and he will intercede for 70 of his family members. – *ibid*

9. The Holy Prophet ﷺ said, "Two tears and two footprints are beloved to Allah ﷻ: (1) tears that fall in the fear of Allah ﷻ, and (2) footprints made while fulfilling responsibility to Him (i.e. treading on the battlefield in Jihad).

10. Rasoolullah ﷺ also said, "The sword erases the sins of a martyr, and on the Day of Judgment, he'll be given the choice of entering Jannah through whichever door he pleases. – *Daarmini, Mishkaat*

11. Also, "The difficulty of death experienced by a martyr is like someone being bitten by an ant."

Who is the 'Leader of the Martyrs' (سيد الشهداء)?

Every flower in the Prophet's ﷺ garden has an enchanting fragrance and hue. So, the Four Khalifas, Hadrat Hamza ﷺ and Imam Husain ﷺ are all

'Leaders of the Martyrs' in different contexts. Hadrat Abu Bakr Siddique ؓ is the leader of the Martyrs because his demise was an example of Rasoolullah's ﷺ – the Holy Prophet's ﷺ martyrdom occurred as a result of Khaibar's poison, and Hadrat Abu Bakr's ؓ martyrdom occurred as a result of the snake's venom in the Cave of Thūr (the venom surfaced at the time of his demise, resulting in his death). Rasoolullah ﷺ passed away on a Monday while Hadrat Abu Bakr ؓ passed away on a Monday night. There wasn't any oil in the home of the Messenger ﷺ at the time of his demise and there wasn't any kafn in the home of Hadrat Abu Bakr Siddique ؓ at the time of his. In short, his status of being the 'second of two' mentioned in Surah Tauba (9) is evident with regards to Hadrat Abu Bakr Siddique ؓ at every juncture.

Hadrat Umar ؓ is the leader of the Martyrs in the sense that his martyrdom occurred in the blessed city of Madina, in Musjidun-Nabawi, on the *musalla* of the Holy Prophet ﷺ, while engaged in Fajr Salaah. He was then buried in the Sacred Rauda next to the Holy Prophet ﷺ and Hadrat Abu Bakr ؓ. The above qualities are uniquely possessed by him.

Hadrat Uthman ؓ is remembered as the leader of the Martyrs in the sense that his demise occurred in the blessed city of Madina while he was reciting the Holy Quran, and indeed, his blood even fell on the Quran Sharif he was reading. He was so forbearing at the time of his martyrdom that he didn't even hurt his killer by lifting his hand against him! In fact, the Khalifa prohibited combating his enemies because he didn't wish to stain Madina with the blood of people.

Imam Husain ؓ is indeed also the leader of the Martyrs as no one from the time of Sayyiduna Adam ﷺ until now endured such an amount of suffering and hardship. In the foreign land of Karbala, he was a rightful soldier, a traveler, one who had kept fast for three successive days, one who sacrificed his family and children in the path of Allah ﷻ, and a unique reader of Salaah (as his martyrdom occurred while he was reading it). The Holy Messenger ﷺ also said, "Hasan ؓ and Husain ؓ are the leaders of the youth of Jannah." Leaders should possess greater eminence than those who fall under their leadership. Before Karbala, Imam Husain ؓ was outwardly not in a foreign land, he wasn't a soldier, etc. In that single occurrence, however, Allah ﷻ willed all of these qualities for him. So, it now cannot be asked, "Why is Husain ؓ the leader of the youth of Jannah when he didn't endure difficulty?" Every quality of Imam Husain ؓ is unique. There has never been a reader of Salaah, one who kept fast, or a rightful soldier like Husain ؓ. Also, the world hasn't seen a procession like the procession of the Prophet's ﷺ family (Ahle-Bait) in Karbala. People make wudhu or tayammum for Salaah, but for his last Salaah, Imam Husain ﷺ had difficulty to perform both of these! Where could he get water from if it was being withheld from him? How could he strike his face and arms with sand when they were bruised with injuries and the earth of Karbala was mixed with his blood?

'Not in the musjid, not in the shade of the Ka'ba's walls. No! The worship of love is completed in the shadow of swords.'

In short, this Salaah was unique as wudhu and tayammum were secondary to it. The fast kept by Imam Husain ﷺ was also unrivalled in the world. Fasting lasts until the setting of the sun, yet his fast lasted only until mid-day. Food and drink is used to open one's fast, but Imam Husain's ﷺ fast was completed when his blessed head was severed.

When a person dies, his widow serves *iddat* at a place for 4 months, 10 days, but when the wife of Imam Husain ﷺ, the mother of Ali Asghar ﷺ, the daughter-in-law of Sayyidah Fathima ﷺ and the pride of all Muslims became a widow, she (as well as others of the Prophet's ﷺ family) were taken captive and paraded from Karbala to Kufa and from Kufa to Damascus. There has never been a procession of a martyr's family like that of Imam Husain's ﷺ. Never have the Earth and Heavens witnessed a brother's head being hoisted on a spear while his grief-stricken sisters walked (bound like criminals) behind it.

At the time of death, a person makes a will for his children, but Imam Husain ﷺ, after suffering 72 injuries, fell from his horse and asked his merciless killer for an opportunity to perform 2 rakaats qasr Salaah! Oath on Allah ﷻ! Millions of our sajdas may be sacrificed on just one of Imam Husain's ﷺ!

And why shouldn't have Imam Husain ﷺ been conscious of his religious duties? He's the fragrant rose of the Holy Prophet's ﷺ garden, the guardian of the Ummah and the custodian of the deen. Indeed, Imam Husain ﷺ turned to the deen in both time of happiness *and* sadness!

Sayyiduna Ismail ﷺ made the following request to his father (Sayyiduna Ibrahim ﷺ) at the time of being sacrificed, "Tie my hands and legs so that I don't become restless from the knife's movement. Everyone becomes uneasy at the time of the soul leaving the body." Imam Husain's ﷺ martyrdom was so unique, however, that at the time of his head being separated from his body, there was no restlessness or movement from him!

After the martyrdom, when his blessed head was placed on the point of a spear, Imam Husain's 🙏 eyes were open and looking at the ground. A poet explains the reason for this,

'His head on the spear, his face turned towards the ground. Why?!
Because he desires to complete the second sajda!'

(Imam Husain 🙏 had only completed the first sajda of the first rakaat when his killer martyred him.)

These are the reasons why Imam Husain 🙏 is known as the Leader of the Martyrs. In fact, the reality is that the martyrdom of the shaheeds reaches the court of Allah 🕋 with the blessings of their martyrdom.

Rasoolullah 🟢 and his entire family are pure. How can I, then – an insignificant, impure sinner – ever articulate their lofty praise! I have very humbly written these few lines and pray that Allah 🕋 accepts this effort and makes it a means of perpetual blessings (صدقة جارية) for me and for the compensation of my sins. He who acquires some benefit from it is requested to make dua for forgiveness for this mendicant slave, as this is the intent of this attempt.

Ahmed Yaar Khan
14ᵗʰ Muharram 1365 A.H

وصلى الله تعالى على خير خلقه ونور عرشه سيدنا محمد وعلى اله
واصحابه اجمعين برحمته وهو ارحم الرحمين

www.ingramcontent.com/pod-product-compliance
Lightning Source LLC
Chambersburg PA
CBHW021216090426
42740CB00006B/242